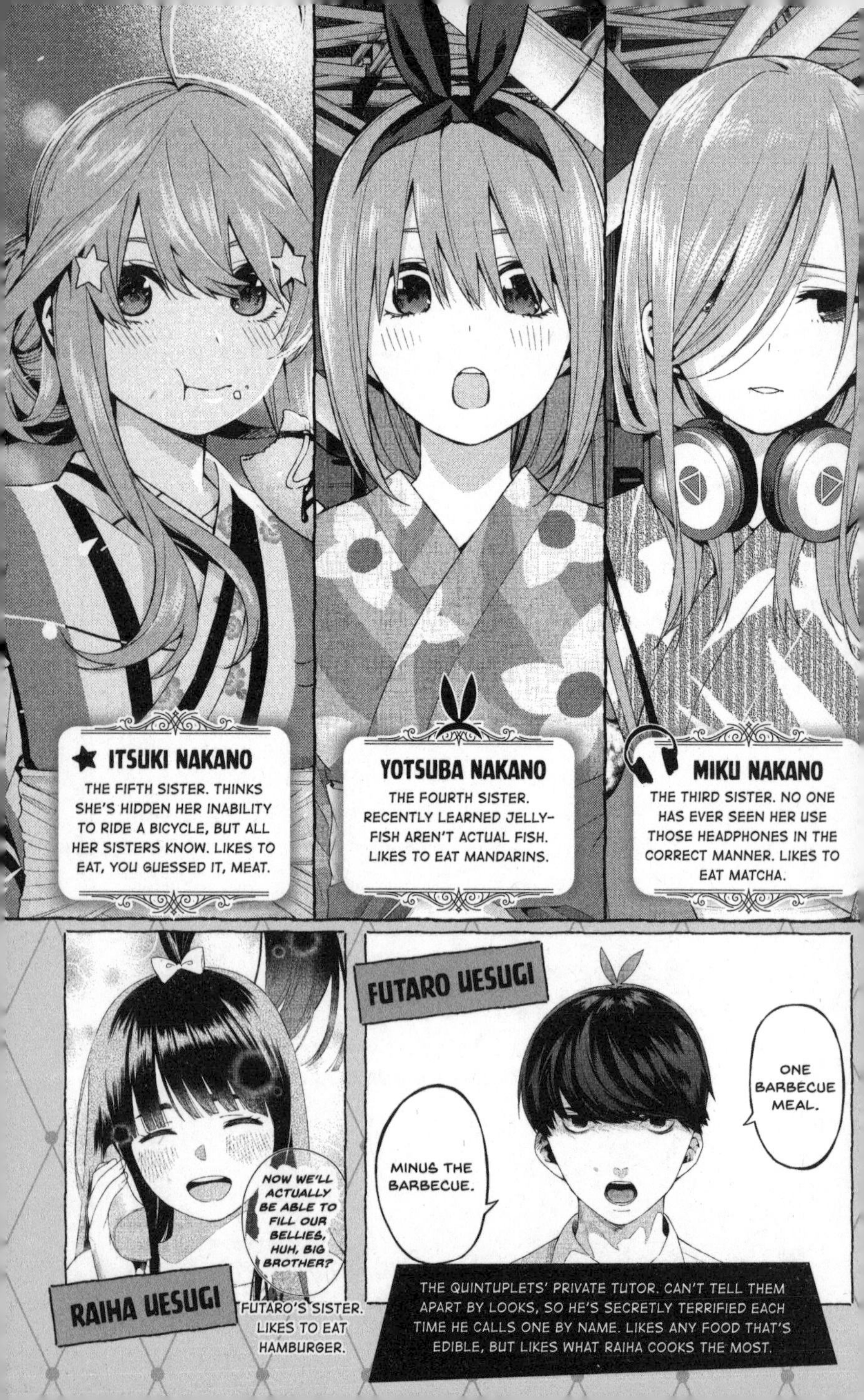
MIKU NAKANO
THE THIRD SISTER. NO ONE HAS EVER SEEN HER USE THOSE HEADPHONES IN THE CORRECT MANNER. LIKES TO EAT MATCHA.
YOTSUBA NAKANO
THE FOURTH SISTER. RECENTLY LEARNED JELLY-FISH AREN'T ACTUAL FISH. LIKES TO EAT MANDARINS.
ITSUKI NAKANO
THE FIFTH SISTER. THINKS SHE'S HIDDEN HER INABILITY TO RIDE A BICYCLE, BUT ALL HER SISTERS KNOW. LIKES TO EAT, YOU GUESSED IT, MEAT.
FUTARO UESUGI
ONE BARBECUE MEAL.
MINUS THE BARBECUE.
THE QUINTUPLETS' PRIVATE TUTOR. CAN'T TELL THEM APART BY LOOKS, SO HE'S SECRETLY TERRIFIED EACH TIME HE CALLS ONE BY NAME. LIKES ANY FOOD THAT'S EDIBLE, BUT LIKES WHAT RAIHA COOKS THE MOST.
NOW WE'LL ACTUALLY BE ABLE TO FILL OUR BELLIES, HUH, BIG BROTHER?
RAIHA UESUGI
FUTARO'S SISTER. LIKES TO EAT HAMBURGER.

CONTENTS

3

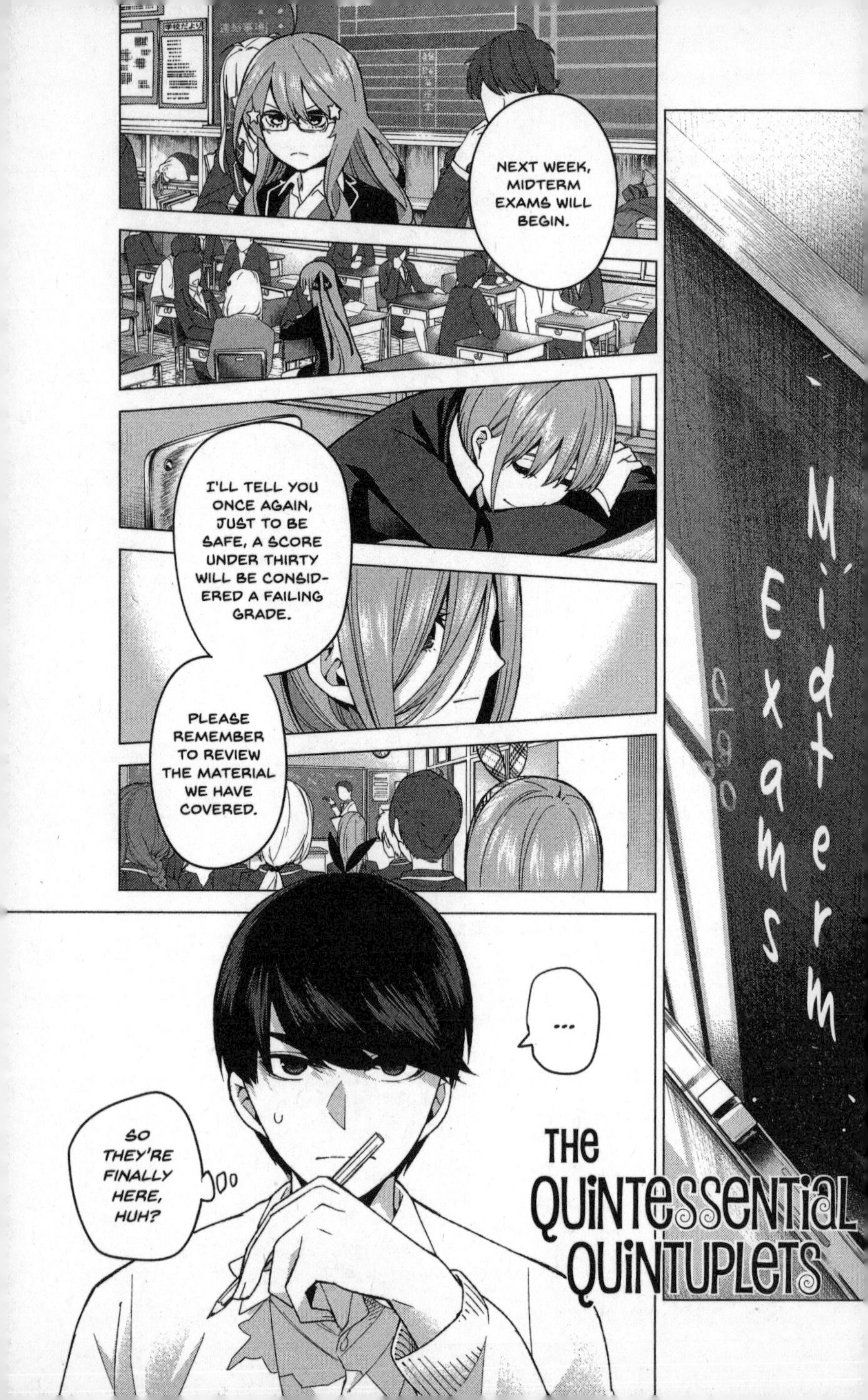

Midterm Exams
NEXT WEEK, MIDTERM EXAMS WILL BEGIN.
I'LL TELL YOU ONCE AGAIN, JUST TO BE SAFE, A SCORE UNDER THIRTY WILL BE CONSIDERED A FAILING GRADE.
PLEASE REMEMBER TO REVIEW THE MATERIAL WE HAVE COVERED.
...
SO THEY'RE FINALLY HERE, HUH?
THE QUINTESSENTIAL QUINTUPLETS

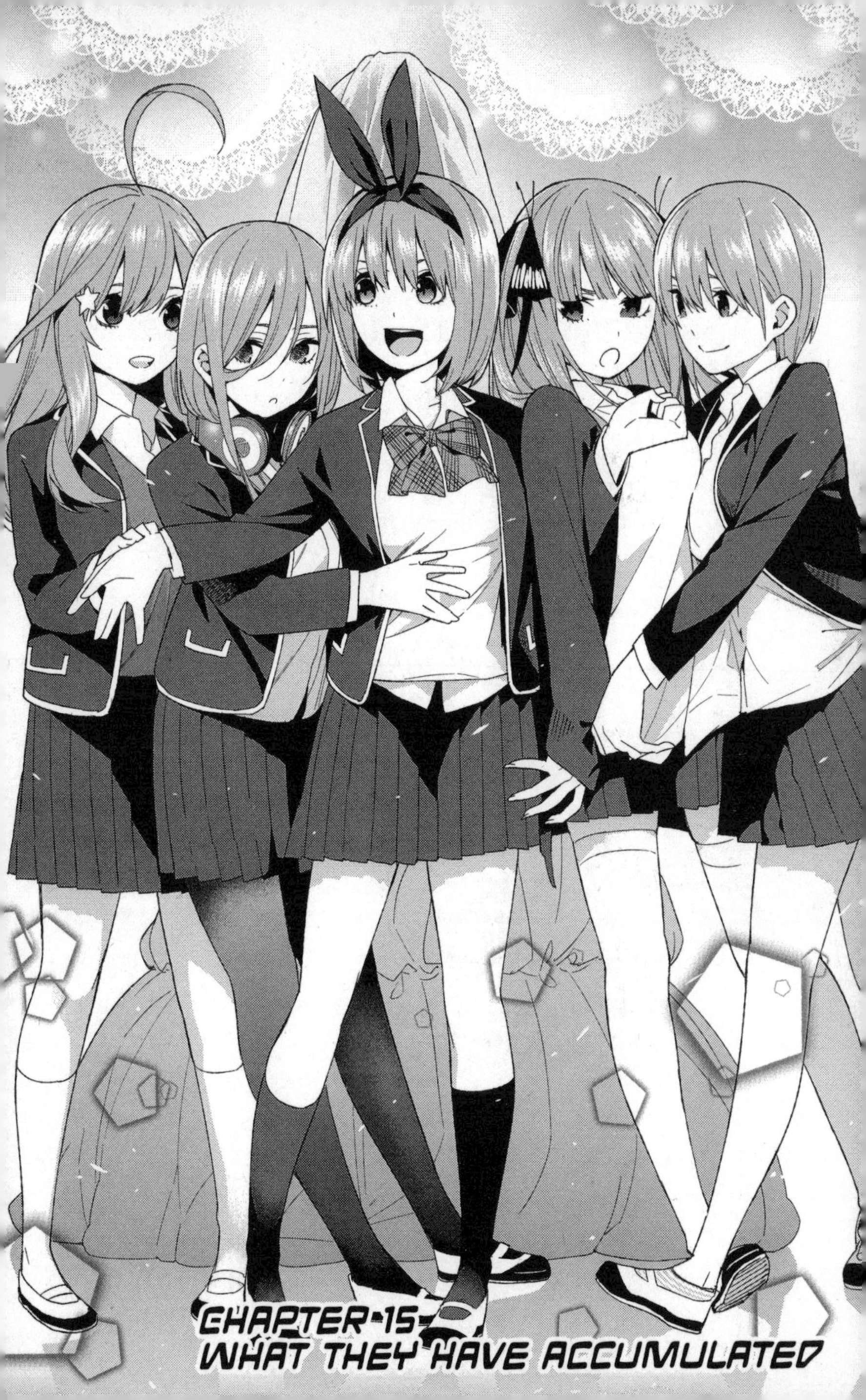
CHAPTER 15
WHAT THEY HAVE ACCUMULATED

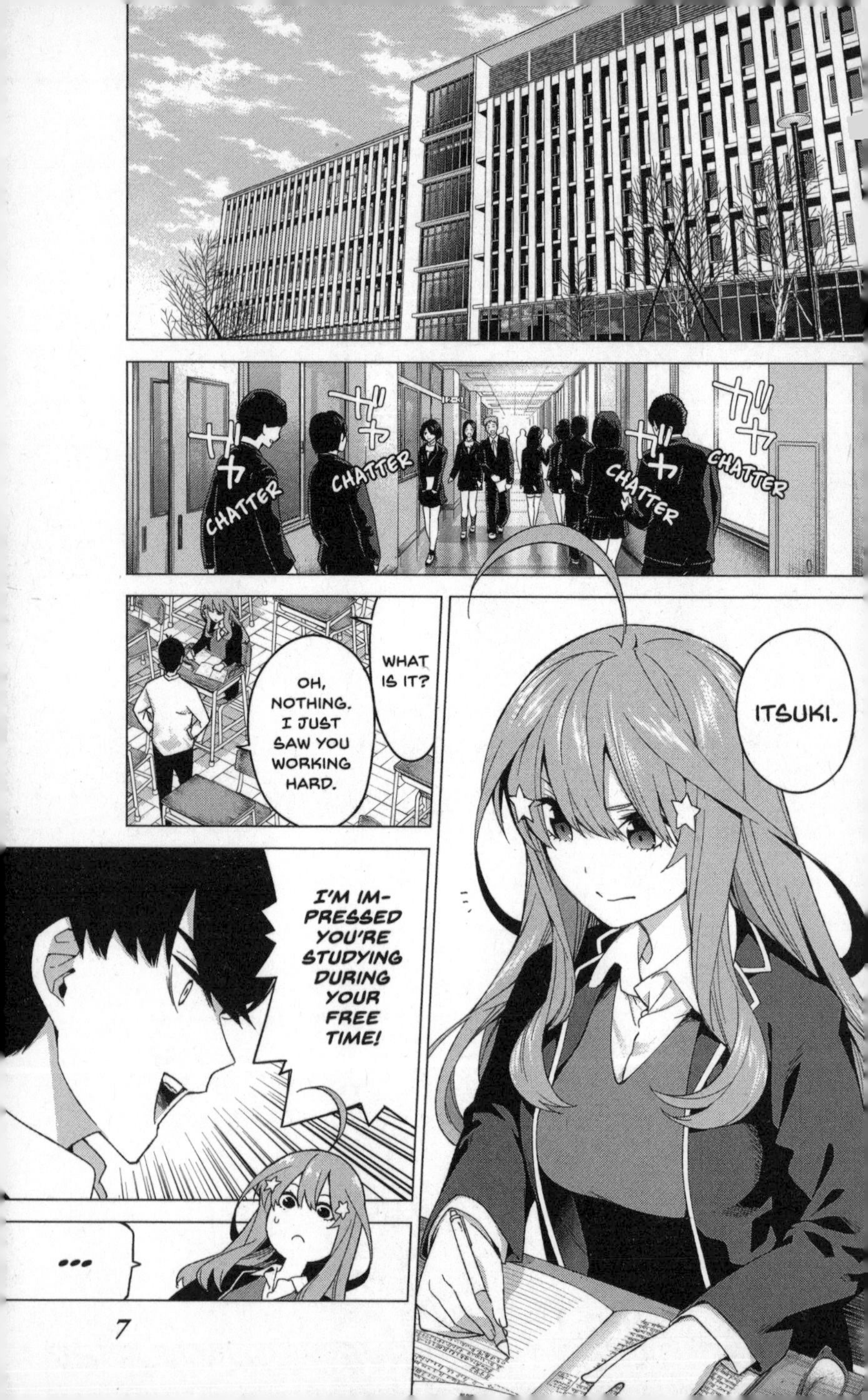
ガヤ
CHATTER
ガヤ
CHATTER
CHATTER
ガヤ
CHATTER
CHATTER
ITSUKI.
WHAT IS IT?
OH, NOTHING. I JUST SAW YOU WORKING HARD.
I'M IM-PRESSED YOU'RE STUDYING DURING YOUR FREE TIME!
...

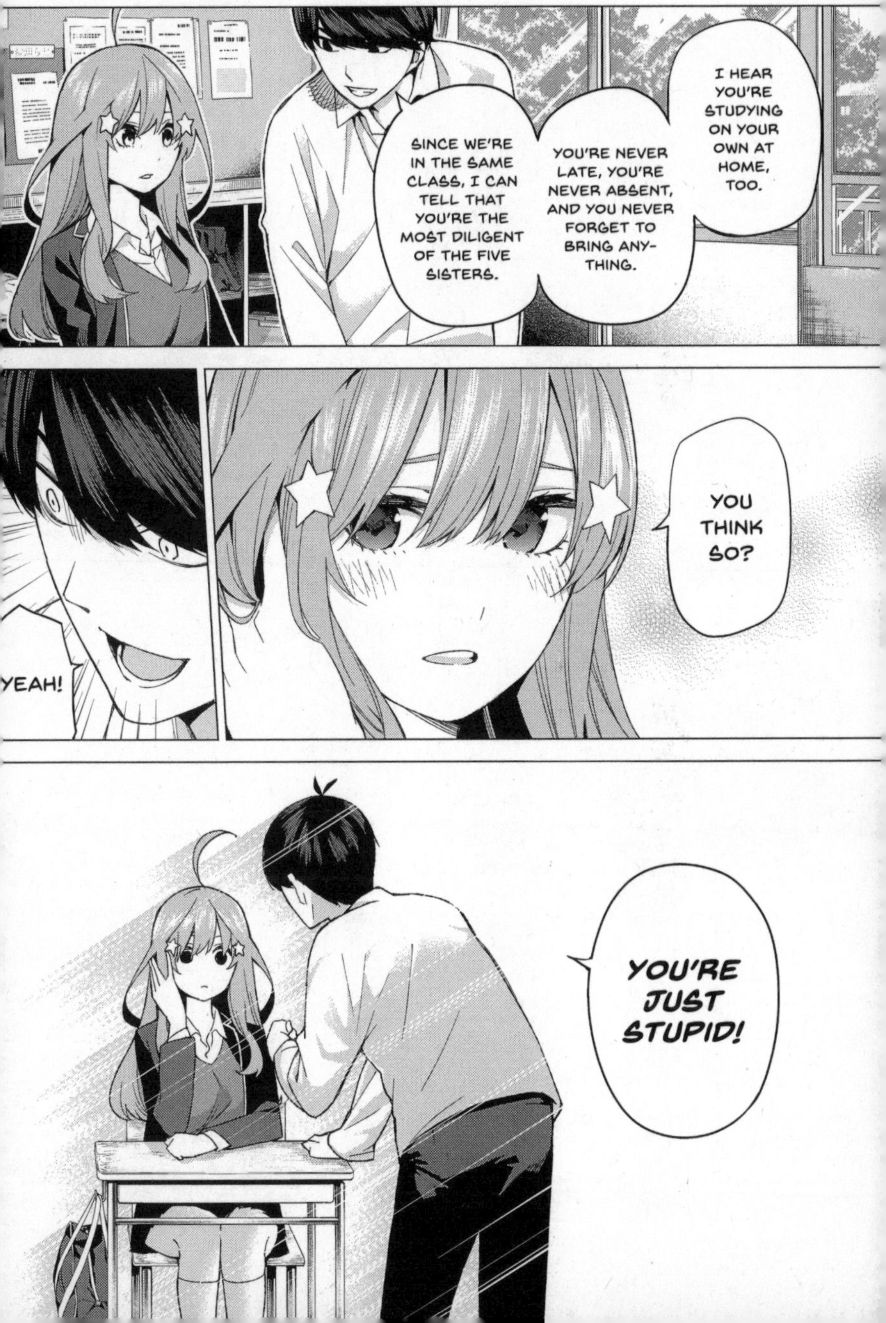
I HEAR YOU'RE STUDYING ON YOUR OWN AT HOME, TOO.
YOU'RE NEVER LATE, YOU'RE NEVER ABSENT, AND YOU NEVER FORGET TO BRING ANY-THING.
SINCE WE'RE IN THE SAME CLASS, I CAN TELL THAT YOU'RE THE MOST DILIGENT OF THE FIVE SISTERS.
YOU THINK SO?
YEAH!
YOU'RE JUST STUPID!

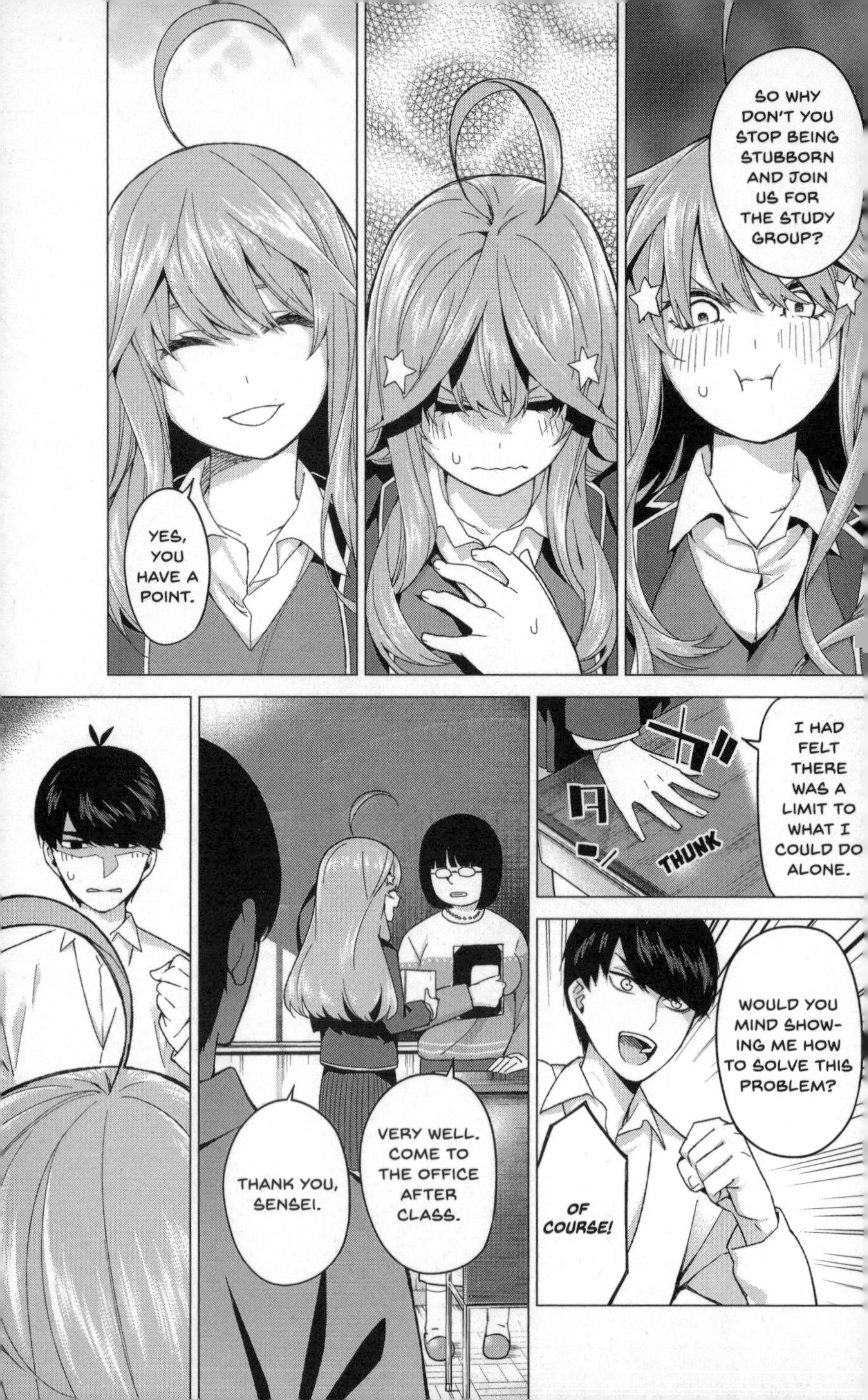
SO WHY DON'T YOU STOP BEING STUBBORN AND JOIN US FOR THE STUDY GROUP?
YES, YOU HAVE A POINT.
I HAD FELT THERE WAS A LIMIT TO WHAT I COULD DO ALONE.
THUNK
WOULD YOU MIND SHOWING ME HOW TO SOLVE THIS PROBLEM?
OF COURSE!
VERY WELL. COME TO THE OFFICE AFTER CLASS.
THANK YOU, SENSEI.

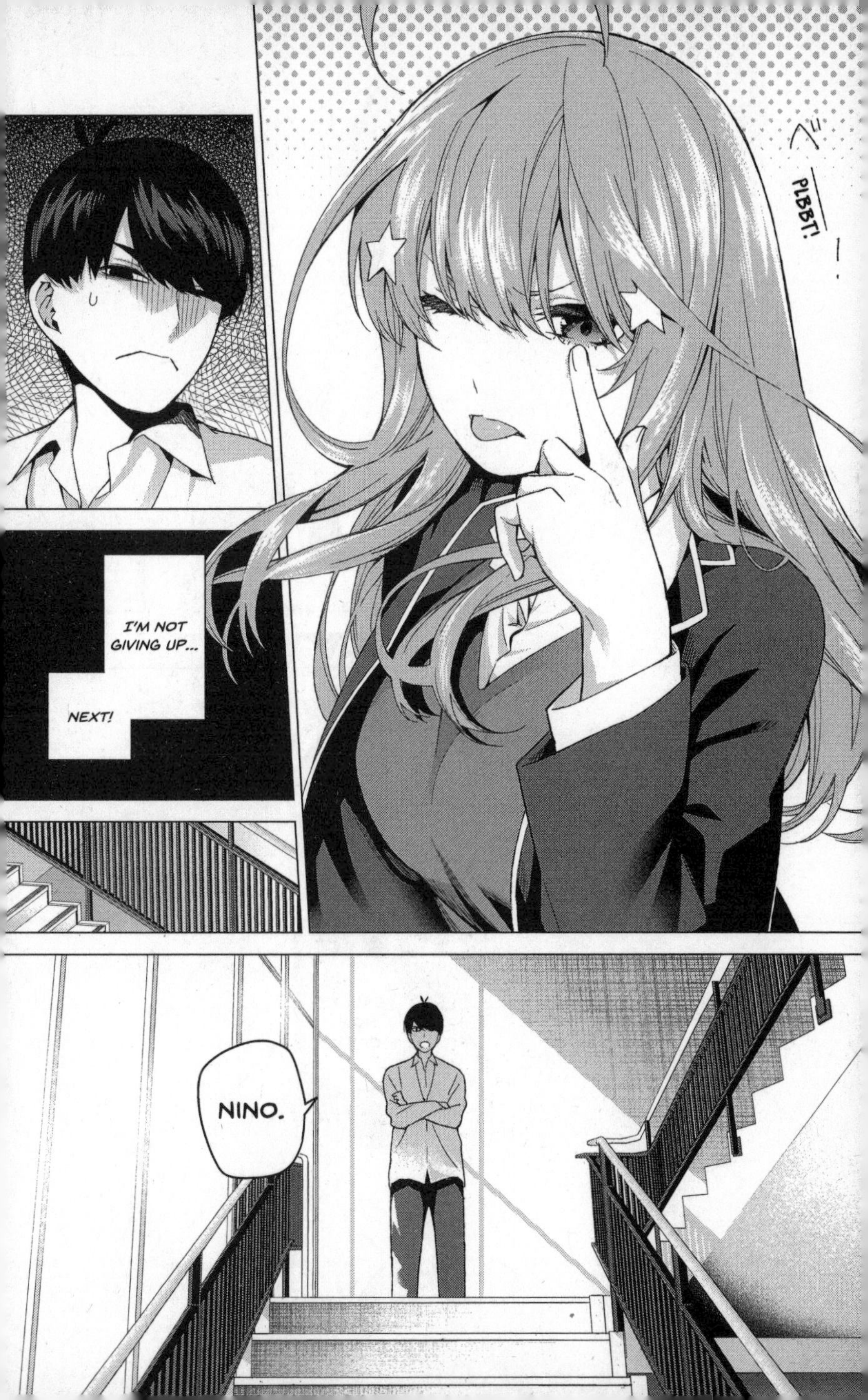

PLBBT!
I'M NOT GIVING UP...
NEXT!
NINO.

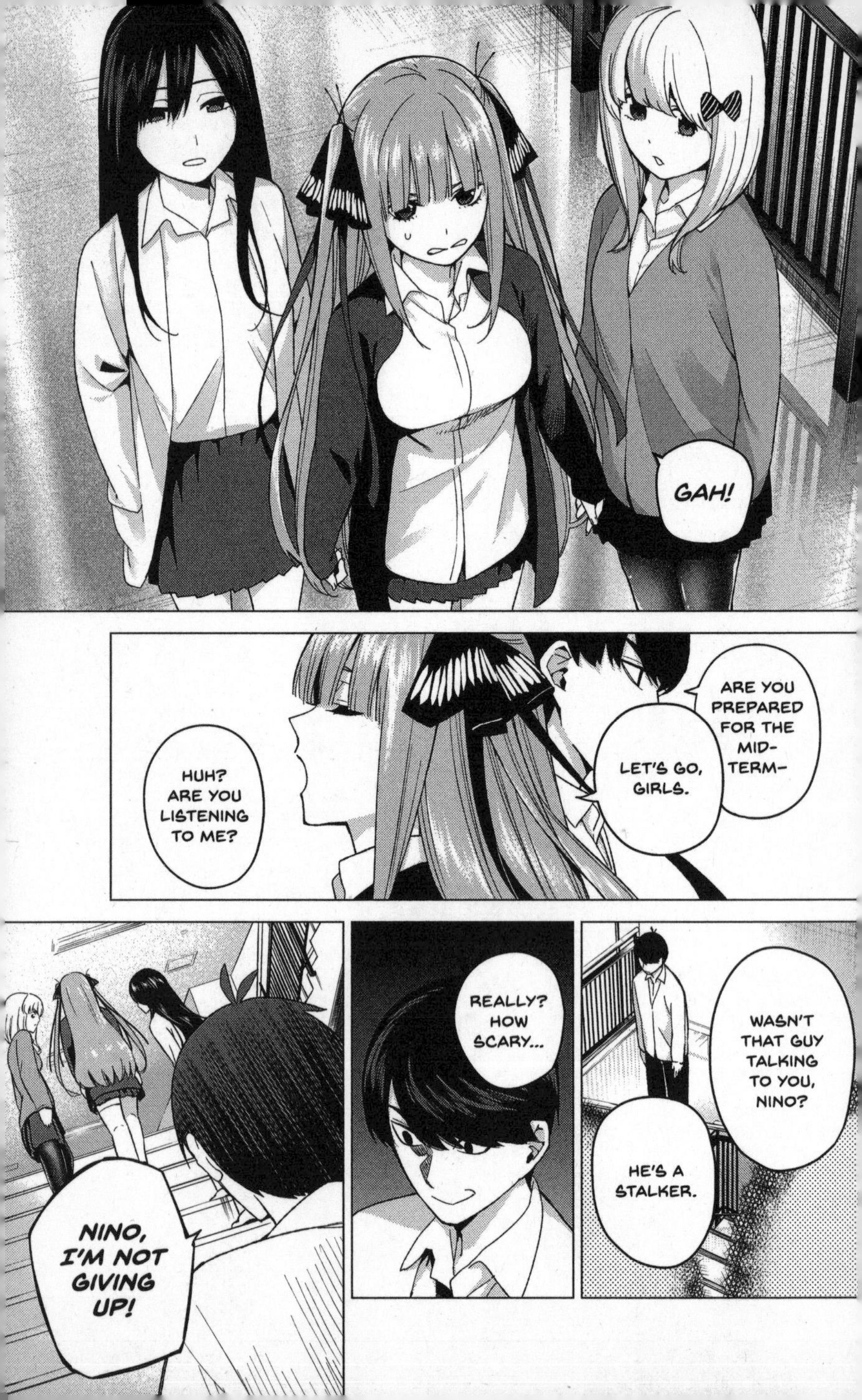
GAH!
ARE YOU PREPARED FOR THE MID-TERM-
LET'S GO, GIRLS.
HUH? ARE YOU LISTENING TO ME?
WASN'T THAT GUY TALKING TO YOU, NINO?
HE'S A STALKER.
REALLY? HOW SCARY...
NINO, I'M NOT GIVING UP!

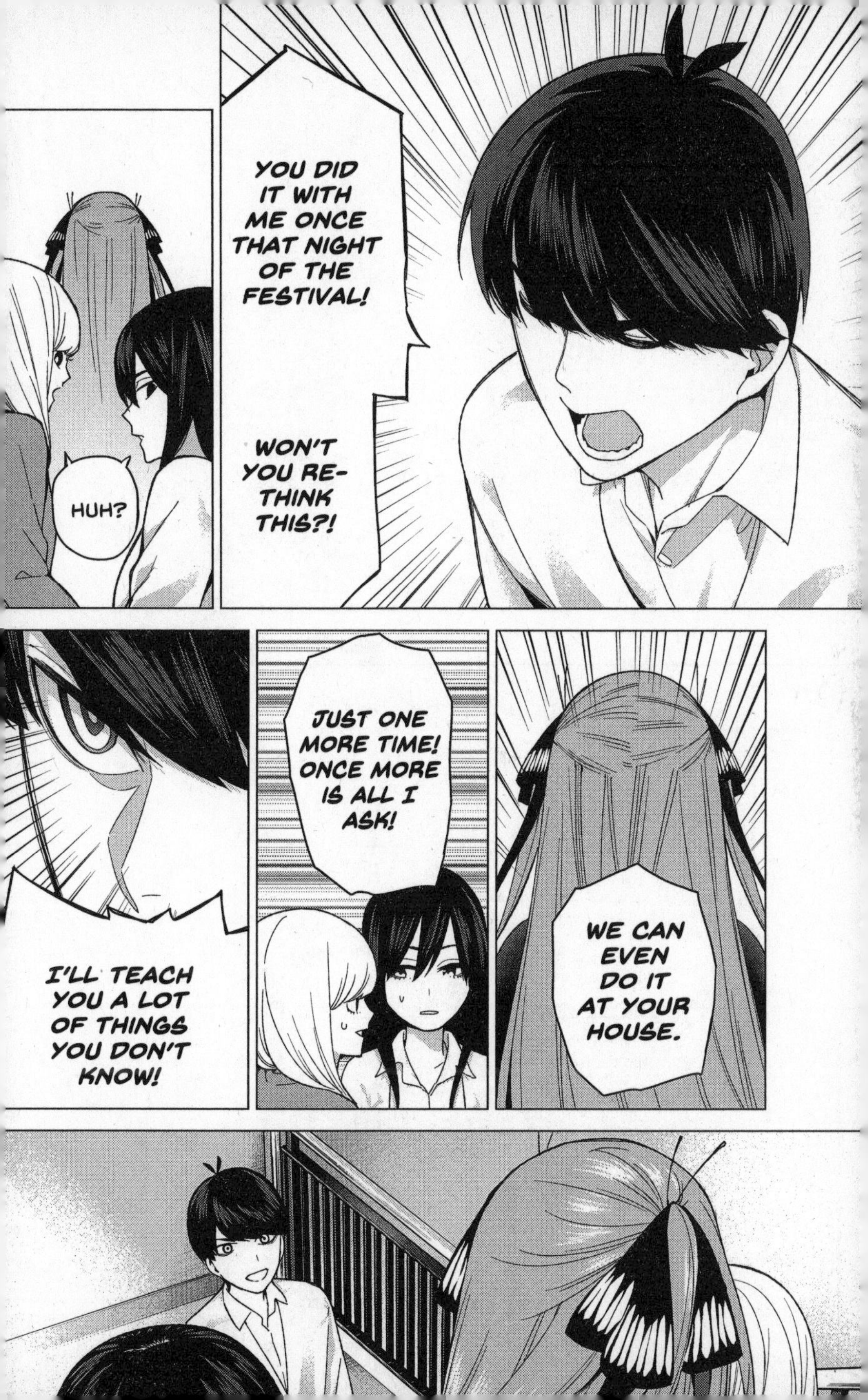
YOU DID IT WITH ME ONCE THAT NIGHT OF THE FESTIVAL!
WON'T YOU RE-THINK THIS?!
HUH?
WE CAN EVEN DO IT AT YOUR HOUSE.
JUST ONE MORE TIME! ONCE MORE IS ALL I ASK!
I'LL TEACH YOU A LOT OF THINGS YOU DON'T KNOW!

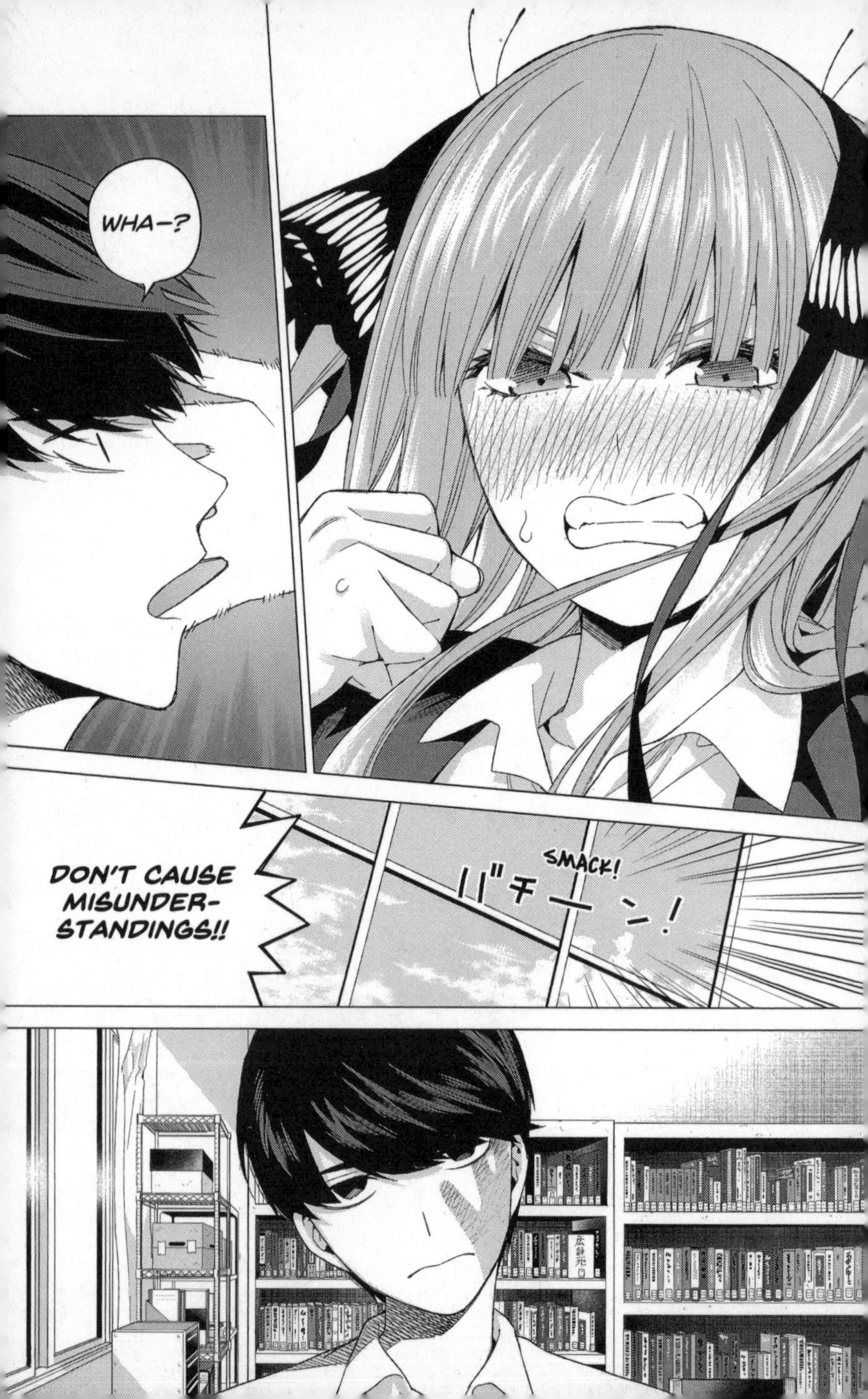
WHA-?
SMACK!
バチーン!
DON'T CAUSE MISUNDER-STANDINGS!!

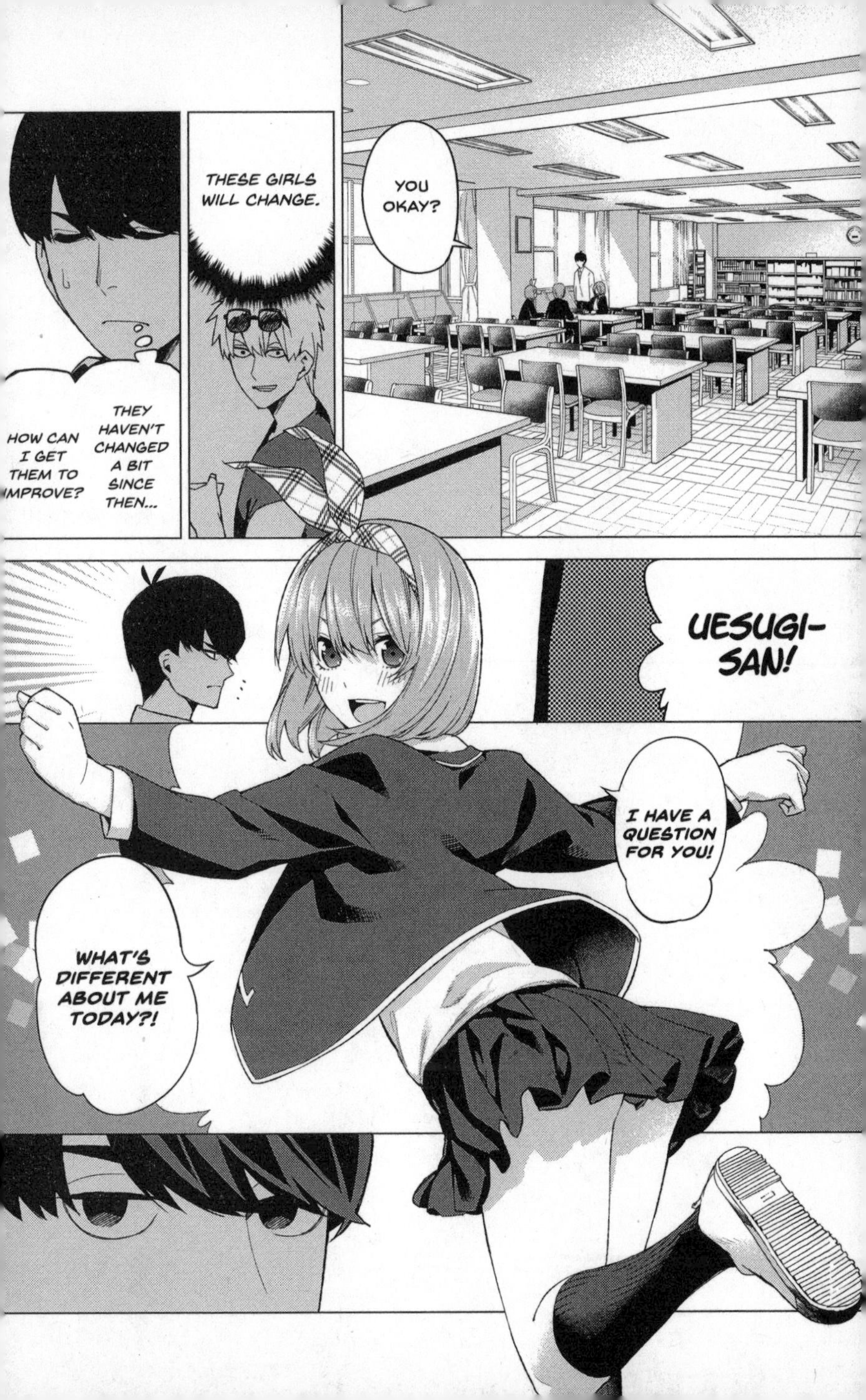
YOU OKAY?
THESE GIRLS WILL CHANGE.
THEY HAVEN'T CHANGED A BIT SINCE THEN...
HOW CAN I GET THEM TO IMPROVE?
UESUGI-SAN!
I HAVE A QUESTION FOR YOU!
WHAT'S DIFFERENT ABOUT ME TODAY?!

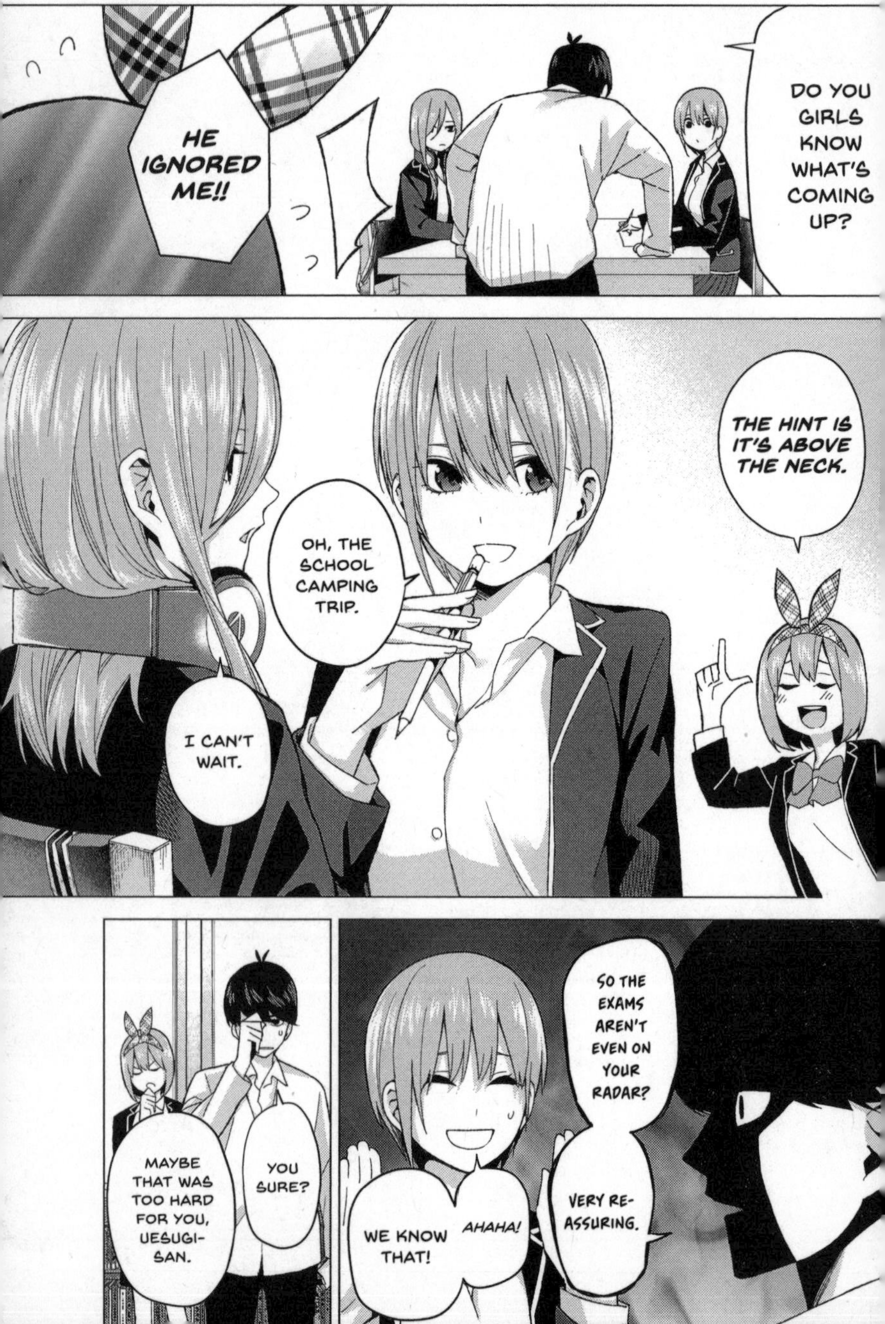
DO YOU GIRLS KNOW WHAT'S COMING UP?
HE IGNORED ME!!
THE HINT IS IT'S ABOVE THE NECK.
OH, THE SCHOOL CAMPING TRIP.
I CAN'T WAIT.
SO THE EXAMS AREN'T EVEN ON YOUR RADAR?
VERY RE-ASSURING.
AHAHA!
WE KNOW THAT!
YOU SURE?
MAYBE THAT WAS TOO HARD FOR YOU, UESUGI-SAN.

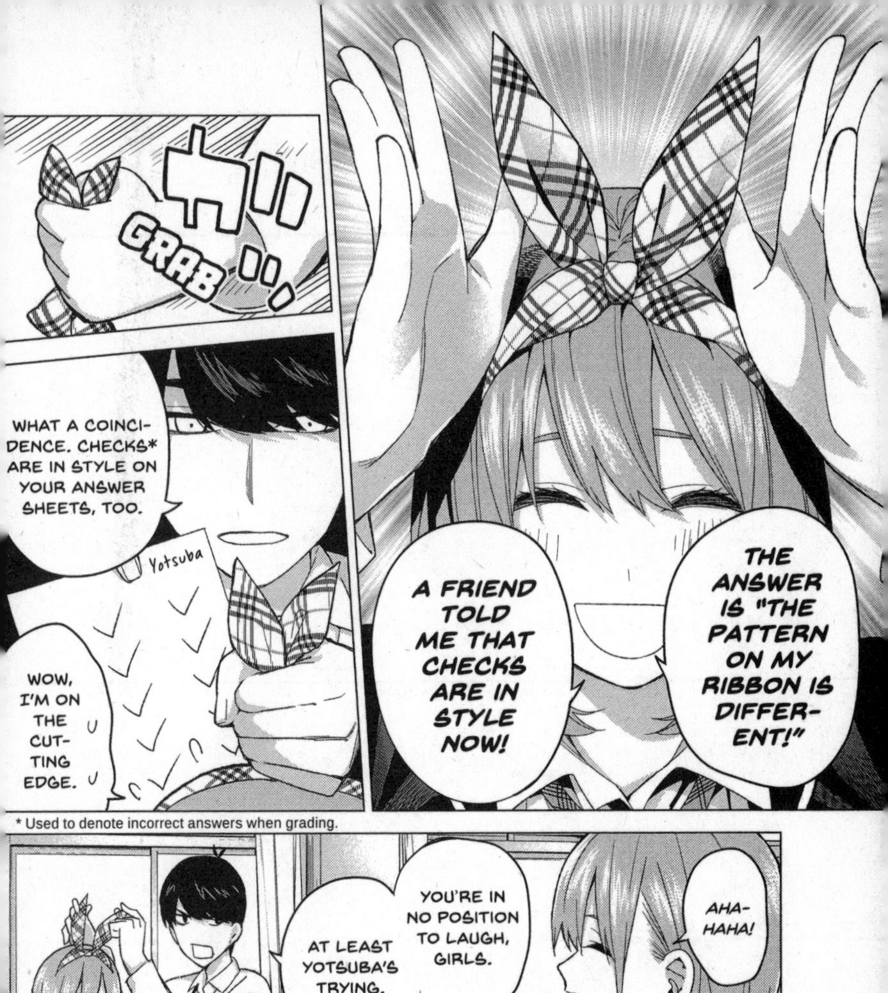
THE ANSWER IS "THE PATTERN ON MY RIBBON IS DIFFER-ENT!"
A FRIEND TOLD ME THAT CHECKS ARE IN STYLE NOW!
GRAB
WHAT A COINCI-DENCE. CHECKS* ARE IN STYLE ON YOUR ANSWER SHEETS, TOO.
Yotsuba
WOW, I'M ON THE CUT-TING EDGE.

* Used to denote incorrect answers when grading.

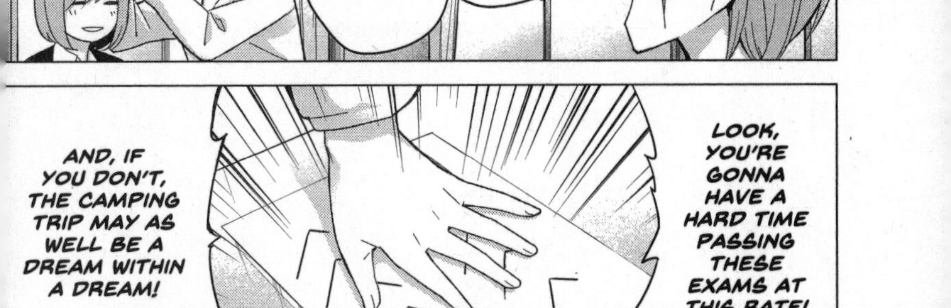
AHA-HAHA!
YOU'RE IN NO POSITION TO LAUGH, GIRLS.
AT LEAST YOTSUBA'S TRYING.
LOOK, YOU'RE GONNA HAVE A HARD TIME PASSING THESE EXAMS AT THIS RATE!
AND, IF YOU DON'T, THE CAMPING TRIP MAY AS WELL BE A DREAM WITHIN A DREAM!

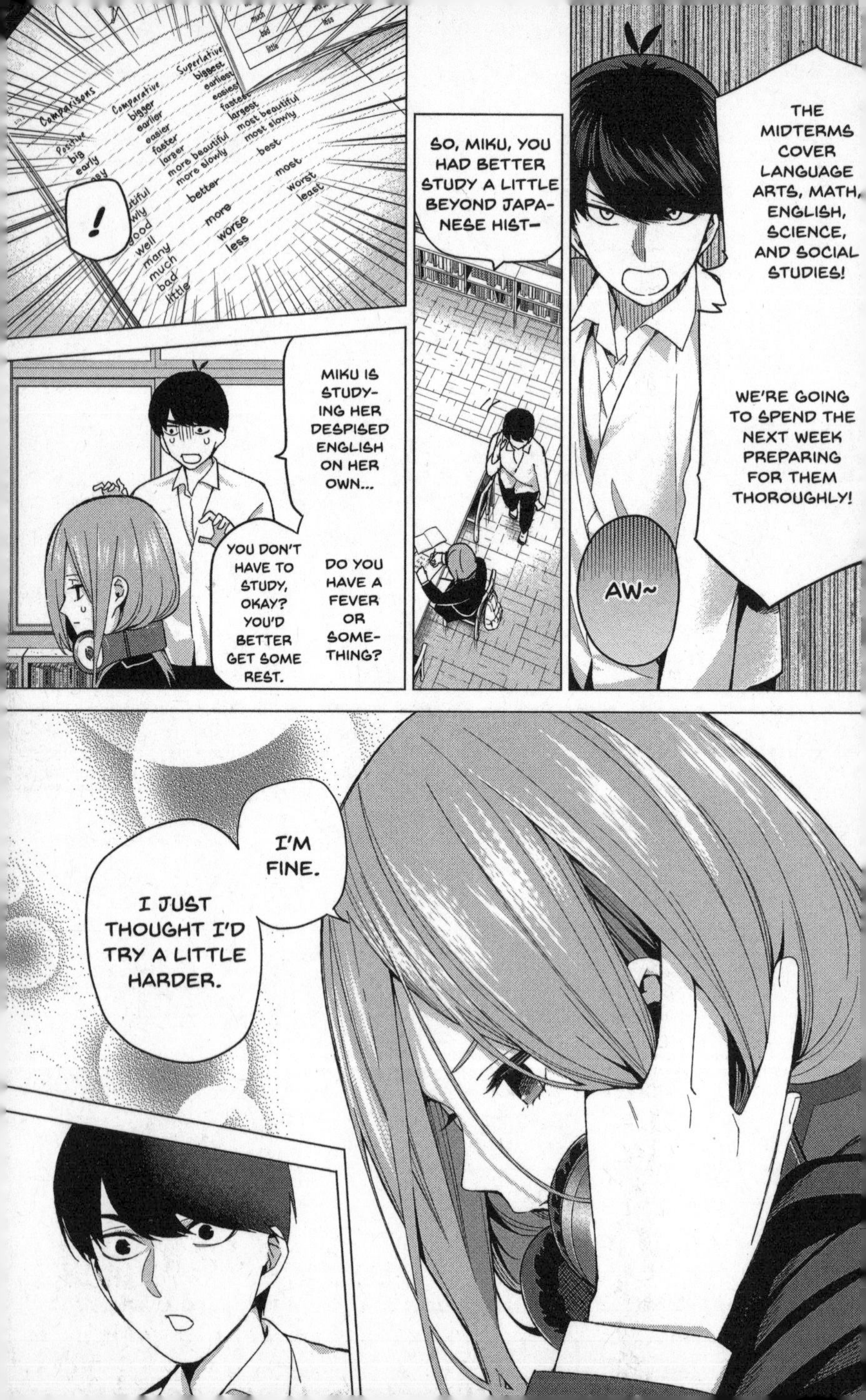

THE MIDTERMS COVER LANGUAGE ARTS, MATH, ENGLISH, SCIENCE, AND SOCIAL STUDIES!
WE'RE GOING TO SPEND THE NEXT WEEK PREPARING FOR THEM THOROUGHLY!
AW~
SO, MIKU, YOU HAD BETTER STUDY A LITTLE BEYOND JAPANESE HIST—
Comparisons
Positive
Comparative
Superlative
big bigger biggest
early earlier earliest
easier easiest
faster fastest
larger largest
more beautiful most beautiful
more slowly most slowly
better best
more most
worse worst
less least
good
well
many
much
bad
little
!
MIKU IS STUDYING HER DESPISED ENGLISH ON HER OWN...
DO YOU HAVE A FEVER OR SOMETHING?
YOU DON'T HAVE TO STUDY, OKAY? YOU'D BETTER GET SOME REST.
I'M FINE.
I JUST THOUGHT I'D TRY A LITTLE HARDER.

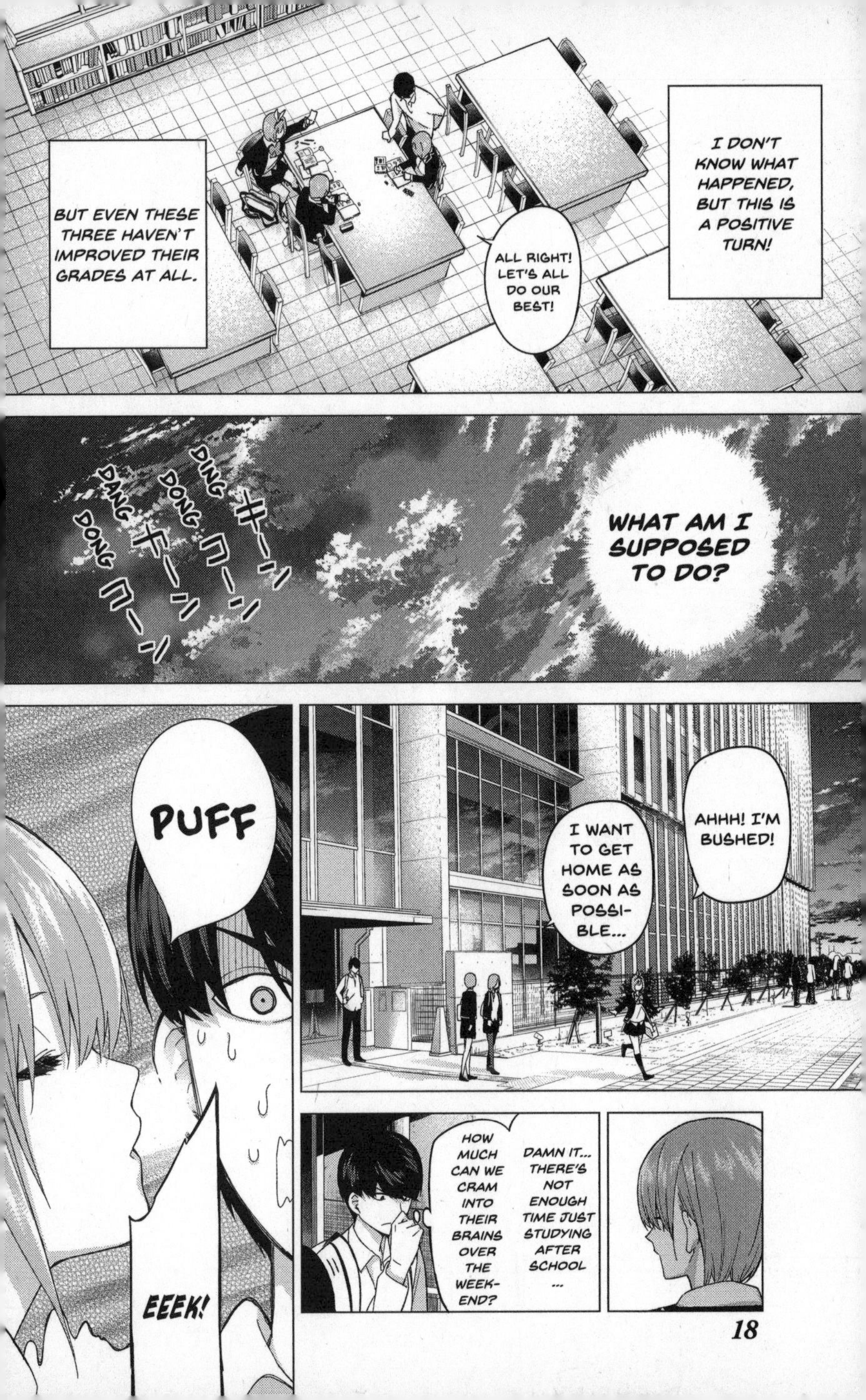
I DON'T KNOW WHAT HAPPENED, BUT THIS IS A POSITIVE TURN!
ALL RIGHT! LET'S ALL DO OUR BEST!
BUT EVEN THESE THREE HAVEN'T IMPROVED THEIR GRADES AT ALL.
WHAT AM I SUPPOSED TO DO?
DING DONG
DANG DONG
AHHH! I'M BUSHED!
I WANT TO GET HOME AS SOON AS POSSI-BLE...
DAMN IT... THERE'S NOT ENOUGH TIME JUST STUDYING AFTER SCHOOL ...
HOW MUCH CAN WE CRAM INTO THEIR BRAINS OVER THE WEEK-END?
PUFF
EEEK!

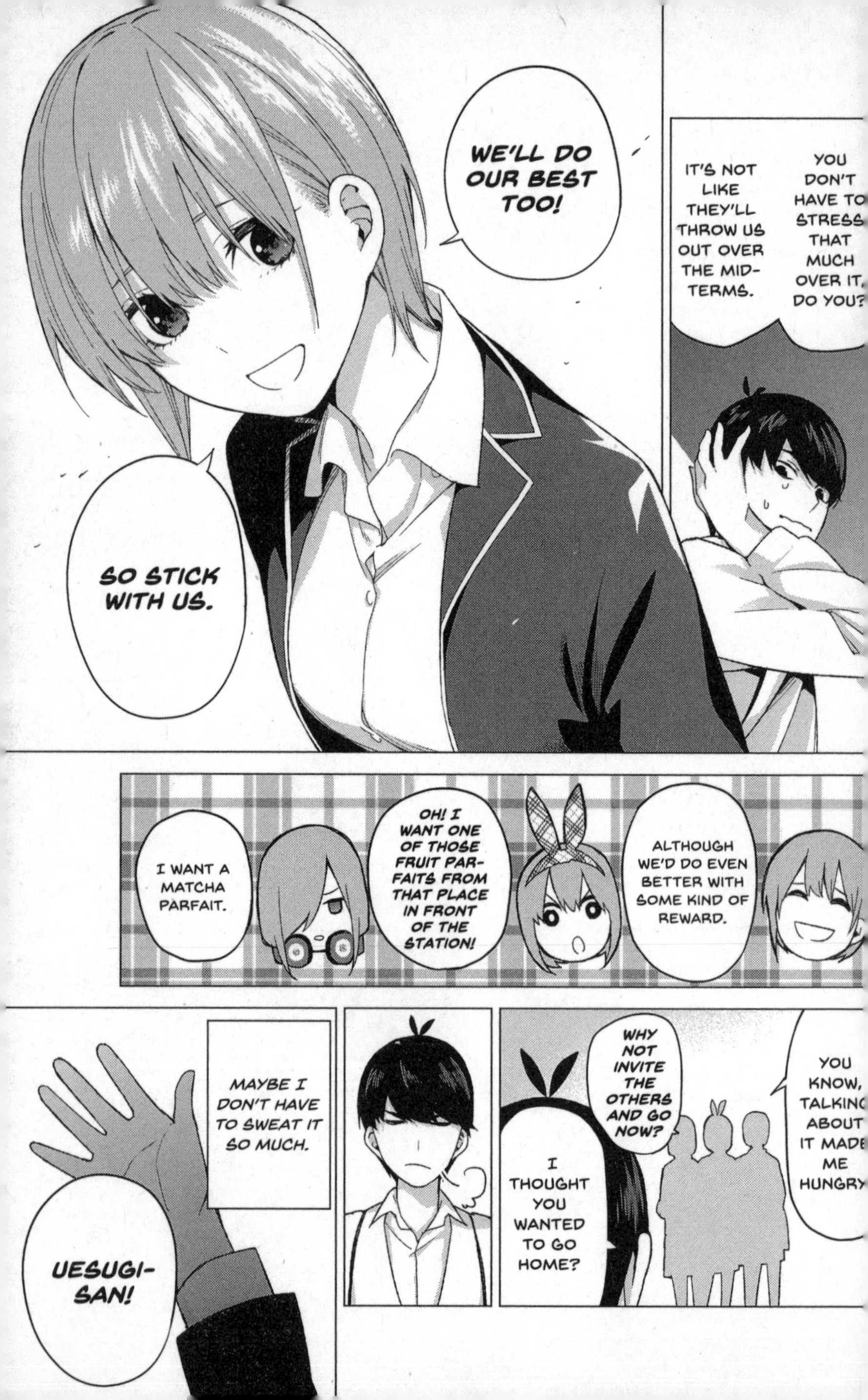
YOU DON'T HAVE TO STRESS THAT MUCH OVER IT, DO YOU?
IT'S NOT LIKE THEY'LL THROW US OUT OVER THE MID-TERMS.
WE'LL DO OUR BEST TOO!
SO STICK WITH US.
ALTHOUGH WE'D DO EVEN BETTER WITH SOME KIND OF REWARD.
OH! I WANT ONE OF THOSE FRUIT PARFAITS FROM THAT PLACE IN FRONT OF THE STATION!
I WANT A MATCHA PARFAIT.
YOU KNOW, TALKING ABOUT IT MADE ME HUNGRY
WHY NOT INVITE THE OTHERS AND GO NOW?
I THOUGHT YOU WANTED TO GO HOME?
MAYBE I DON'T HAVE TO SWEAT IT SO MUCH.
UESUGI-SAN!

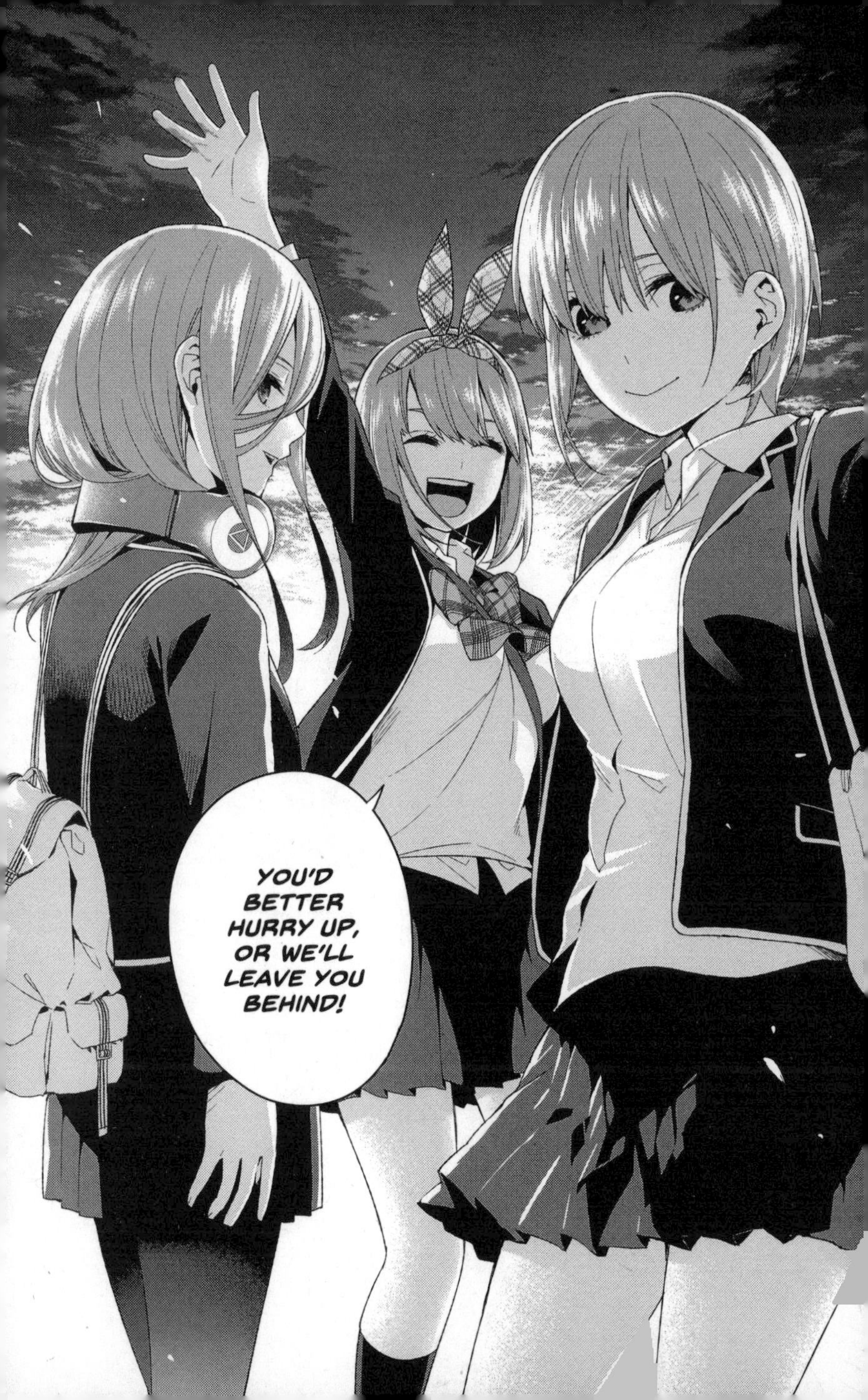
YOU'D BETTER HURRY UP, OR WE'LL LEAVE YOU BEHIND!

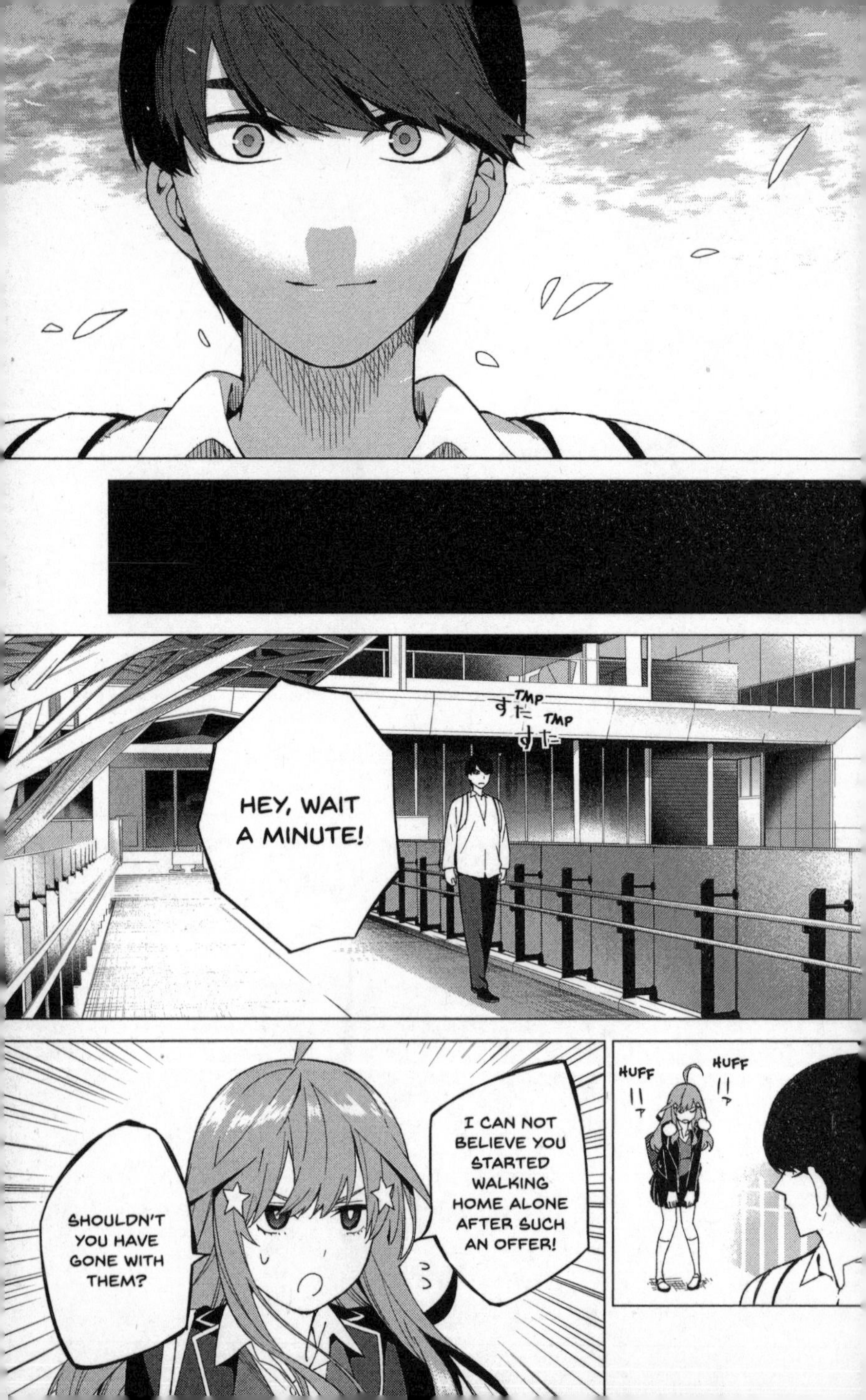

TMP すた
TMP すた
HEY, WAIT A MINUTE!
HUFF
HUFF
I CAN NOT BELIEVE YOU STARTED WALKING HOME ALONE AFTER SUCH AN OFFER!
SHOULDN'T YOU HAVE GONE WITH THEM?

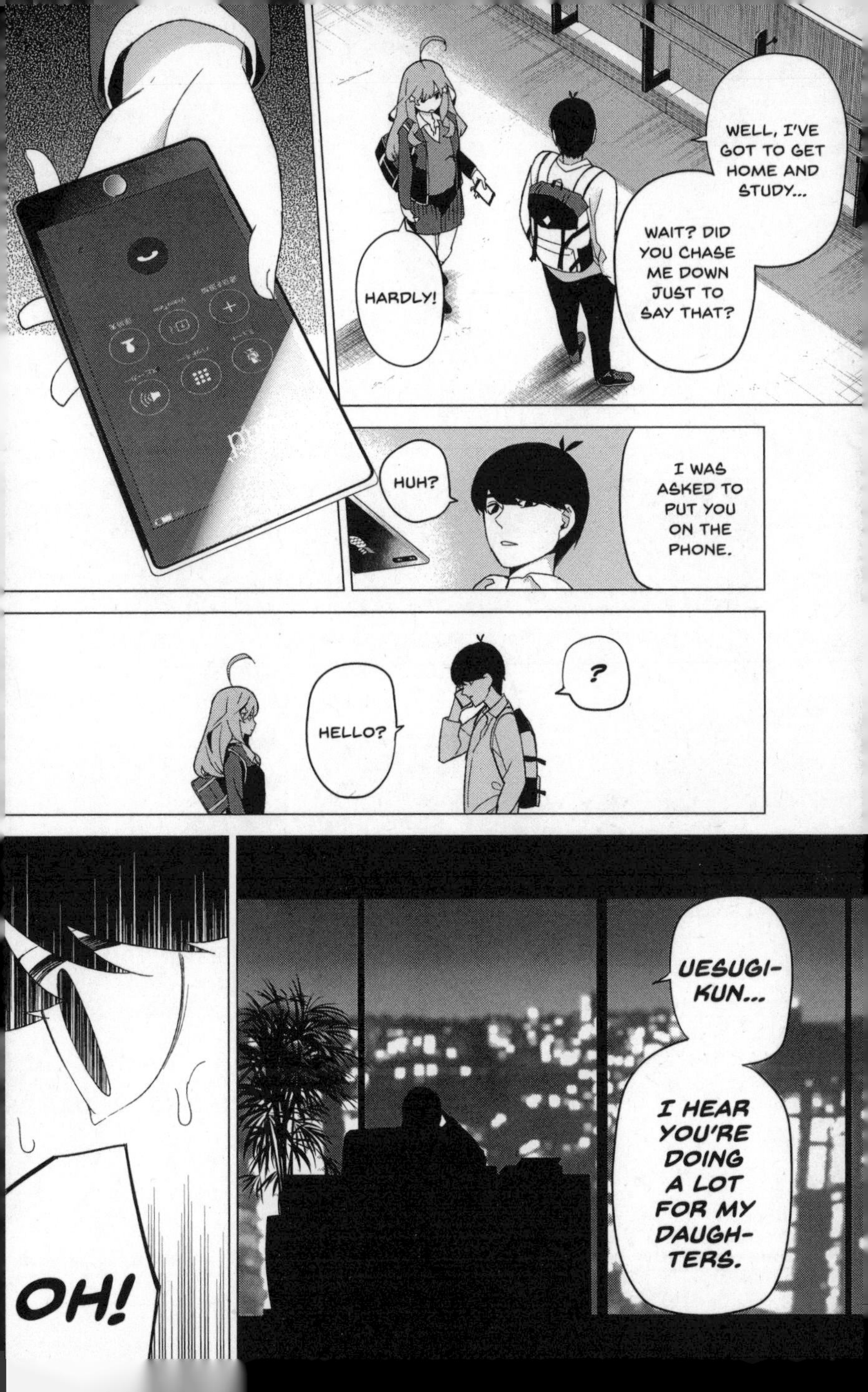
WELL, I'VE GOT TO GET HOME AND STUDY...
WAIT? DID YOU CHASE ME DOWN JUST TO SAY THAT?
HARDLY!
I WAS ASKED TO PUT YOU ON THE PHONE.
HUH?
?
HELLO?
UESUGI-KUN...
I HEAR YOU'RE DOING A LOT FOR MY DAUGHTERS.
OH!

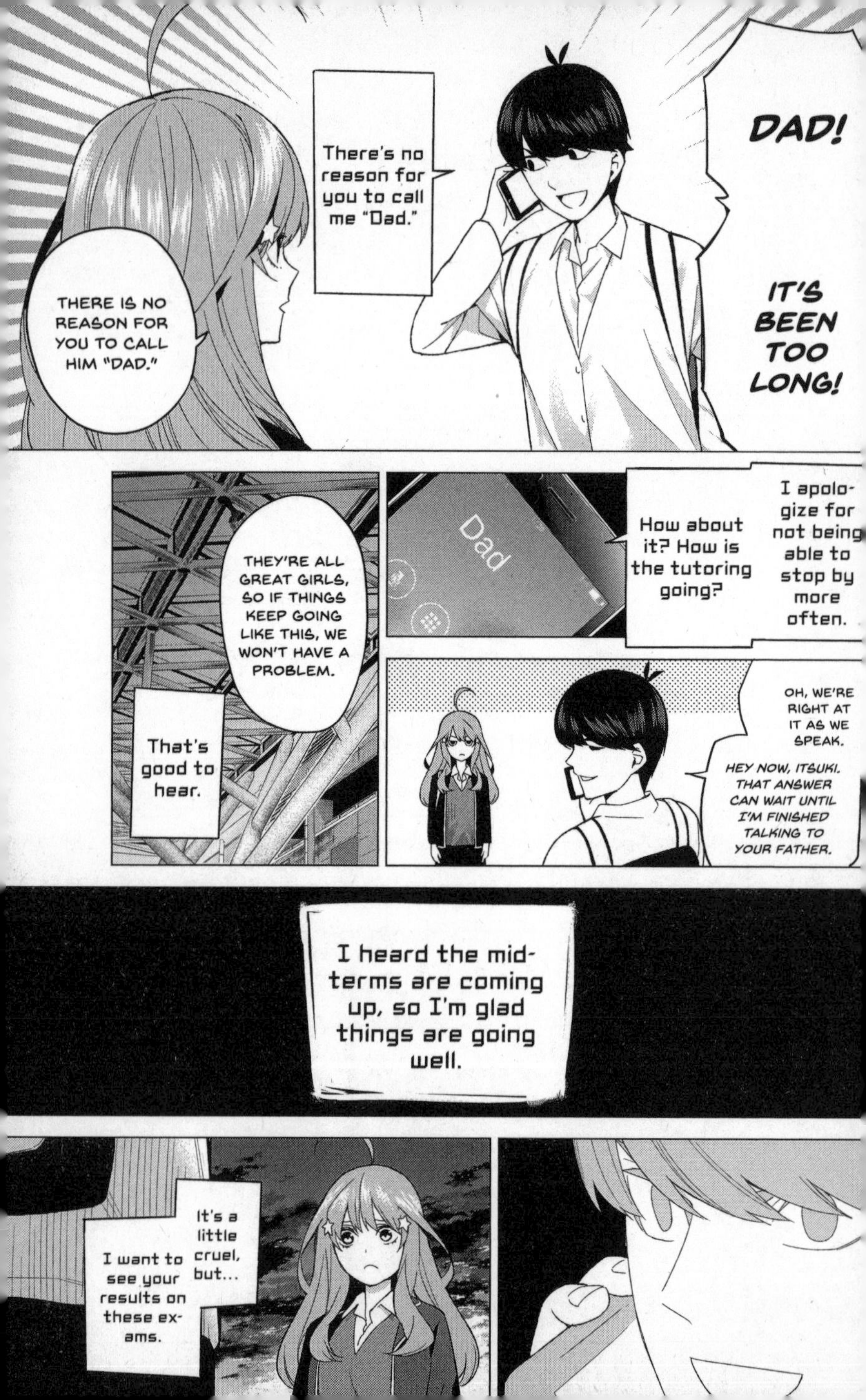
DAD!
IT'S BEEN TOO LONG!
There's no reason for you to call me "Dad."
THERE IS NO REASON FOR YOU TO CALL HIM "DAD."
I apologize for not being able to stop by more often.
How about it? How is the tutoring going?
Dad
OH, WE'RE RIGHT AT IT AS WE SPEAK.
HEY NOW, ITSUKI. THAT ANSWER CAN WAIT UNTIL I'M FINISHED TALKING TO YOUR FATHER.
THEY'RE ALL GREAT GIRLS, SO IF THINGS KEEP GOING LIKE THIS, WE WON'T HAVE A PROBLEM.
That's good to hear.
I heard the midterms are coming up, so I'm glad things are going well.
It's a little cruel, but...
I want to see your results on these exams.

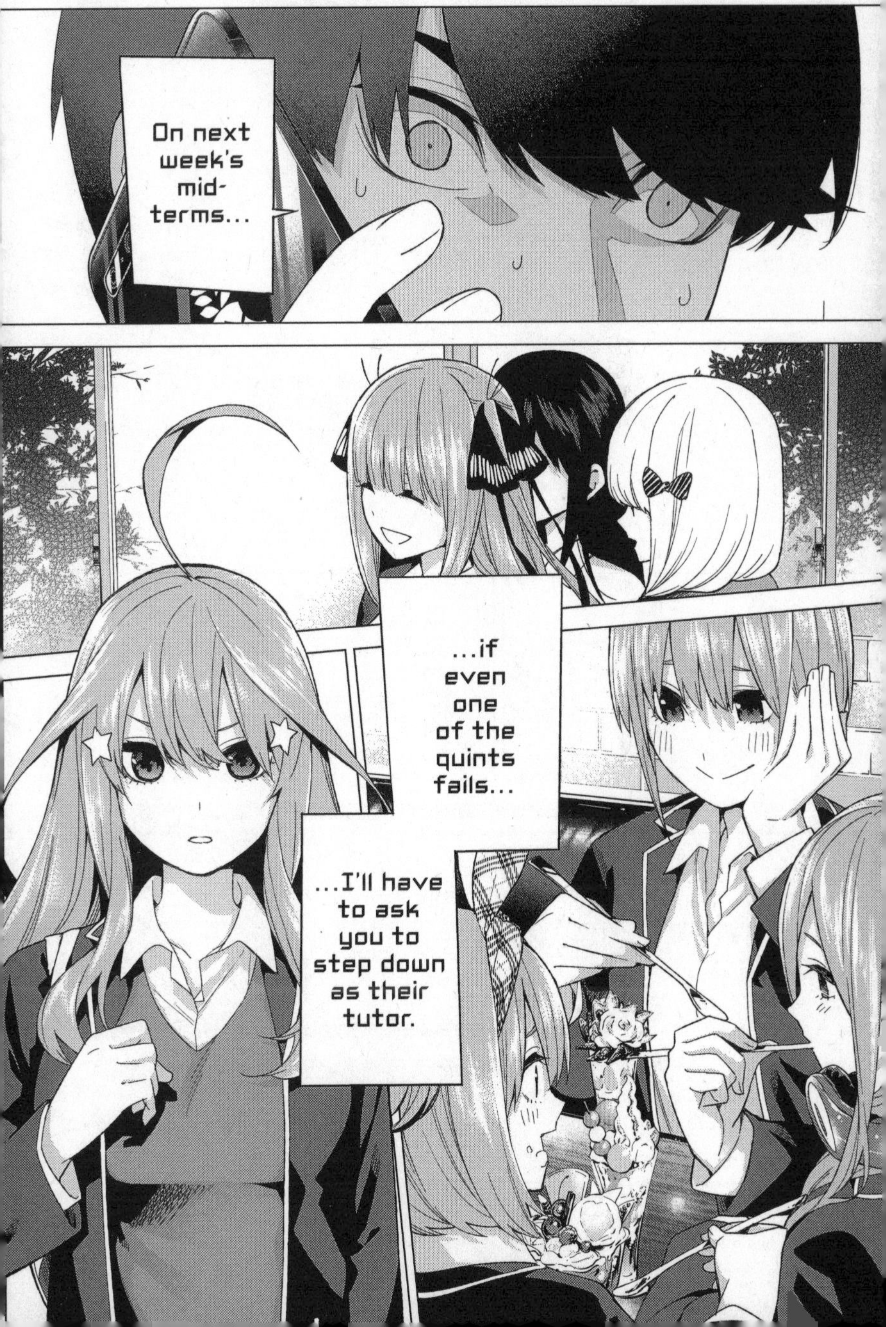
On next week's mid-terms...
...if even one of the quints fails...
...I'll have to ask you to step down as their tutor.

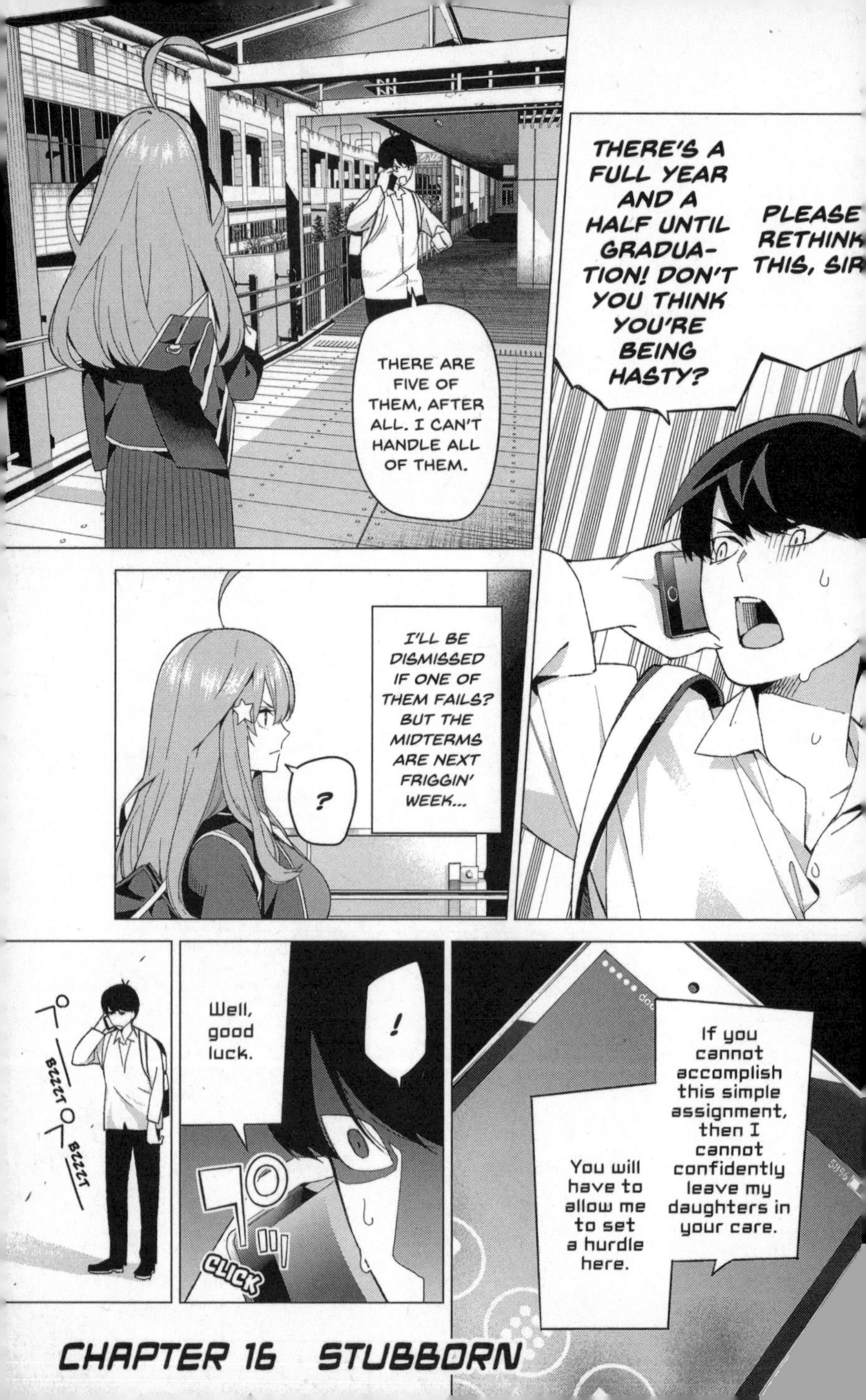
PLEASE RETHINK THIS, SIR
THERE'S A FULL YEAR AND A HALF UNTIL GRADUATION! DON'T YOU THINK YOU'RE BEING HASTY?
THERE ARE FIVE OF THEM, AFTER ALL. I CAN'T HANDLE ALL OF THEM.
I'LL BE DISMISSED IF ONE OF THEM FAILS? BUT THE MIDTERMS ARE NEXT FRIGGIN' WEEK...
?
If you cannot accomplish this simple assignment, then I cannot confidently leave my daughters in your care.
You will have to allow me to set a hurdle here.
!
Well, good luck.
CLICK
BZZZT
BZZZT

CHAPTER 16 STUBBORN

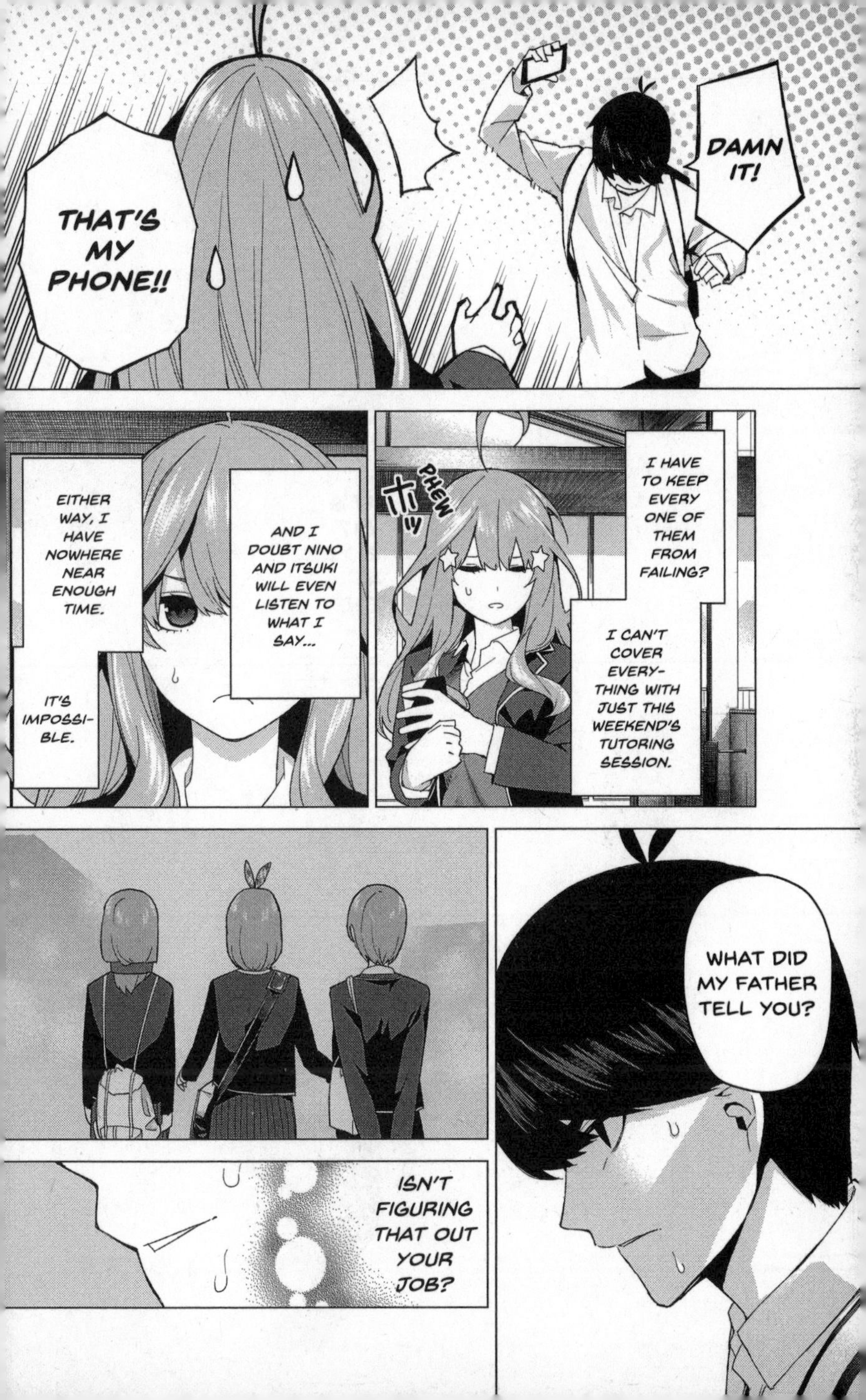
DAMN IT!
THAT'S MY PHONE!!
I HAVE TO KEEP EVERY ONE OF THEM FROM FAILING?
PHEW
ホッ
I CAN'T COVER EVERY-THING WITH JUST THIS WEEKEND'S TUTORING SESSION.
AND I DOUBT NINO AND ITSUKI WILL EVEN LISTEN TO WHAT I SAY...
EITHER WAY, I HAVE NOWHERE NEAR ENOUGH TIME.
IT'S IMPOSSI-BLE.
WHAT DID MY FATHER TELL YOU?
ISN'T FIGURING THAT OUT YOUR JOB?

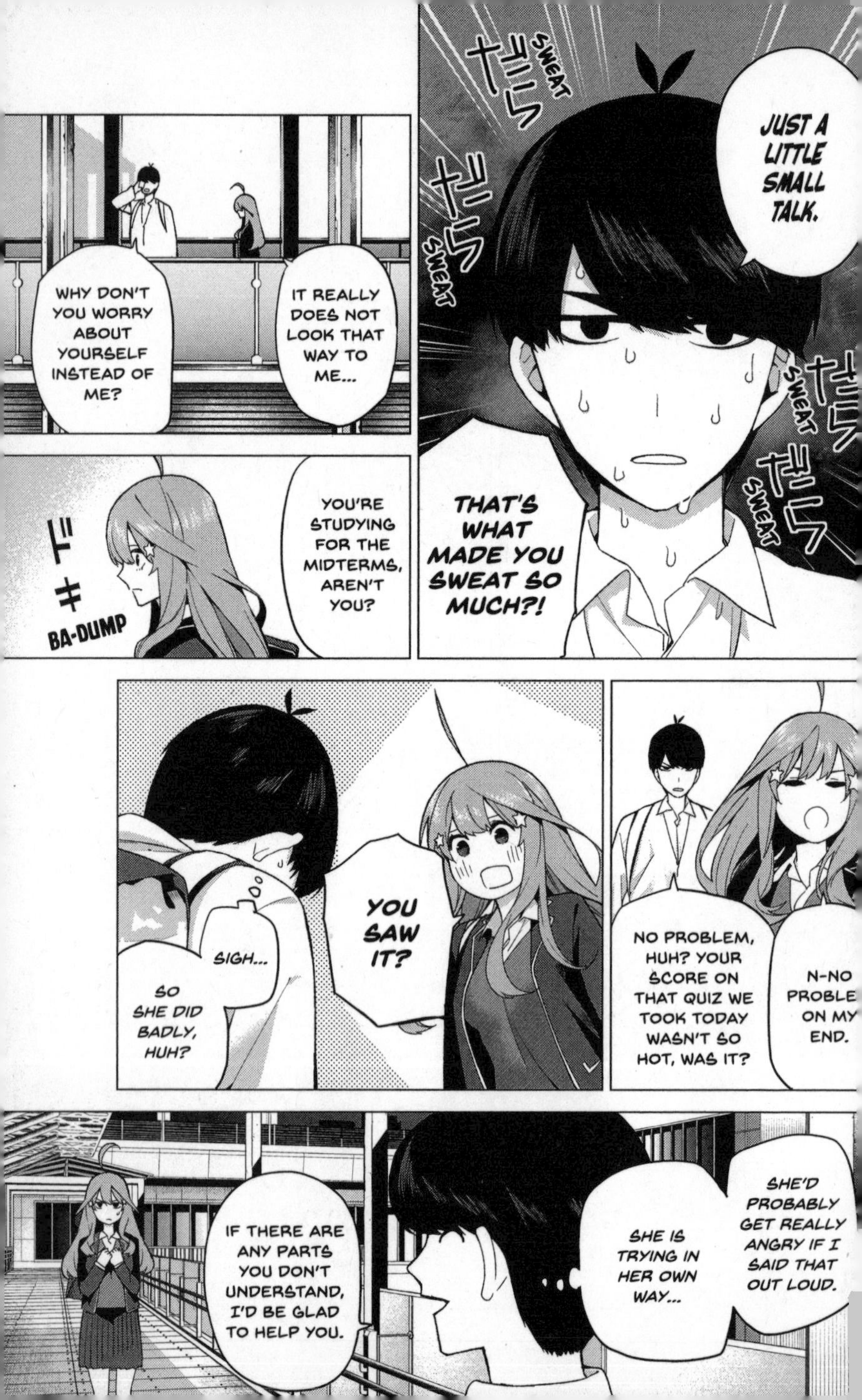
JUST A LITTLE SMALL TALK.
SWEAT
SWEAT
SWEAT
SWEAT
THAT'S WHAT MADE YOU SWEAT SO MUCH?!
IT REALLY DOES NOT LOOK THAT WAY TO ME...
WHY DON'T YOU WORRY ABOUT YOURSELF INSTEAD OF ME?
YOU'RE STUDYING FOR THE MIDTERMS, AREN'T YOU?
ドキ
BA-DUMP
N-NO PROBLE ON MY END.
NO PROBLEM, HUH? YOUR SCORE ON THAT QUIZ WE TOOK TODAY WASN'T SO HOT, WAS IT?
YOU SAW IT?
SIGH...
SO SHE DID BADLY, HUH?
SHE'D PROBABLY GET REALLY ANGRY IF I SAID THAT OUT LOUD.
SHE IS TRYING IN HER OWN WAY...
IF THERE ARE ANY PARTS YOU DON'T UNDERSTAND, I'D BE GLAD TO HELP YOU.

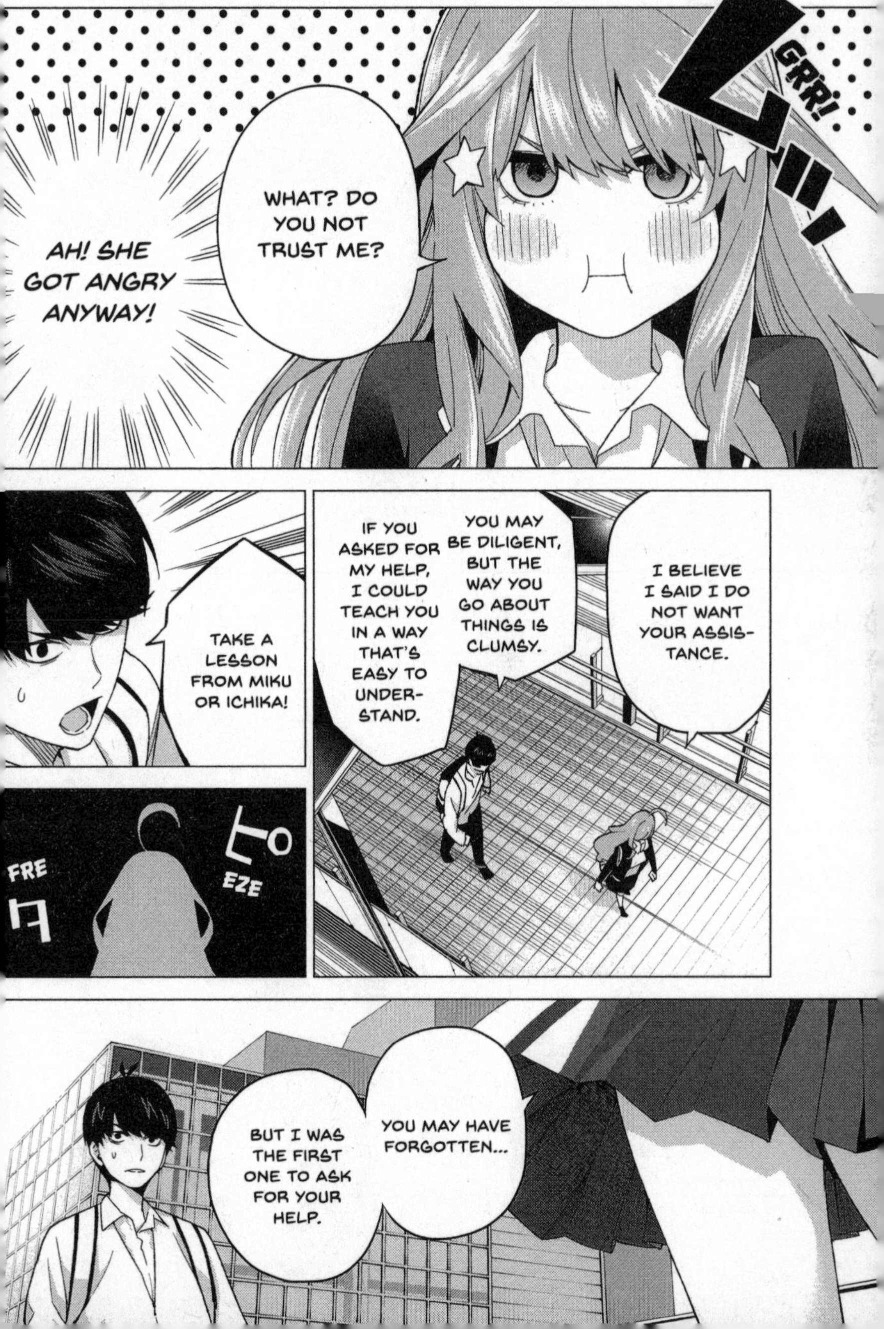
GRR!
WHAT? DO YOU NOT TRUST ME?
AH! SHE GOT ANGRY ANYWAY!
I BELIEVE I SAID I DO NOT WANT YOUR ASSIS-TANCE.
YOU MAY BE DILIGENT, BUT THE WAY YOU GO ABOUT THINGS IS CLUMSY.
IF YOU ASKED FOR MY HELP, I COULD TEACH YOU IN A WAY THAT'S EASY TO UNDER-STAND.
TAKE A LESSON FROM MIKU OR ICHIKA!
FREEZE
YOU MAY HAVE FORGOTTEN...
BUT I WAS THE FIRST ONE TO ASK FOR YOUR HELP.

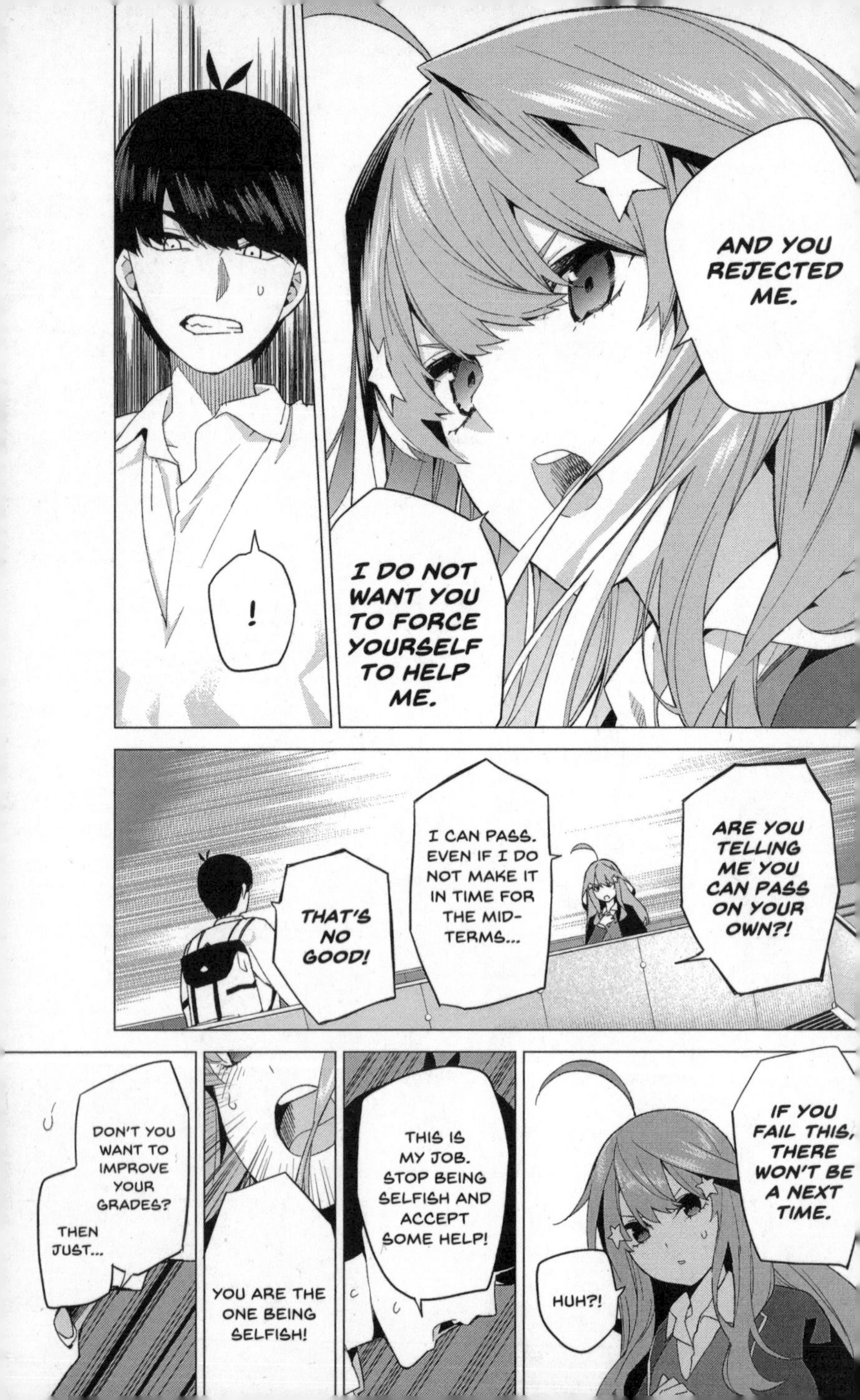
AND YOU REJECTED ME.
I DO NOT WANT YOU TO FORCE YOURSELF TO HELP ME.
!
ARE YOU TELLING ME YOU CAN PASS ON YOUR OWN?!
I CAN PASS. EVEN IF I DO NOT MAKE IT IN TIME FOR THE MID-TERMS...
THAT'S NO GOOD!
IF YOU FAIL THIS, THERE WON'T BE A NEXT TIME.
HUH?!
THIS IS MY JOB. STOP BEING SELFISH AND ACCEPT SOME HELP!
YOU ARE THE ONE BEING SELFISH!
DON'T YOU WANT TO IMPROVE YOUR GRADES?
THEN JUST...

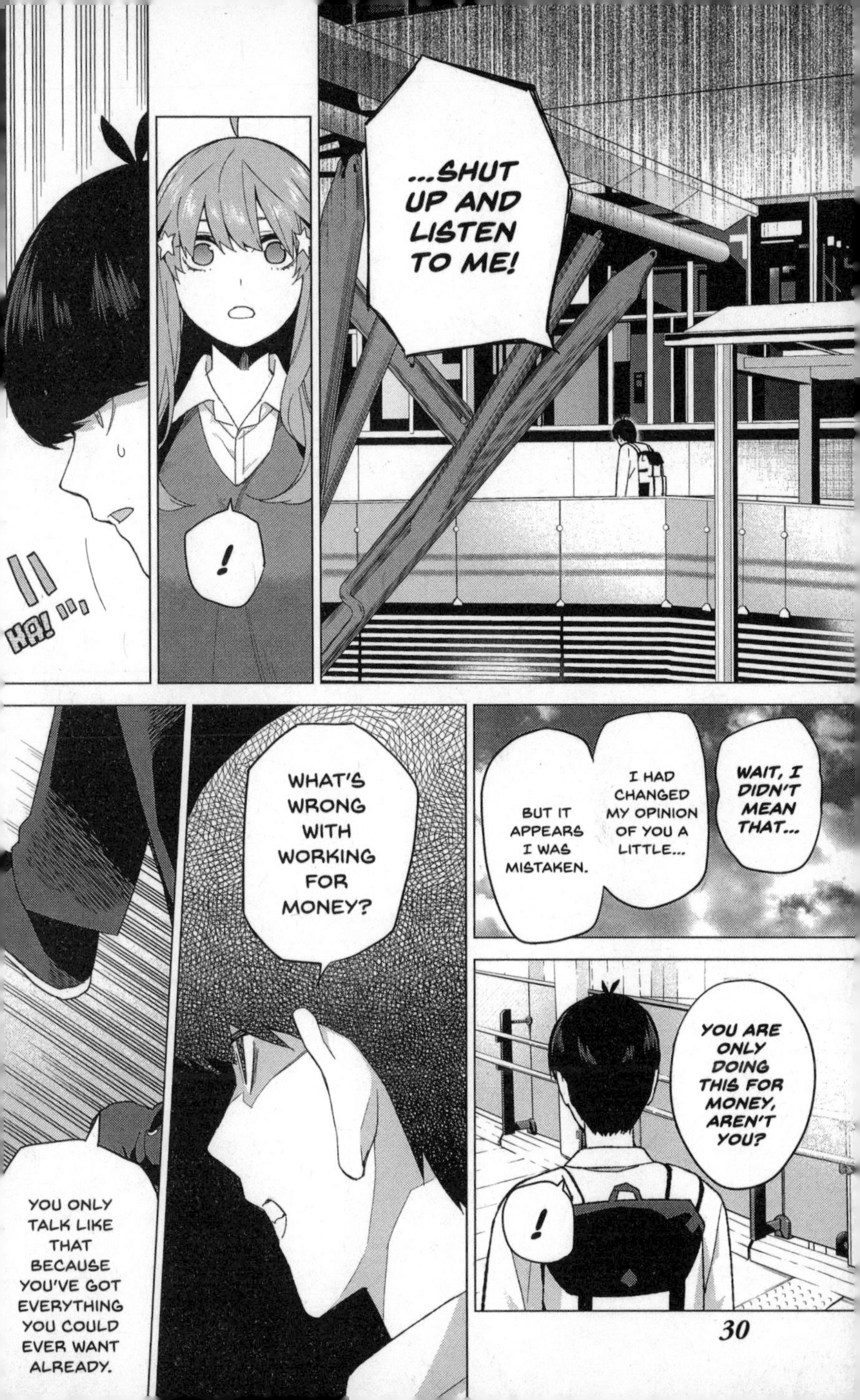
...SHUT UP AND LISTEN TO ME!
!
HA!
WAIT, I DIDN'T MEAN THAT...
I HAD CHANGED MY OPINION OF YOU A LITTLE...
BUT IT APPEARS I WAS MISTAKEN.
YOU ARE ONLY DOING THIS FOR MONEY, AREN'T YOU?
!
WHAT'S WRONG WITH WORKING FOR MONEY?
YOU ONLY TALK LIKE THAT BECAUSE YOU'VE GOT EVERYTHING YOU COULD EVER WANT ALREADY.

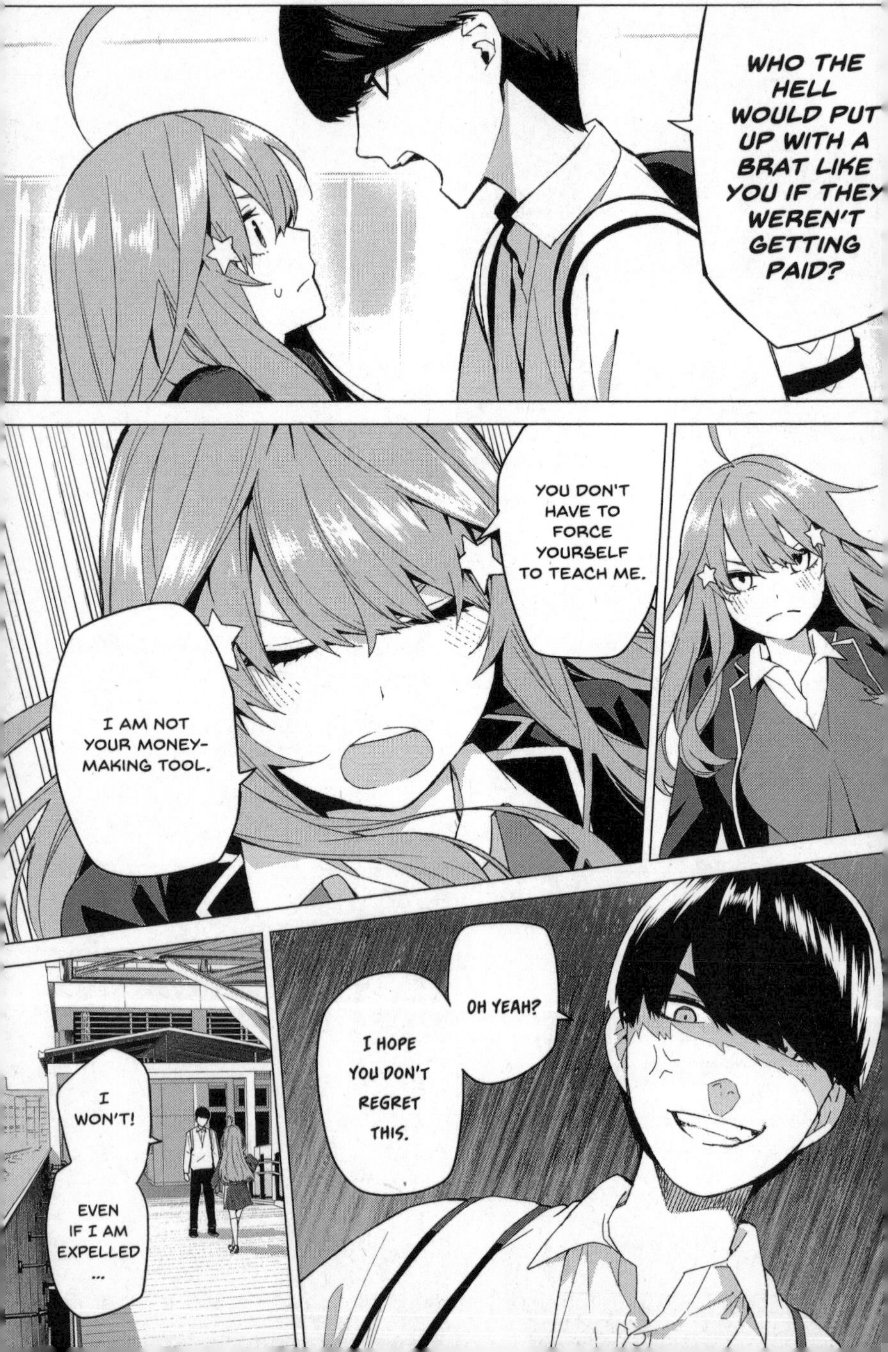
WHO THE HELL WOULD PUT UP WITH A BRAT LIKE YOU IF THEY WEREN'T GETTING PAID?
YOU DON'T HAVE TO FORCE YOURSELF TO TEACH ME.
I AM NOT YOUR MONEY-MAKING TOOL.
OH YEAH?
I HOPE YOU DON'T REGRET THIS.
I WON'T!
EVEN IF I AM EXPELLED ...

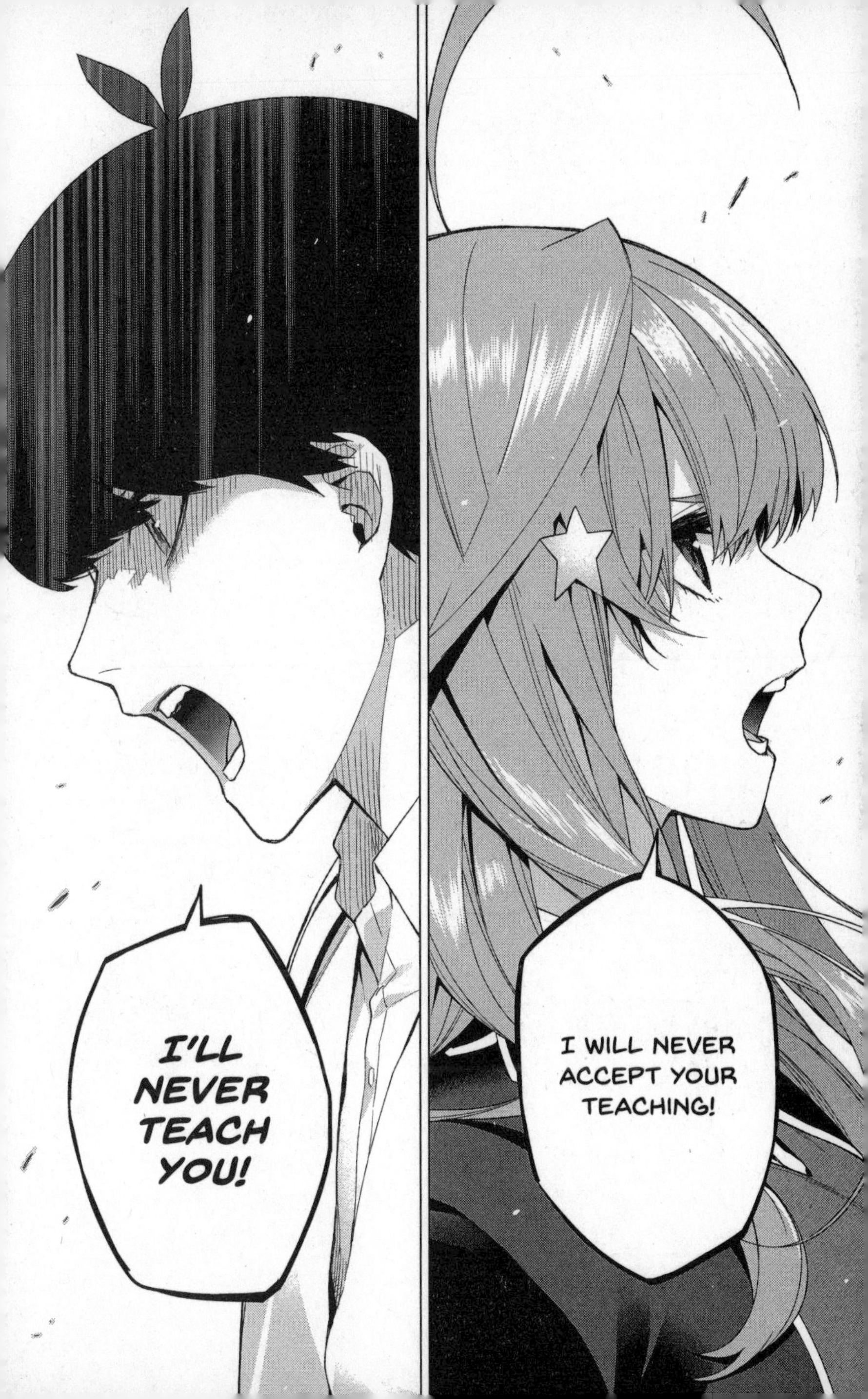
I WILL NEVER ACCEPT YOUR TEACHING!
I'LL NEVER TEACH YOU!

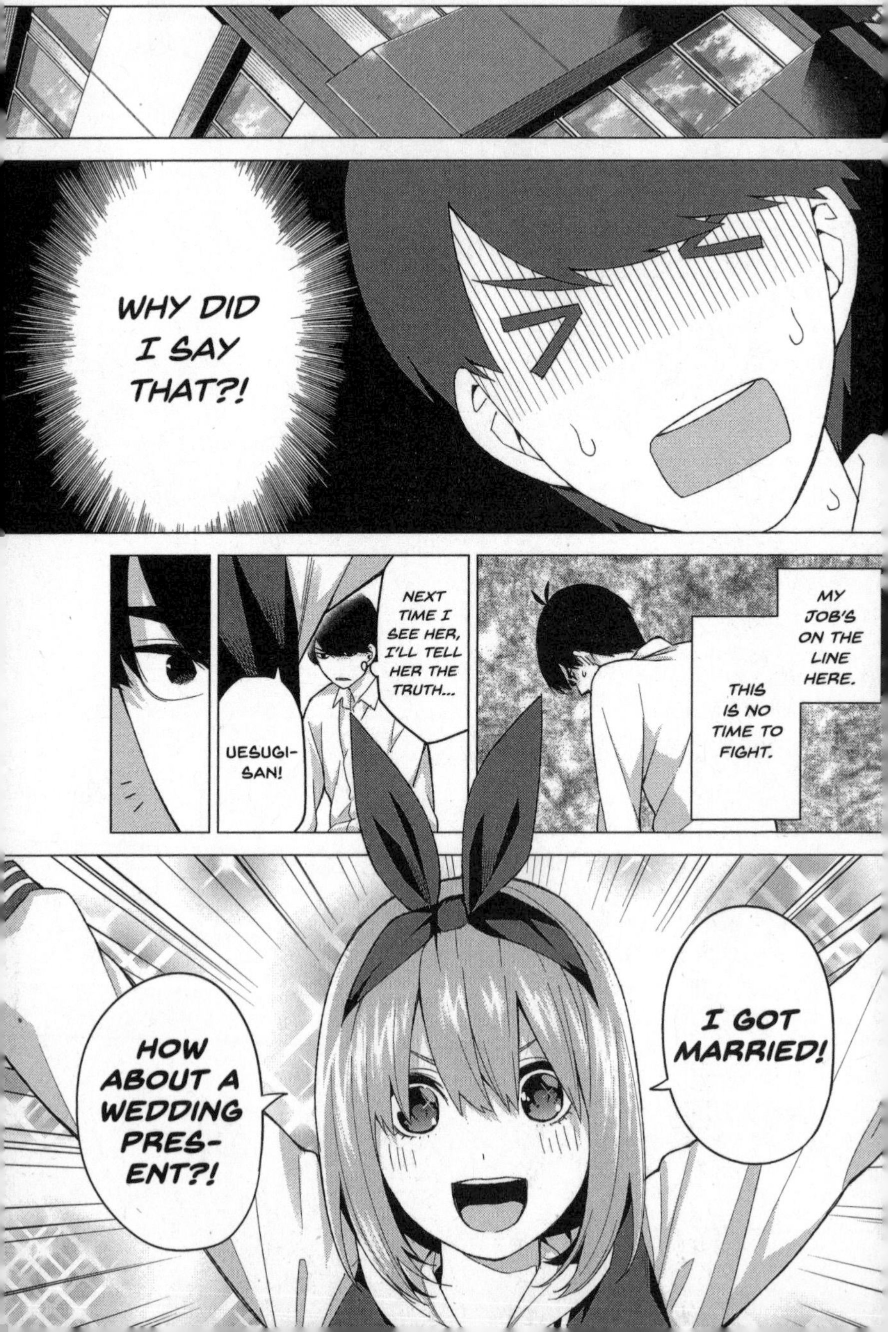
WHY DID I SAY THAT?!
MY JOB'S ON THE LINE HERE.
THIS IS NO TIME TO FIGHT.
NEXT TIME I SEE HER, I'LL TELL HER THE TRUTH...
UESUGI-SAN!
I GOT MARRIED!
HOW ABOUT A WEDDING PRESENT?!

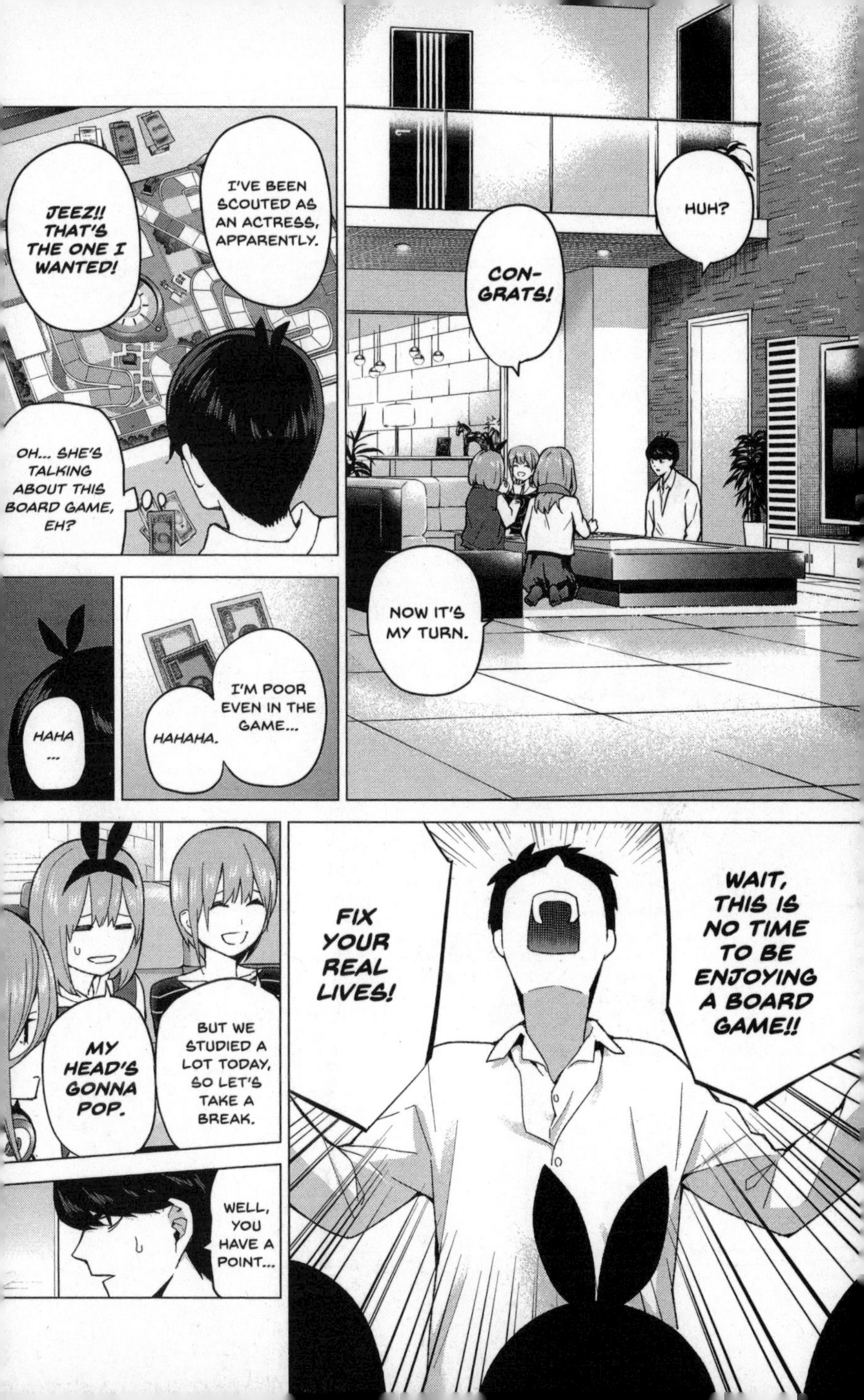
HUH?
CON-GRATS!
NOW IT'S MY TURN.
I'VE BEEN SCOUTED AS AN ACTRESS, APPARENTLY.
JEEZ!! THAT'S THE ONE I WANTED!
OH... SHE'S TALKING ABOUT THIS BOARD GAME, EH?
I'M POOR EVEN IN THE GAME...
HAHAHA.
HAHA ...
WAIT, THIS IS NO TIME TO BE ENJOYING A BOARD GAME!!
FIX YOUR REAL LIVES!
BUT WE STUDIED A LOT TODAY, SO LET'S TAKE A BREAK.
MY HEAD'S GONNA POP.
WELL, YOU HAVE A POINT...

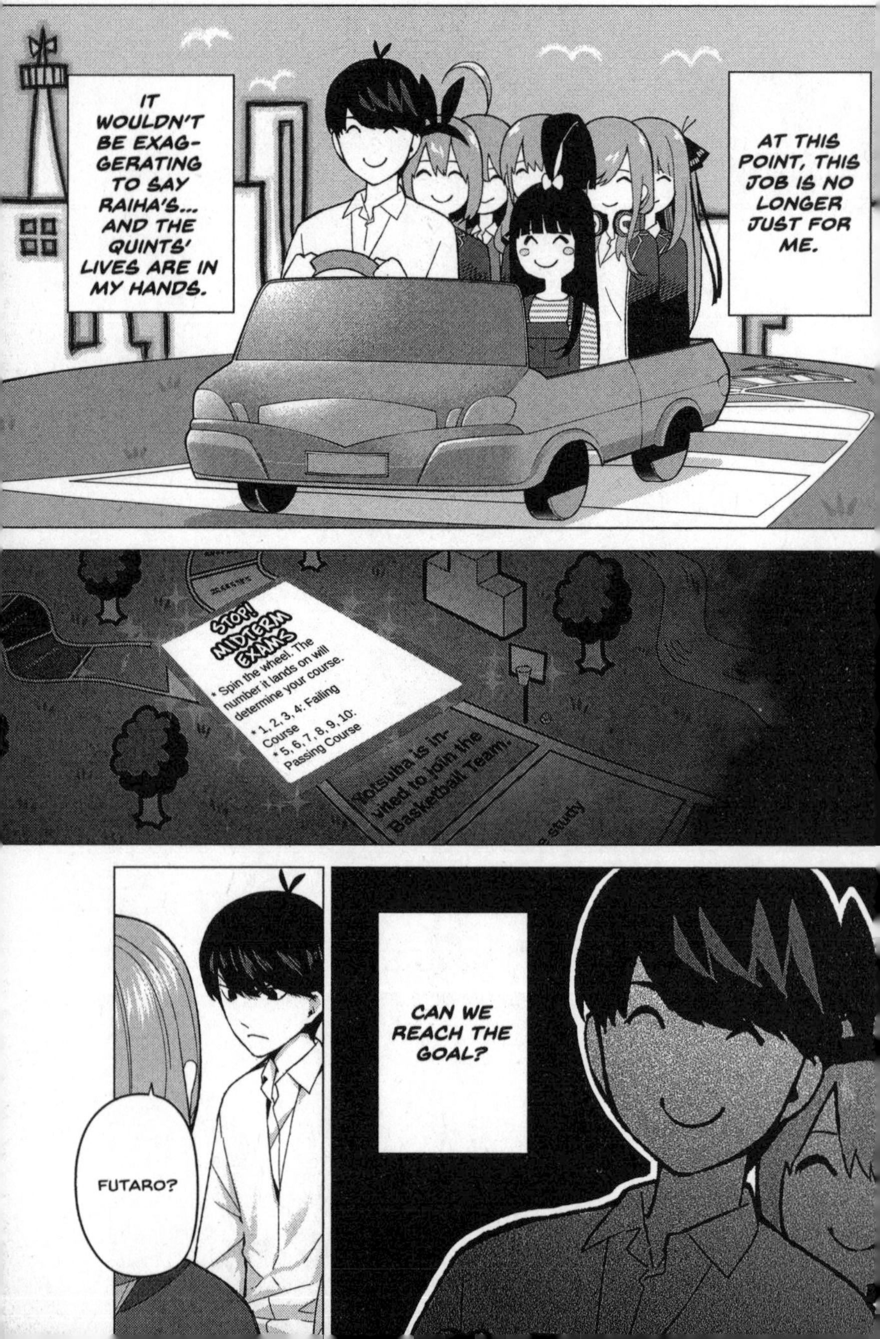
AT THIS POINT, THIS JOB IS NO LONGER JUST FOR ME.
IT WOULDN'T BE EXAG-GERATING TO SAY RAIHA'S... AND THE QUINTS' LIVES ARE IN MY HANDS.
STOP! MIDTERM EXAMS
* Spin the wheel. The number it lands on will determine your course.
* 1, 2, 3, 4: Failing Course
* 5, 6, 7, 8, 9, 10: Passing Course
Yotsuba is in-vited to join the Basketball Team.
CAN WE REACH THE GOAL?
FUTARO?

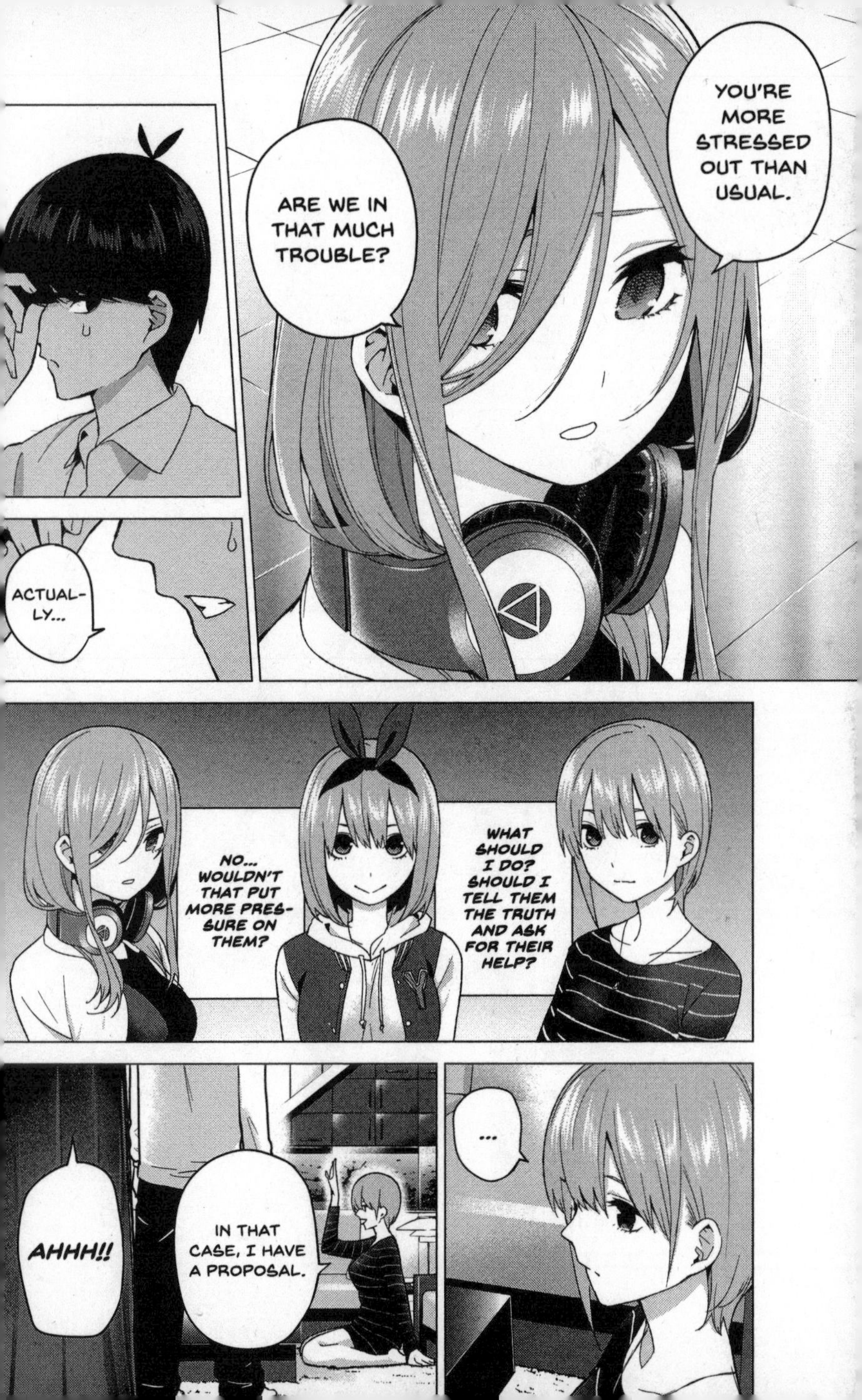
YOU'RE MORE STRESSED OUT THAN USUAL.
ARE WE IN THAT MUCH TROUBLE?
ACTUAL-LY...
WHAT SHOULD I DO? SHOULD I TELL THEM THE TRUTH AND ASK FOR THEIR HELP?
NO... WOULDN'T THAT PUT MORE PRES-SURE ON THEM?
...
IN THAT CASE, I HAVE A PROPOSAL.
AHHH!!

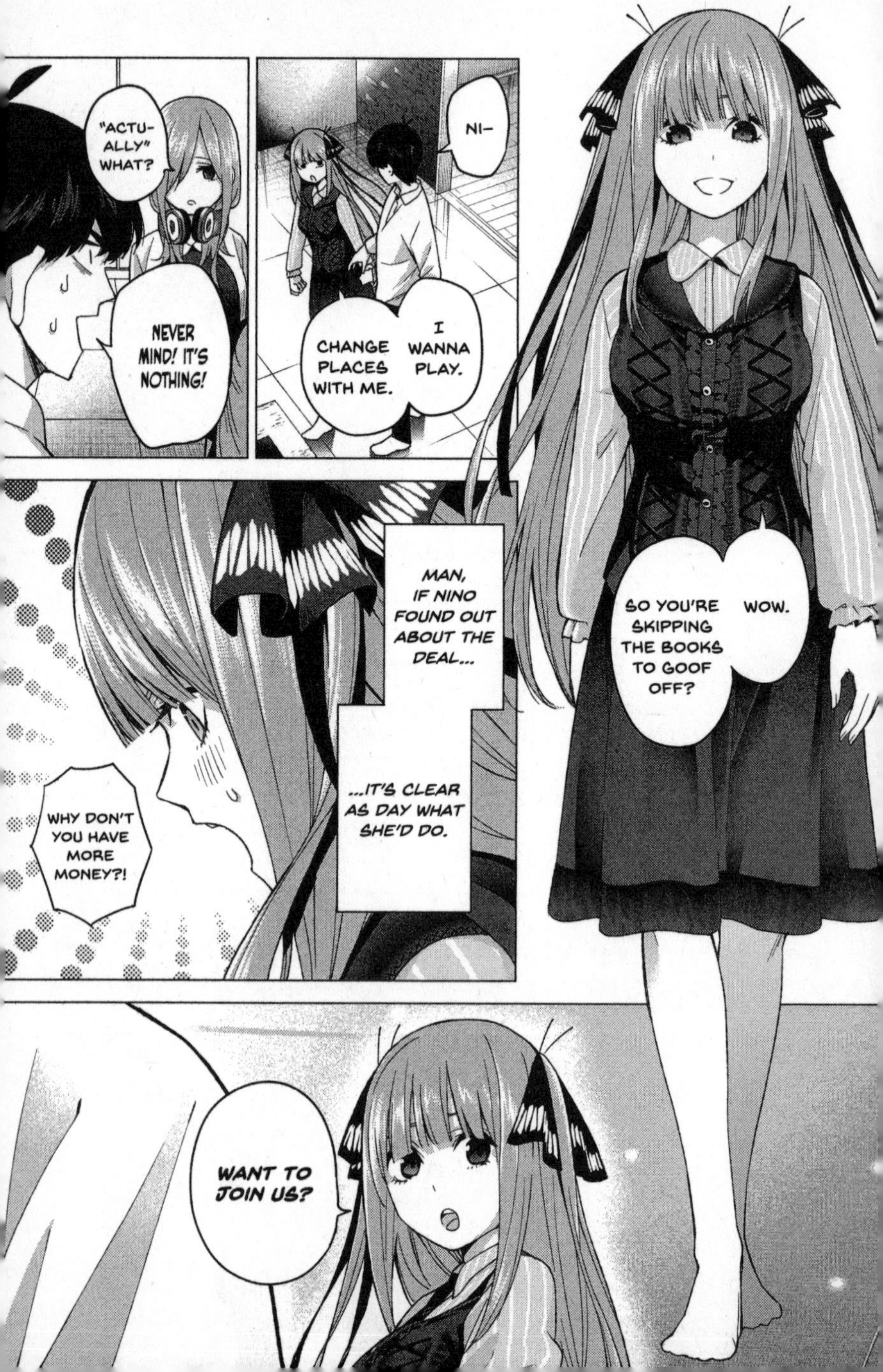
WOW.
SO YOU'RE SKIPPING THE BOOKS TO GOOF OFF?
NI–
I WANNA PLAY.
CHANGE PLACES WITH ME.
"ACTU-ALLY" WHAT?
NEVER MIND! IT'S NOTHING!
MAN, IF NINO FOUND OUT ABOUT THE DEAL...
...IT'S CLEAR AS DAY WHAT SHE'D DO.
WHY DON'T YOU HAVE MORE MONEY?!
WANT TO JOIN US?

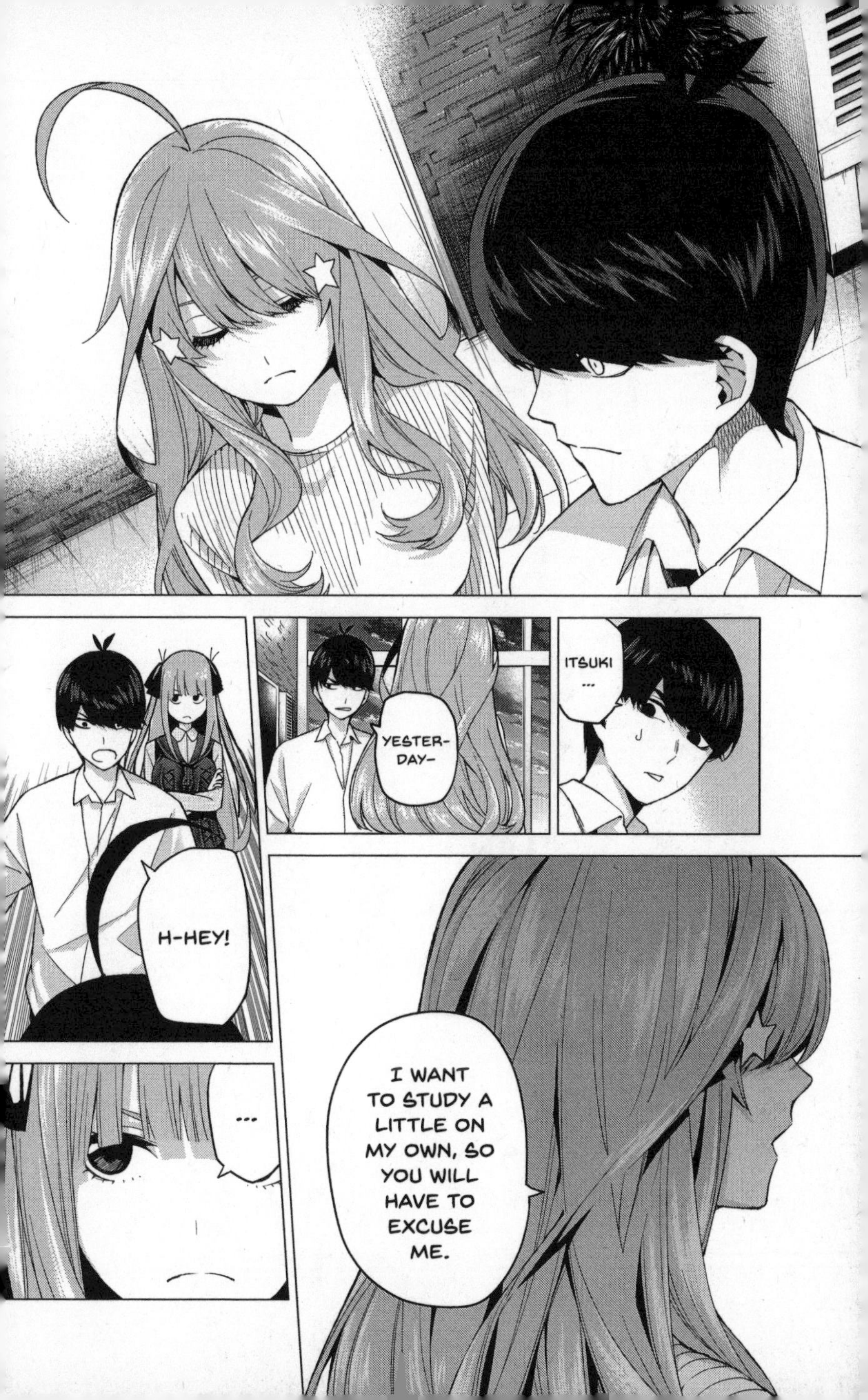
ITSUKI ...
YESTER-DAY-
I WANT TO STUDY A LITTLE ON MY OWN, SO YOU WILL HAVE TO EXCUSE ME.
H-HEY!
...

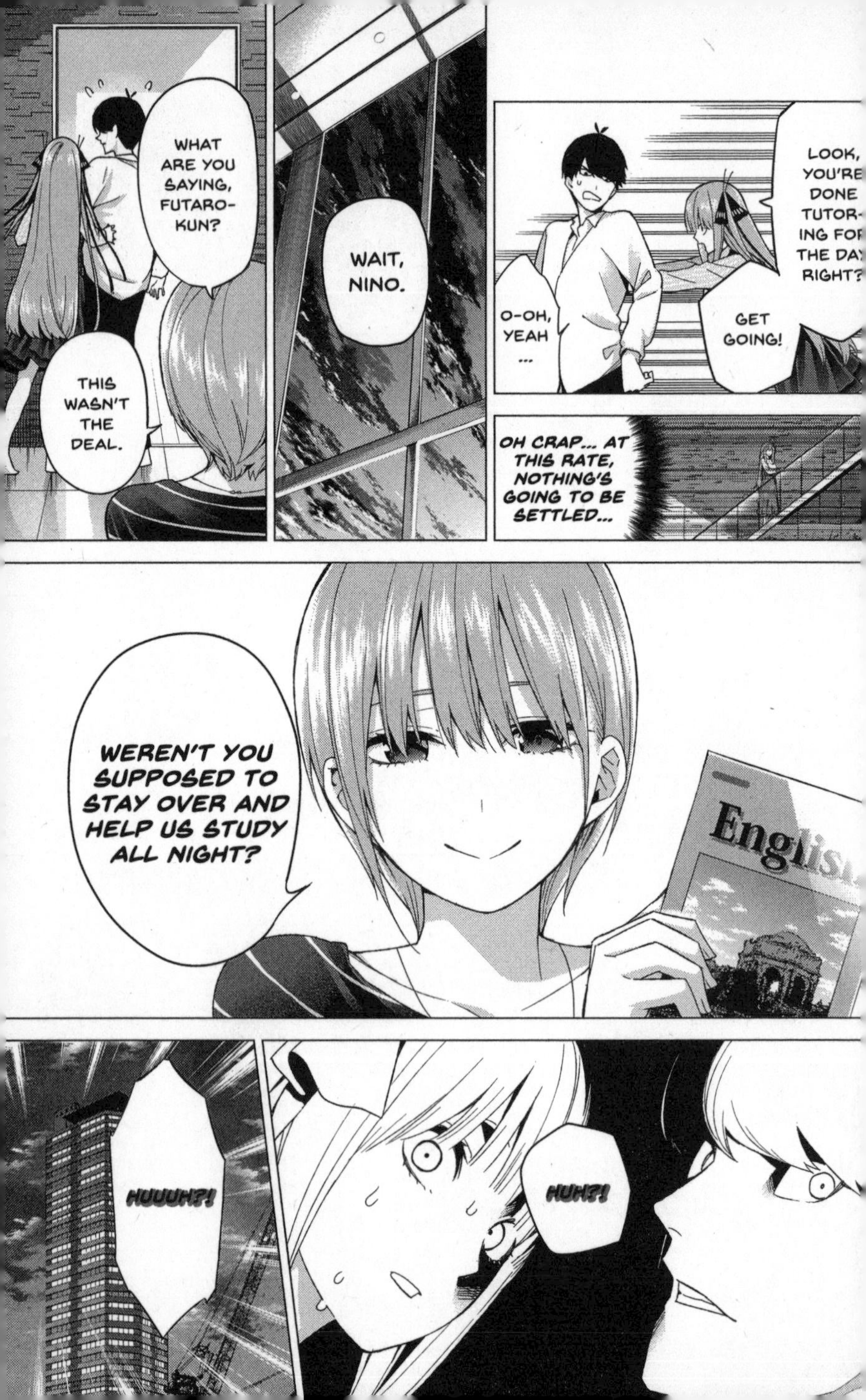
LOOK, YOU'RE DONE TUTOR-ING FOR THE DAY RIGHT?
GET GOING!
O-OH, YEAH ...
OH CRAP... AT THIS RATE, NOTHING'S GOING TO BE SETTLED...
WAIT, NINO.
WHAT ARE YOU SAYING, FUTARO-KUN?
THIS WASN'T THE DEAL.
WEREN'T YOU SUPPOSED TO STAY OVER AND HELP US STUDY ALL NIGHT?
Engli
HUH?!
HUUUH?!

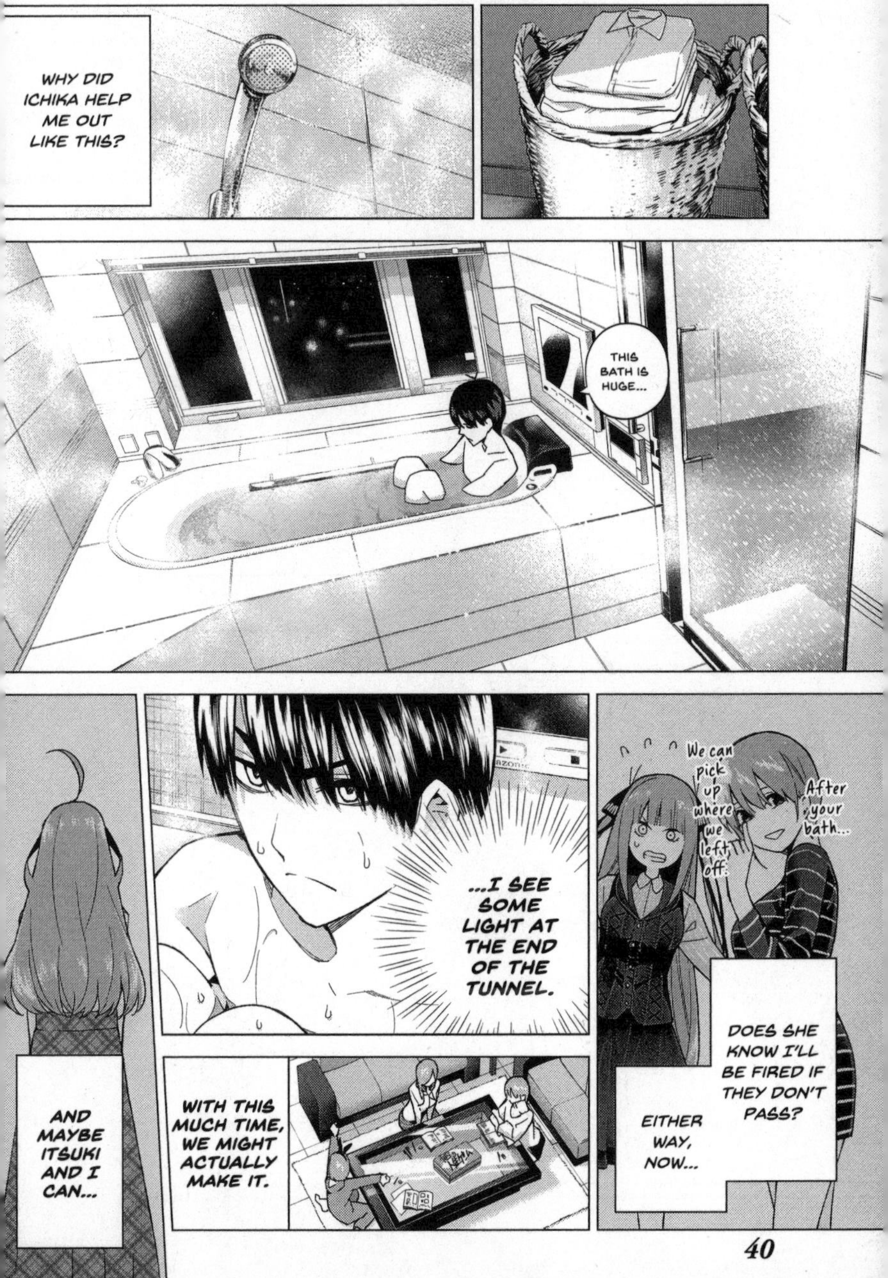
WHY DID ICHIKA HELP ME OUT LIKE THIS?
THIS BATH IS HUGE...
After your bath...
We can pick up where we left off.
DOES SHE KNOW I'LL BE FIRED IF THEY DON'T PASS?
EITHER WAY, NOW...
...I SEE SOME LIGHT AT THE END OF THE TUNNEL.
WITH THIS MUCH TIME, WE MIGHT ACTUALLY MAKE IT.
AND MAYBE ITSUKI AND I CAN...

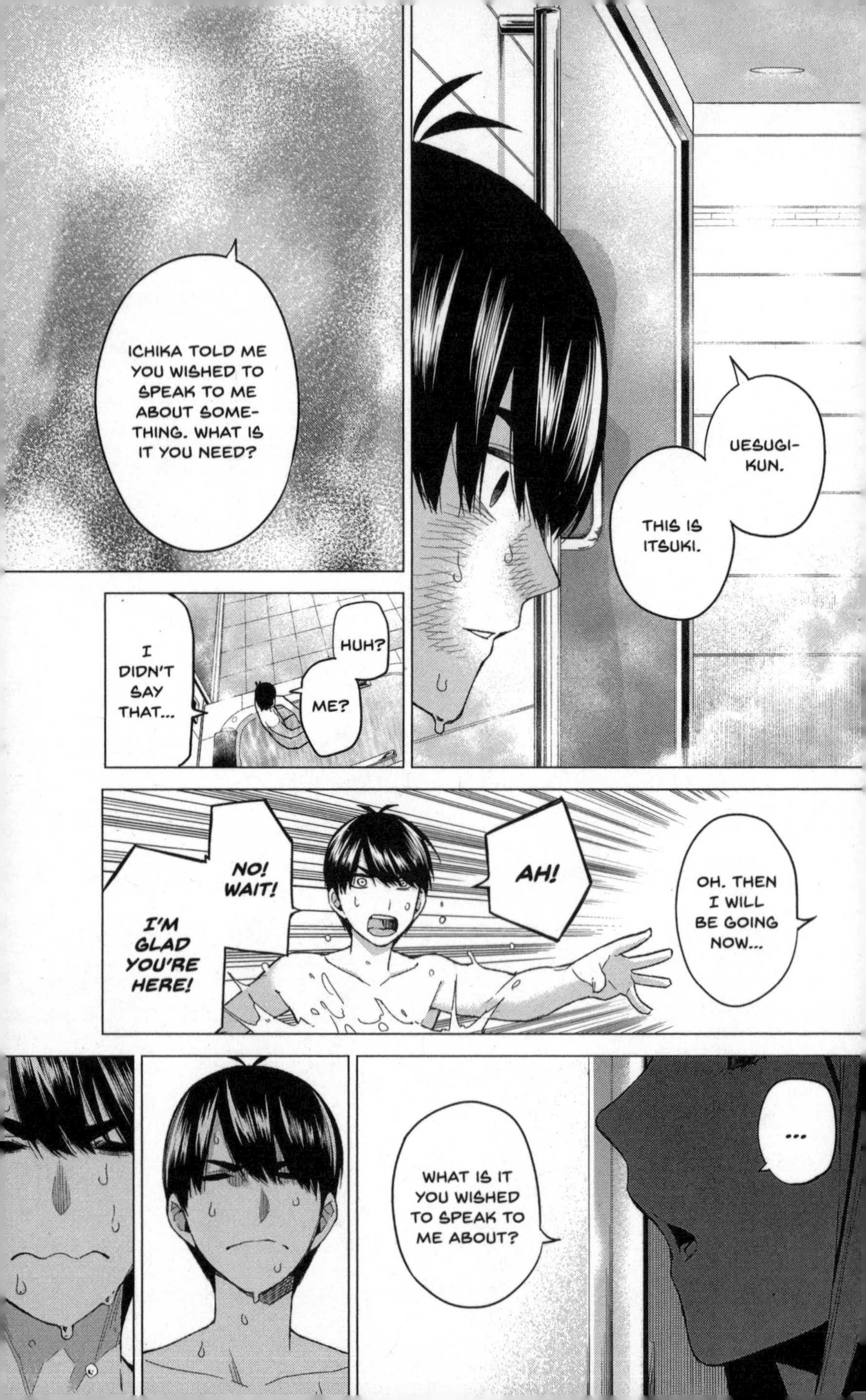
UESUGI-KUN.
THIS IS ITSUKI.
ICHIKA TOLD ME YOU WISHED TO SPEAK TO ME ABOUT SOME-THING. WHAT IS IT YOU NEED?
HUH?
ME?
I DIDN'T SAY THAT...
OH. THEN I WILL BE GOING NOW...
AH!
NO! WAIT!
I'M GLAD YOU'RE HERE!
...
WHAT IS IT YOU WISHED TO SPEAK TO ME ABOUT?

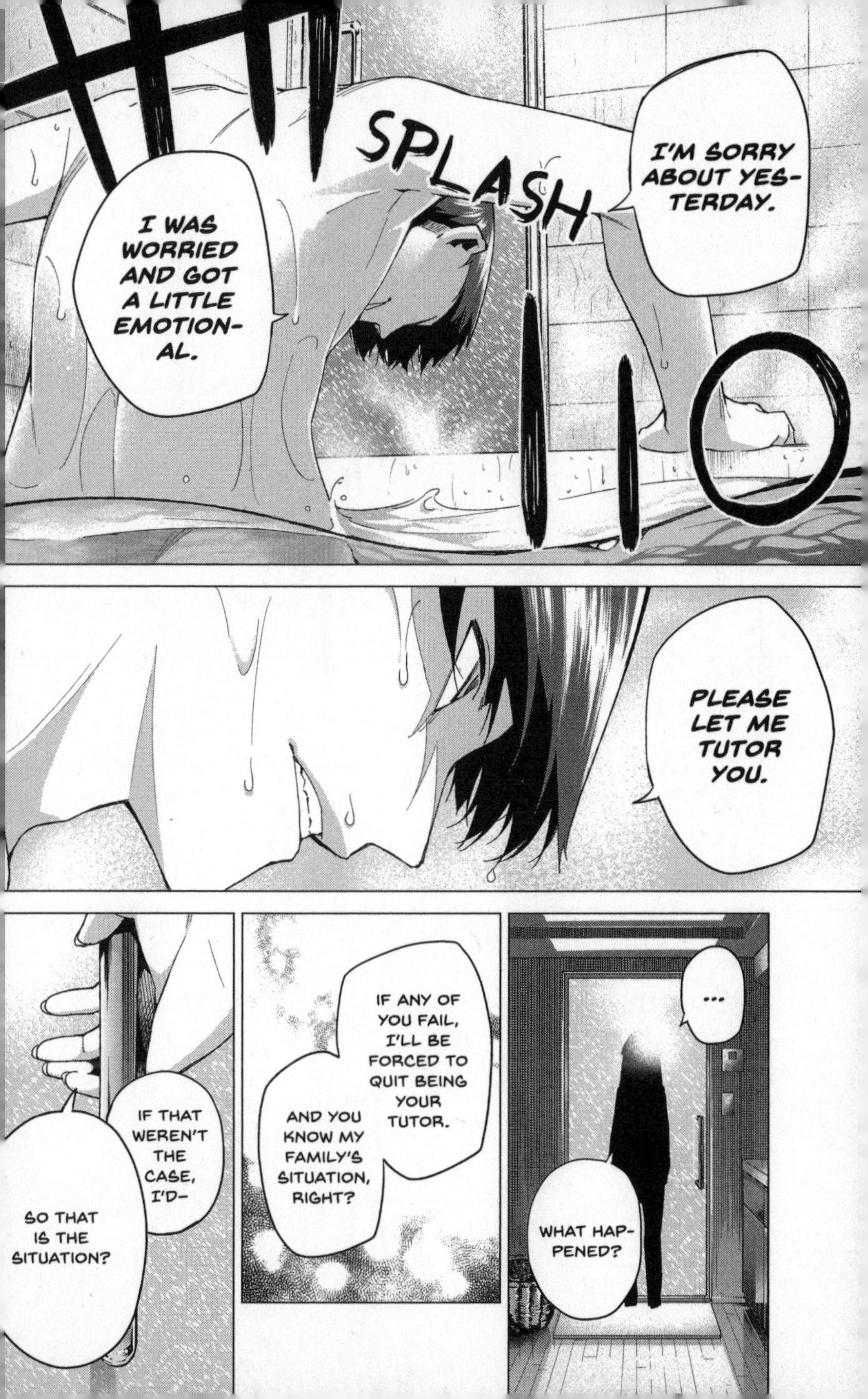
I'M SORRY ABOUT YESTERDAY.
SPLASH
I WAS WORRIED AND GOT A LITTLE EMOTIONAL.
PLEASE LET ME TUTOR YOU.
...
WHAT HAPPENED?
IF ANY OF YOU FAIL, I'LL BE FORCED TO QUIT BEING YOUR TUTOR.
AND YOU KNOW MY FAMILY'S SITUATION, RIGHT?
IF THAT WEREN'T THE CASE, I'D—
SO THAT IS THE SITUATION?

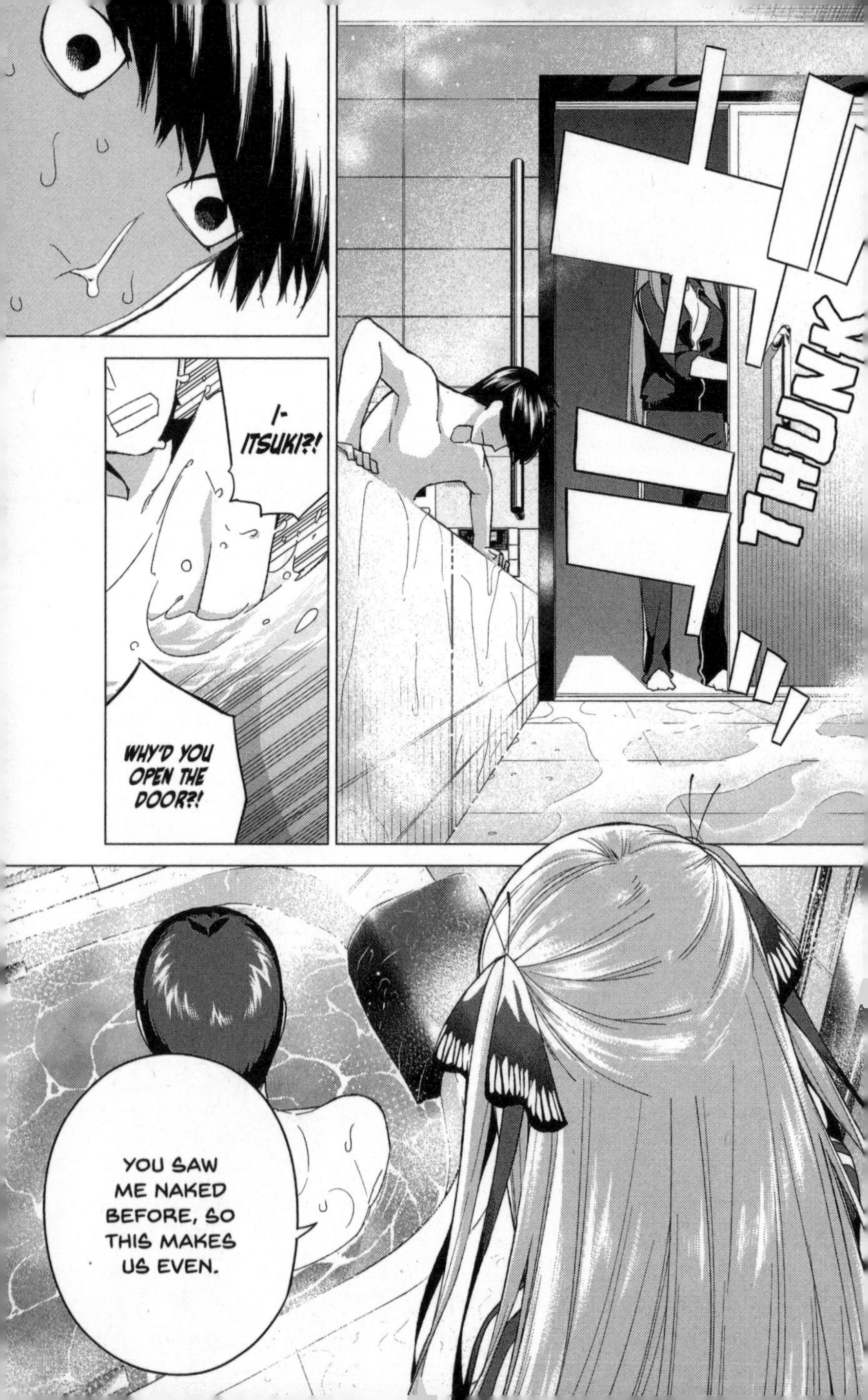
THUNK
I- ITSUKI?!
WHY'D YOU OPEN THE DOOR?!
YOU SAW ME NAKED BEFORE, SO THIS MAKES US EVEN.

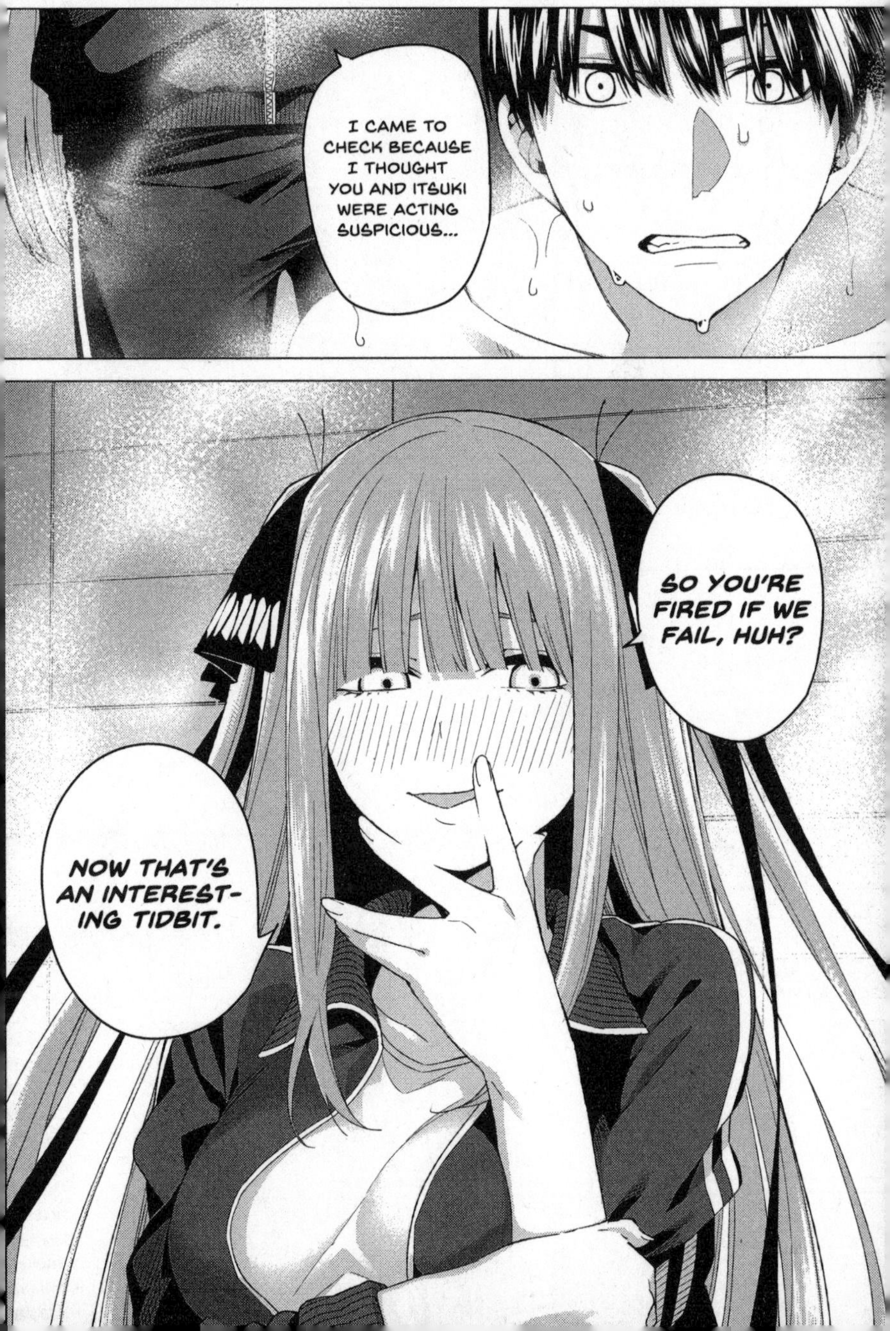
I CAME TO CHECK BECAUSE I THOUGHT YOU AND ITSUKI WERE ACTING SUSPICIOUS...
SO YOU'RE FIRED IF WE FAIL, HUH?
NOW THAT'S AN INTEREST-ING TIDBIT.

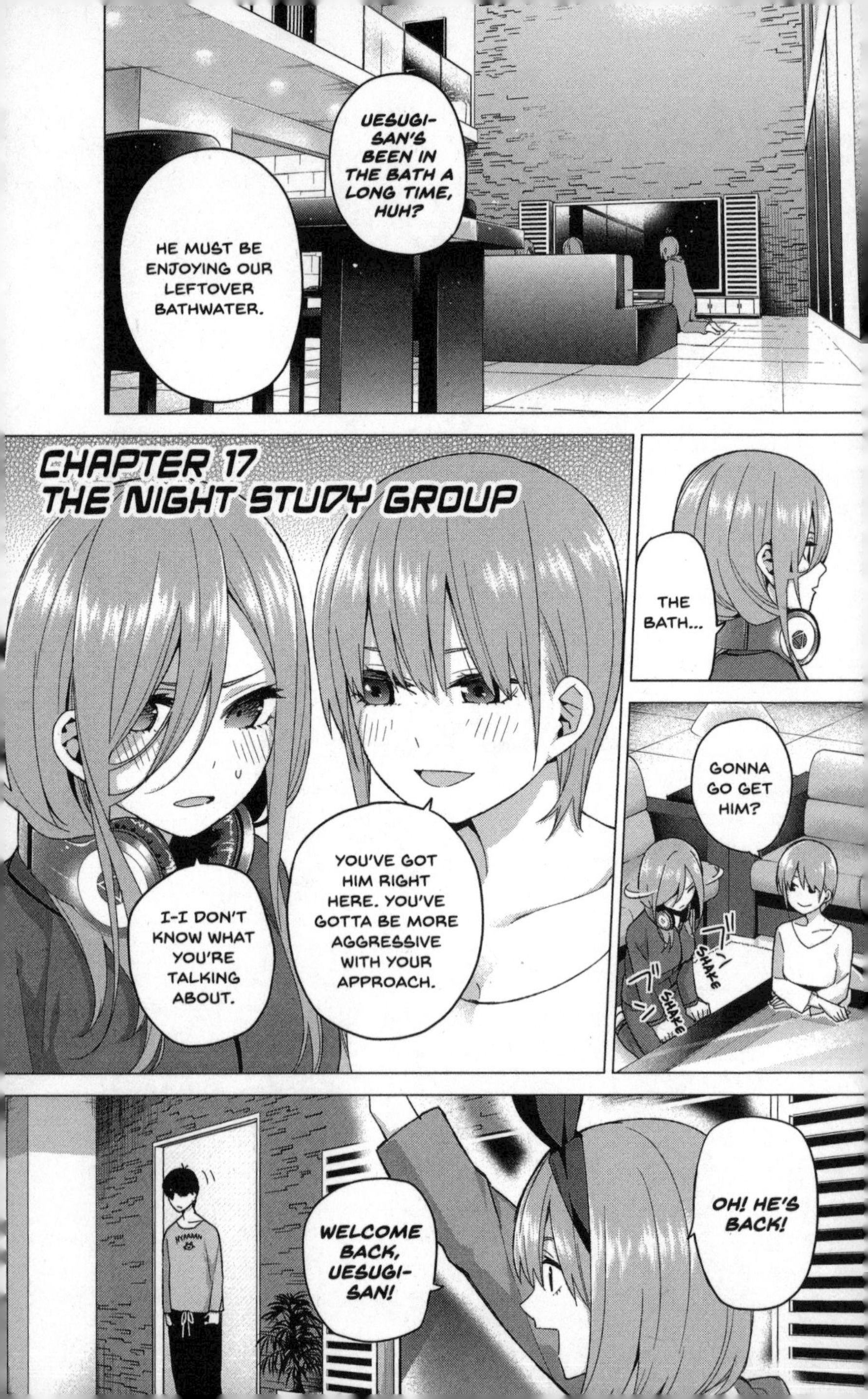
UESUGI-SAN'S BEEN IN THE BATH A LONG TIME, HUH?
HE MUST BE ENJOYING OUR LEFTOVER BATHWATER.
THE BATH...
GONNA GO GET HIM?
SHAKE
SHAKE
CHAPTER 17
THE NIGHT STUDY GROUP
YOU'VE GOT HIM RIGHT HERE. YOU'VE GOTTA BE MORE AGGRESSIVE WITH YOUR APPROACH.
I-I DON'T KNOW WHAT YOU'RE TALKING ABOUT.
OH! HE'S BACK!
WELCOME BACK, UESUGI-SAN!

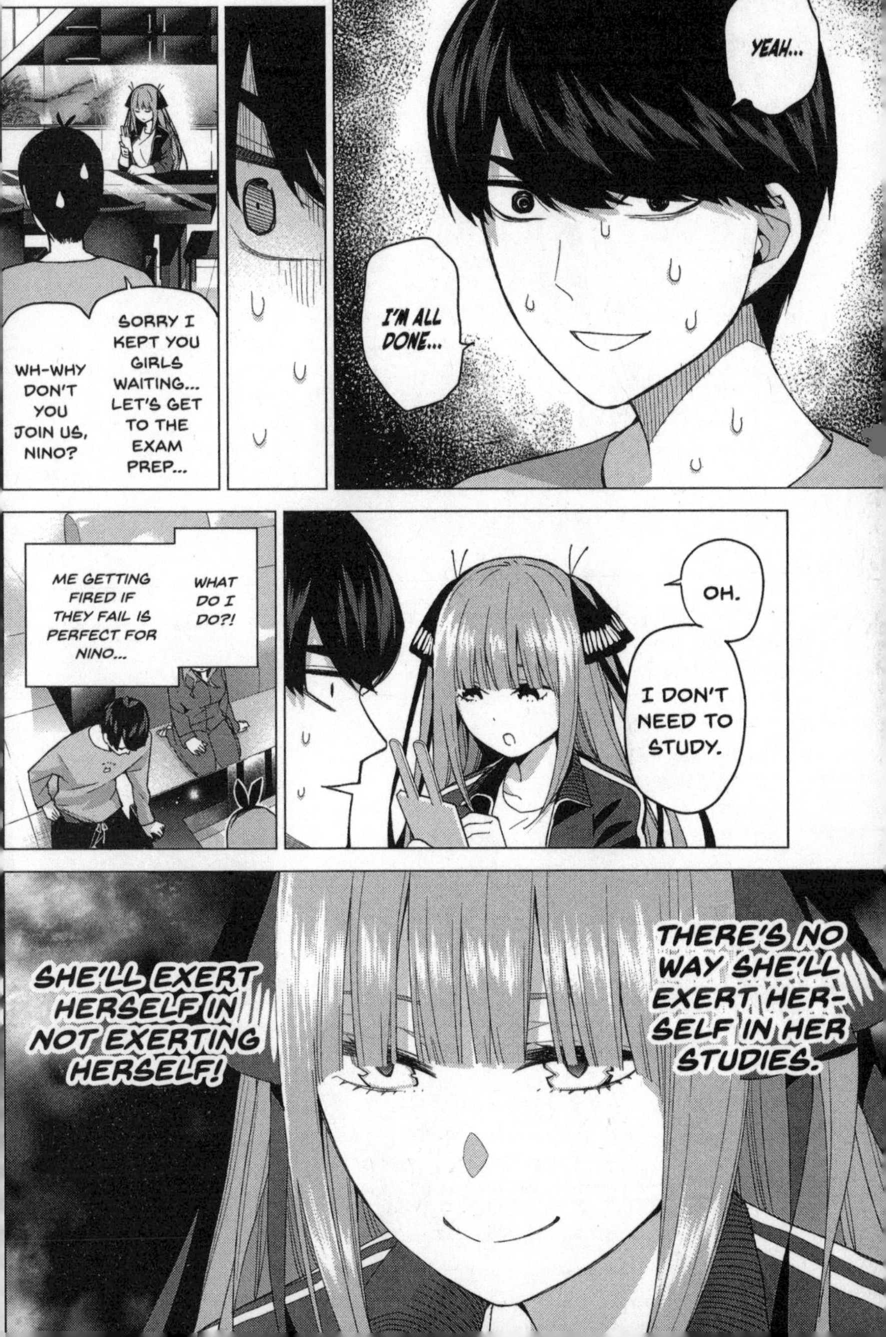
YEAH...
I'M ALL DONE...
SORRY I KEPT YOU GIRLS WAITING... LET'S GET TO THE EXAM PREP...
WH-WHY DON'T YOU JOIN US, NINO?
OH.
I DON'T NEED TO STUDY.
WHAT DO I DO?!
ME GETTING FIRED IF THEY FAIL IS PERFECT FOR NINO...
THERE'S NO WAY SHE'LL EXERT HER-SELF IN HER STUDIES.
SHE'LL EXERT HERSELF IN NOT EXERTING HERSELF!

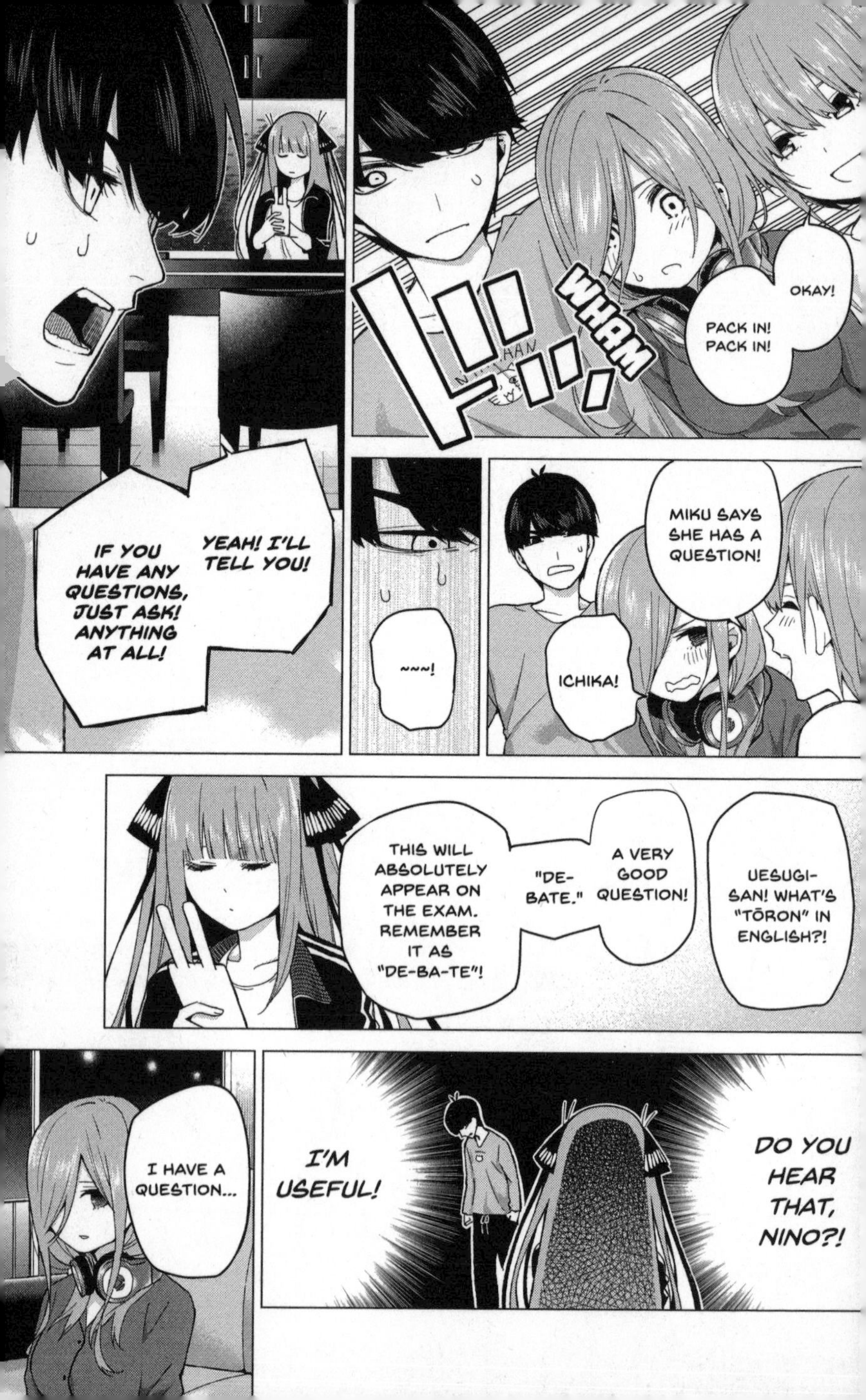
WHAM
OKAY!
PACK IN! PACK IN!
MIKU SAYS SHE HAS A QUESTION!
ICHIKA!
~~~!
YEAH! I'LL TELL YOU!
IF YOU HAVE ANY QUESTIONS, JUST ASK! ANYTHING AT ALL!
UESUGI-SAN! WHAT'S "TŌRON" IN ENGLISH?!
A VERY GOOD QUESTION!
"DE-BATE."
THIS WILL ABSOLUTELY APPEAR ON THE EXAM. REMEMBER IT AS "DE-BA-TE"!
DO YOU HEAR THAT, NINO?!
I'M USEFUL!
I HAVE A QUESTION...
~~~

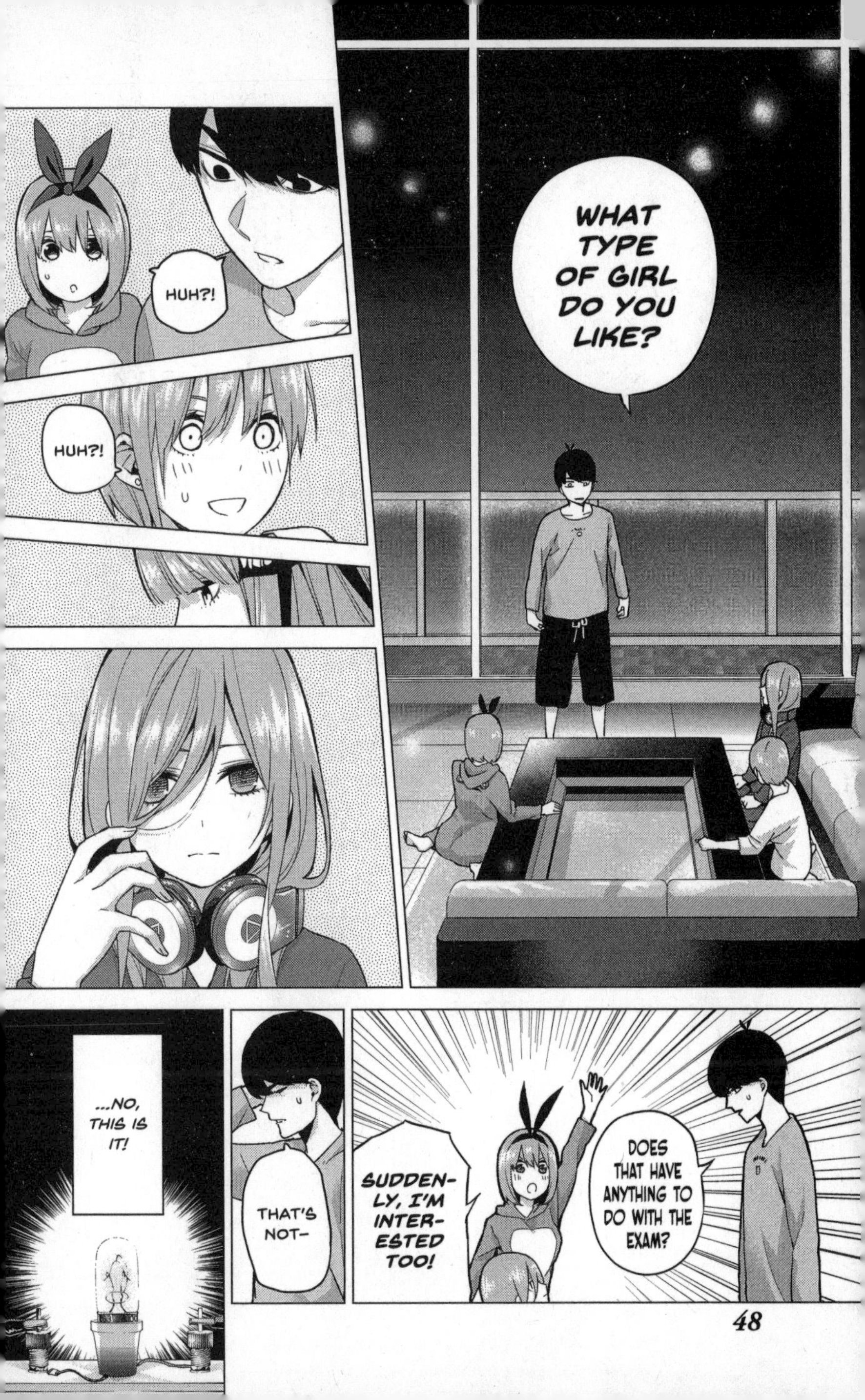
WHAT TYPE OF GIRL DO YOU LIKE?
HUH?!
HUH?!
DOES THAT HAVE ANYTHING TO DO WITH THE EXAM?
SUDDEN-LY, I'M INTER-ESTED TOO!
THAT'S NOT-
...NO, THIS IS IT!

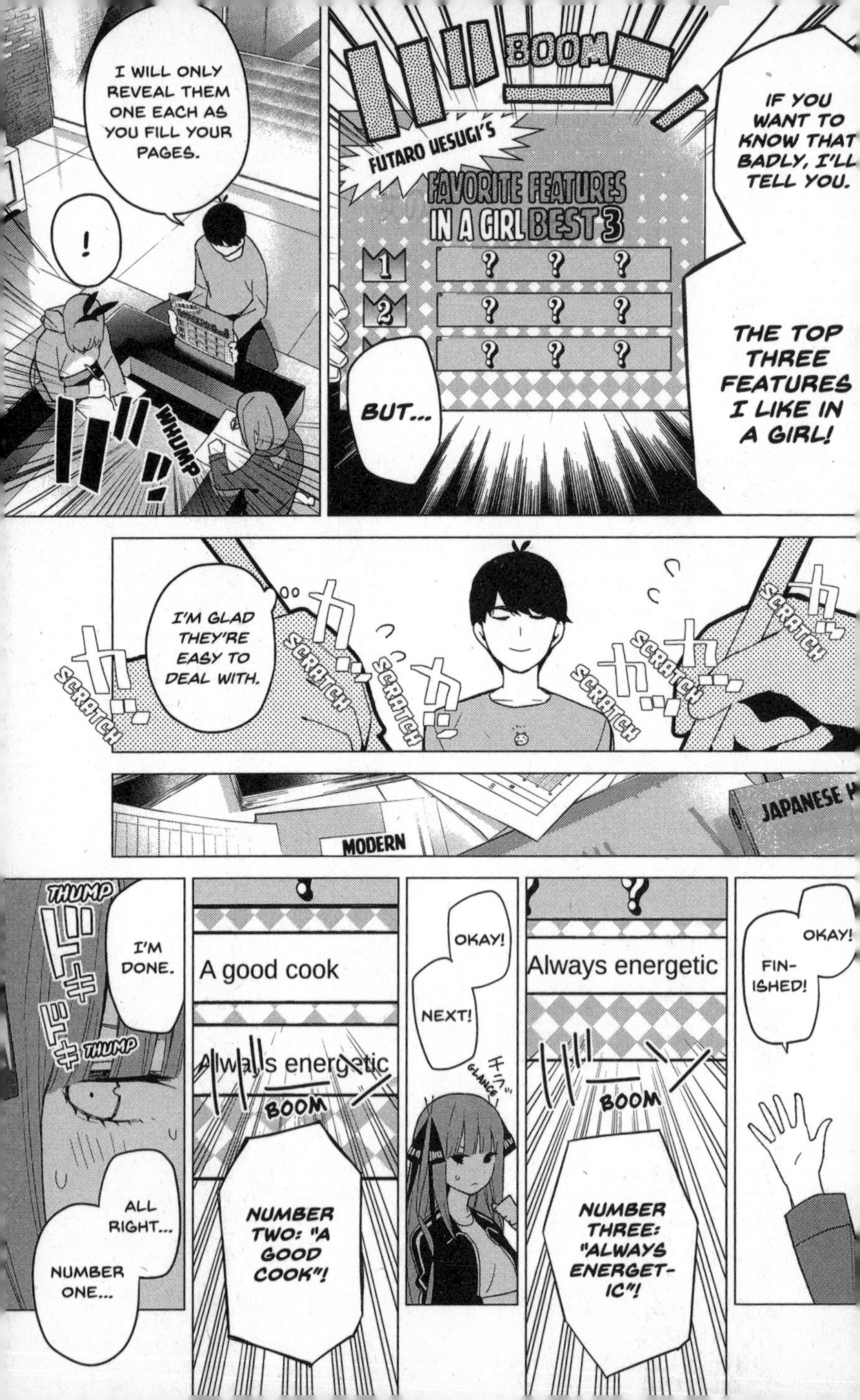
IF YOU WANT TO KNOW THAT BADLY, I'LL TELL YOU.
THE TOP THREE FEATURES I LIKE IN A GIRL!
BOOM
FUTARO UESUGI'S
FAVORITE FEATURES IN A GIRL BEST 3
1 ? ? ?
2 ? ? ?
? ? ?
BUT...
I WILL ONLY REVEAL THEM ONE EACH AS YOU FILL YOUR PAGES.
!
WHUMP
SCRATCH
SCRATCH
I'M GLAD THEY'RE EASY TO DEAL WITH.
SCRATCH
SCRATCH
MODERN
OKAY! FIN-ISHED!
Always energetic
BOOM
NUMBER THREE: "ALWAYS ENERGET-IC"!
OKAY! NEXT!
GLANCE
A good cook
Always energetic
BOOM
NUMBER TWO: "A GOOD COOK"!
I'M DONE.
THUMP
THUMP
ALL RIGHT... NUMBER ONE...

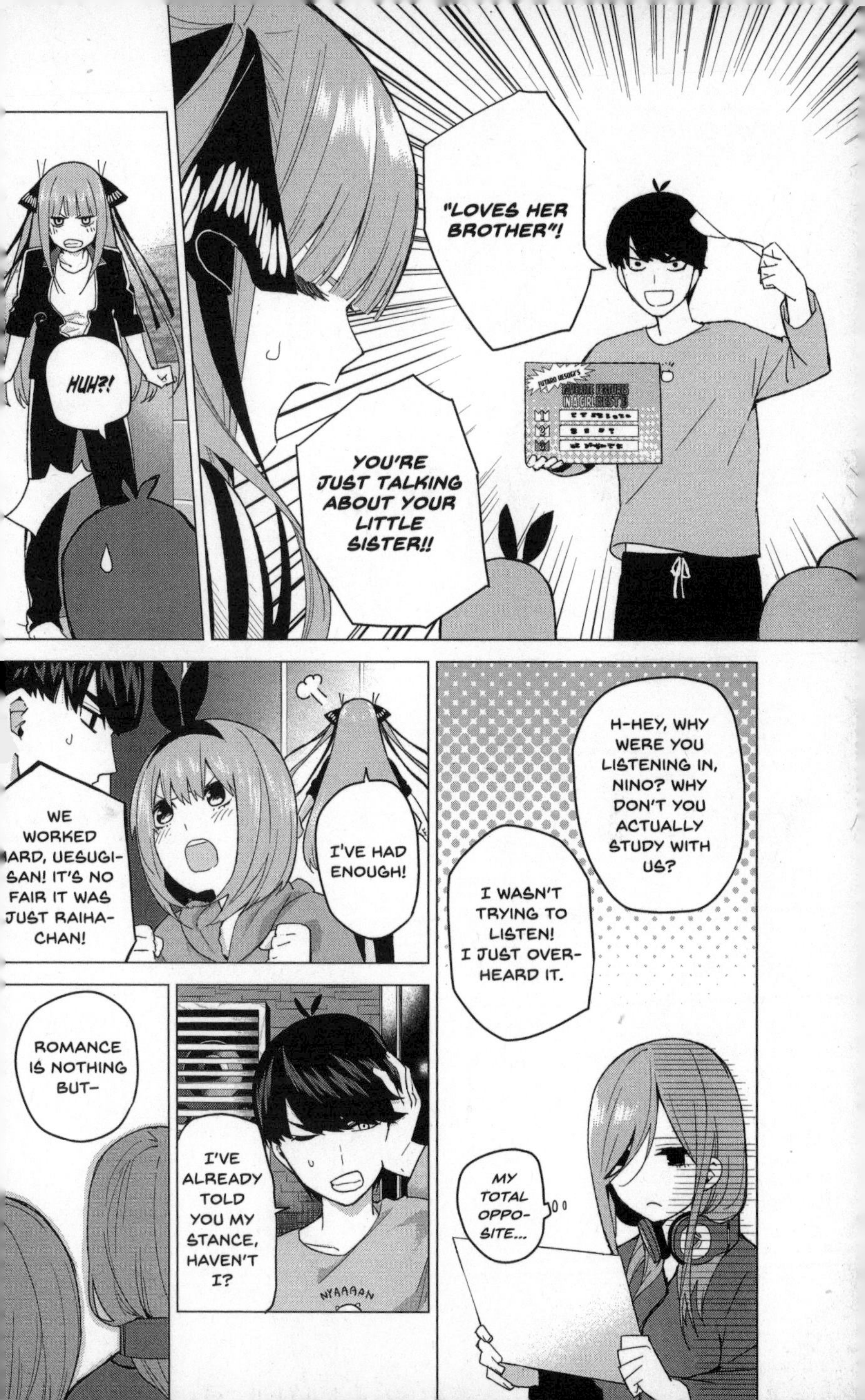

"LOVES HER BROTHER"!
FUTARO UESUGI'S
FAVORITE FEATURES IN A GIRL BEST 3
YOU'RE JUST TALKING ABOUT YOUR LITTLE SISTER!!
HUH?!
H-HEY, WHY WERE YOU LISTENING IN, NINO? WHY DON'T YOU ACTUALLY STUDY WITH US?
I WASN'T TRYING TO LISTEN! I JUST OVER-HEARD IT.
MY TOTAL OPPO-SITE...
I'VE HAD ENOUGH!
WE WORKED HARD, UESUGI-SAN! IT'S NO FAIR IT WAS JUST RAIHA-CHAN!
I'VE ALREADY TOLD YOU MY STANCE, HAVEN'T I?
NYAAAAN
ROMANCE IS NOTHING BUT-

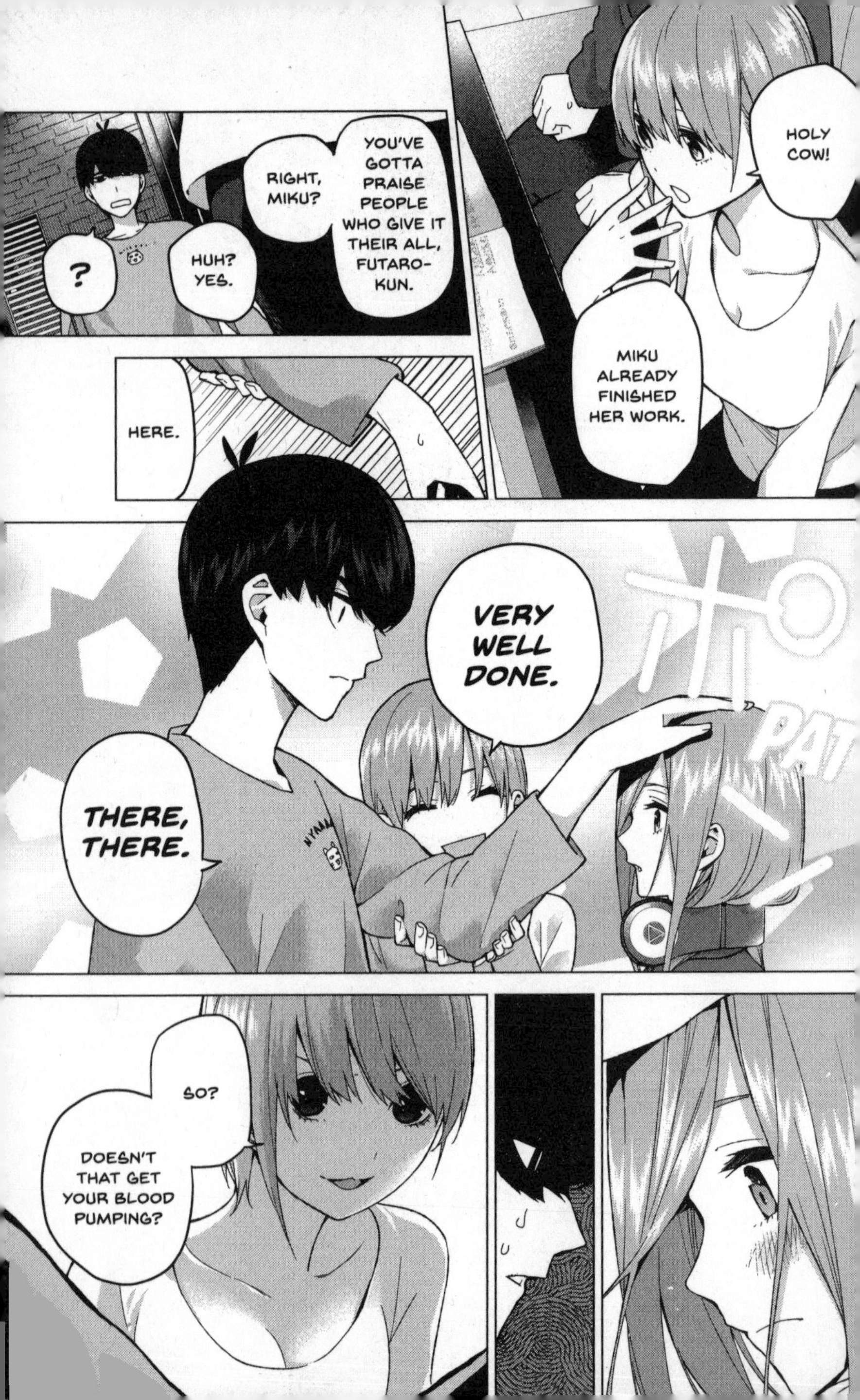
HOLY COW!
MIKU ALREADY FINISHED HER WORK.
YOU'VE GOTTA PRAISE PEOPLE WHO GIVE IT THEIR ALL, FUTARO-KUN.
RIGHT, MIKU?
HUH? YES.
?
HERE.
VERY WELL DONE.
PAT
THERE, THERE.
SO?
DOESN'T THAT GET YOUR BLOOD PUMPING?

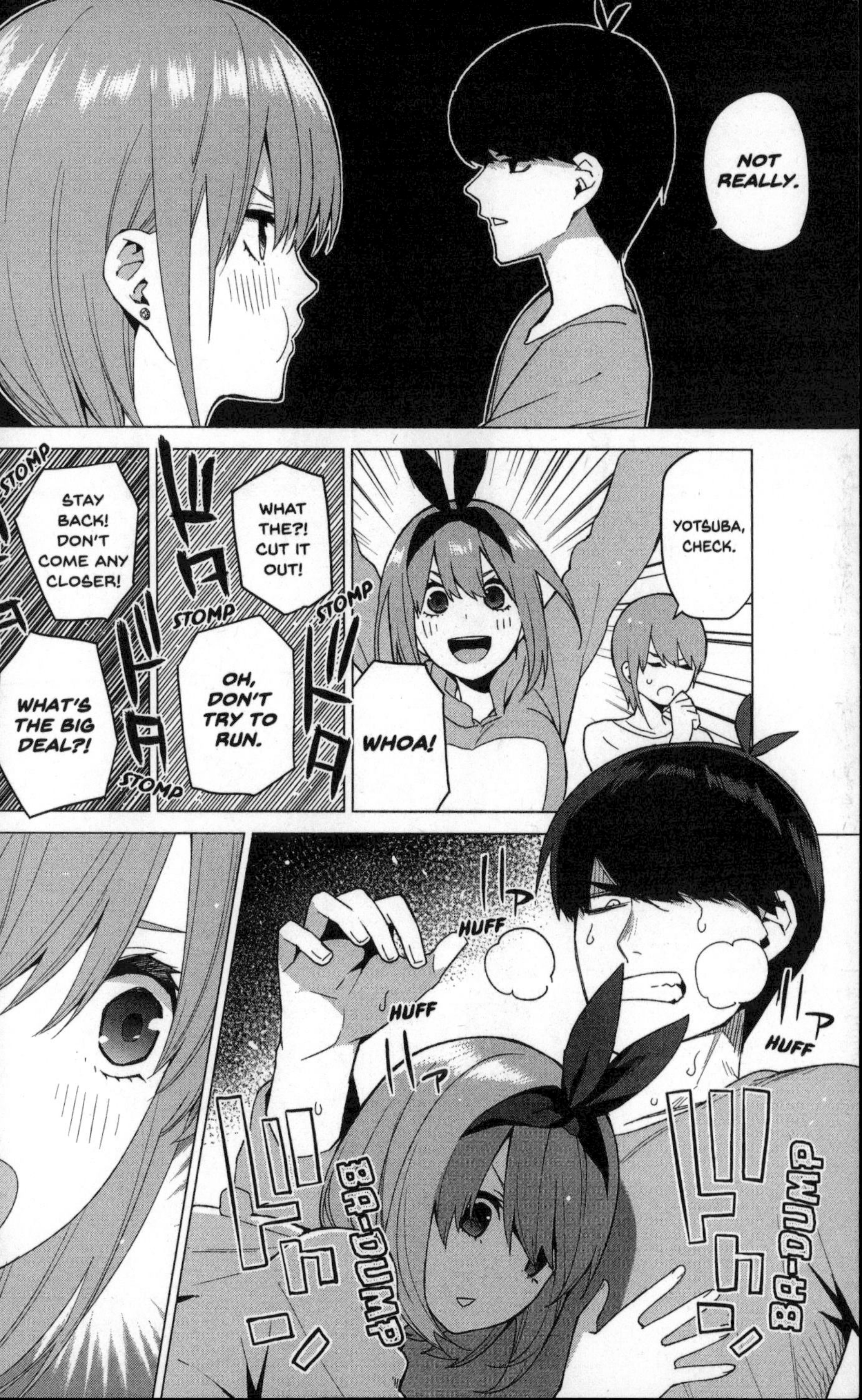
NOT REALLY.
YOTSUBA, CHECK.
STOMP
WHOA!
WHAT THE?! CUT IT OUT!
STOMP
OH, DON'T TRY TO RUN.
STOMP
STAY BACK! DON'T COME ANY CLOSER!
STOMP
WHAT'S THE BIG DEAL?!
HUFF
HUFF
HUFF
BA-DUMP
BA-DUMP

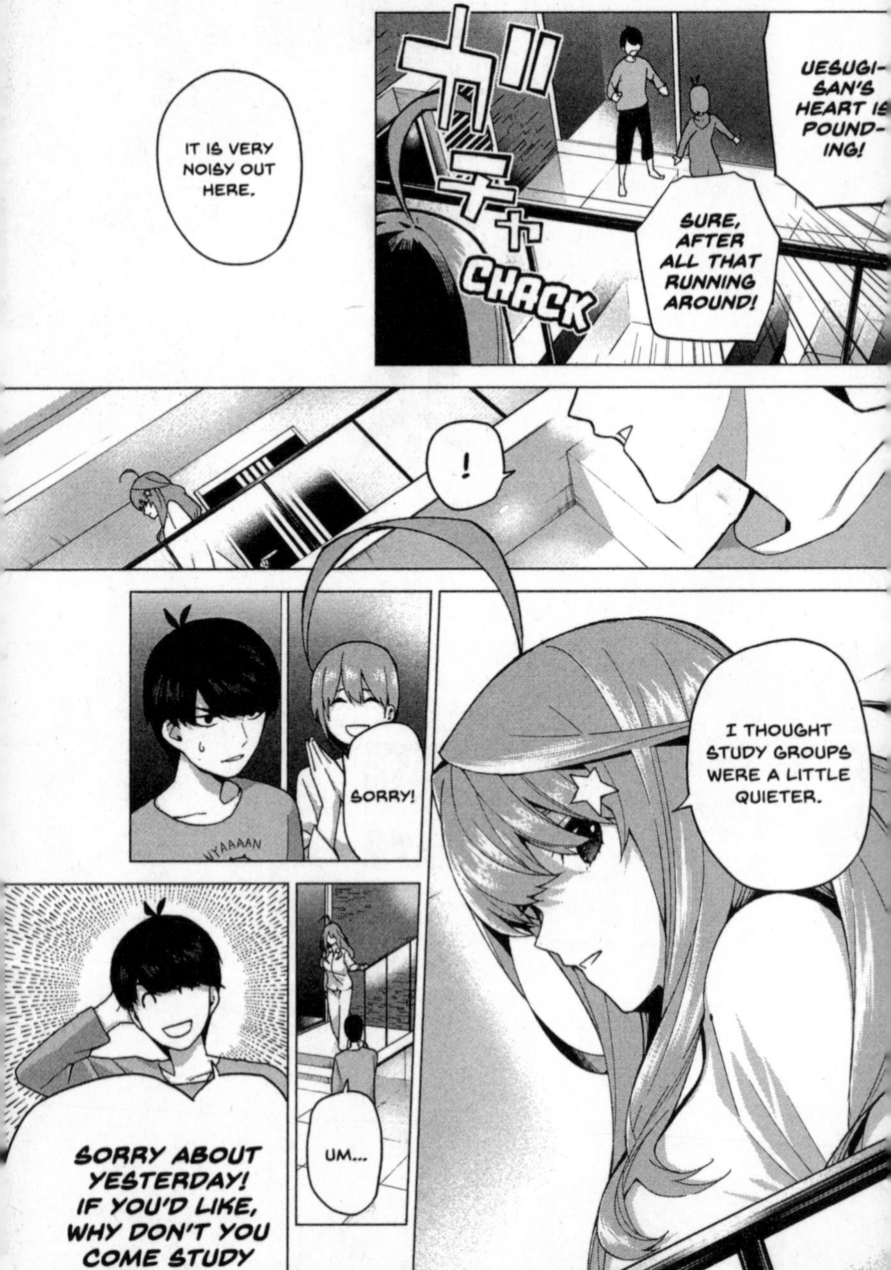
UESUGI-SAN'S HEART IS POUNDING!
SURE, AFTER ALL THAT RUNNING AROUND!
CHACK
IT IS VERY NOISY OUT HERE.
!
I THOUGHT STUDY GROUPS WERE A LITTLE QUIETER.
SORRY!
UM...
SORRY ABOUT YESTERDAY! IF YOU'D LIKE, WHY DON'T YOU COME STUDY WITH US?

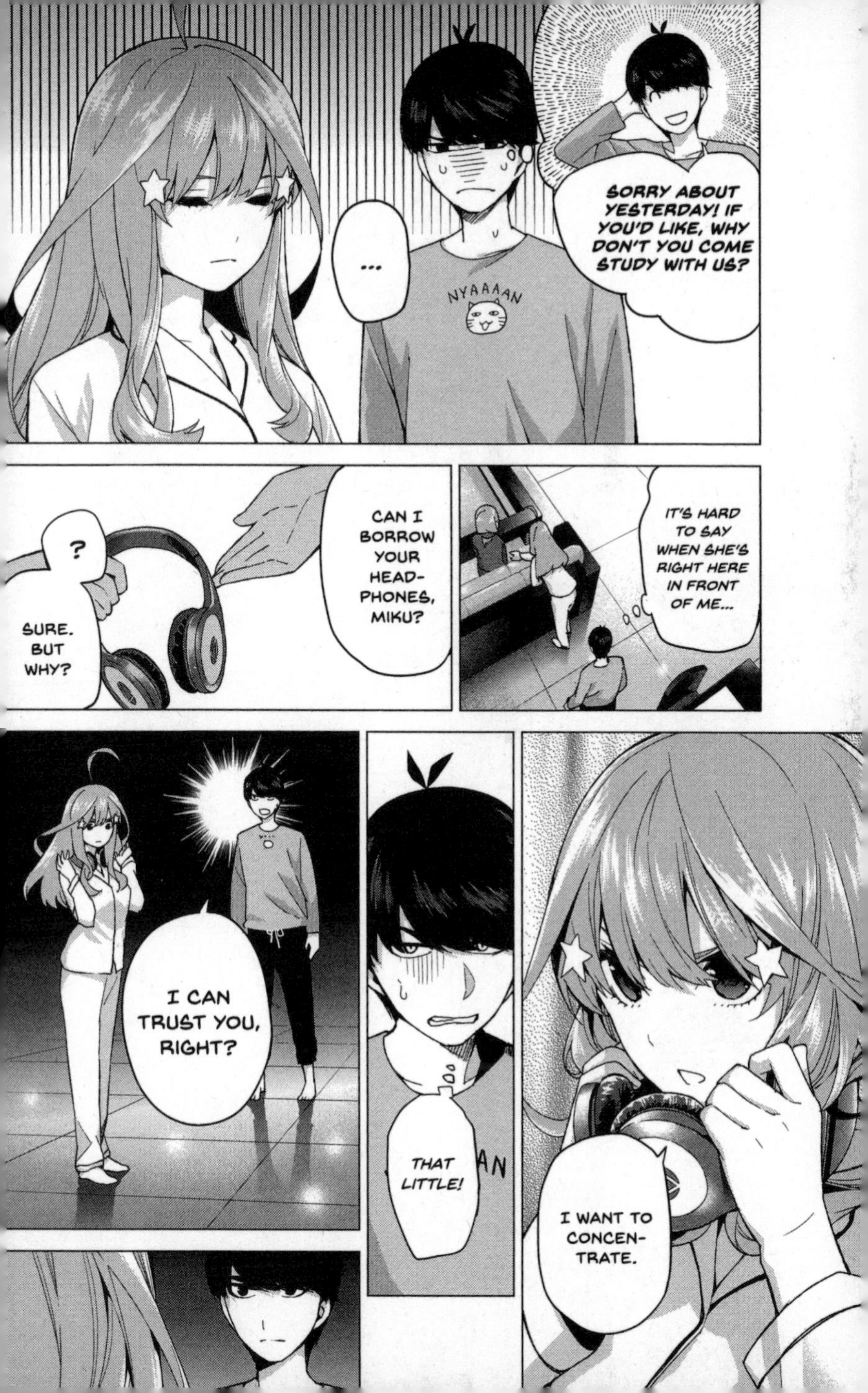
SORRY ABOUT YESTERDAY! IF YOU'D LIKE, WHY DON'T YOU COME STUDY WITH US?
...
NYAAAAN
IT'S HARD TO SAY WHEN SHE'S RIGHT HERE IN FRONT OF ME...
CAN I BORROW YOUR HEAD-PHONES, MIKU?
?
SURE. BUT WHY?
I WANT TO CONCEN-TRATE.
THAT LITTLE!
I CAN TRUST YOU, RIGHT?

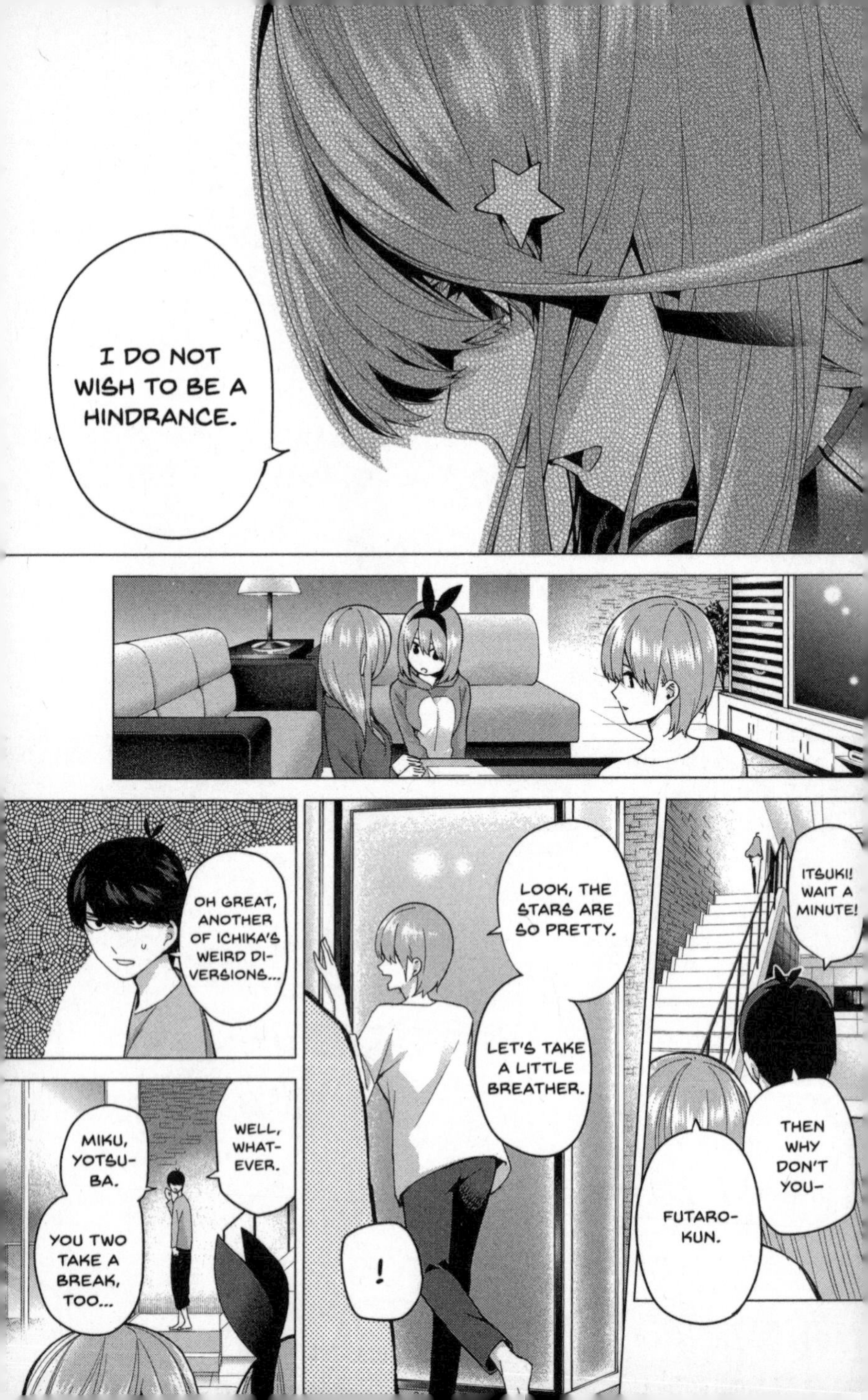
I DO NOT WISH TO BE A HINDRANCE.
ITSUKI! WAIT A MINUTE!
THEN WHY DON'T YOU-
FUTARO-KUN.
LOOK, THE STARS ARE SO PRETTY.
LET'S TAKE A LITTLE BREATHER.
!
OH GREAT, ANOTHER OF ICHIKA'S WEIRD DI-VERSIONS...
WELL, WHAT-EVER.
MIKU, YOTSU-BA.
YOU TWO TAKE A BREAK, TOO...

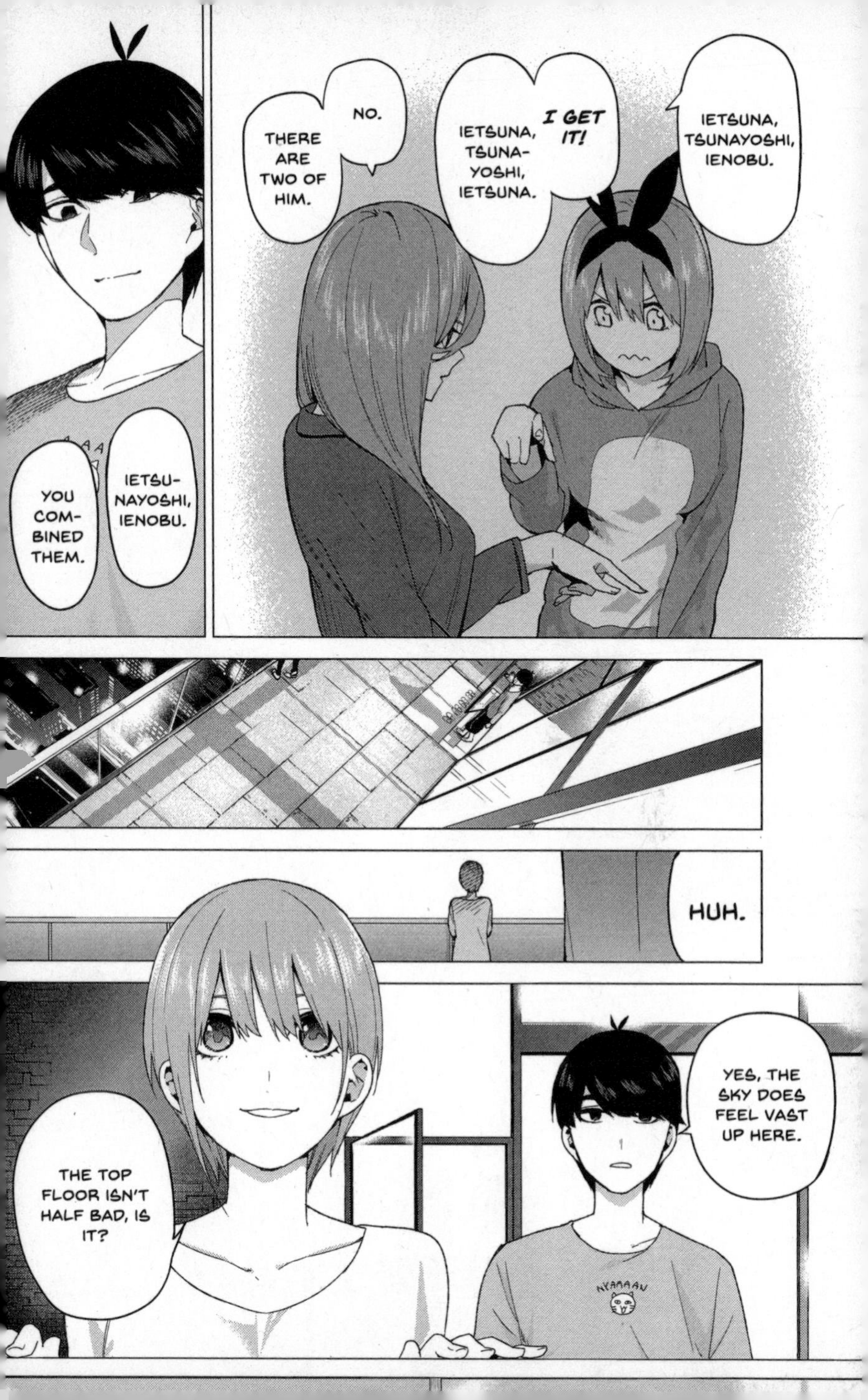
IETSUNA, TSUNAYOSHI, IENOBU.
I GET IT!
IETSUNA, TSUNA-YOSHI, IETSUNA.
NO.
THERE ARE TWO OF HIM.
IETSU-NAYOSHI, IENOBU.
YOU COM-BINED THEM.
HUH.
YES, THE SKY DOES FEEL VAST UP HERE.
THE TOP FLOOR ISN'T HALF BAD, IS IT?

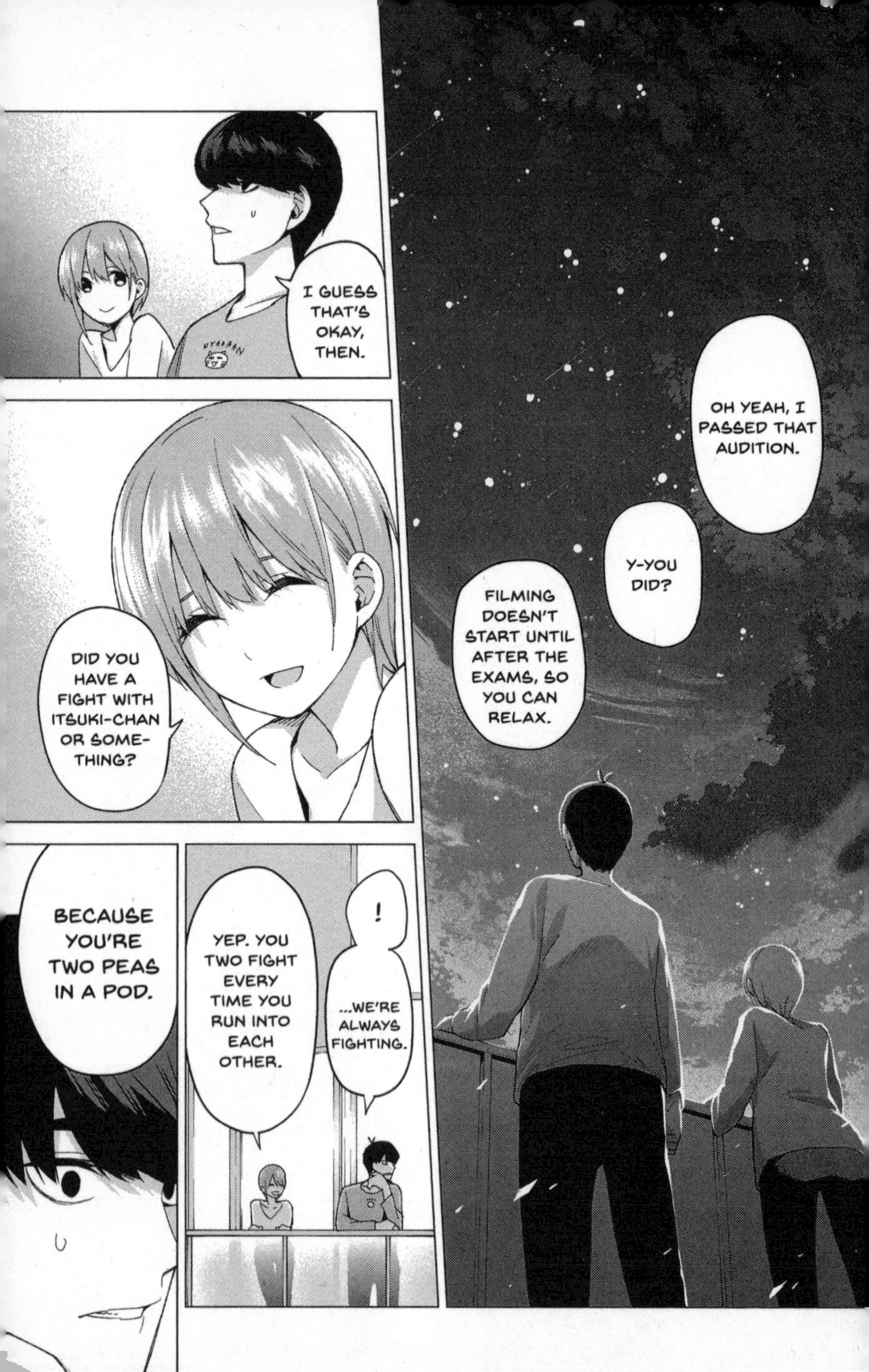
OH YEAH, I PASSED THAT AUDITION.
Y-YOU DID?
FILMING DOESN'T START UNTIL AFTER THE EXAMS, SO YOU CAN RELAX.
I GUESS THAT'S OKAY, THEN.
DID YOU HAVE A FIGHT WITH ITSUKI-CHAN OR SOME-THING?
!
...WE'RE ALWAYS FIGHTING.
YEP. YOU TWO FIGHT EVERY TIME YOU RUN INTO EACH OTHER.
BECAUSE YOU'RE TWO PEAS IN A POD.

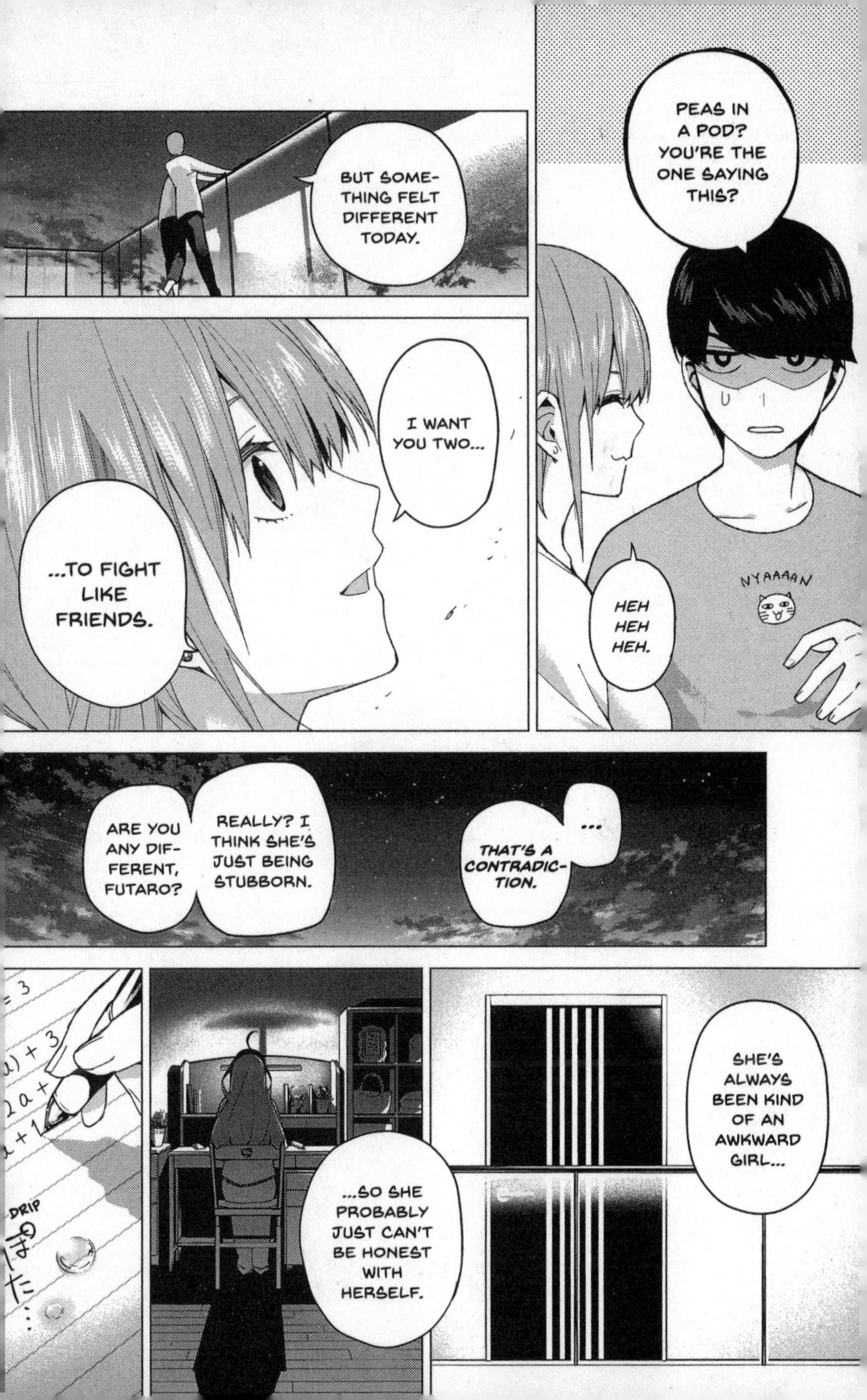
PEAS IN A POD? YOU'RE THE ONE SAYING THIS?
HEH HEH HEH.
NYAAAAN
BUT SOMETHING FELT DIFFERENT TODAY.
I WANT YOU TWO...
...TO FIGHT LIKE FRIENDS.
...
THAT'S A CONTRADICTION.
REALLY? I THINK SHE'S JUST BEING STUBBORN.
ARE YOU ANY DIFFERENT, FUTARO?
SHE'S ALWAYS BEEN KIND OF AN AWKWARD GIRL...
...SO SHE PROBABLY JUST CAN'T BE HONEST WITH HERSELF.
DRIP

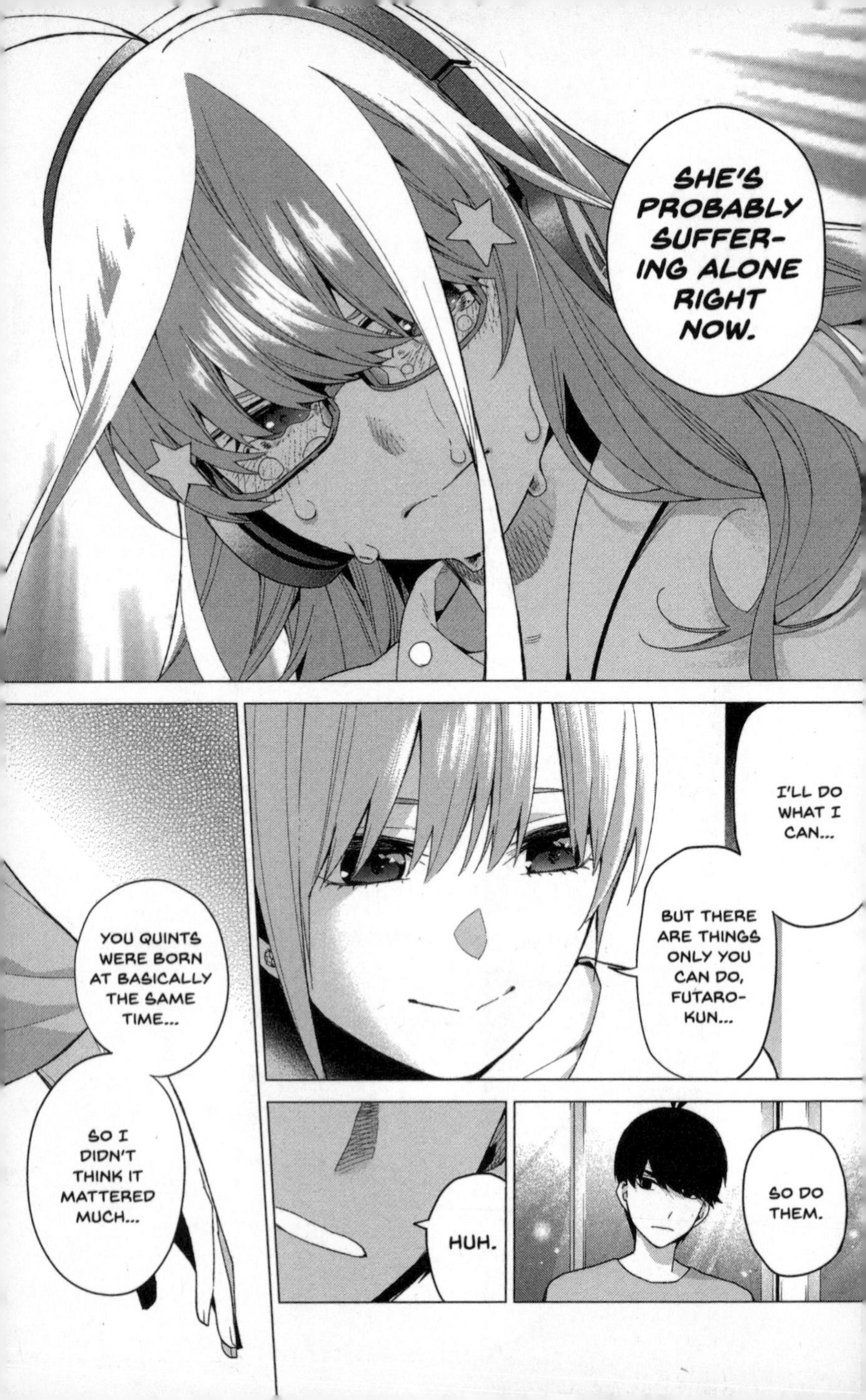
SHE'S PROBABLY SUFFERING ALONE RIGHT NOW.
I'LL DO WHAT I CAN...
BUT THERE ARE THINGS ONLY YOU CAN DO, FUTARO-KUN...
SO DO THEM.
HUH.
YOU QUINTS WERE BORN AT BASICALLY THE SAME TIME...
SO I DIDN'T THINK IT MATTERED MUCH...

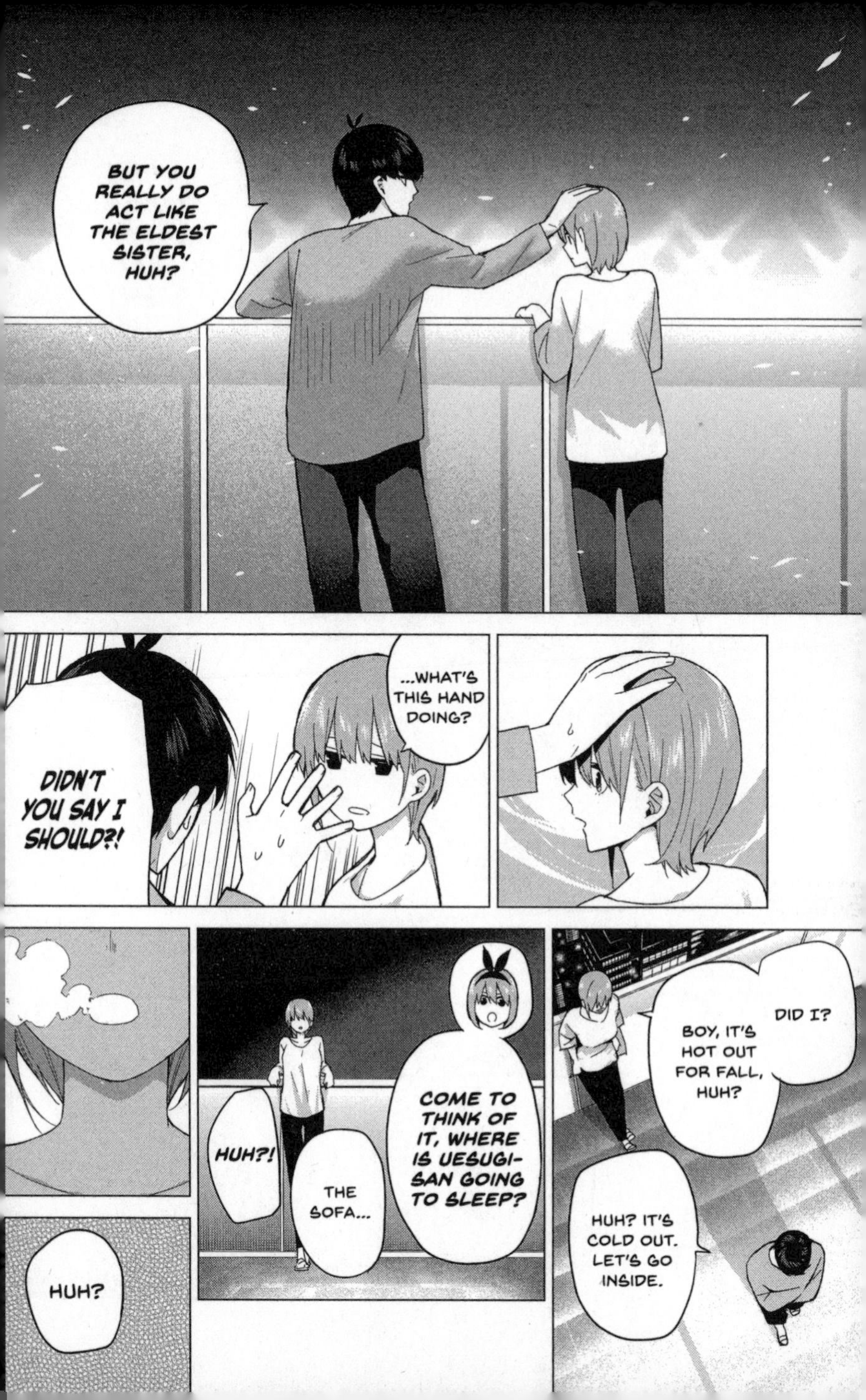
BUT YOU REALLY DO ACT LIKE THE ELDEST SISTER, HUH?
...WHAT'S THIS HAND DOING?
DIDN'T YOU SAY I SHOULD?!
DID I?
BOY, IT'S HOT OUT FOR FALL, HUH?
HUH? IT'S COLD OUT. LET'S GO INSIDE.
COME TO THINK OF IT, WHERE IS UESUGI-SAN GOING TO SLEEP?
THE SOFA...
HUH?!
HUH?

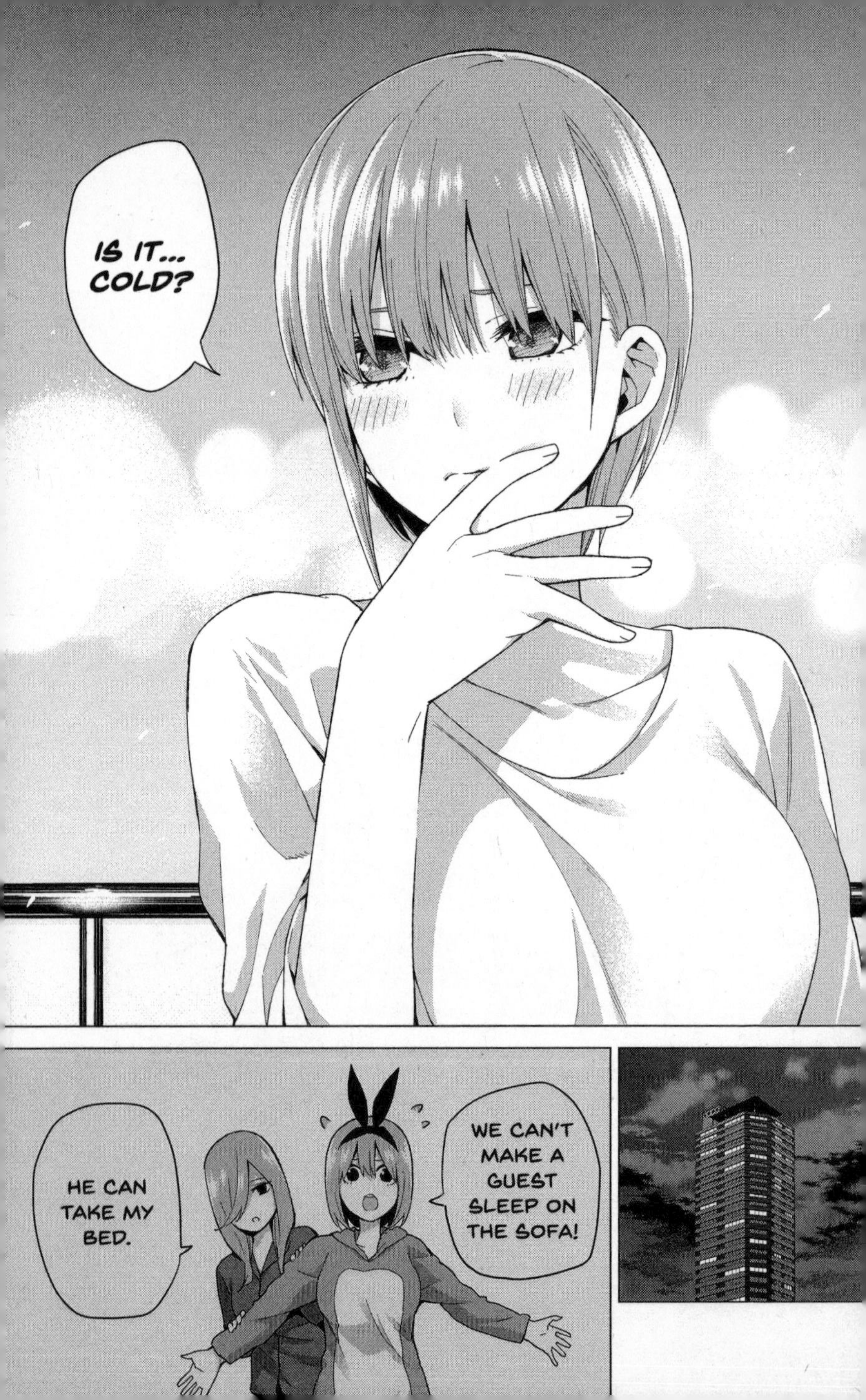
IS IT... COLD?
WE CAN'T MAKE A GUEST SLEEP ON THE SOFA!
HE CAN TAKE MY BED.

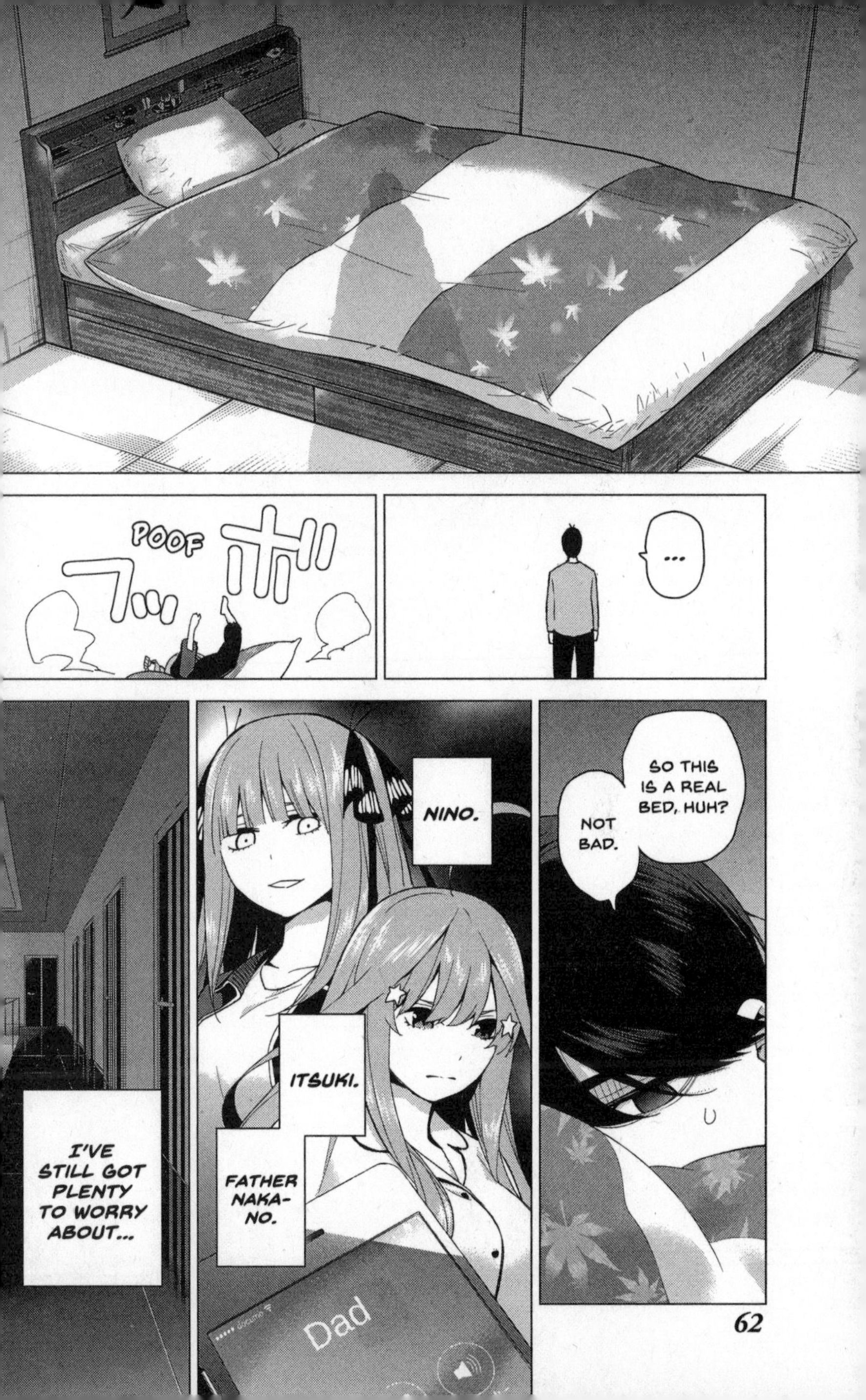
...
POOF
SO THIS IS A REAL BED, HUH?
NOT BAD.
NINO.
ITSUKI.
FATHER NAKA-NO.
I'VE STILL GOT PLENTY TO WORRY ABOUT...
Dad

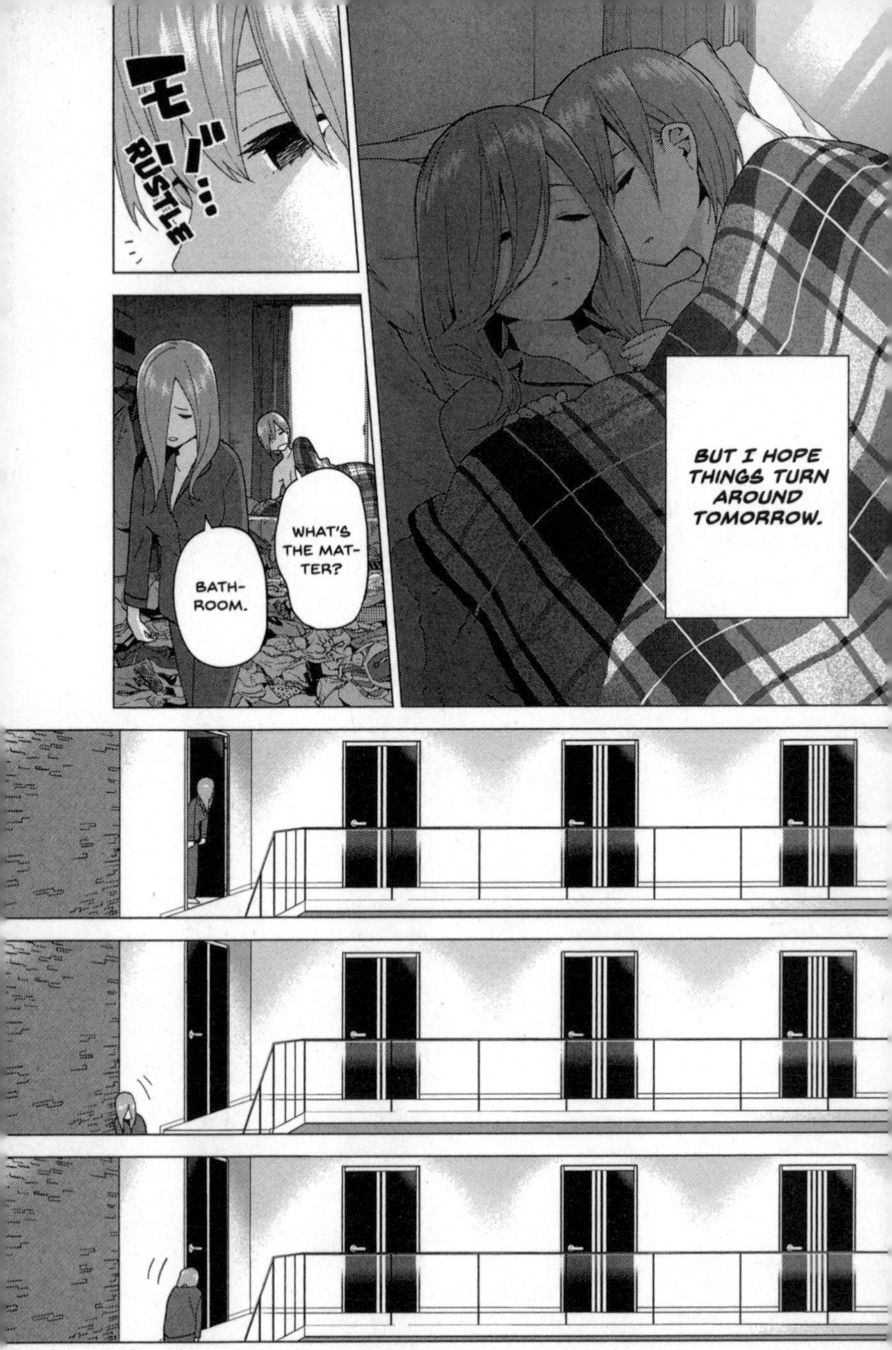
BUT I HOPE THINGS TURN AROUND TOMORROW.
モゾ…
RUSTLE
WHAT'S THE MAT-TER?
BATH-ROOM.

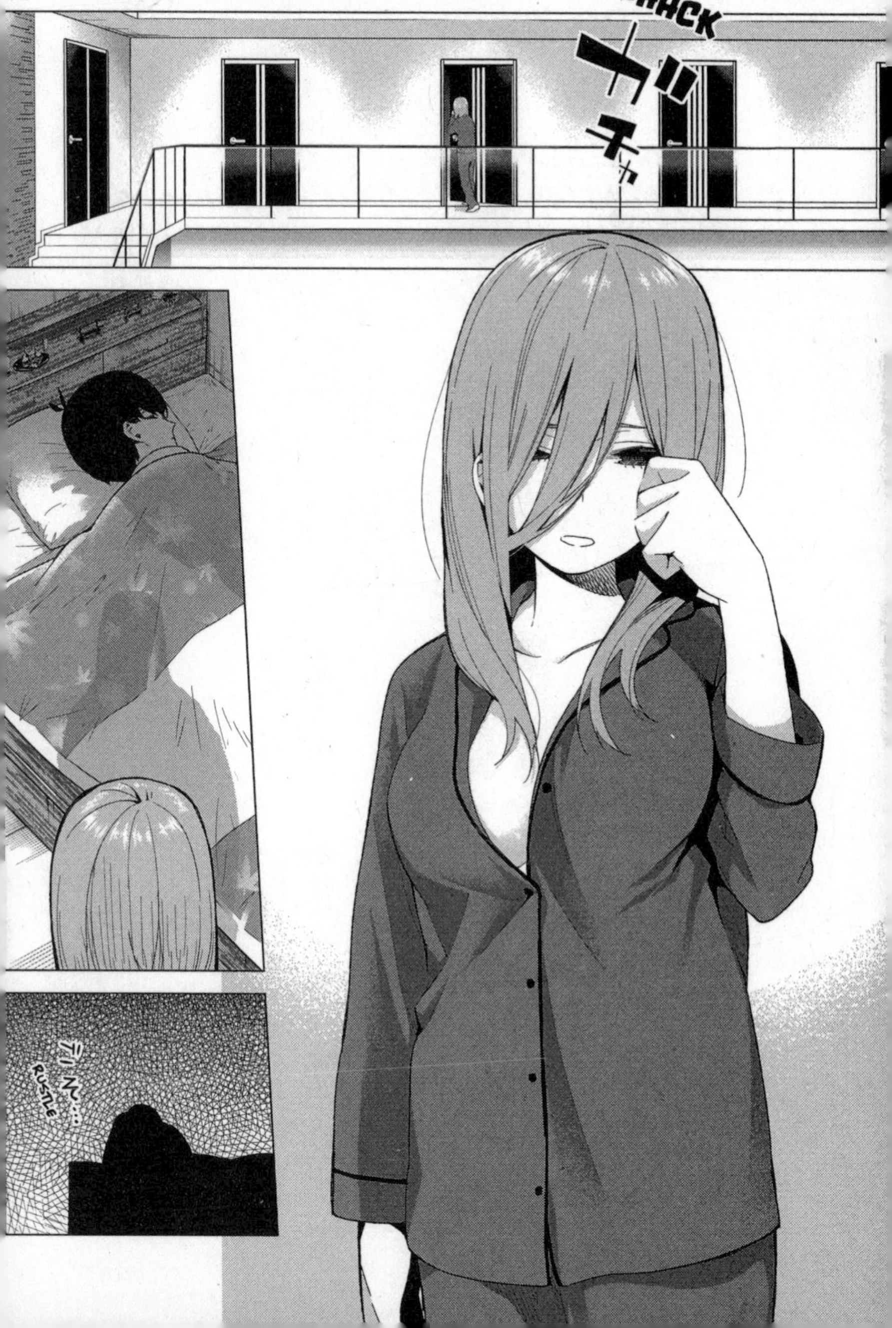
CHACK
ガチャ
RUSTLE

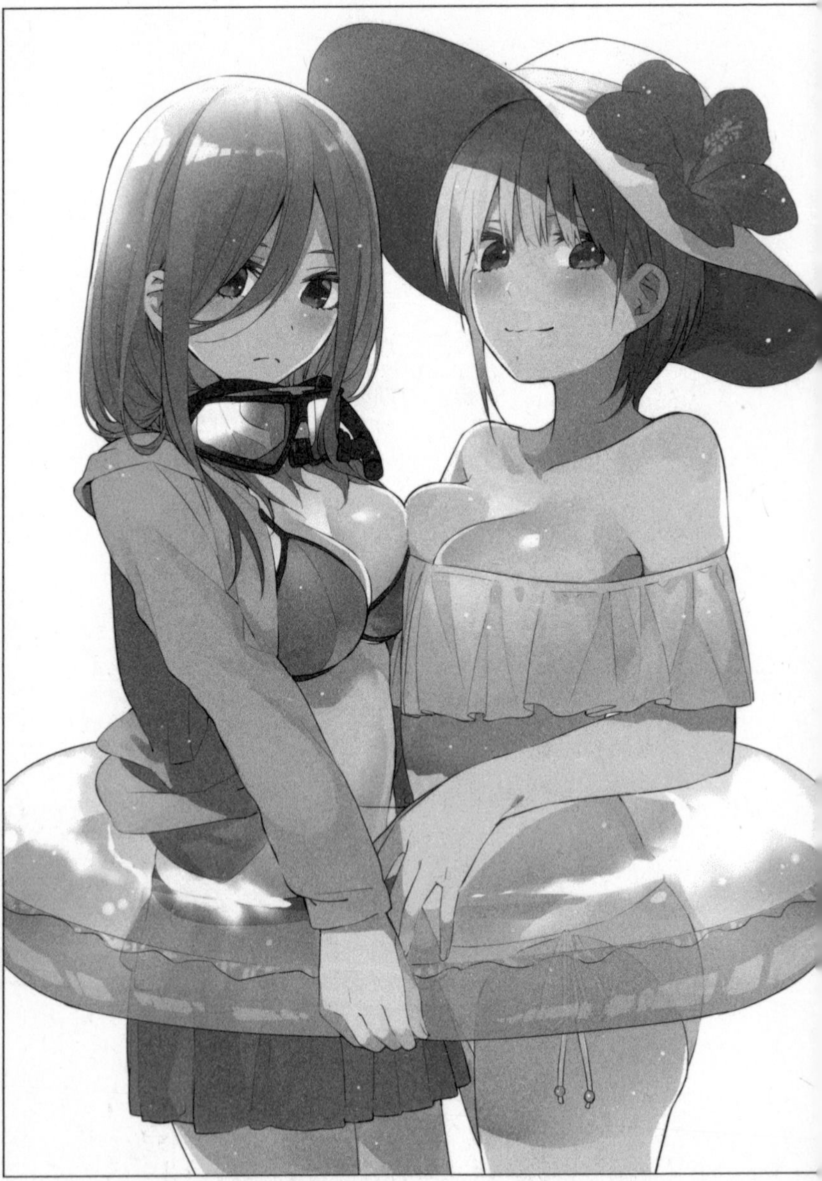

CHAPTER 18 FUTARO THE LYING LIAR

EXTRA BONUS ART

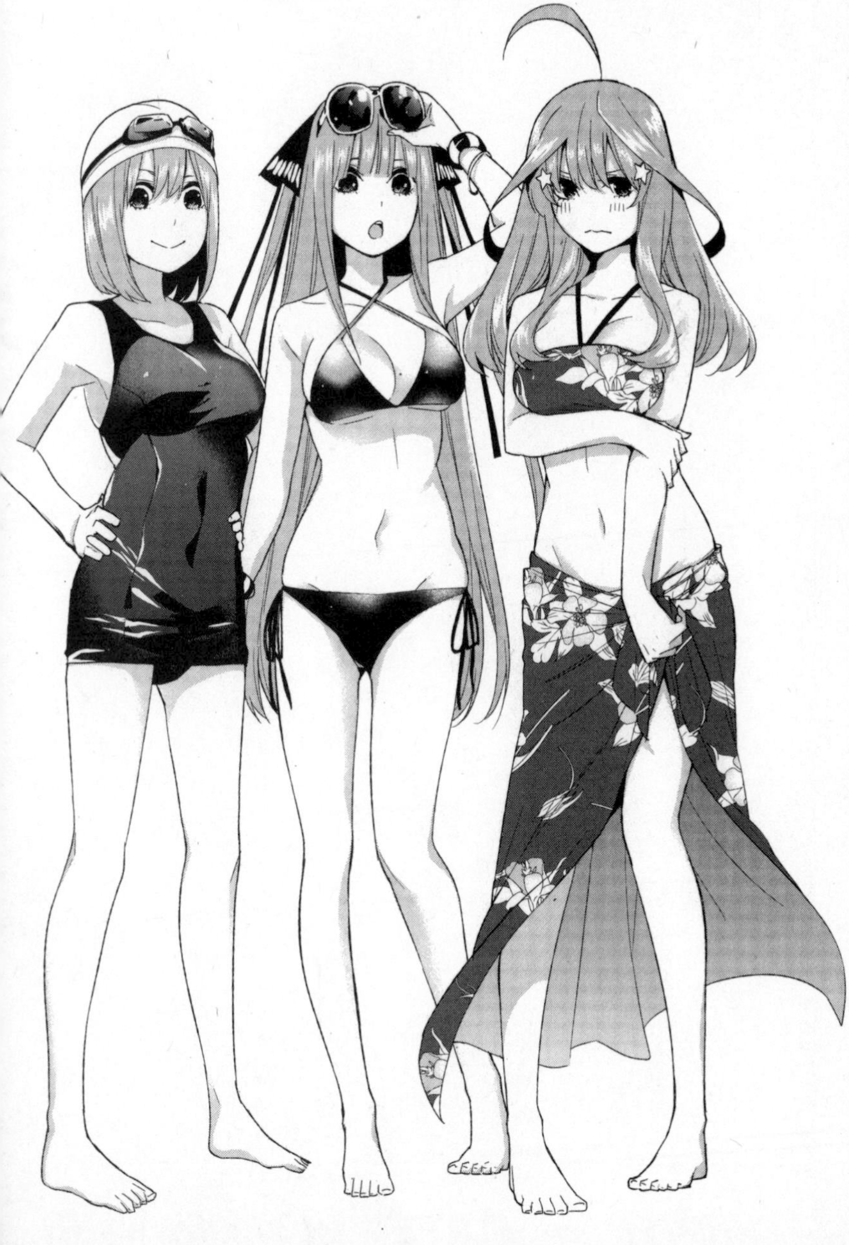

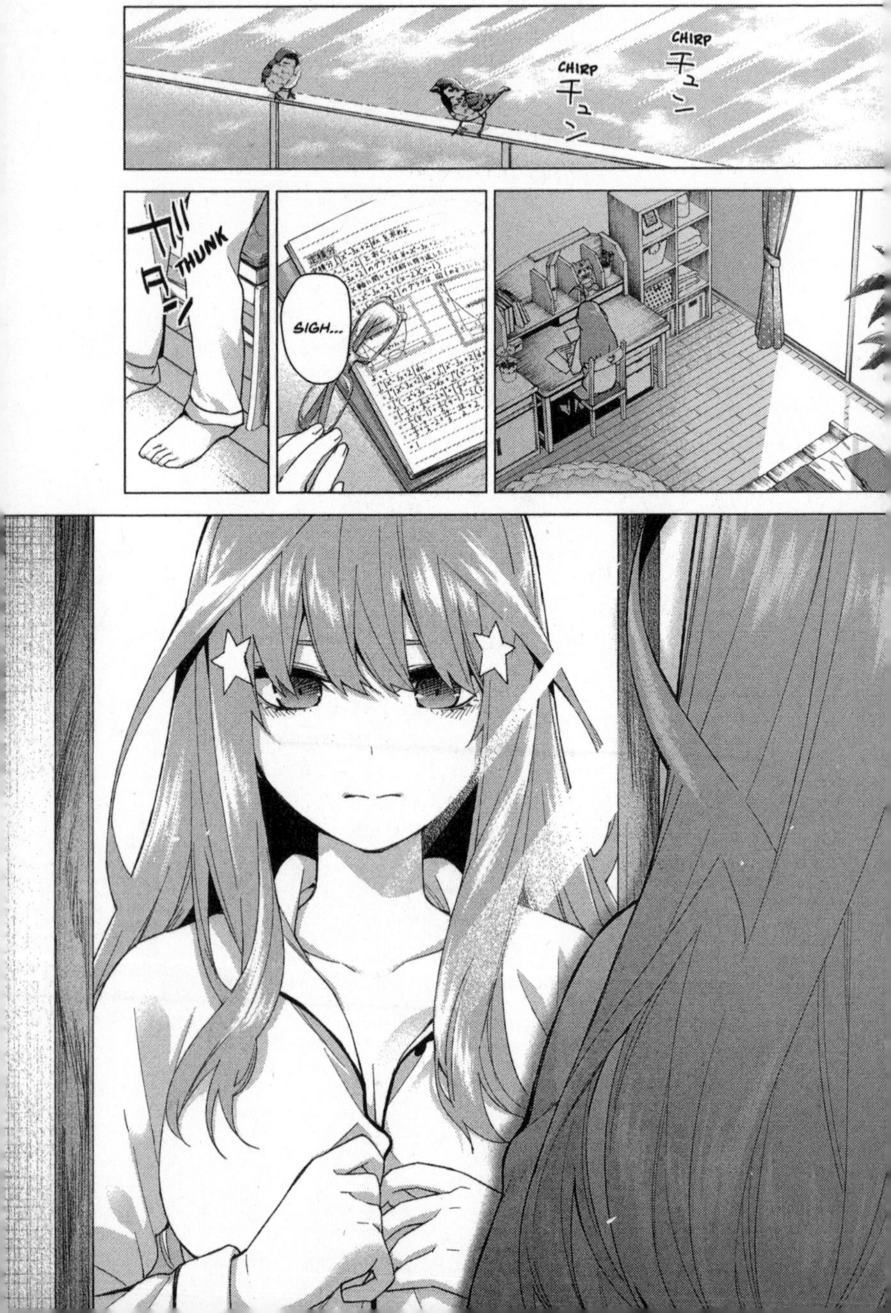
CHIRP
チュン
CHIRP
チュン
SIGH...
THUNK
ガタン

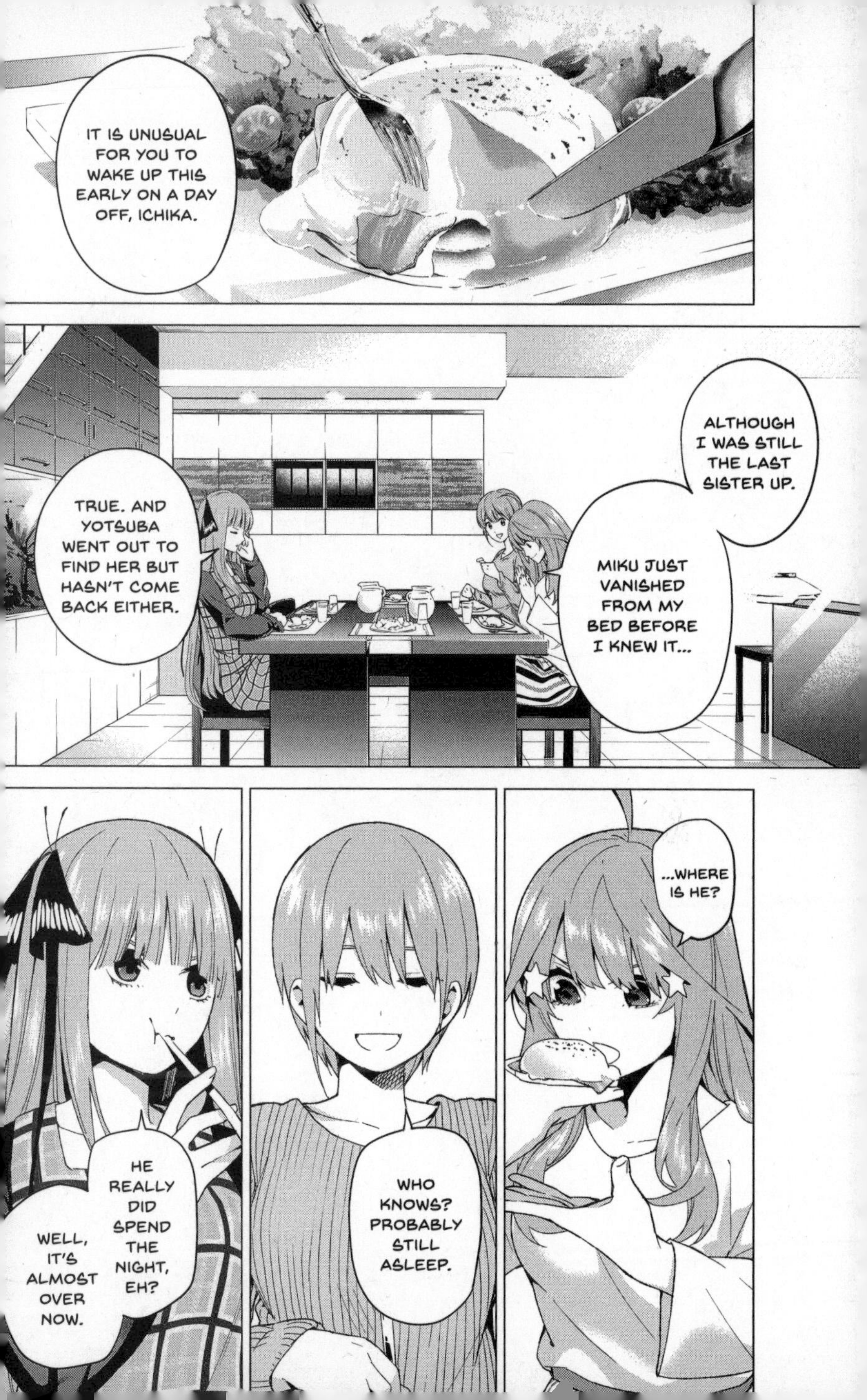
IT IS UNUSUAL FOR YOU TO WAKE UP THIS EARLY ON A DAY OFF, ICHIKA.
ALTHOUGH I WAS STILL THE LAST SISTER UP.
MIKU JUST VANISHED FROM MY BED BEFORE I KNEW IT...
TRUE. AND YOTSUBA WENT OUT TO FIND HER BUT HASN'T COME BACK EITHER.
...WHERE IS HE?
WHO KNOWS? PROBABLY STILL ASLEEP.
HE REALLY DID SPEND THE NIGHT, EH?
WELL, IT'S ALMOST OVER NOW.

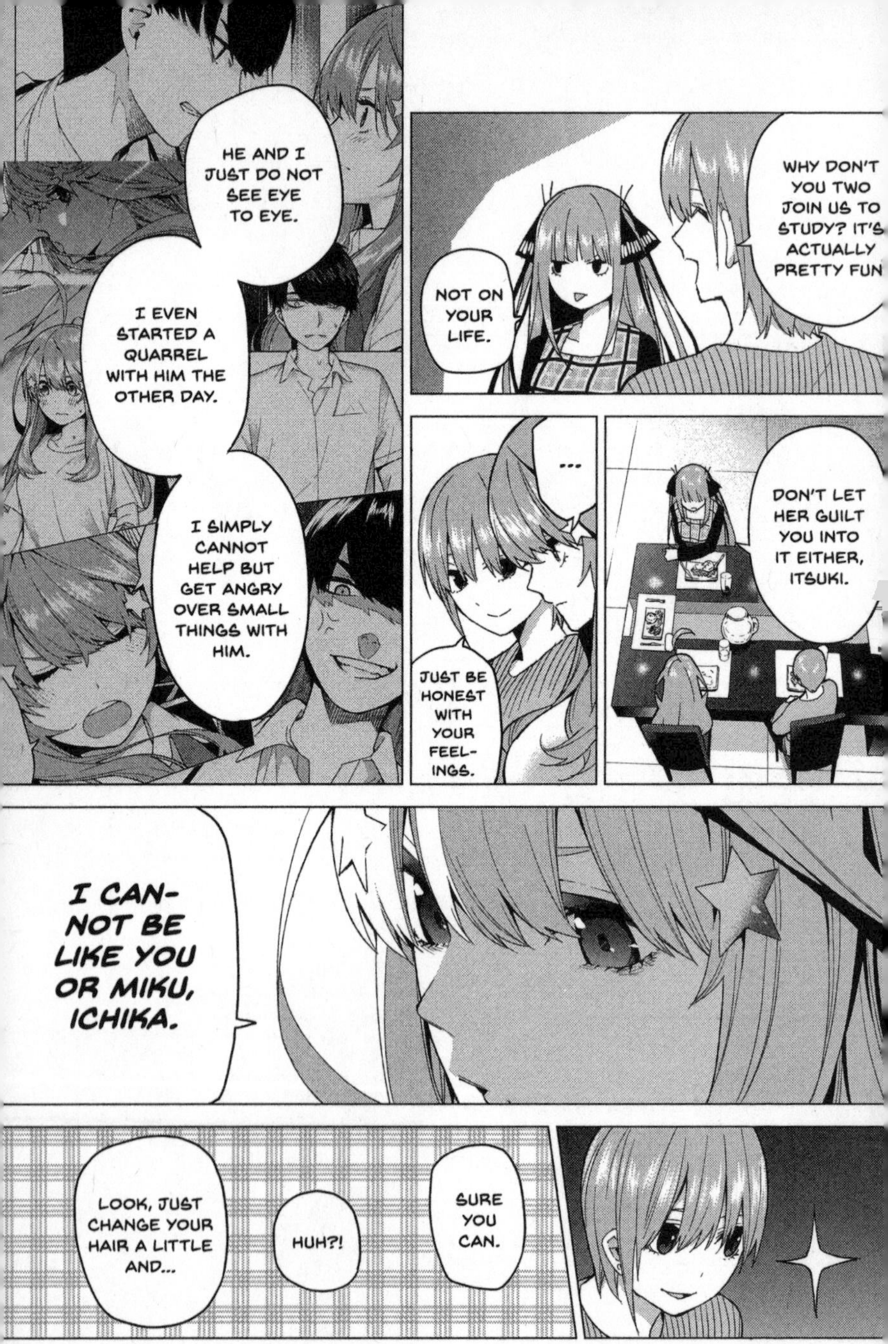
WHY DON'T YOU TWO JOIN US TO STUDY? IT'S ACTUALLY PRETTY FUN
NOT ON YOUR LIFE.
DON'T LET HER GUILT YOU INTO IT EITHER, ITSUKI.
...
JUST BE HONEST WITH YOUR FEEL-INGS.
HE AND I JUST DO NOT SEE EYE TO EYE.
I EVEN STARTED A QUARREL WITH HIM THE OTHER DAY.
I SIMPLY CANNOT HELP BUT GET ANGRY OVER SMALL THINGS WITH HIM.
I CAN-NOT BE LIKE YOU OR MIKU, ICHIKA.
SURE YOU CAN.
HUH?!
LOOK, JUST CHANGE YOUR HAIR A LITTLE AND...

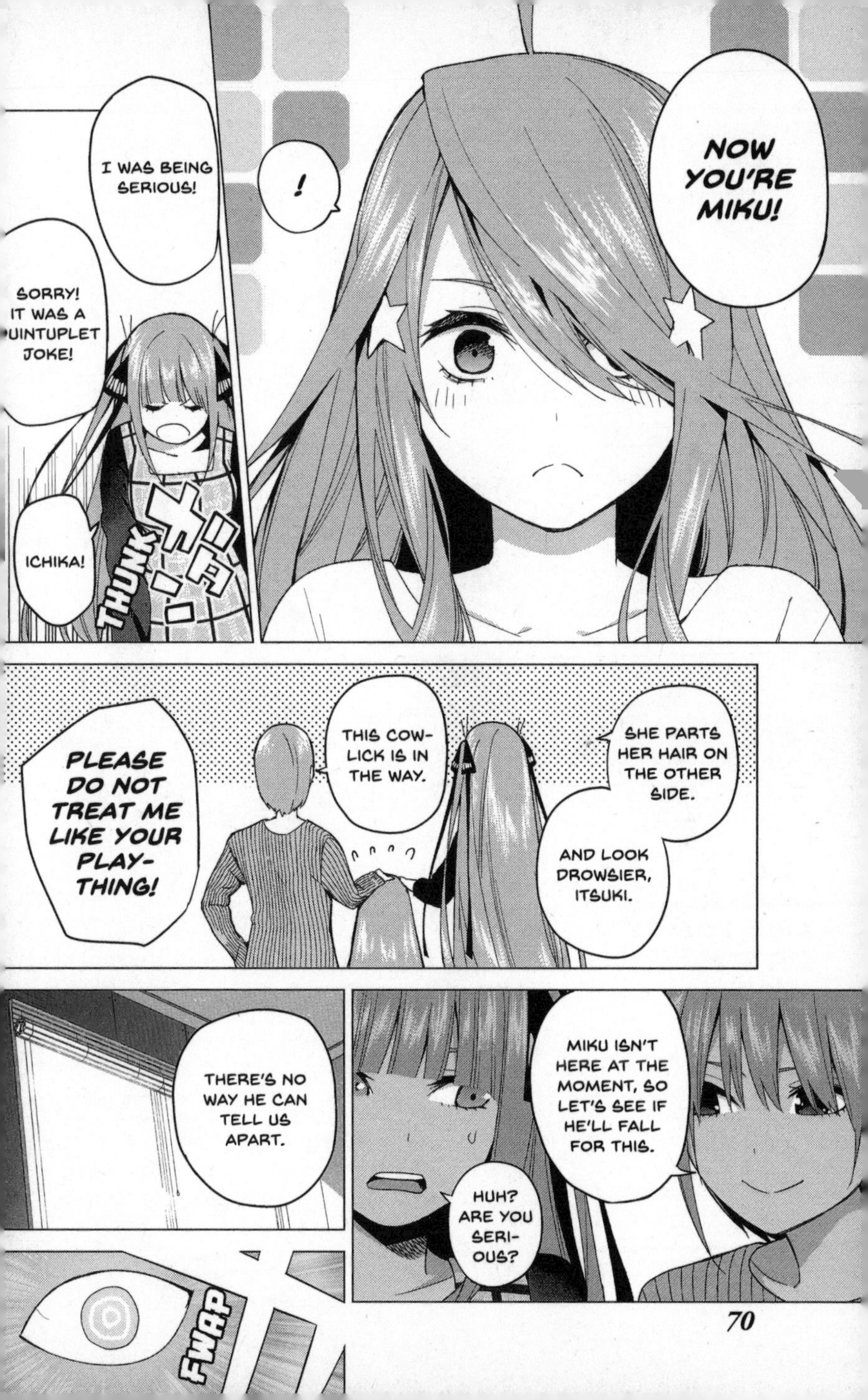
NOW YOU'RE MIKU!
!
I WAS BEING SERIOUS!
SORRY! IT WAS A UINTUPLET JOKE!
THUNK
ICHIKA!
SHE PARTS HER HAIR ON THE OTHER SIDE.
AND LOOK DROWSIER, ITSUKI.
THIS COW-LICK IS IN THE WAY.
PLEASE DO NOT TREAT ME LIKE YOUR PLAY-THING!
MIKU ISN'T HERE AT THE MOMENT, SO LET'S SEE IF HE'LL FALL FOR THIS.
HUH? ARE YOU SERI-OUS?
THERE'S NO WAY HE CAN TELL US APART.
FWAP

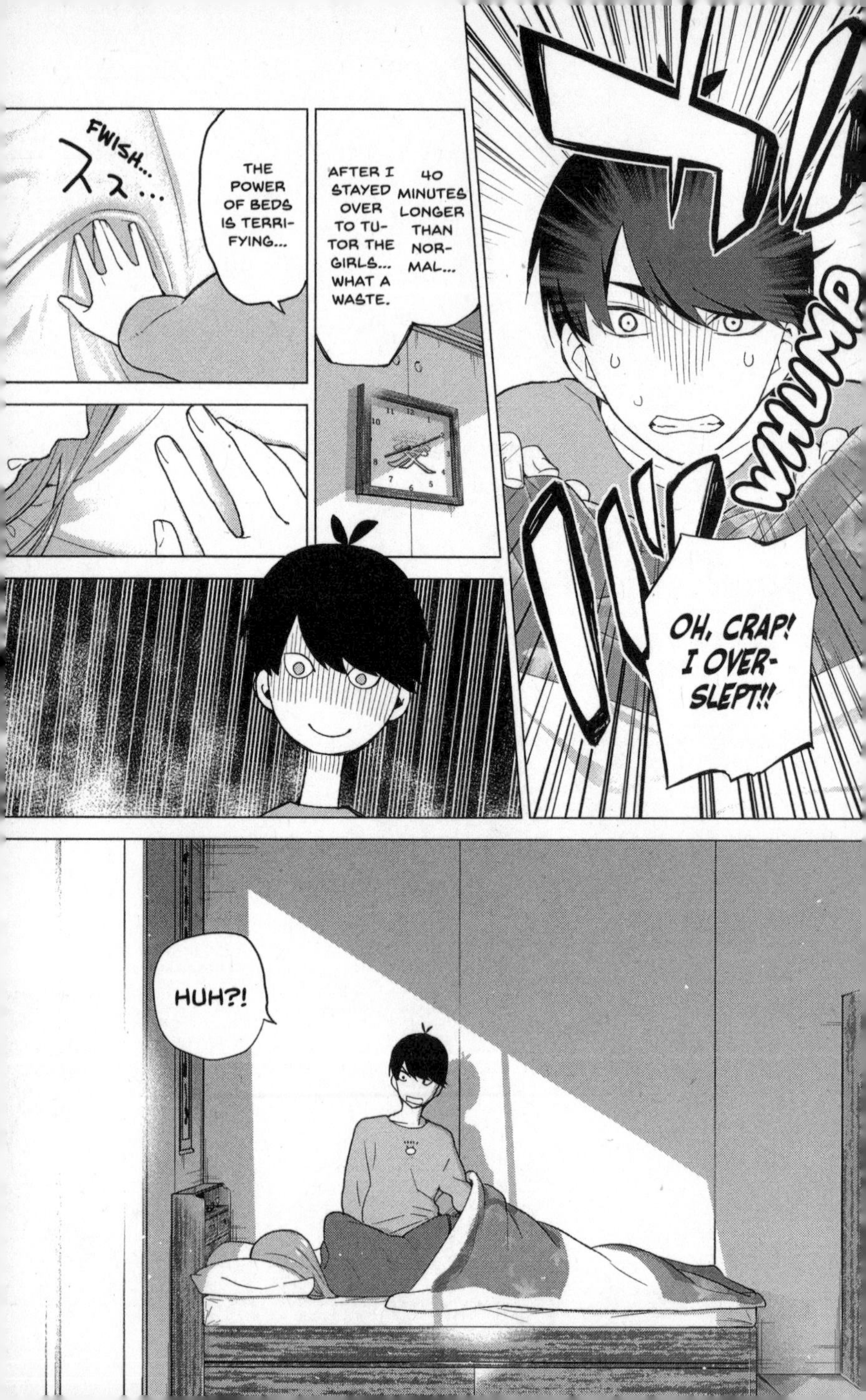

WHUMP
OH, CRAP! I OVER-SLEPT!!
40 MINUTES LONGER THAN NOR-MAL...
AFTER I STAYED OVER TO TU-TOR THE GIRLS... WHAT A WASTE.
FWISH... スス...
THE POWER OF BEDS IS TERRI-FYING...
HUH?!

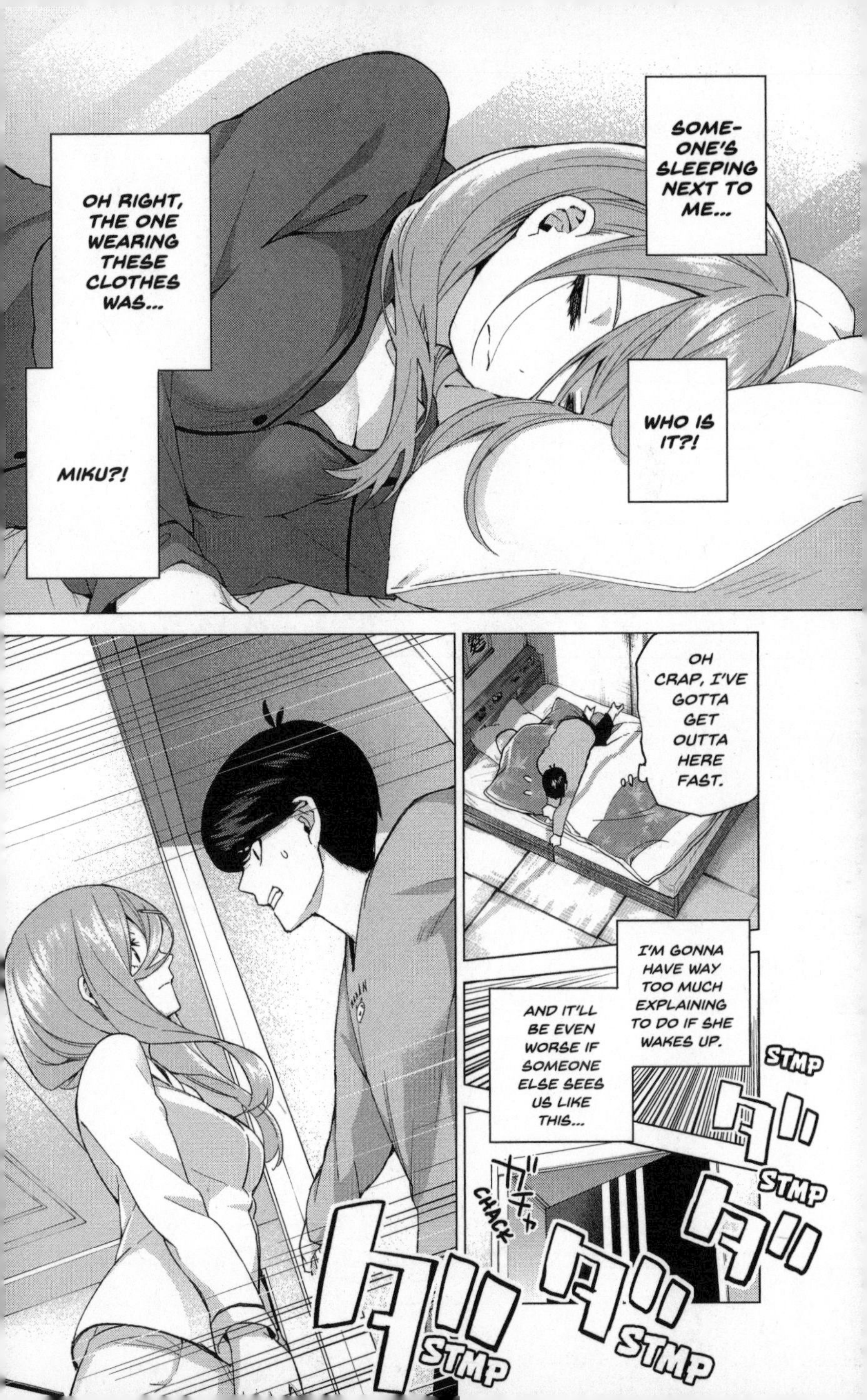
SOME-ONE'S SLEEPING NEXT TO ME...
WHO IS IT?!
OH RIGHT, THE ONE WEARING THESE CLOTHES WAS...
MIKU?!
OH CRAP, I'VE GOTTA GET OUTTA HERE FAST.
I'M GONNA HAVE WAY TOO MUCH EXPLAINING TO DO IF SHE WAKES UP.
AND IT'LL BE EVEN WORSE IF SOMEONE ELSE SEES US LIKE THIS...
STMP
STMP
CHACK
STMP
STMP

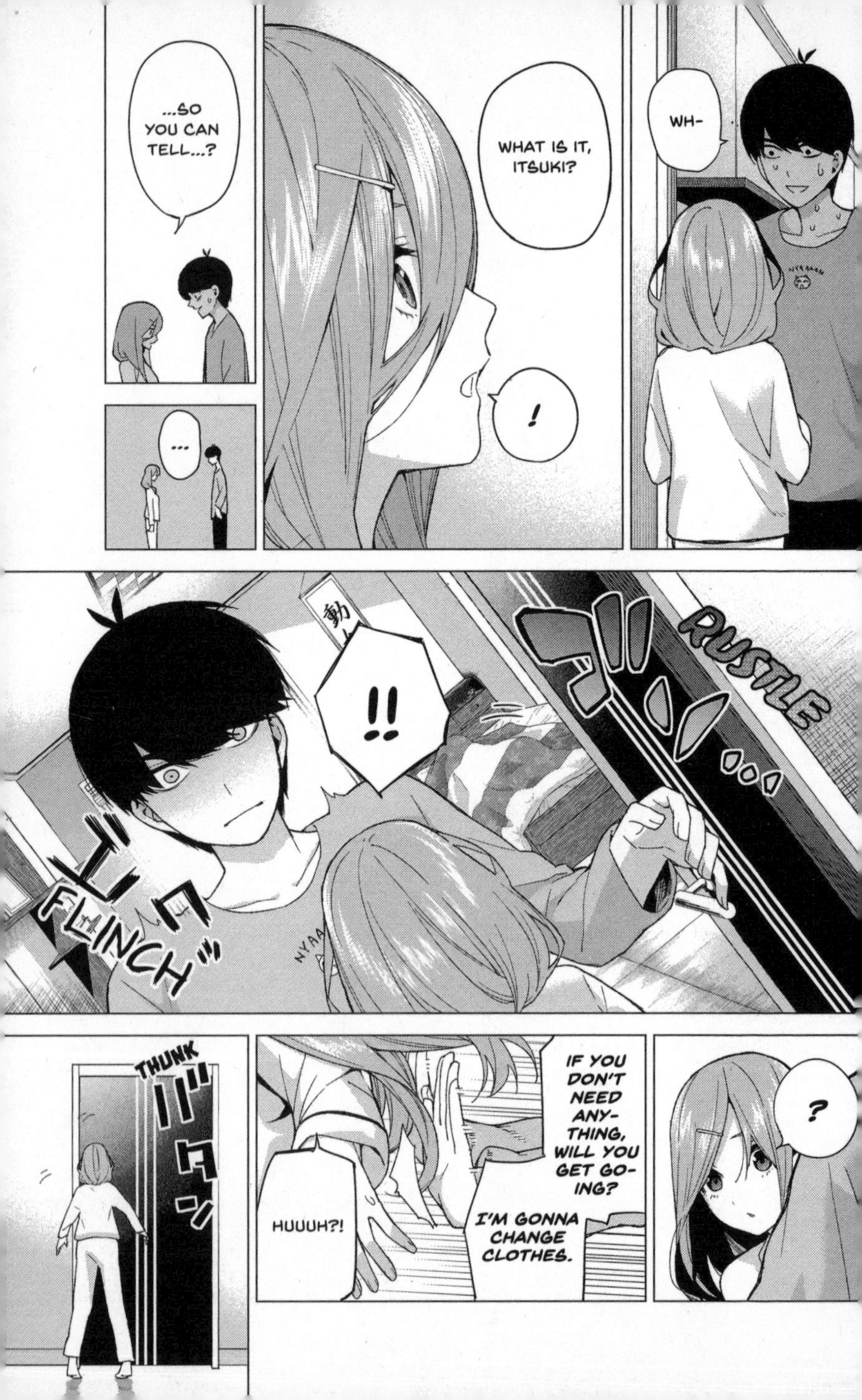
WH-
WHAT IS IT, ITSUKI?
!
...SO YOU CAN TELL...?
...
RUSTLE
!!
FLINCH
?
IF YOU DON'T NEED ANY-THING, WILL YOU GET GO-ING?
I'M GONNA CHANGE CLOTHES.
HUUUH?!
THUNK

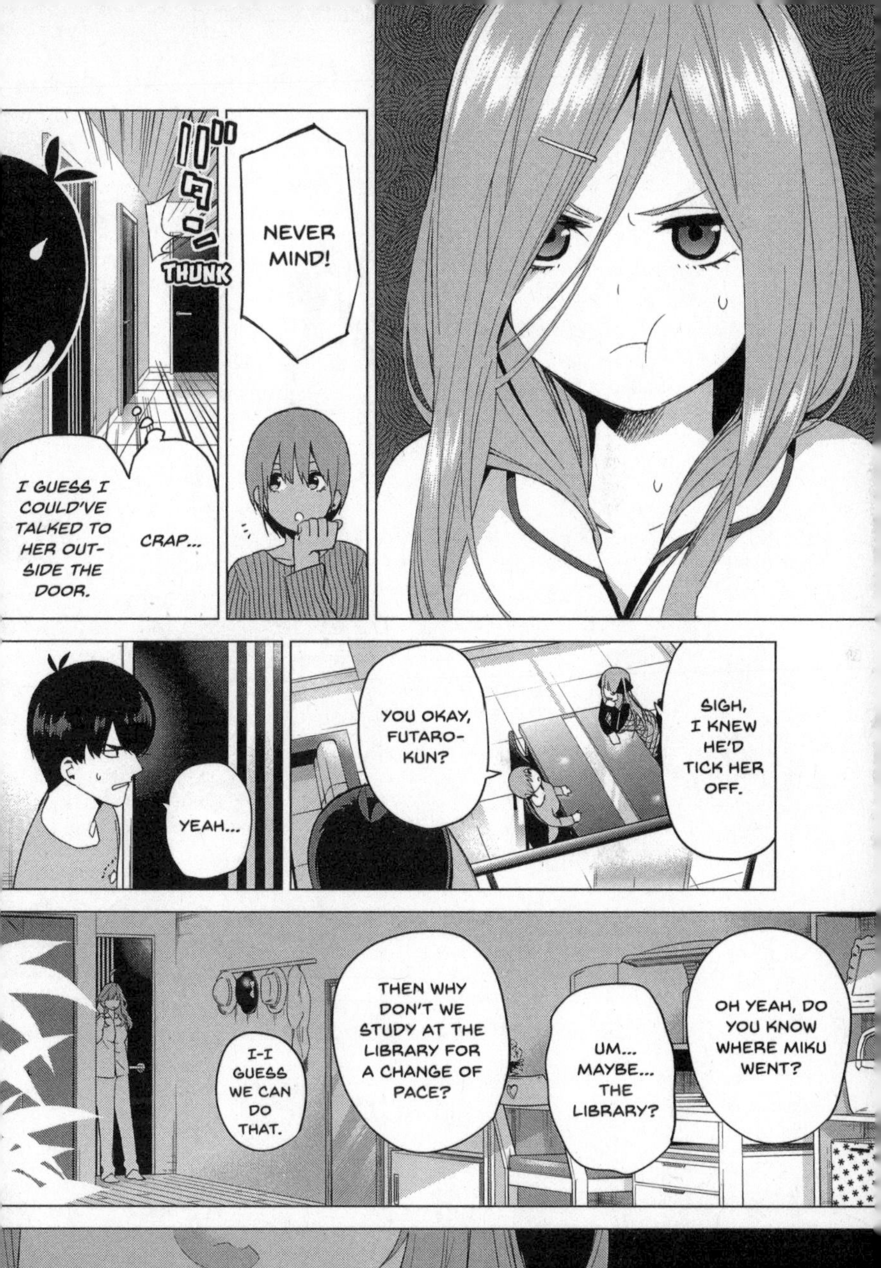
NEVER MIND!
THUNK
CRAP...
I GUESS I COULD'VE TALKED TO HER OUT-SIDE THE DOOR.
SIGH, I KNEW HE'D TICK HER OFF.
YOU OKAY, FUTARO-KUN?
YEAH...
OH YEAH, DO YOU KNOW WHERE MIKU WENT?
UM... MAYBE... THE LIBRARY?
THEN WHY DON'T WE STUDY AT THE LIBRARY FOR A CHANGE OF PACE?
I-I GUESS WE CAN DO THAT.

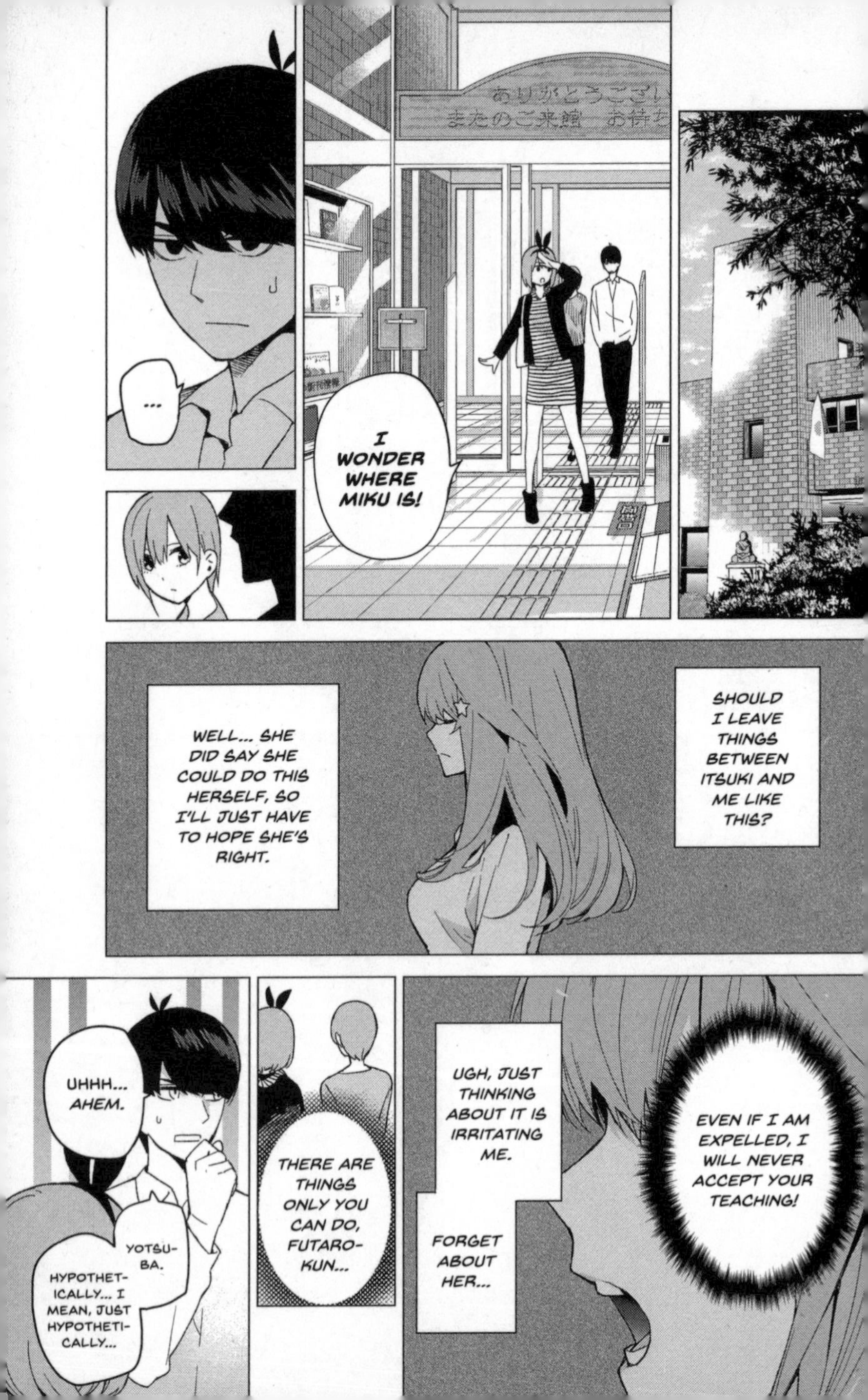

I WONDER WHERE MIKU IS!
...
SHOULD I LEAVE THINGS BETWEEN ITSUKI AND ME LIKE THIS?
WELL... SHE DID SAY SHE COULD DO THIS HERSELF, SO I'LL JUST HAVE TO HOPE SHE'S RIGHT.
EVEN IF I AM EXPELLED, I WILL NEVER ACCEPT YOUR TEACHING!
UGH, JUST THINKING ABOUT IT IS IRRITATING ME.
FORGET ABOUT HER...
THERE ARE THINGS ONLY YOU CAN DO, FUTARO-KUN...
UHHH... AHEM.
YOTSUBA. HYPOTHETICALLY... I MEAN, JUST HYPOTHETICALLY...

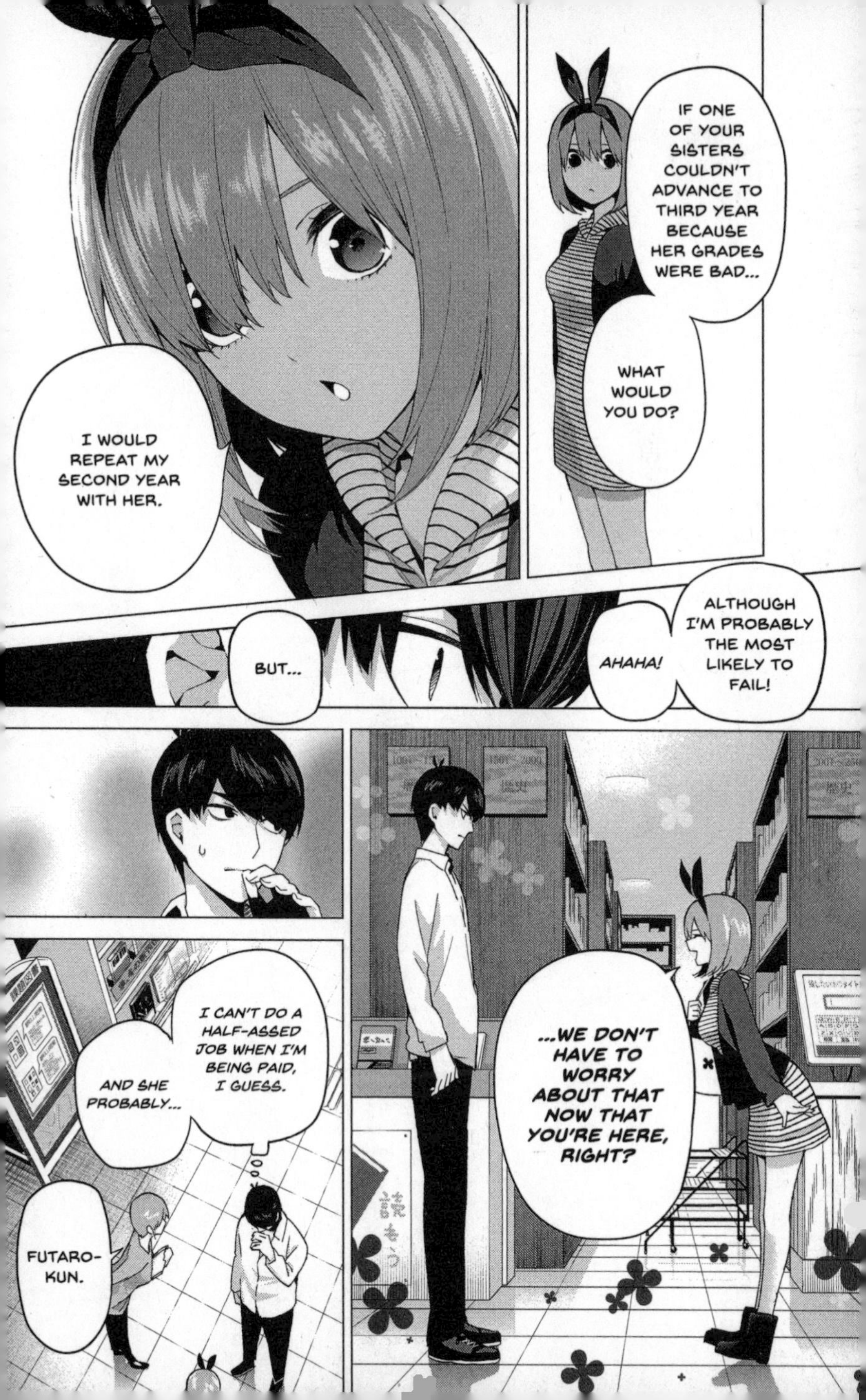
IF ONE OF YOUR SISTERS COULDN'T ADVANCE TO THIRD YEAR BECAUSE HER GRADES WERE BAD...
WHAT WOULD YOU DO?
I WOULD REPEAT MY SECOND YEAR WITH HER.
ALTHOUGH I'M PROBABLY THE MOST LIKELY TO FAIL!
AHAHA!
BUT...
...WE DON'T HAVE TO WORRY ABOUT THAT NOW THAT YOU'RE HERE, RIGHT?
I CAN'T DO A HALF-ASSED JOB WHEN I'M BEING PAID, I GUESS.
AND SHE PROBABLY...
FUTARO-KUN.

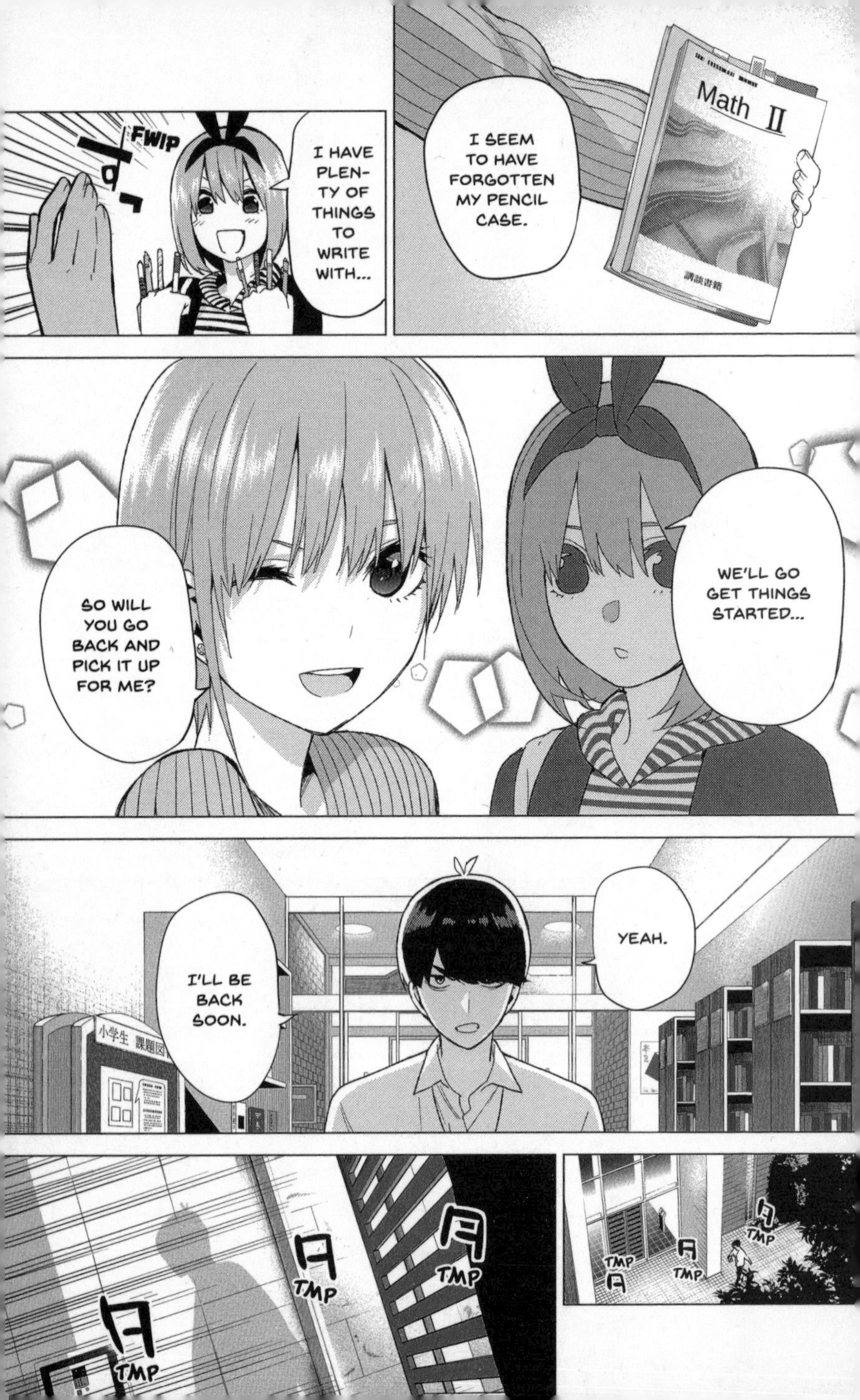
Math II
講談書籍
I SEEM TO HAVE FORGOTTEN MY PENCIL CASE.
FWIP
I HAVE PLENTY OF THINGS TO WRITE WITH...
WE'LL GO GET THINGS STARTED...
SO WILL YOU GO BACK AND PICK IT UP FOR ME?
YEAH.
I'LL BE BACK SOON.
小学生 課題図
TMP
TMP
TMP
TMP
TMP
TMP
TMP
TMP

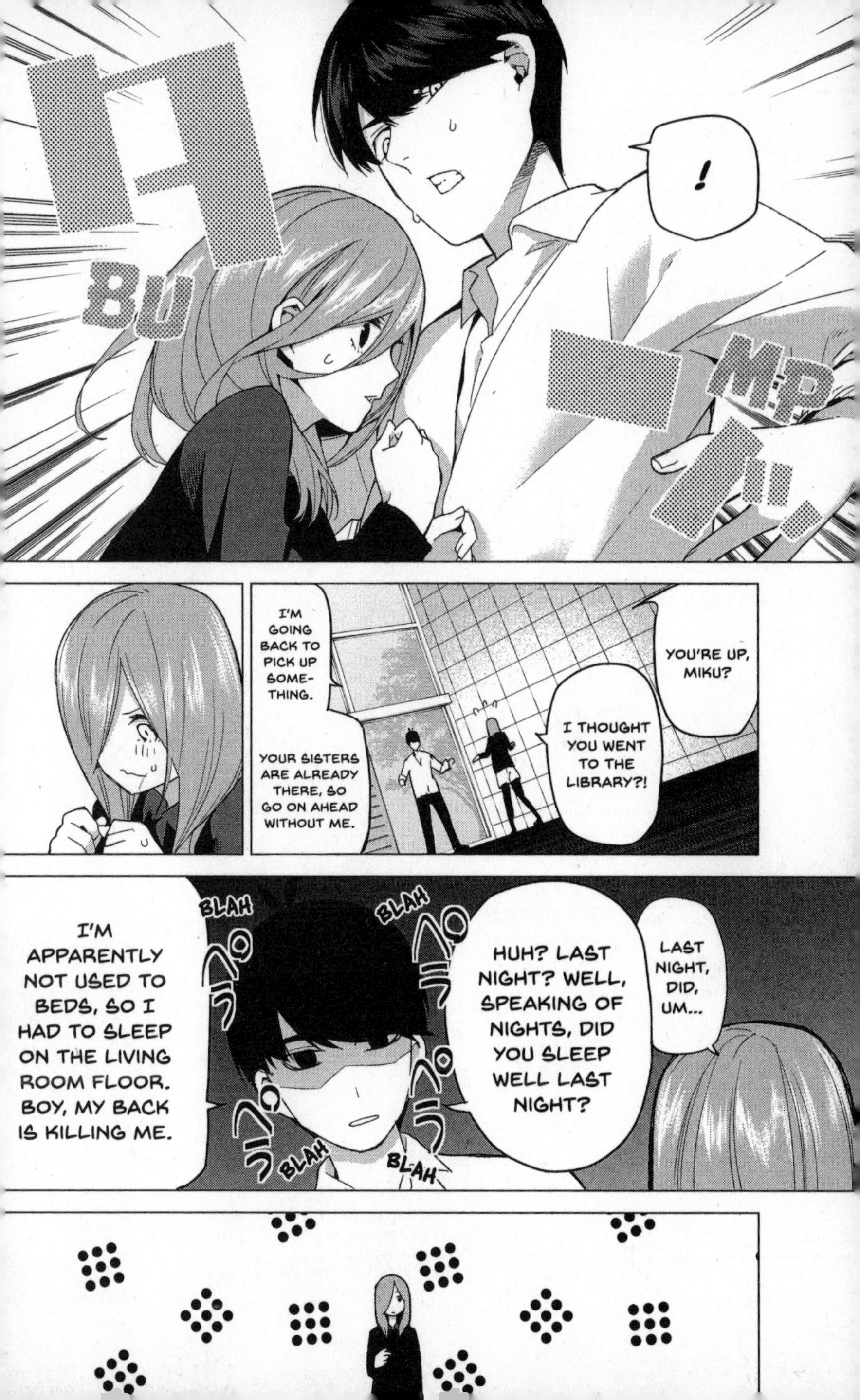
!
BU
MP
YOU'RE UP, MIKU?
I THOUGHT YOU WENT TO THE LIBRARY?!
I'M GOING BACK TO PICK UP SOME-THING.
YOUR SISTERS ARE ALREADY THERE, SO GO ON AHEAD WITHOUT ME.
LAST NIGHT, DID, UM...
HUH? LAST NIGHT? WELL, SPEAKING OF NIGHTS, DID YOU SLEEP WELL LAST NIGHT?
BLAH
BLAH
BLAH
BLAH
I'M APPARENTLY NOT USED TO BEDS, SO I HAD TO SLEEP ON THE LIVING ROOM FLOOR. BOY, MY BACK IS KILLING ME.

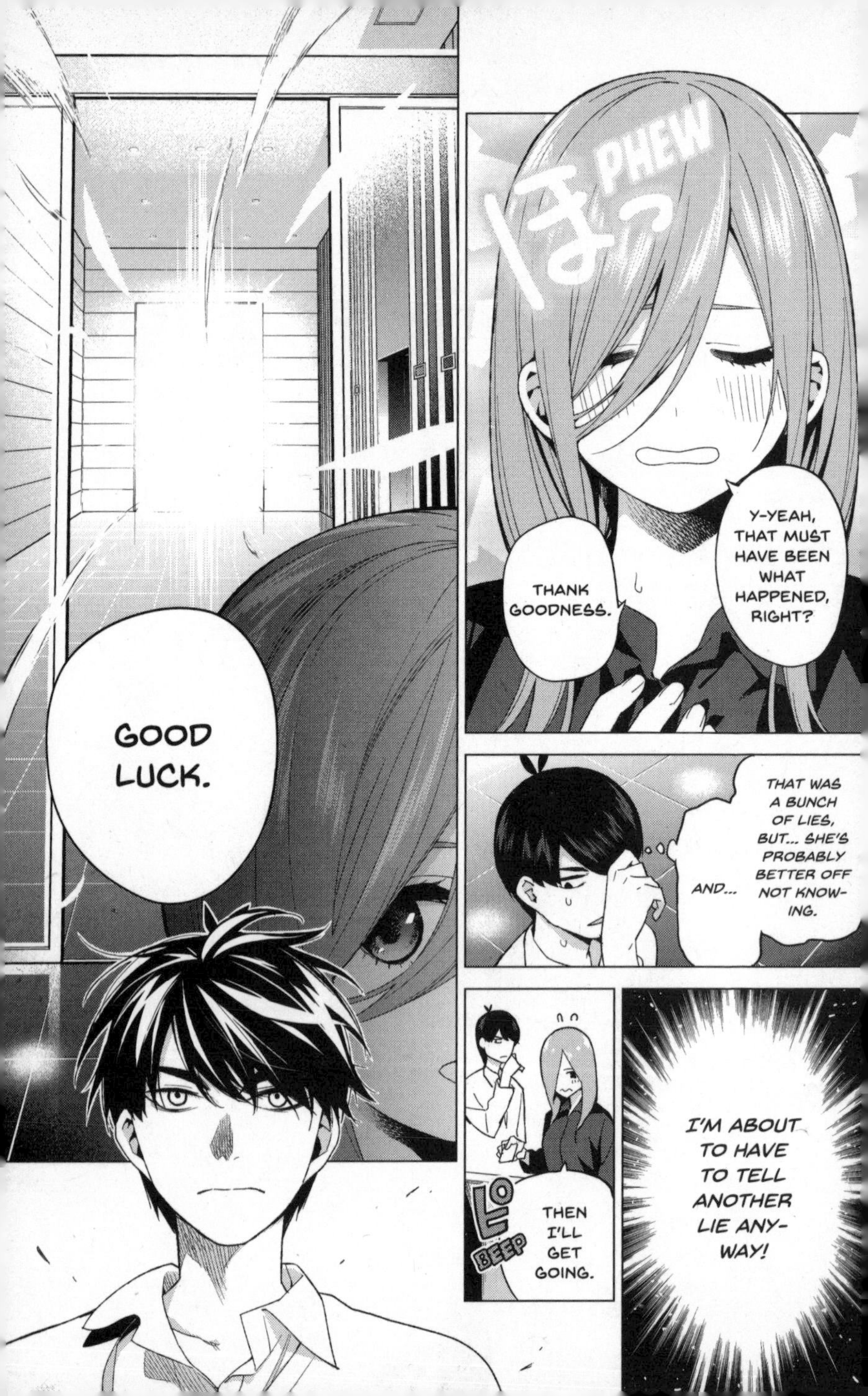
ほっ
PHEW
Y-YEAH, THAT MUST HAVE BEEN WHAT HAPPENED, RIGHT?
THANK GOODNESS.
THAT WAS A BUNCH OF LIES, BUT... SHE'S PROBABLY BETTER OFF NOT KNOWING.
AND...
I'M ABOUT TO HAVE TO TELL ANOTHER LIE ANYWAY!
ピッ
BEEP
THEN I'LL GET GOING.
GOOD LUCK.

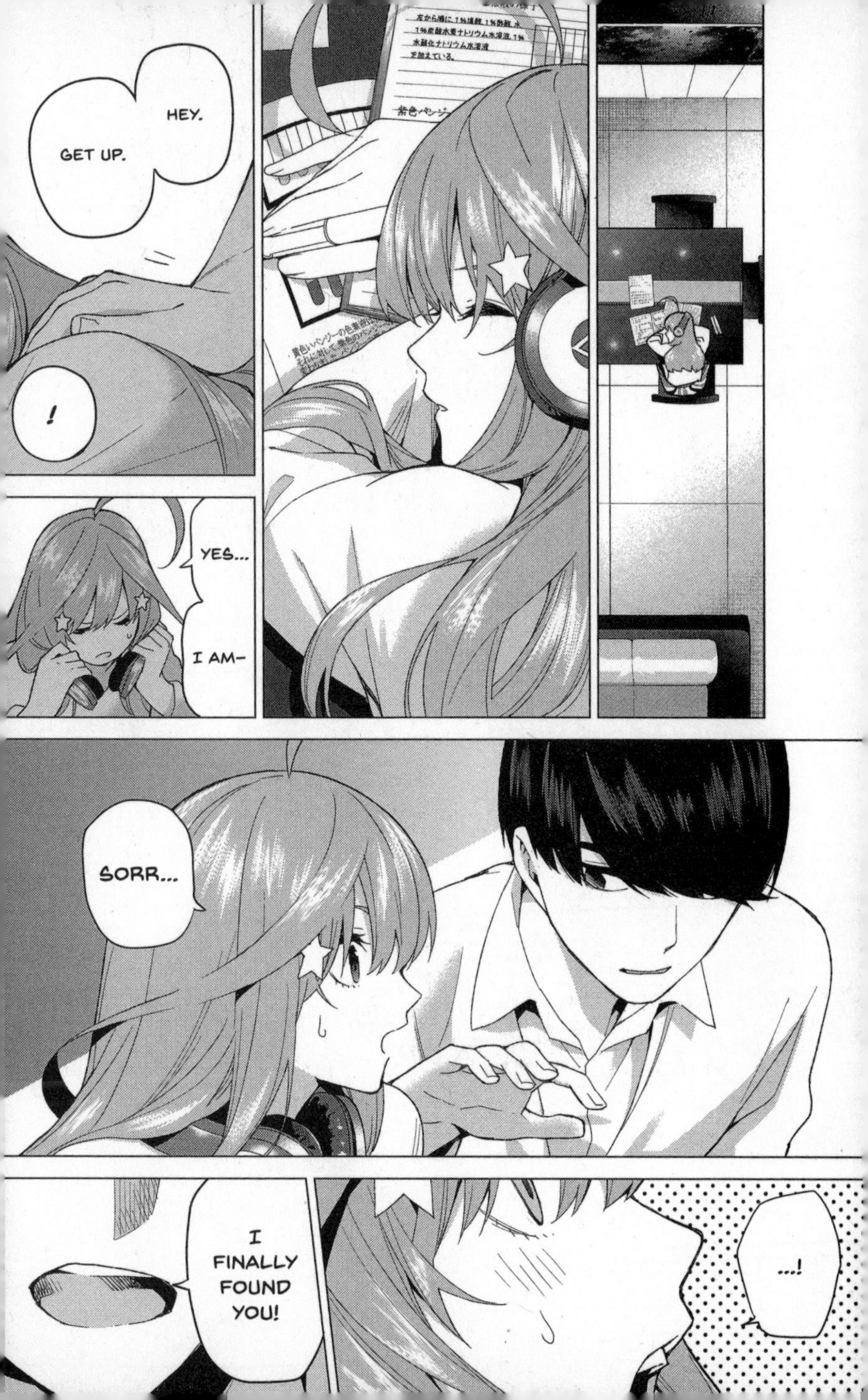
HEY.
GET UP.
!
YES... I AM-
SORR...
...!
I FINALLY FOUND YOU!

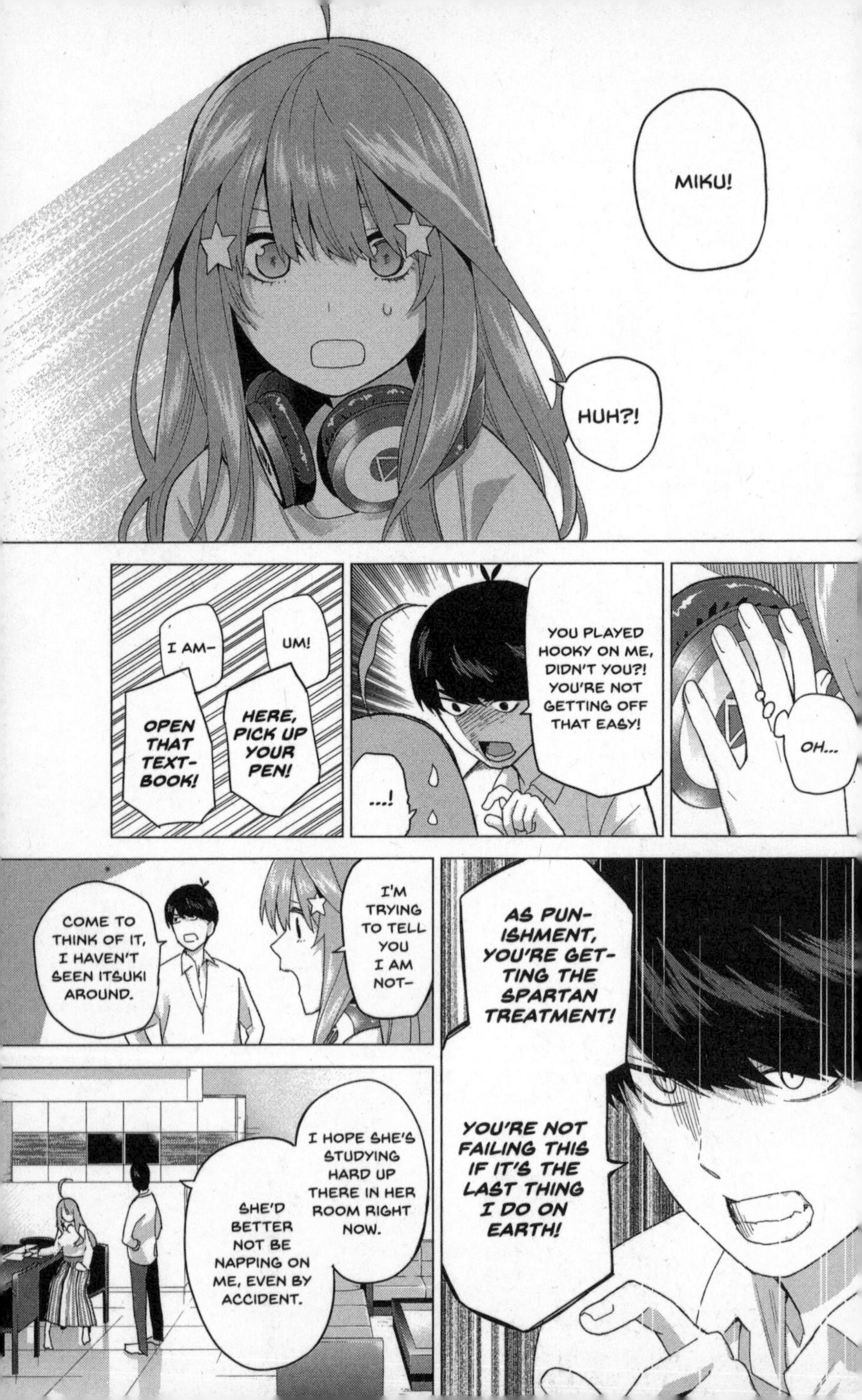
MIKU!
HUH?!
OH...
YOU PLAYED HOOKY ON ME, DIDN'T YOU?! YOU'RE NOT GETTING OFF THAT EASY!
...!
UM!
I AM-
HERE, PICK UP YOUR PEN!
OPEN THAT TEXT-BOOK!
AS PUN-ISHMENT, YOU'RE GET-TING THE SPARTAN TREATMENT!
YOU'RE NOT FAILING THIS IF IT'S THE LAST THING I DO ON EARTH!
I'M TRYING TO TELL YOU I AM NOT-
COME TO THINK OF IT, I HAVEN'T SEEN ITSUKI AROUND.
I HOPE SHE'S STUDYING HARD UP THERE IN HER ROOM RIGHT NOW.
SHE'D BETTER NOT BE NAPPING ON ME, EVEN BY ACCIDENT.

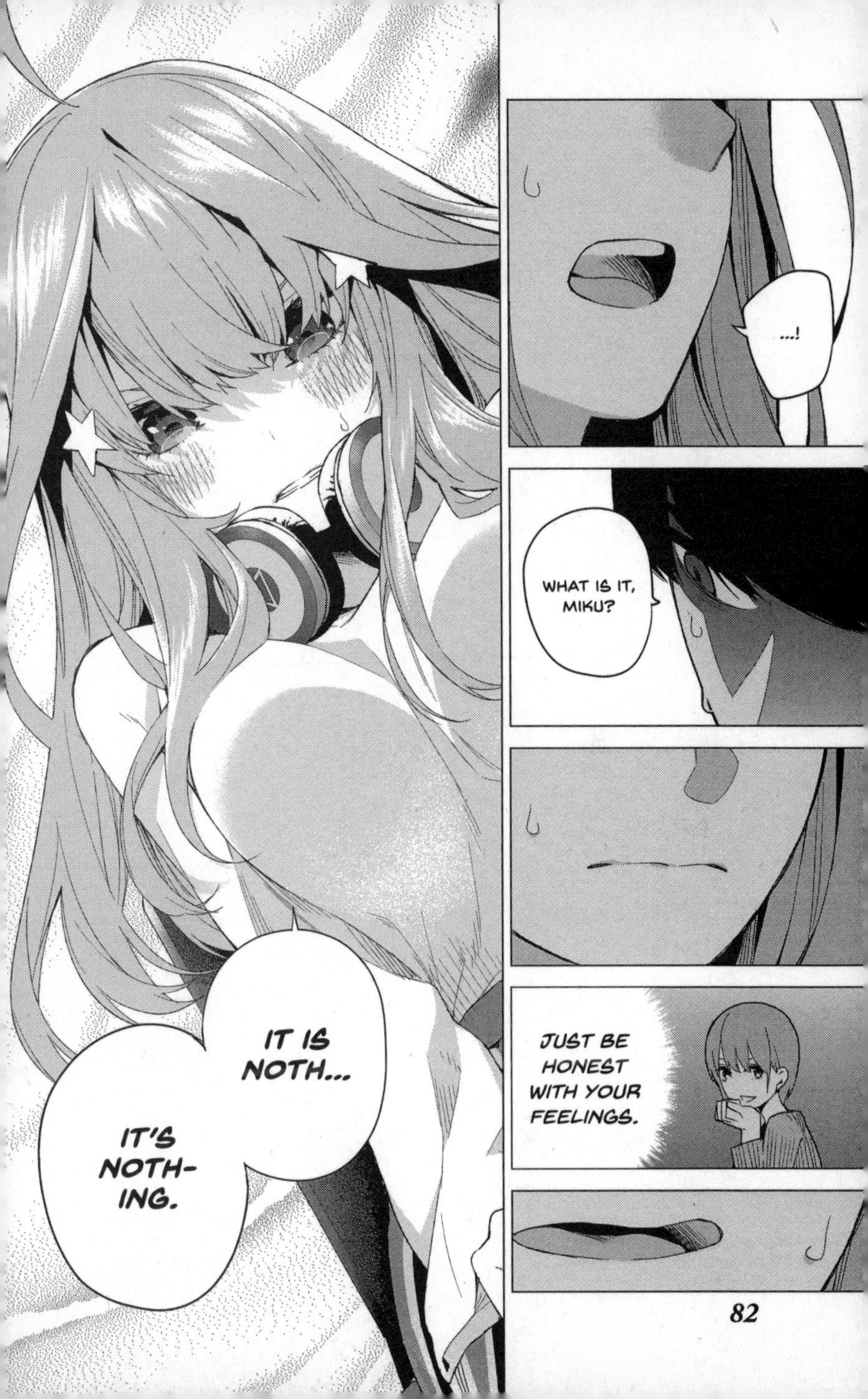
...!
WHAT IS IT, MIKU?
JUST BE HONEST WITH YOUR FEELINGS.
IT IS NOTH...
IT'S NOTH-ING.

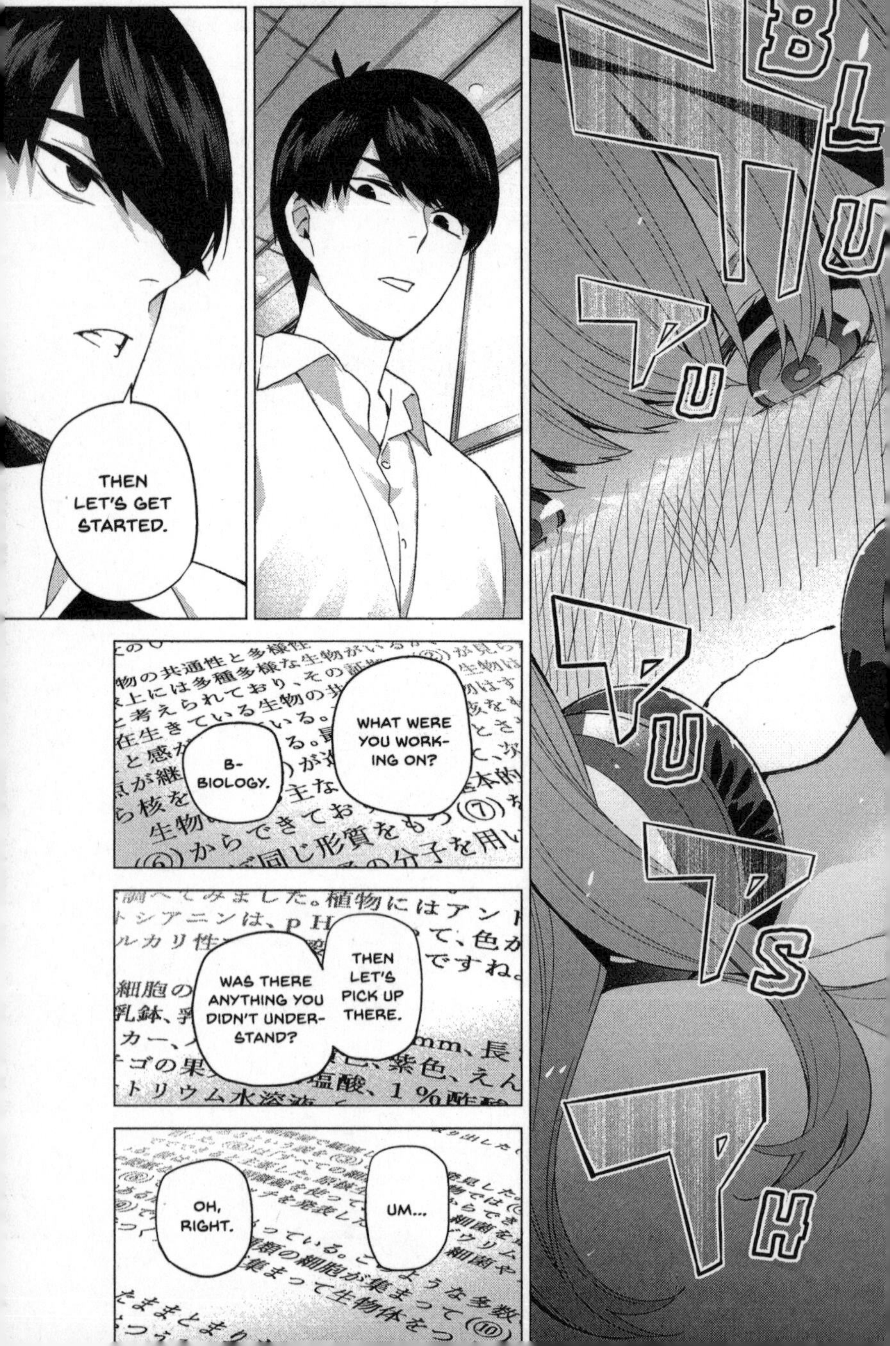
BLUUUSH
THEN LET'S GET STARTED.
WHAT WERE YOU WORKING ON?
B-BIOLOGY.
THEN LET'S PICK UP THERE.
WAS THERE ANYTHING YOU DIDN'T UNDERSTAND?
UM...
OH, RIGHT.

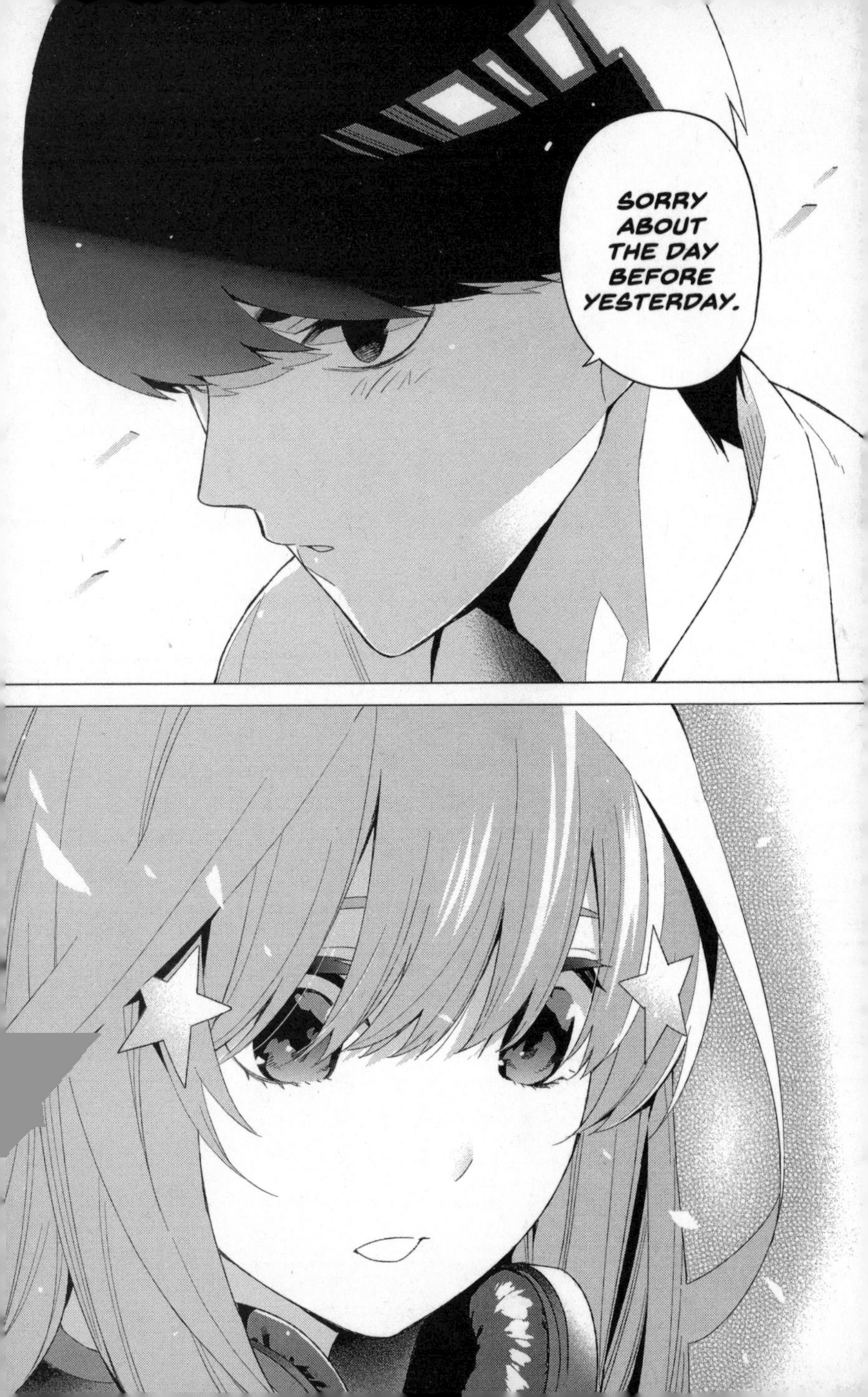
SORRY ABOUT THE DAY BEFORE YESTERDAY.

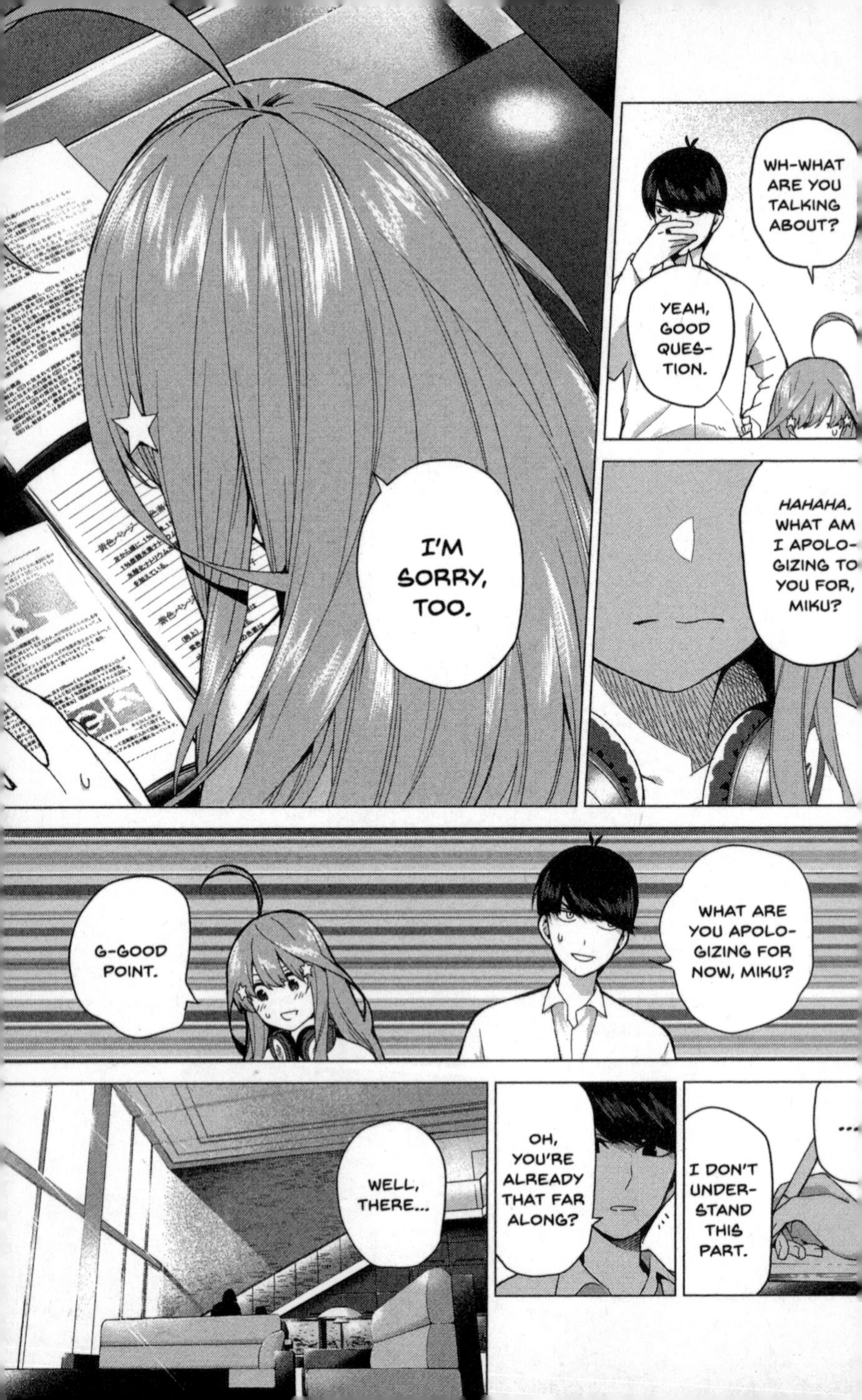

WH-WHAT ARE YOU TALKING ABOUT?
YEAH, GOOD QUES-TION.
HAHAHA. WHAT AM I APOLO-GIZING TO YOU FOR, MIKU?
I'M SORRY, TOO.
WHAT ARE YOU APOLO-GIZING FOR NOW, MIKU?
G-GOOD POINT.
...
I DON'T UNDER-STAND THIS PART.
OH, YOU'RE ALREADY THAT FAR ALONG?
WELL, THERE...

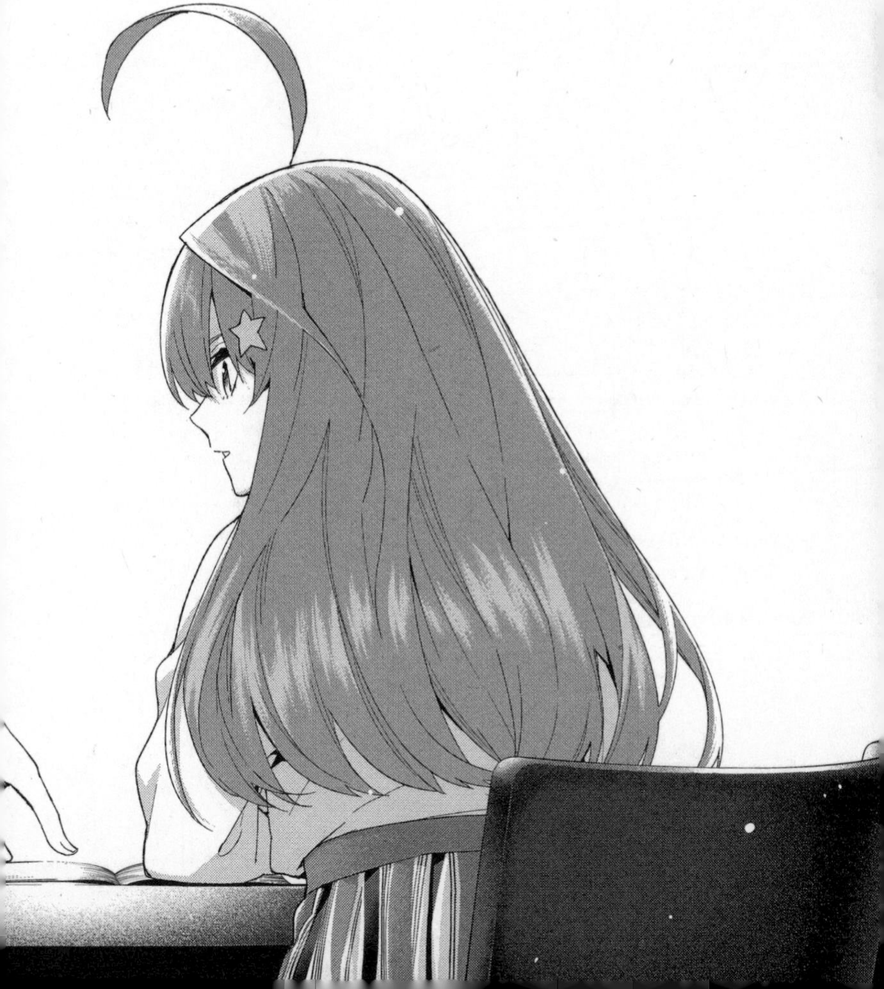

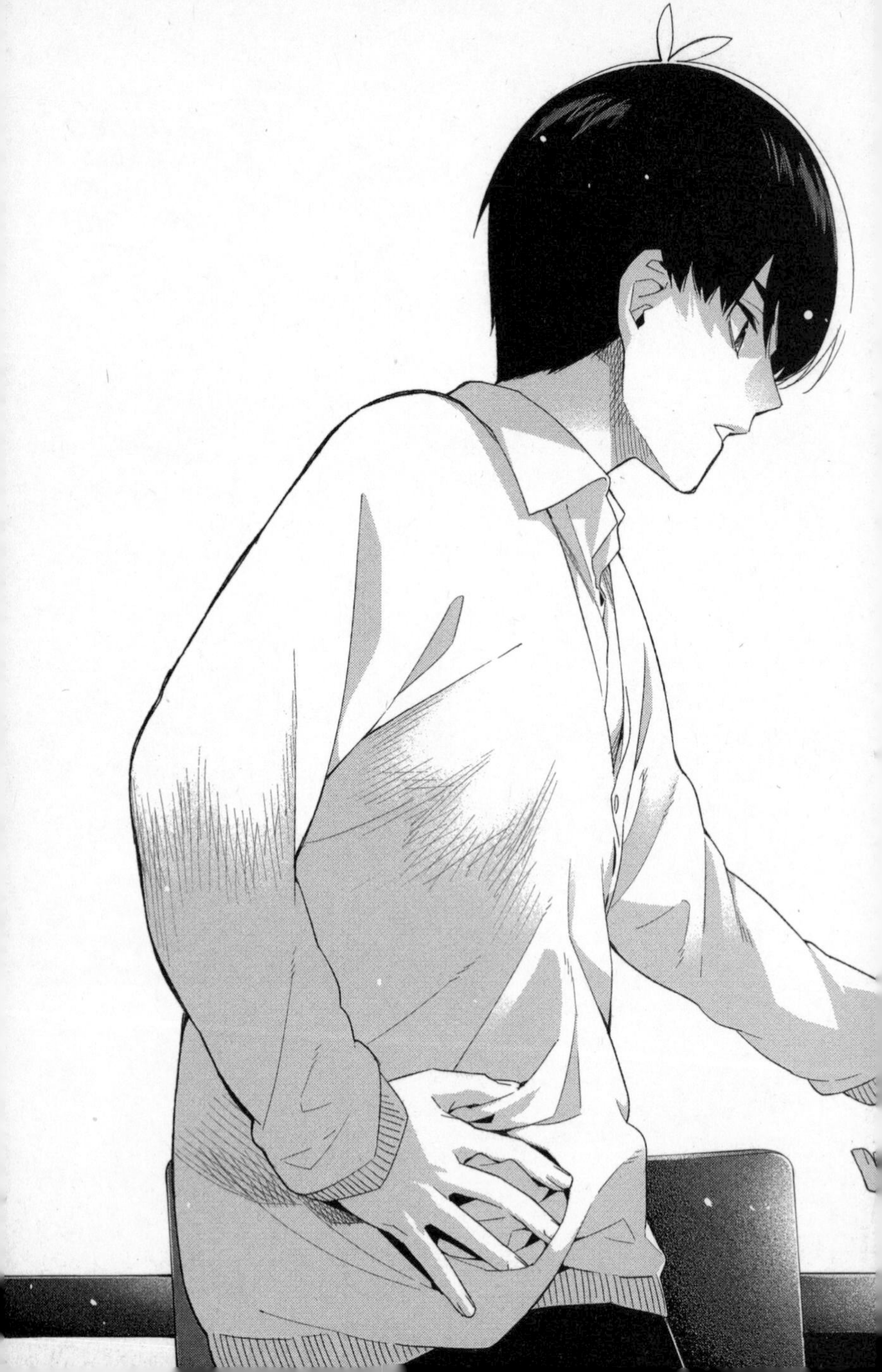

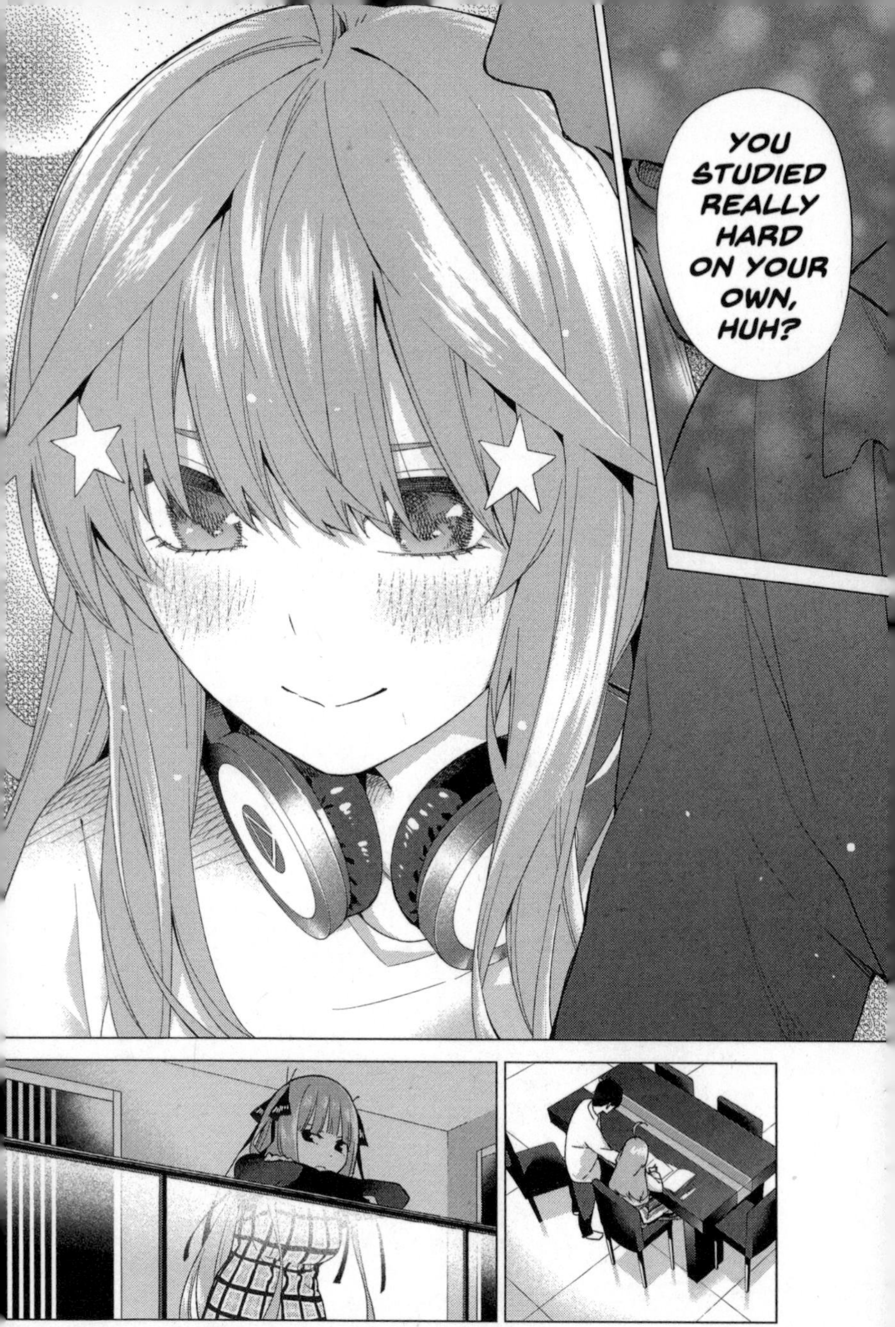
YOU STUDIED REALLY HARD ON YOUR OWN, HUH?

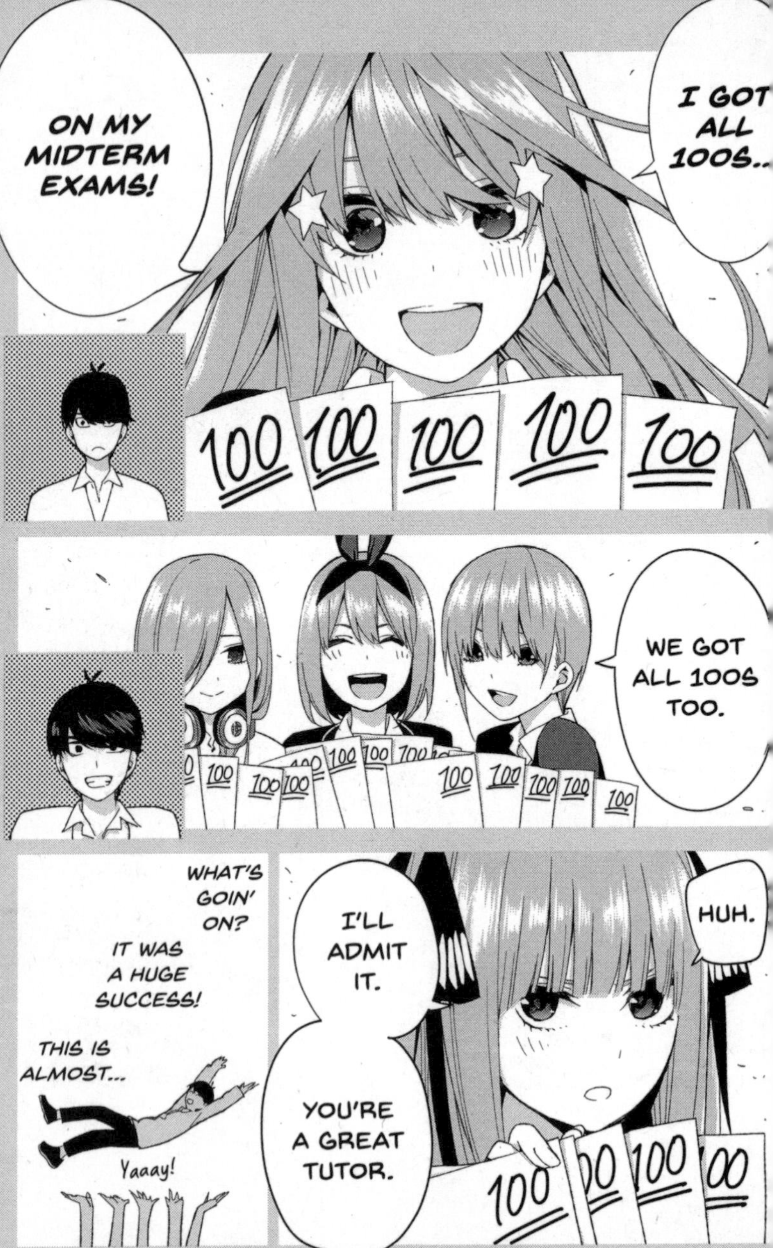
I GOT ALL 100S...
ON MY MIDTERM EXAMS!
WE GOT ALL 100S TOO.
HUH.
I'LL ADMIT IT.
YOU'RE A GREAT TUTOR.
WHAT'S GOIN' ON?
IT WAS A HUGE SUCCESS!
THIS IS ALMOST...
Yaaay!

CHAPTER 19 THE DEATH ROAD OF PANI

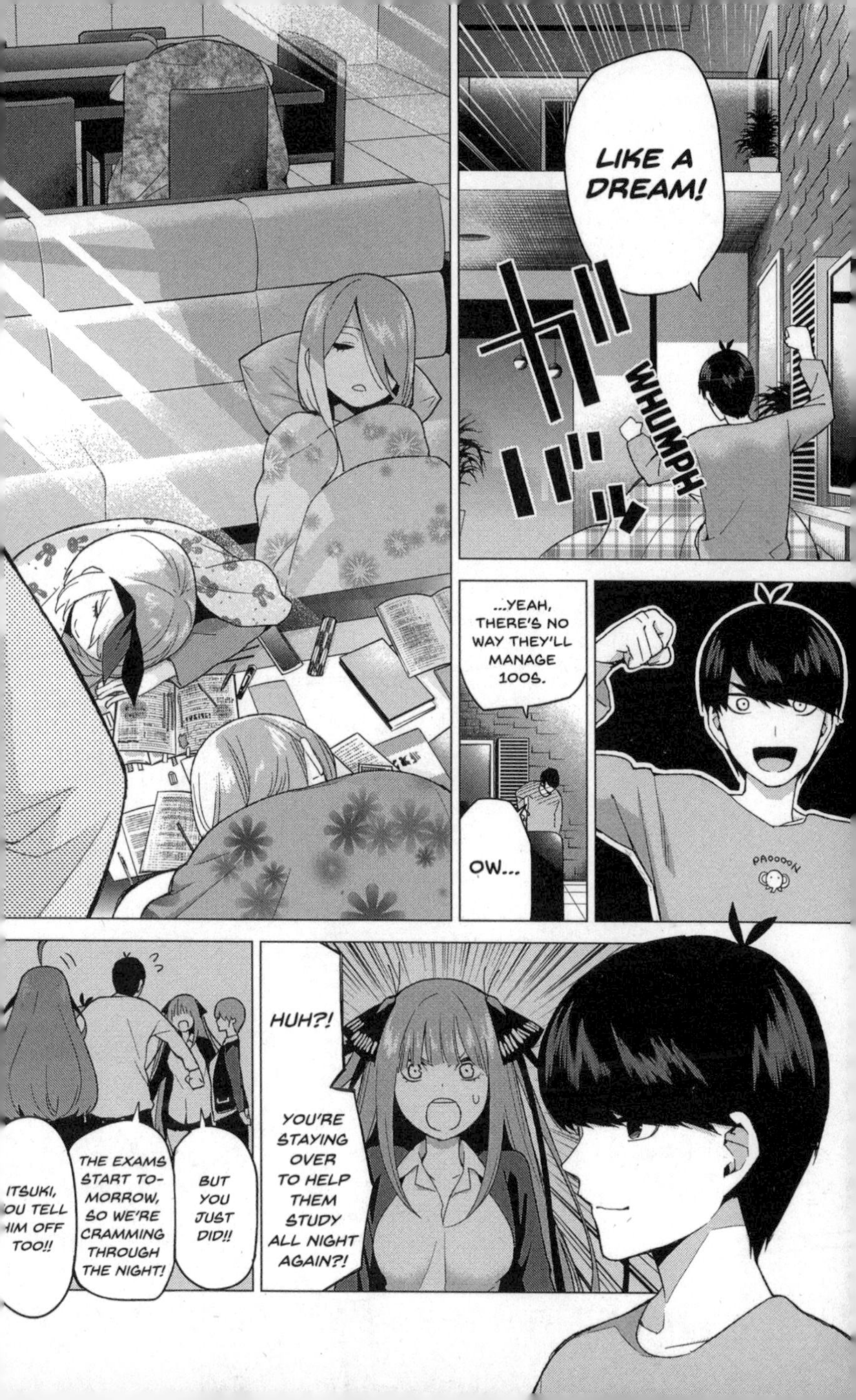
LIKE A DREAM!
WHUMPH
PAOOOON
...YEAH, THERE'S NO WAY THEY'LL MANAGE 100S.
OW...
HUH?!
YOU'RE STAYING OVER TO HELP THEM STUDY ALL NIGHT AGAIN?!
BUT YOU JUST DID!!
THE EXAMS START TO-MORROW, SO WE'RE CRAMMING THROUGH THE NIGHT!
ITSUKI, OU TELL IM OFF TOO!!

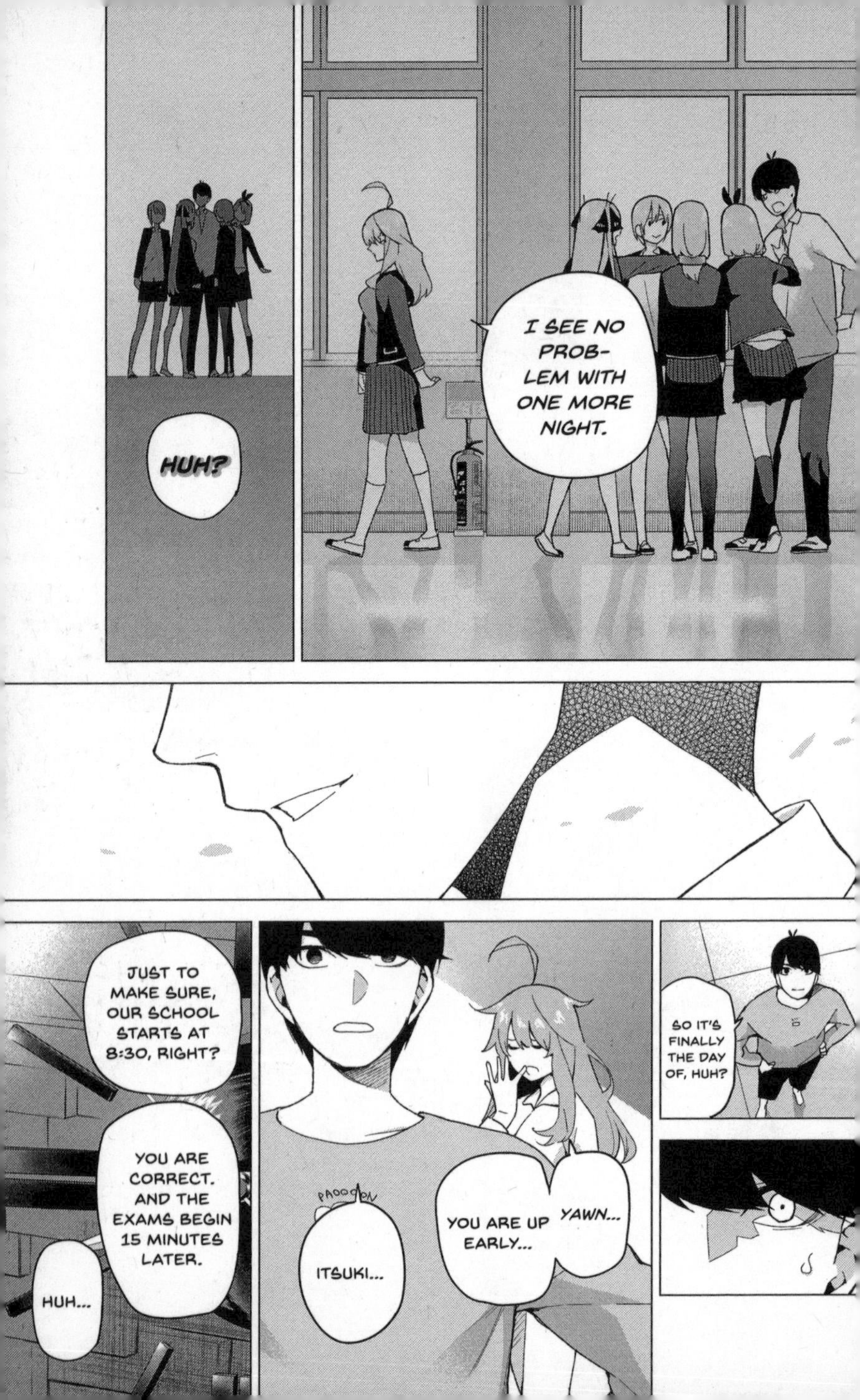
I SEE NO PROBLEM WITH ONE MORE NIGHT.
HUH?
SO IT'S FINALLY THE DAY OF, HUH?
YAWN...
YOU ARE UP EARLY...
PAOOOON
ITSUKI...
JUST TO MAKE SURE, OUR SCHOOL STARTS AT 8:30, RIGHT?
YOU ARE CORRECT. AND THE EXAMS BEGIN 15 MINUTES LATER.
HUH...

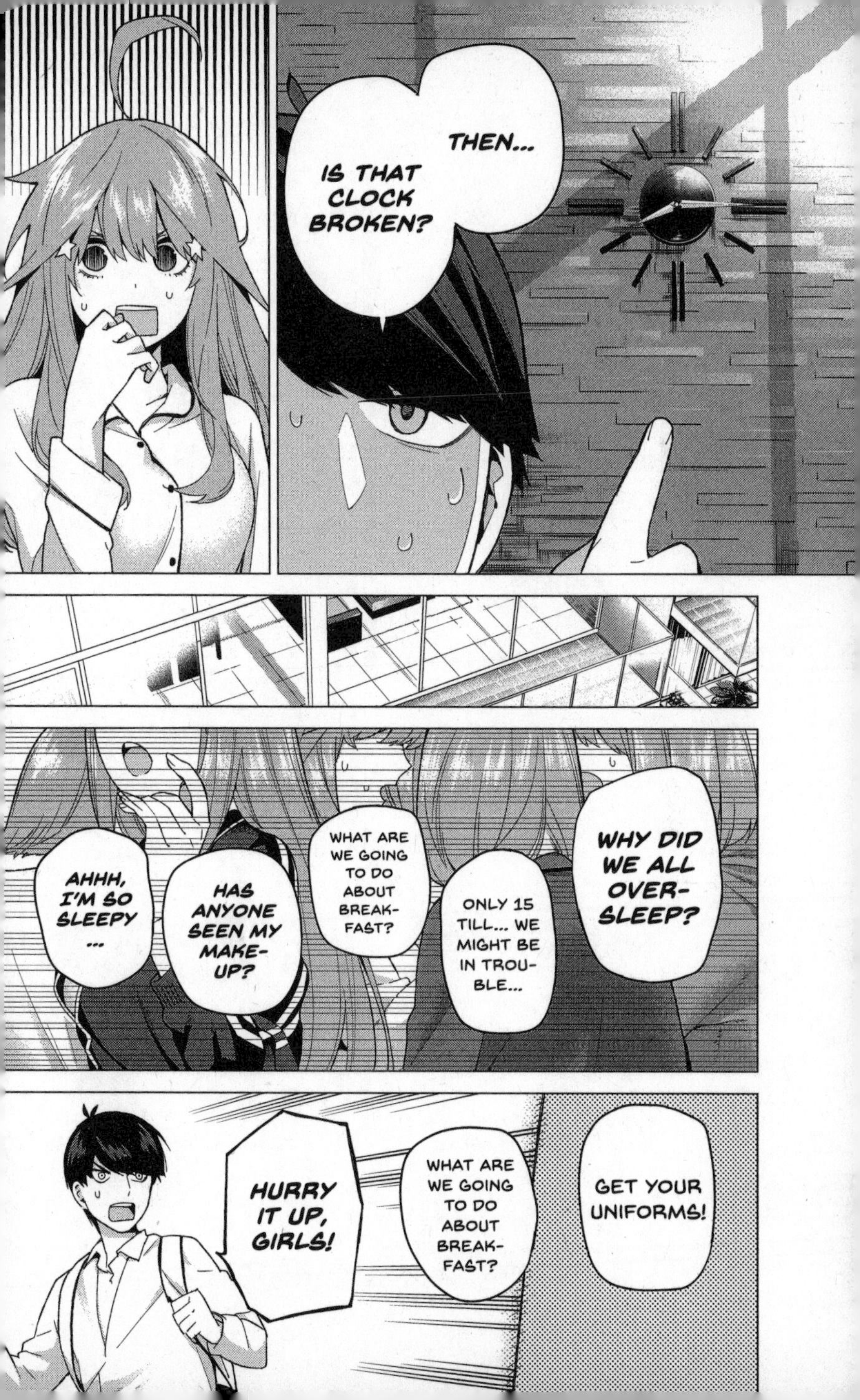
THEN... IS THAT CLOCK BROKEN?
WHY DID WE ALL OVER-SLEEP?
ONLY 15 TILL... WE MIGHT BE IN TROU-BLE...
WHAT ARE WE GOING TO DO ABOUT BREAK-FAST?
HAS ANYONE SEEN MY MAKE-UP?
AHHH, I'M SO SLEEPY ...
GET YOUR UNIFORMS!
WHAT ARE WE GOING TO DO ABOUT BREAK-FAST?
HURRY IT UP, GIRLS!

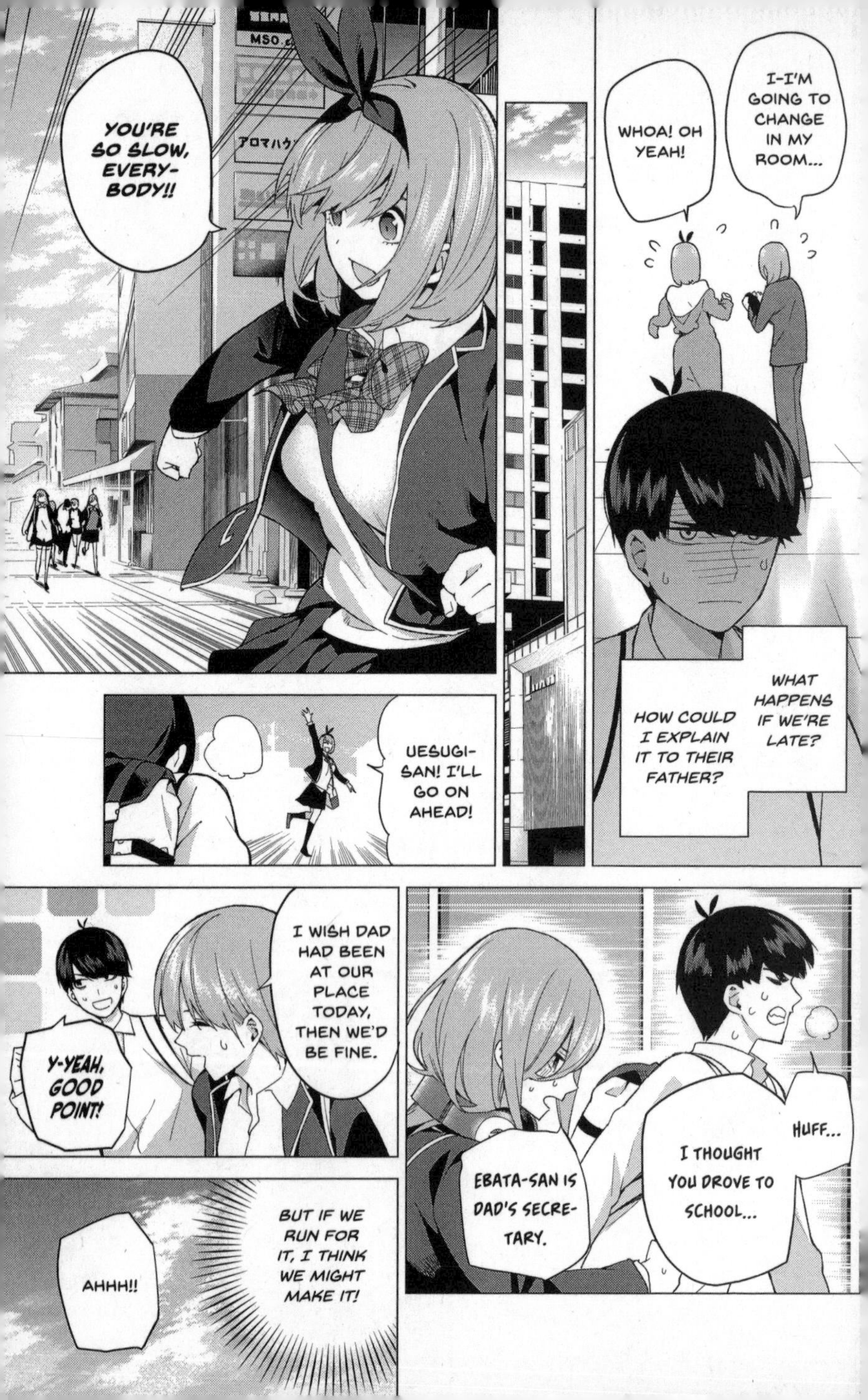
I-I'M GOING TO CHANGE IN MY ROOM...
WHOA! OH YEAH!
WHAT HAPPENS IF WE'RE LATE?
HOW COULD I EXPLAIN IT TO THEIR FATHER?
YOU'RE SO SLOW, EVERY-BODY!!
UESUGI-SAN! I'LL GO ON AHEAD!
HUFF...
I THOUGHT YOU DROVE TO SCHOOL...
EBATA-SAN IS DAD'S SECRE-TARY.
I WISH DAD HAD BEEN AT OUR PLACE TODAY, THEN WE'D BE FINE.
Y-YEAH, GOOD POINT!
BUT IF WE RUN FOR IT, I THINK WE MIGHT MAKE IT!
AHHH!!

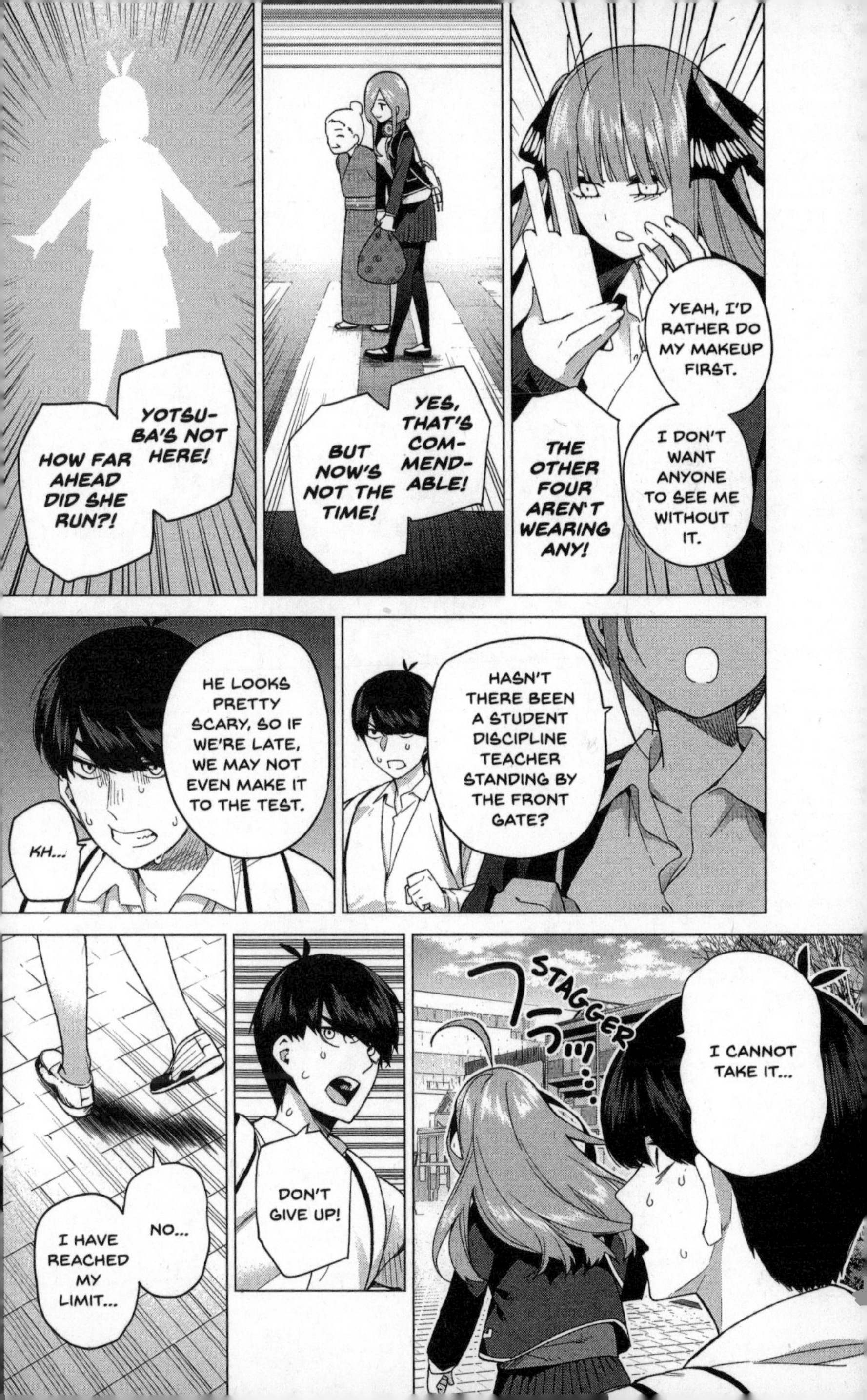
YEAH, I'D RATHER DO MY MAKEUP FIRST.
I DON'T WANT ANYONE TO SEE ME WITHOUT IT.
THE OTHER FOUR AREN'T WEARING ANY!
YES, THAT'S COMMENDABLE!
BUT NOW'S NOT THE TIME!
YOTSUBA'S NOT HERE!
HOW FAR AHEAD DID SHE RUN?!
HASN'T THERE BEEN A STUDENT DISCIPLINE TEACHER STANDING BY THE FRONT GATE?
HE LOOKS PRETTY SCARY, SO IF WE'RE LATE, WE MAY NOT EVEN MAKE IT TO THE TEST.
KH...
STAGGER
I CANNOT TAKE IT...
DON'T GIVE UP!
NO...
I HAVE REACHED MY LIMIT...

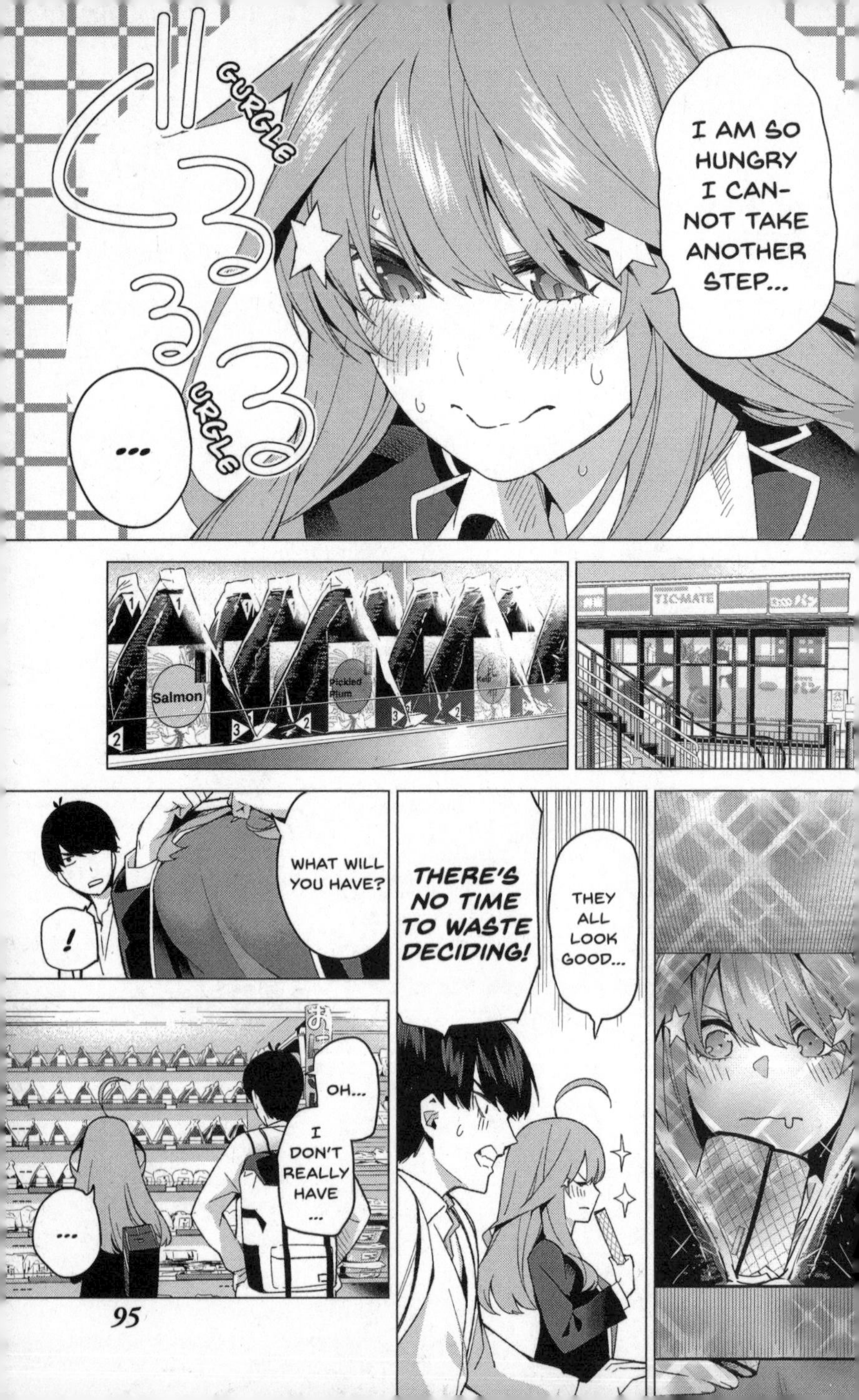
I AM SO HUNGRY I CAN-NOT TAKE ANOTHER STEP...
GURGLE
URGLE
...
TIC-MATE
Salmon
Pickled Plum
Kelp
THEY ALL LOOK GOOD...
THERE'S NO TIME TO WASTE DECIDING!
WHAT WILL YOU HAVE?
!
OH...
I DON'T REALLY HAVE ...
...

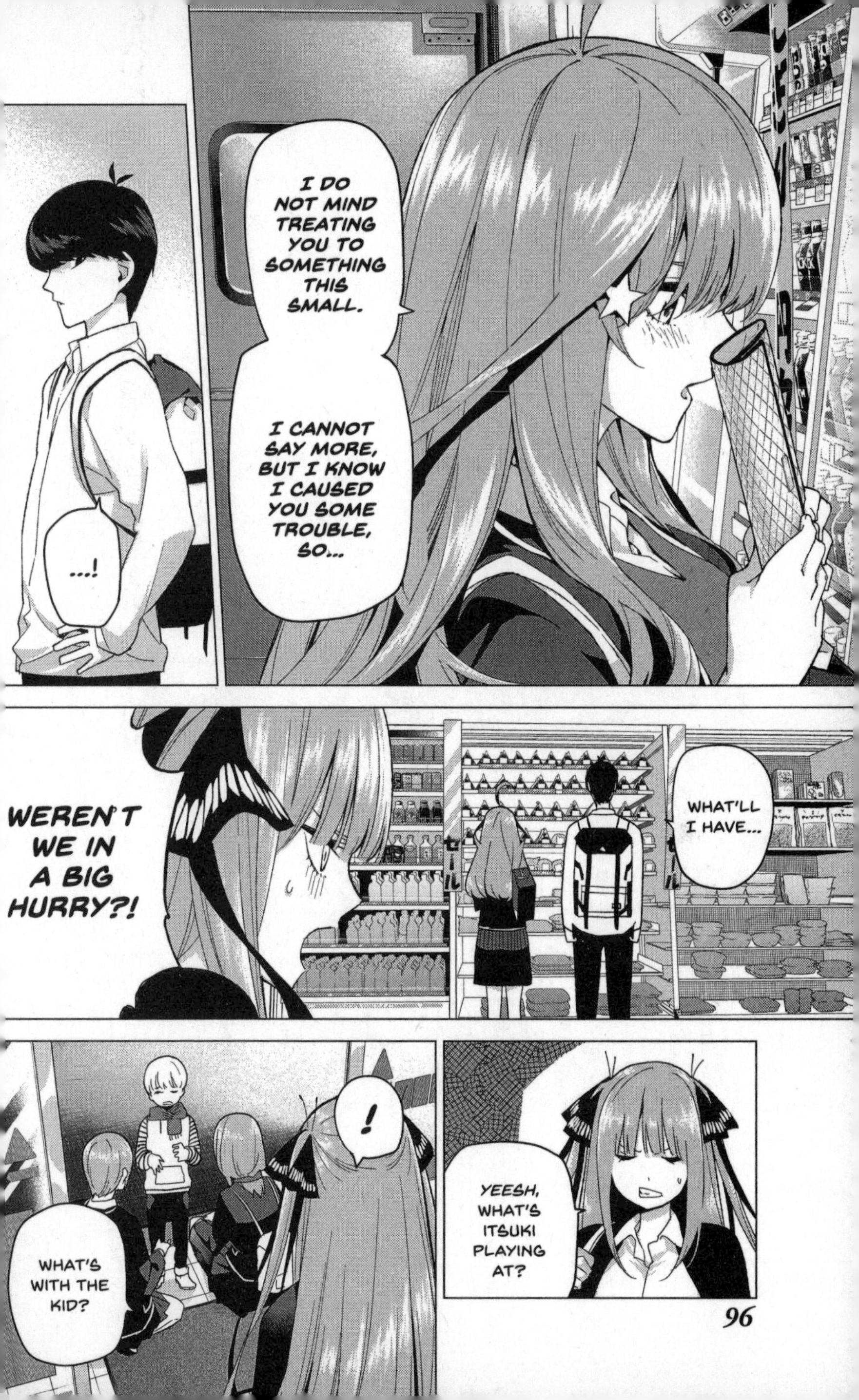
I DO NOT MIND TREATING YOU TO SOMETHING THIS SMALL.
I CANNOT SAY MORE, BUT I KNOW I CAUSED YOU SOME TROUBLE, SO...
...!
WHAT'LL I HAVE...
WEREN'T WE IN A BIG HURRY?!
YEESH, WHAT'S ITSUKI PLAYING AT?
!
WHAT'S WITH THE KID?

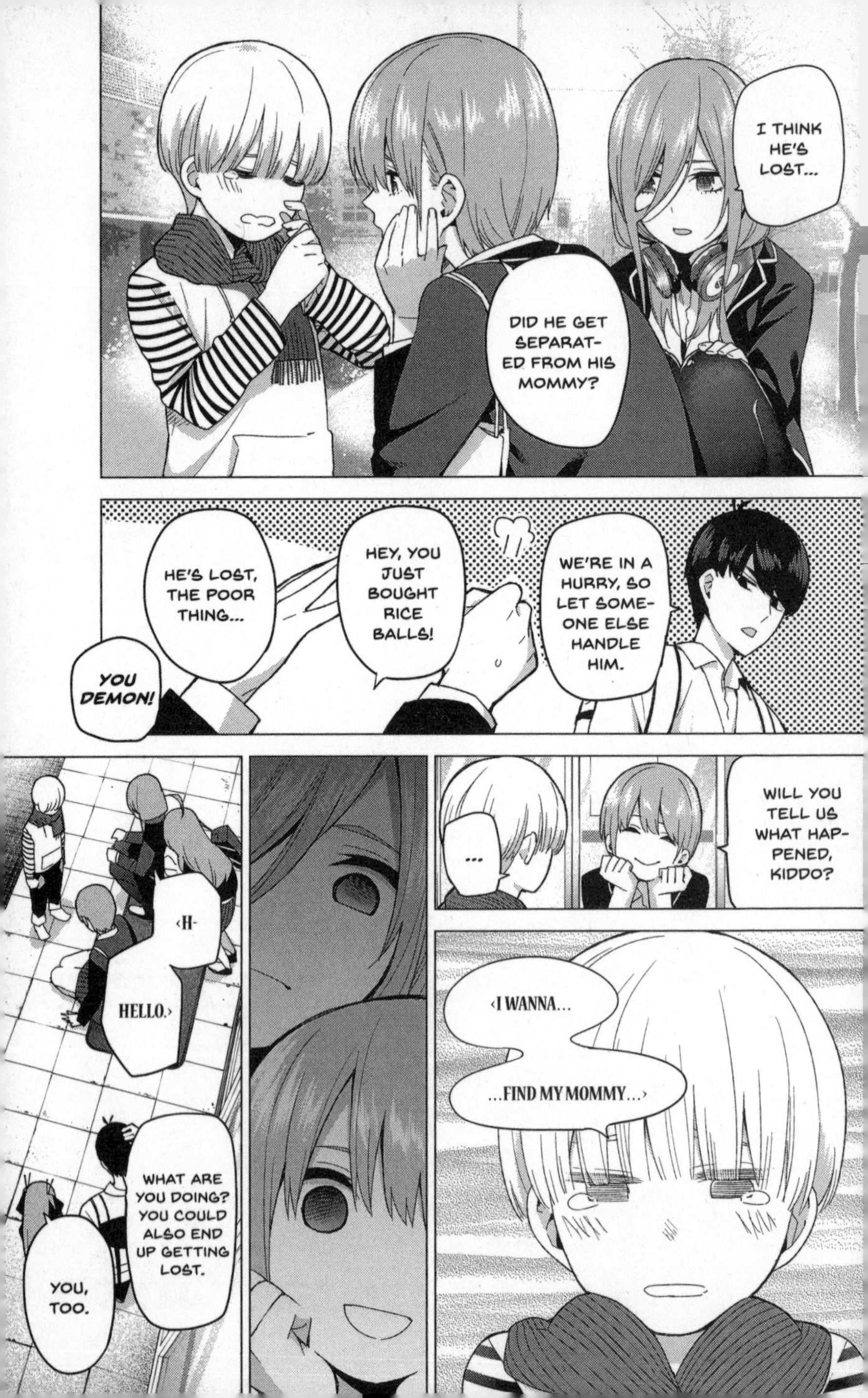
I THINK HE'S LOST...
DID HE GET SEPARATED FROM HIS MOMMY?
WE'RE IN A HURRY, SO LET SOMEONE ELSE HANDLE HIM.
HEY, YOU JUST BOUGHT RICE BALLS!
HE'S LOST, THE POOR THING...
YOU DEMON!
WILL YOU TELL US WHAT HAPPENED, KIDDO?
...
‹I WANNA...
...FIND MY MOMMY...›
‹H-
HELLO.›
WHAT ARE YOU DOING? YOU COULD ALSO END UP GETTING LOST.
YOU, TOO.

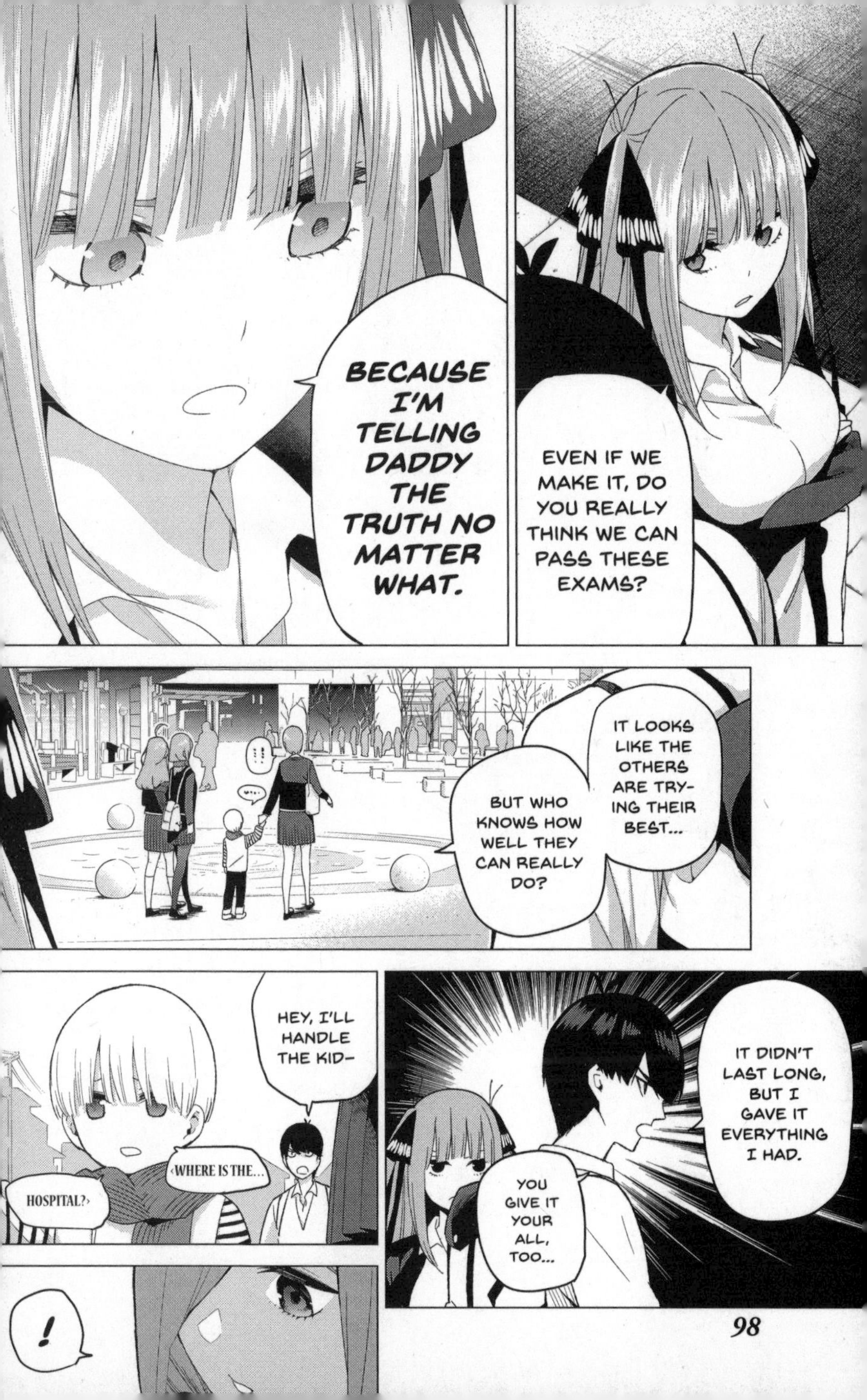
EVEN IF WE MAKE IT, DO YOU REALLY THINK WE CAN PASS THESE EXAMS?
BECAUSE I'M TELLING DADDY THE TRUTH NO MATTER WHAT.
IT LOOKS LIKE THE OTHERS ARE TRY-ING THEIR BEST...
BUT WHO KNOWS HOW WELL THEY CAN REALLY DO?
IT DIDN'T LAST LONG, BUT I GAVE IT EVERYTHING I HAD.
YOU GIVE IT YOUR ALL, TOO...
HEY, I'LL HANDLE THE KID-
‹WHERE IS THE...
HOSPITAL?›
!

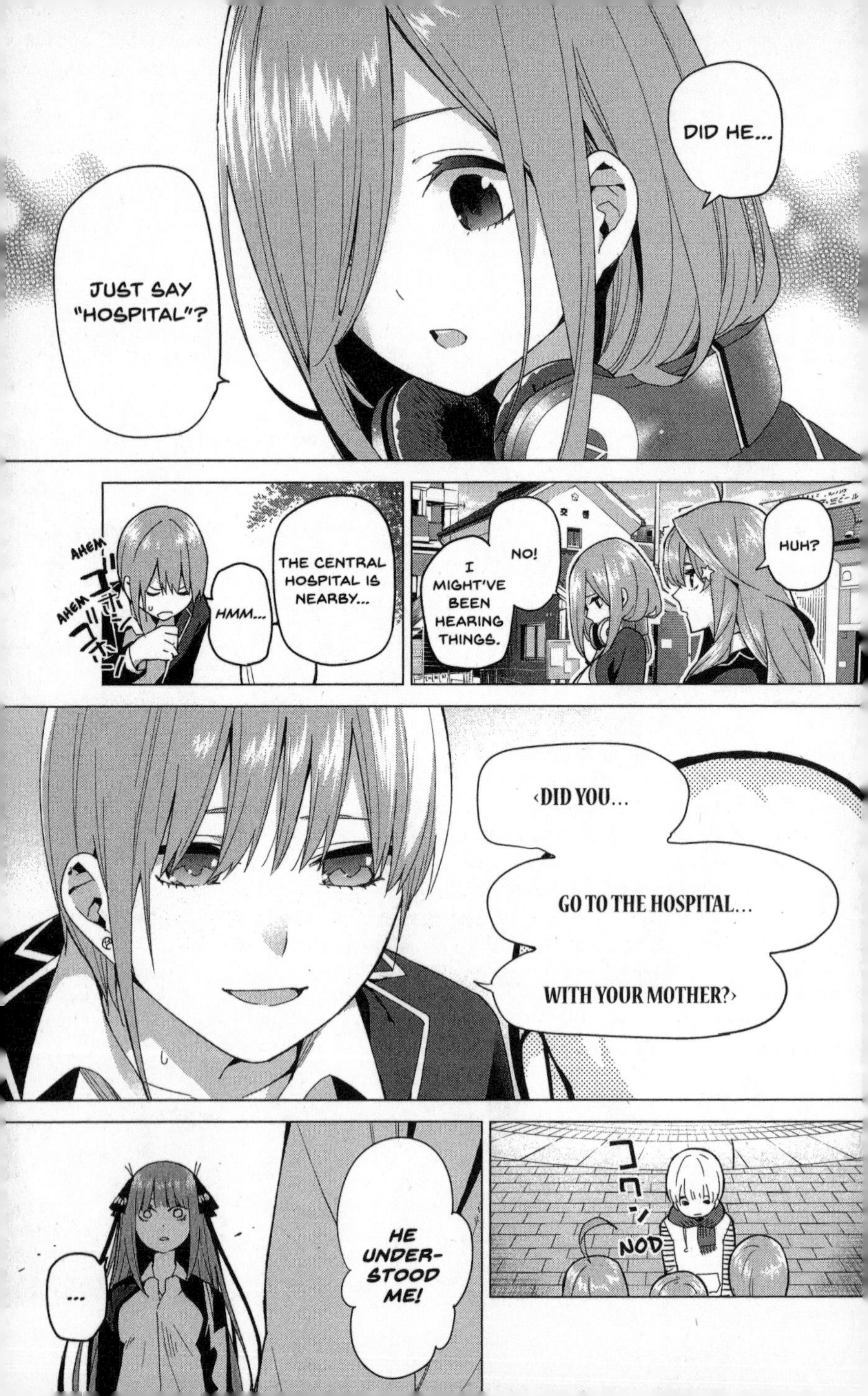
DID HE...
JUST SAY "HOSPITAL"?
HUH?
NO!
I MIGHT'VE BEEN HEARING THINGS.
THE CENTRAL HOSPITAL IS NEARBY...
HMM...
AHEM
AHEM
‹DID YOU...
GO TO THE HOSPITAL...
WITH YOUR MOTHER?›
NOD
HE UNDER-STOOD ME!
...

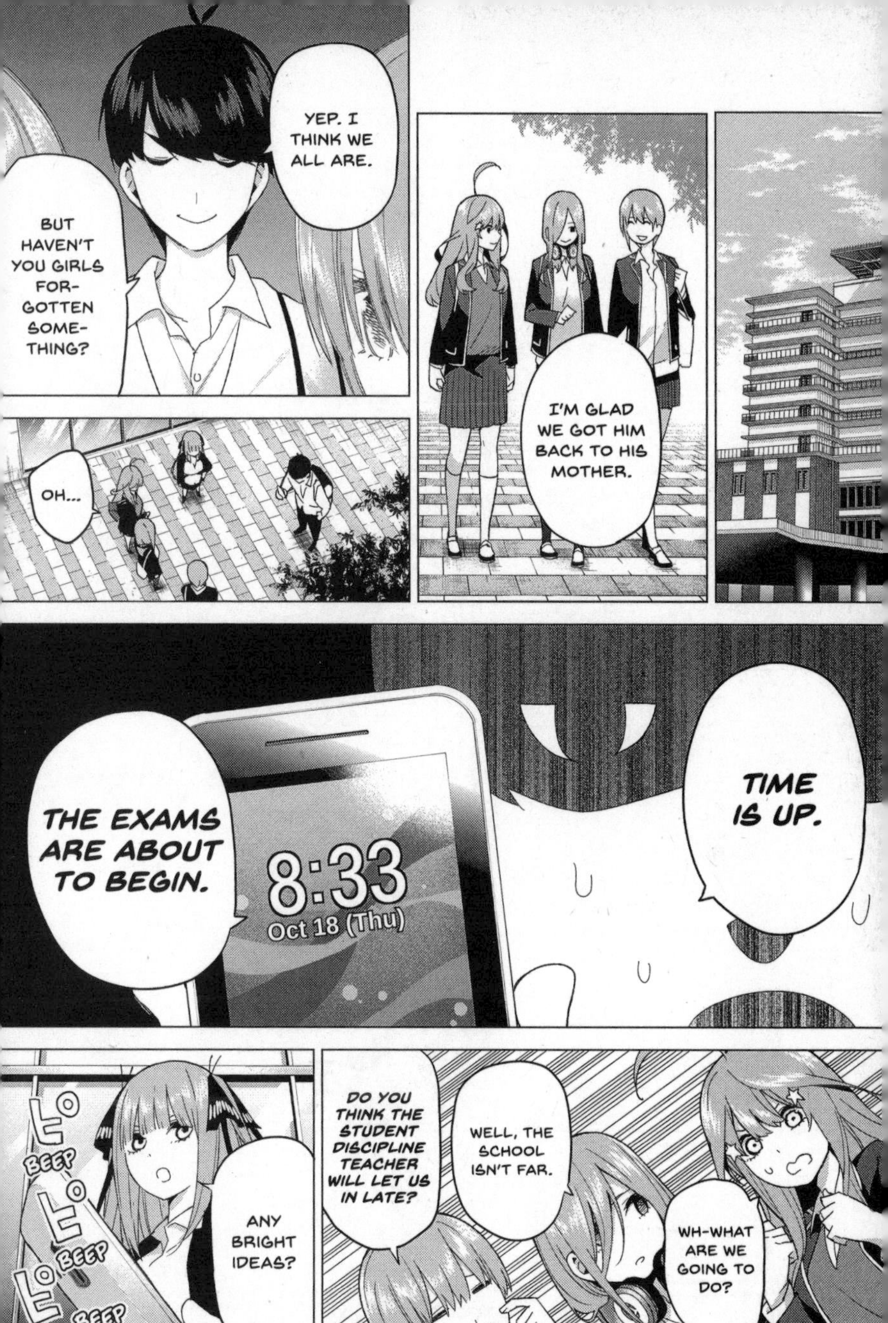
I'M GLAD WE GOT HIM BACK TO HIS MOTHER.
YEP. I THINK WE ALL ARE.
BUT HAVEN'T YOU GIRLS FOR-GOTTEN SOME-THING?
OH...
TIME IS UP.
THE EXAMS ARE ABOUT TO BEGIN.
8:33
Oct 18 (Thu)
WH-WHAT ARE WE GOING TO DO?
WELL, THE SCHOOL ISN'T FAR.
DO YOU THINK THE STUDENT DISCIPLINE TEACHER WILL LET US IN LATE?
ANY BRIGHT IDEAS?
BEEP
BEEP
BEEP

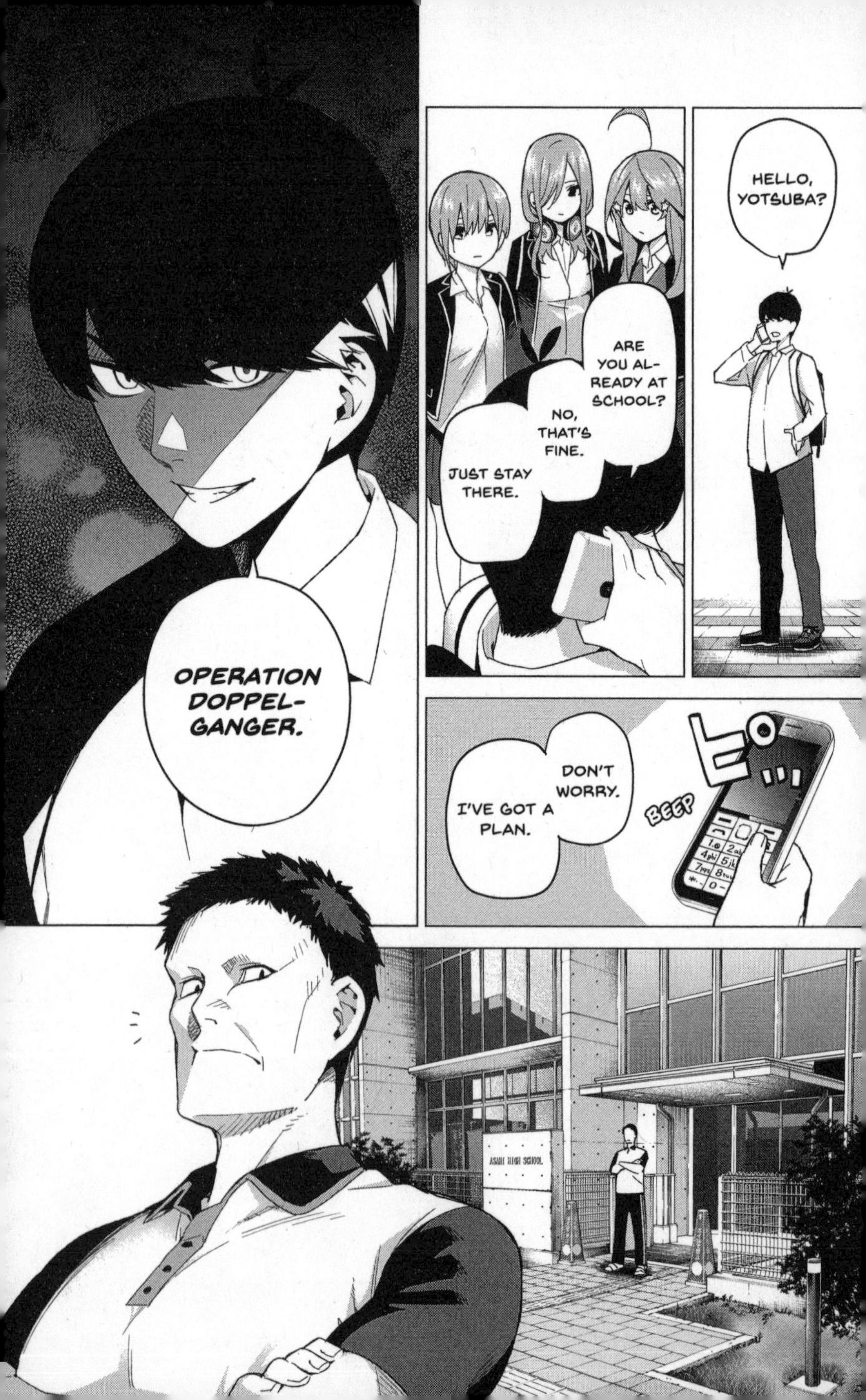
HELLO, YOTSUBA?
ARE YOU ALREADY AT SCHOOL?
NO, THAT'S FINE.
JUST STAY THERE.
DON'T WORRY.
I'VE GOT A PLAN.
BEEP
OPERATION DOPPEL-GANGER.
ASAHI HIGH SCHOOL

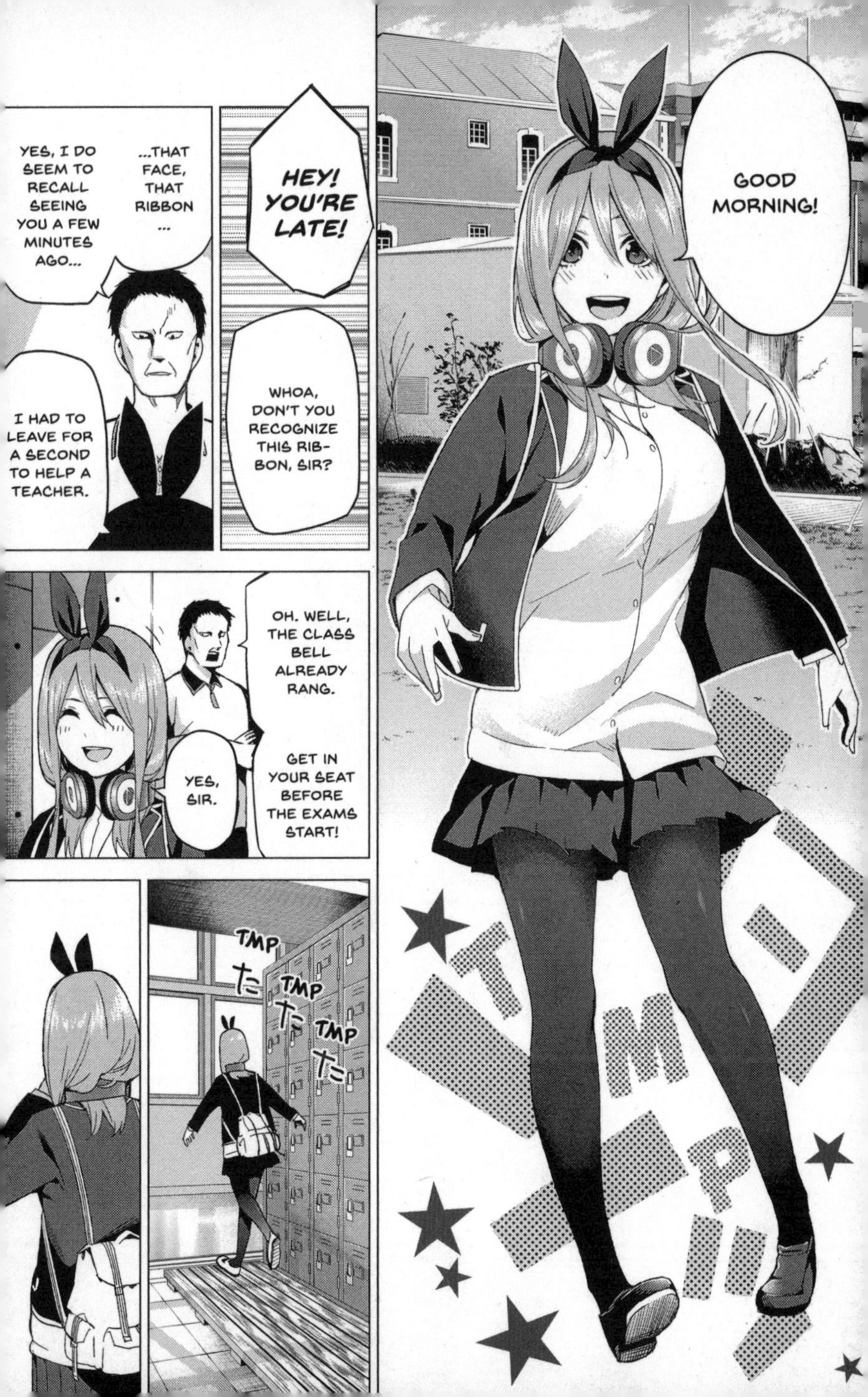
GOOD MORNING!
TMP!!
HEY! YOU'RE LATE!
WHOA, DON'T YOU RECOGNIZE THIS RIB-BON, SIR?
...THAT FACE, THAT RIBBON ...
YES, I DO SEEM TO RECALL SEEING YOU A FEW MINUTES AGO...
I HAD TO LEAVE FOR A SECOND TO HELP A TEACHER.
OH. WELL, THE CLASS BELL ALREADY RANG.
GET IN YOUR SEAT BEFORE THE EXAMS START!
YES, SIR.
TMP
TMP
TMP

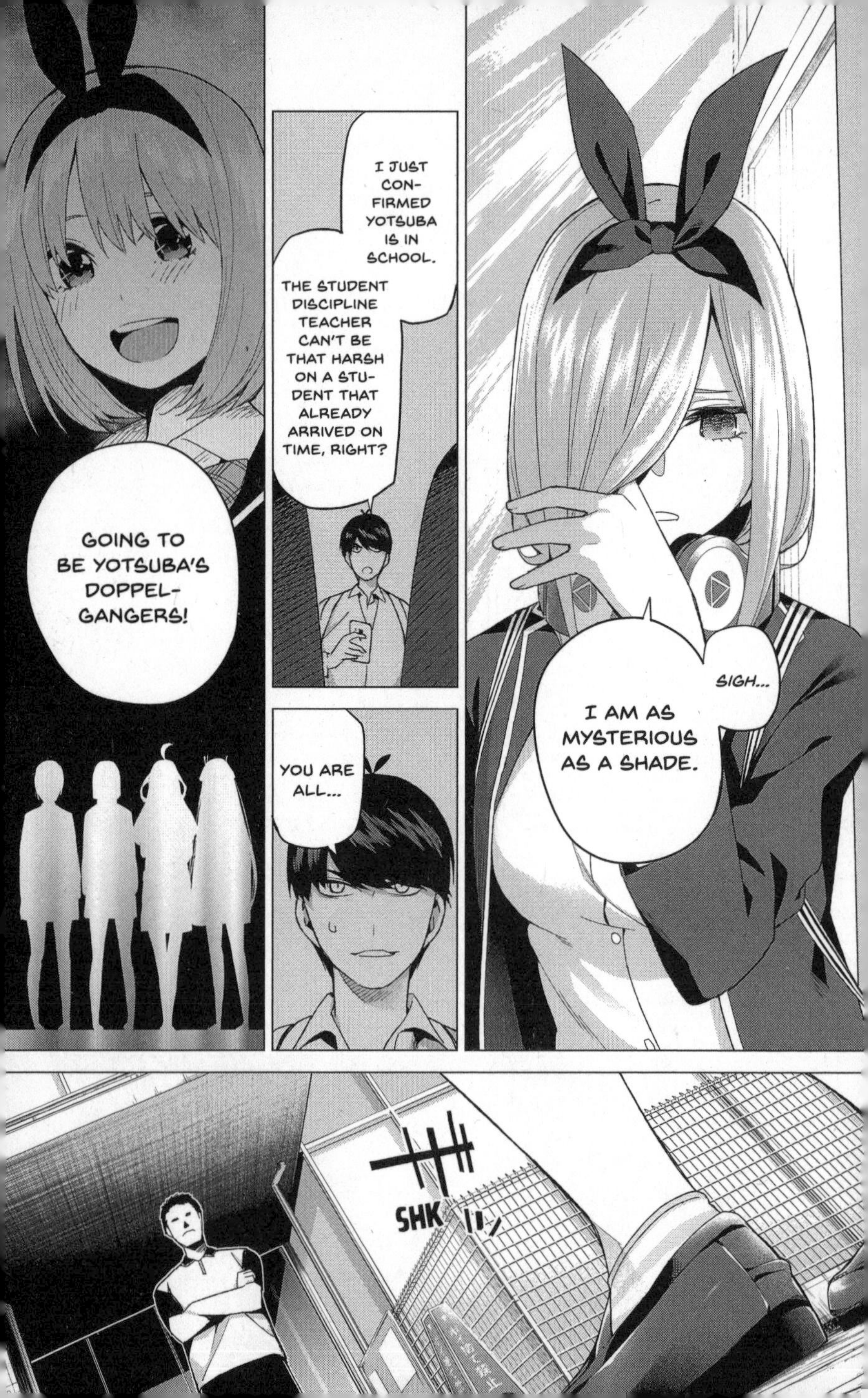
SIGH...
I AM AS MYSTERIOUS AS A SHADE.
I JUST CON-FIRMED YOTSUBA IS IN SCHOOL.
THE STUDENT DISCIPLINE TEACHER CAN'T BE THAT HARSH ON A STU-DENT THAT ALREADY ARRIVED ON TIME, RIGHT?
YOU ARE ALL...
GOING TO BE YOTSUBA'S DOPPEL-GANGERS!
SHK

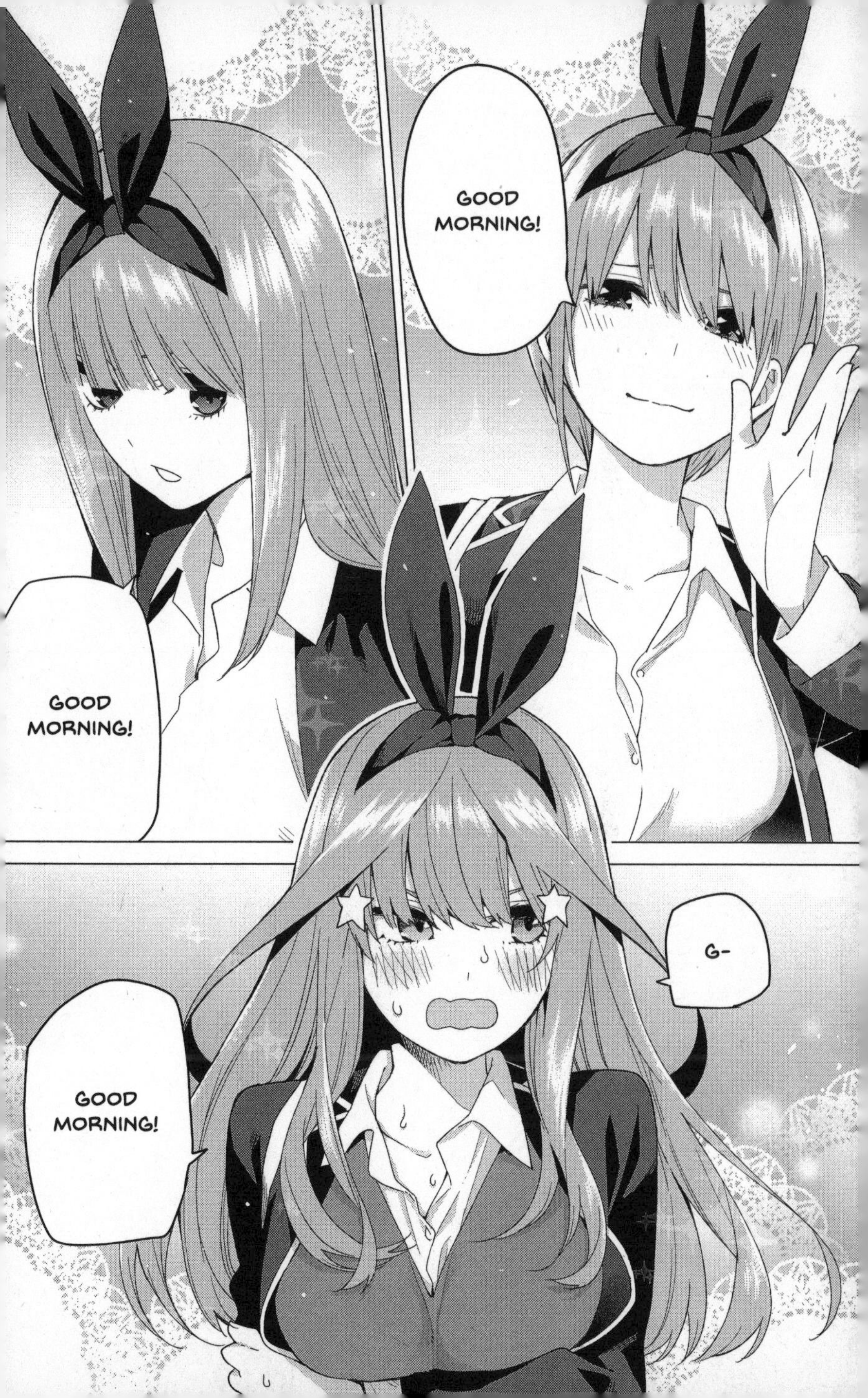
GOOD MORNING!
GOOD MORNING!
G-
GOOD MORNING!

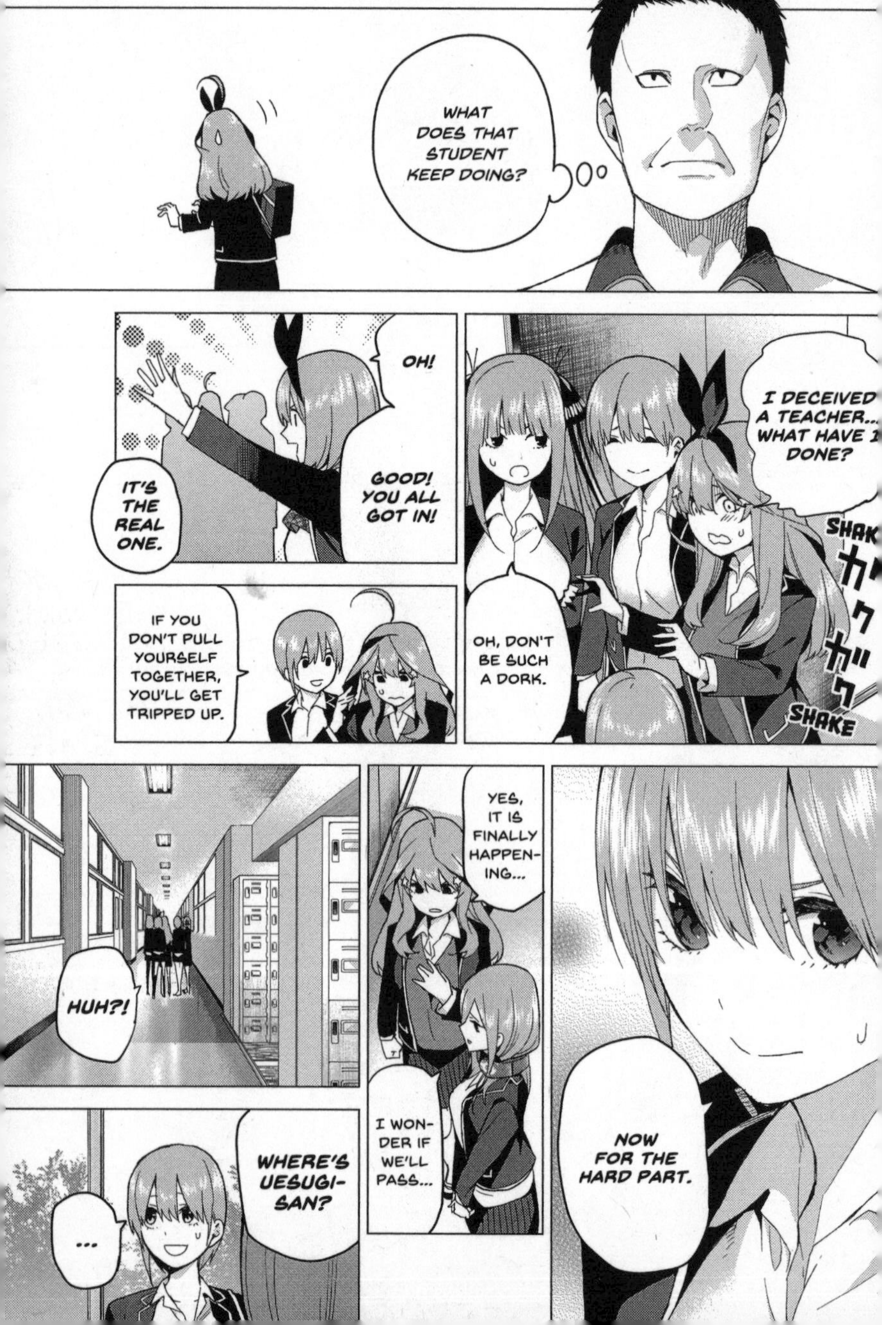
WHAT DOES THAT STUDENT KEEP DOING?
I DECEIVED A TEACHER... WHAT HAVE I DONE?
SHAK
ガクガク
SHAKE
OH, DON'T BE SUCH A DORK.
OH!
GOOD! YOU ALL GOT IN!
IT'S THE REAL ONE.
IF YOU DON'T PULL YOURSELF TOGETHER, YOU'LL GET TRIPPED UP.
NOW FOR THE HARD PART.
YES, IT IS FINALLY HAPPEN-ING...
I WON-DER IF WE'LL PASS...
HUH?!
WHERE'S UESUGI-SAN?
...

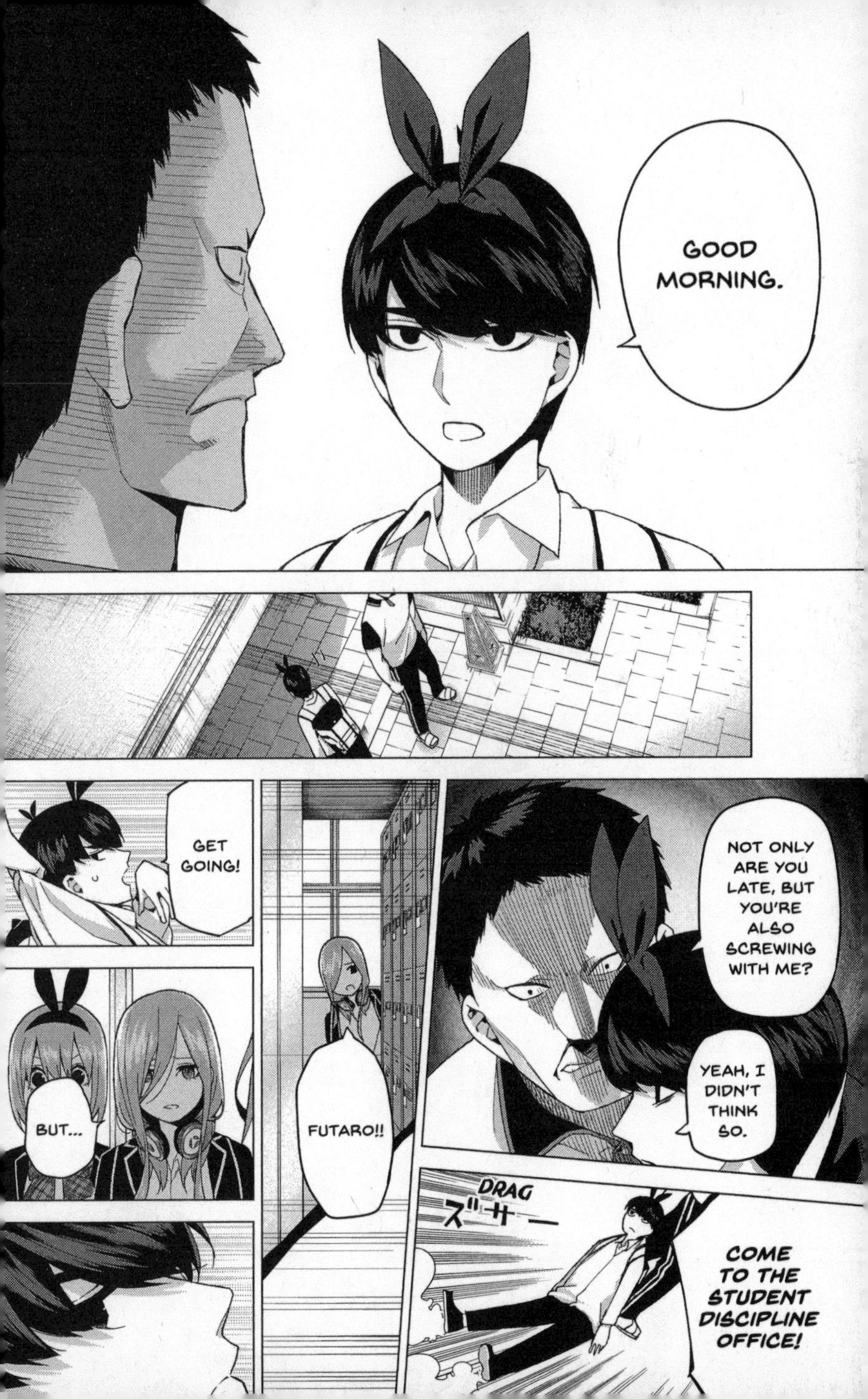
GOOD MORNING.
NOT ONLY ARE YOU LATE, BUT YOU'RE ALSO SCREWING WITH ME?
YEAH, I DIDN'T THINK SO.
DRAG
ズサー
COME TO THE STUDENT DISCIPLINE OFFICE!
FUTARO!!
GET GOING!
BUT...

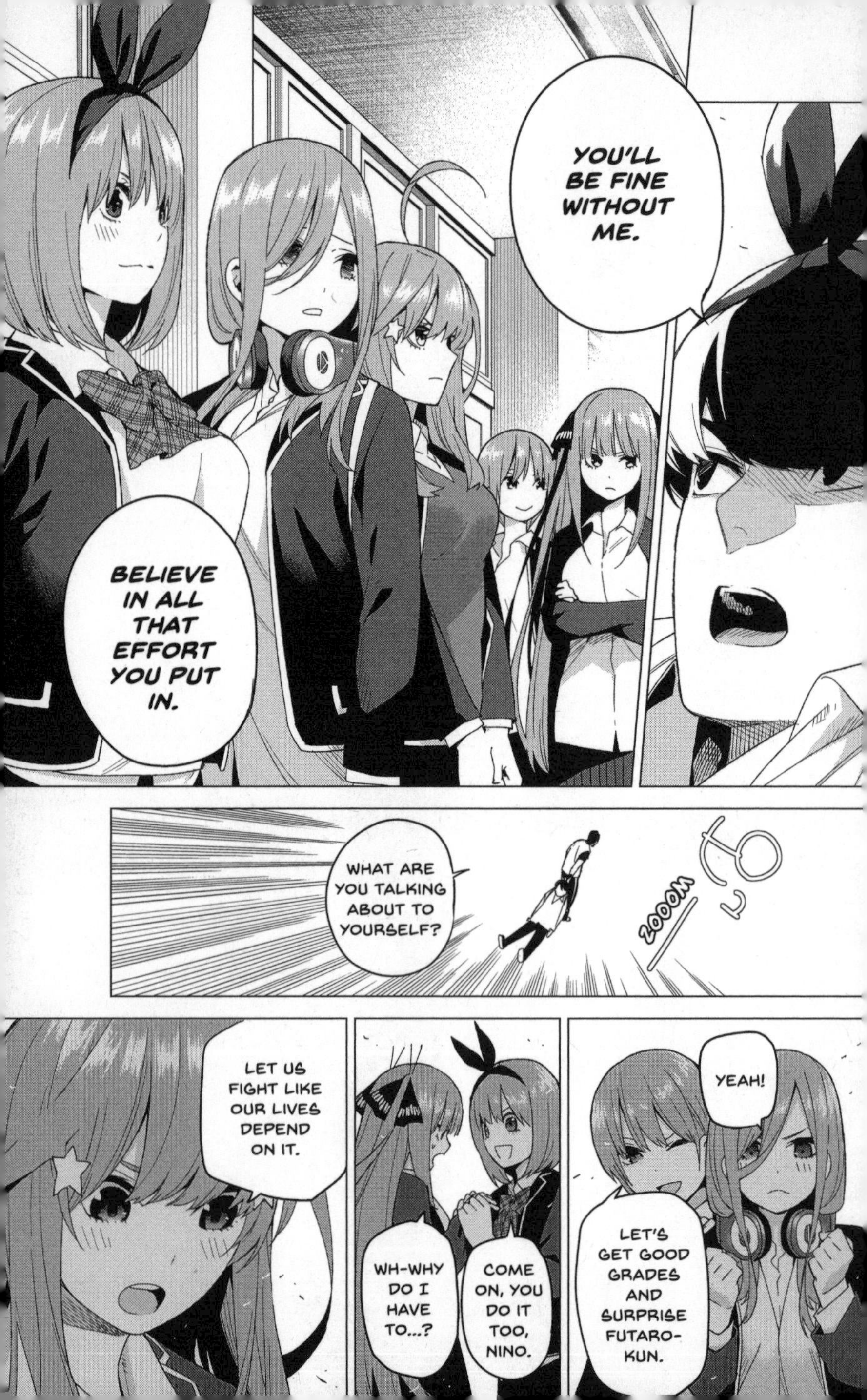
YOU'LL BE FINE WITHOUT ME.
BELIEVE IN ALL THAT EFFORT YOU PUT IN.
ZOOOM
WHAT ARE YOU TALKING ABOUT TO YOURSELF?
YEAH!
LET'S GET GOOD GRADES AND SURPRISE FUTARO-KUN.
COME ON, YOU DO IT TOO, NINO.
WH-WHY DO I HAVE TO...?
LET US FIGHT LIKE OUR LIVES DEPEND ON IT.

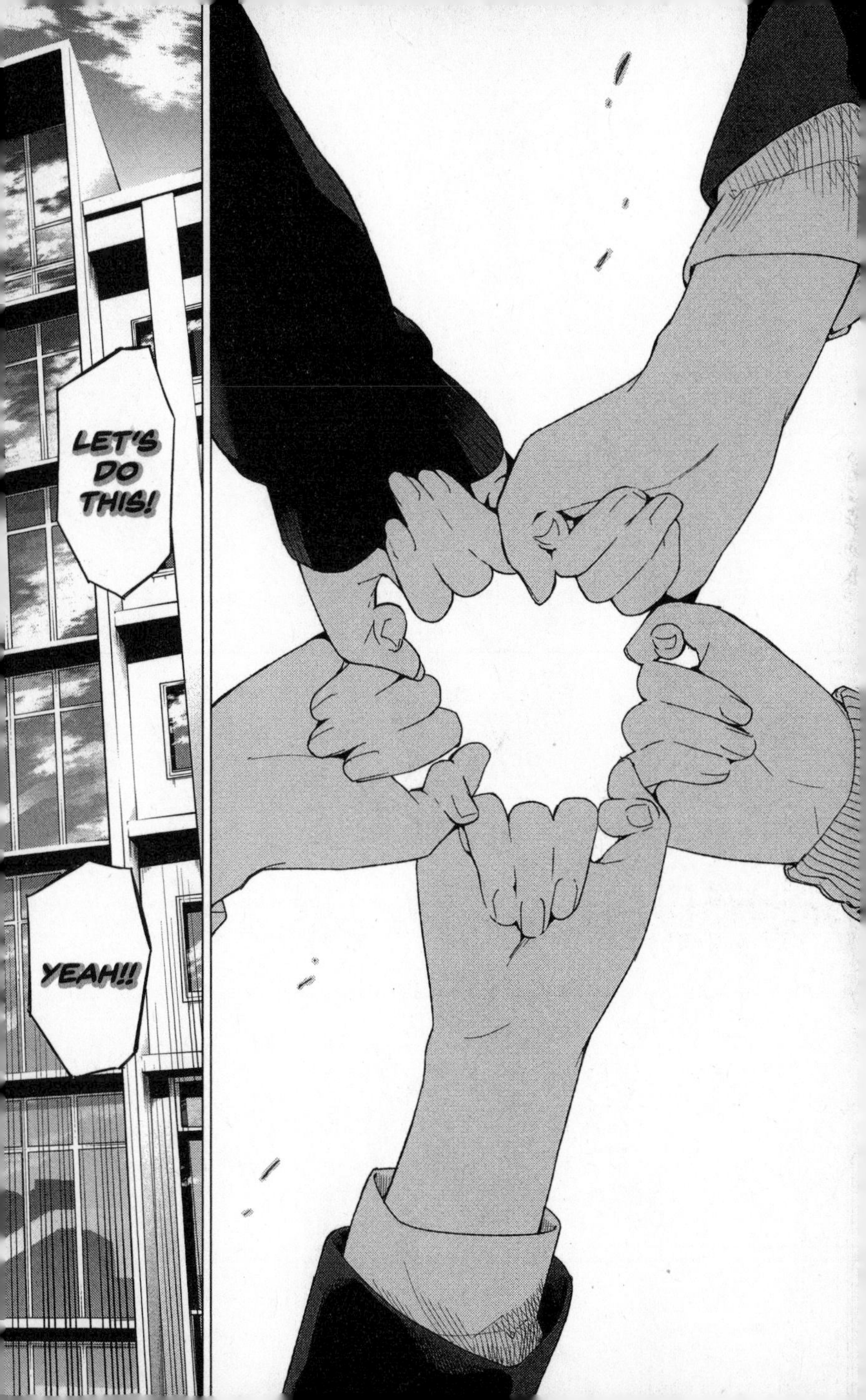
LET'S DO THIS!
YEAH!!

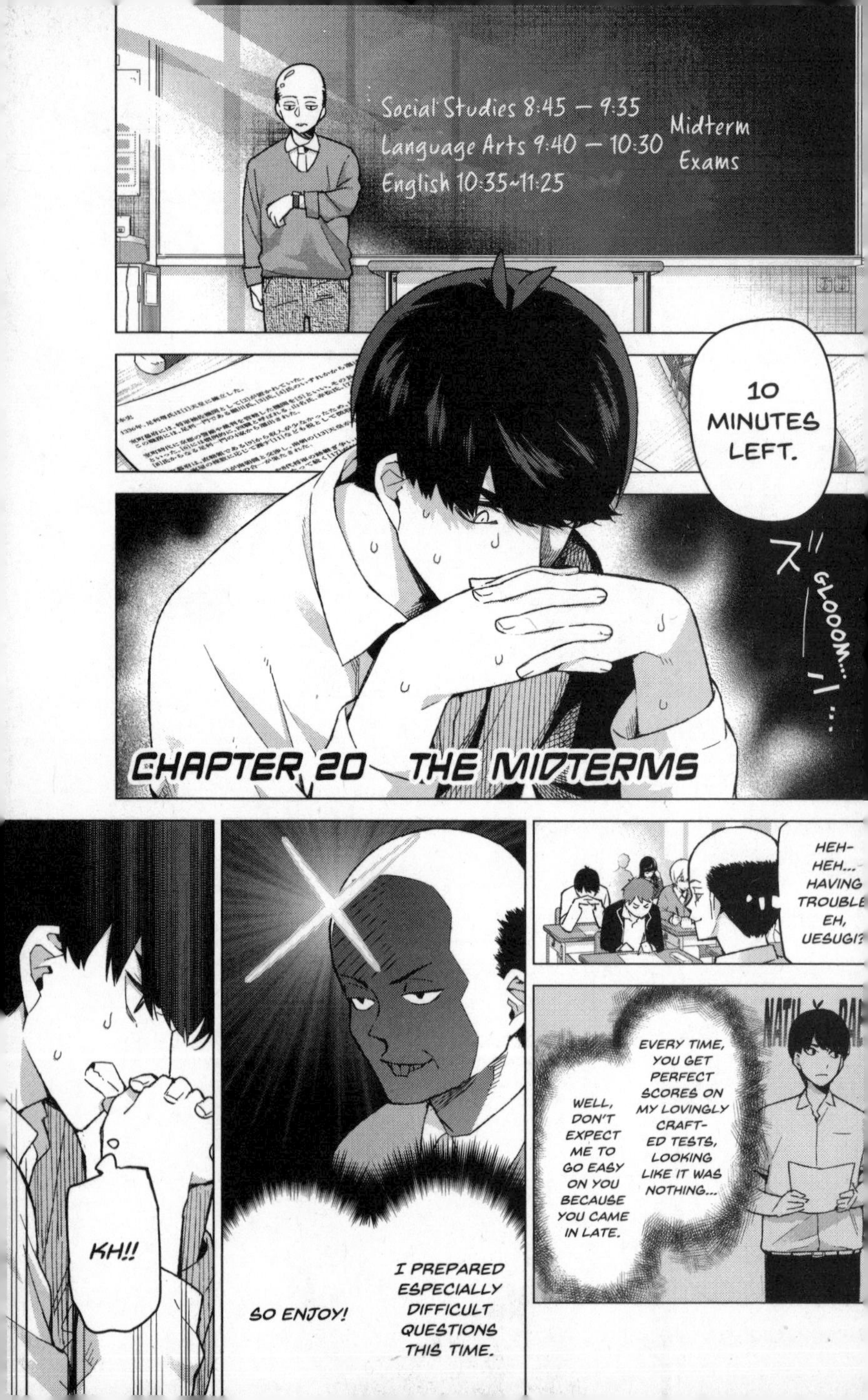
Social Studies 8:45 — 9:35
Language Arts 9:40 — 10:30
English 10:35~11:25
Midterm Exams
10 MINUTES LEFT.
ズ
GLOOOM...
CHAPTER 20 THE MIDTERMS
HEH-HEH... HAVING TROUBLE EH, UESUGI?
EVERY TIME, YOU GET PERFECT SCORES ON MY LOVINGLY CRAFT-ED TESTS, LOOKING LIKE IT WAS NOTHING...
WELL, DON'T EXPECT ME TO GO EASY ON YOU BECAUSE YOU CAME IN LATE.
I PREPARED ESPECIALLY DIFFICULT QUESTIONS THIS TIME.
SO ENJOY!
KH!!

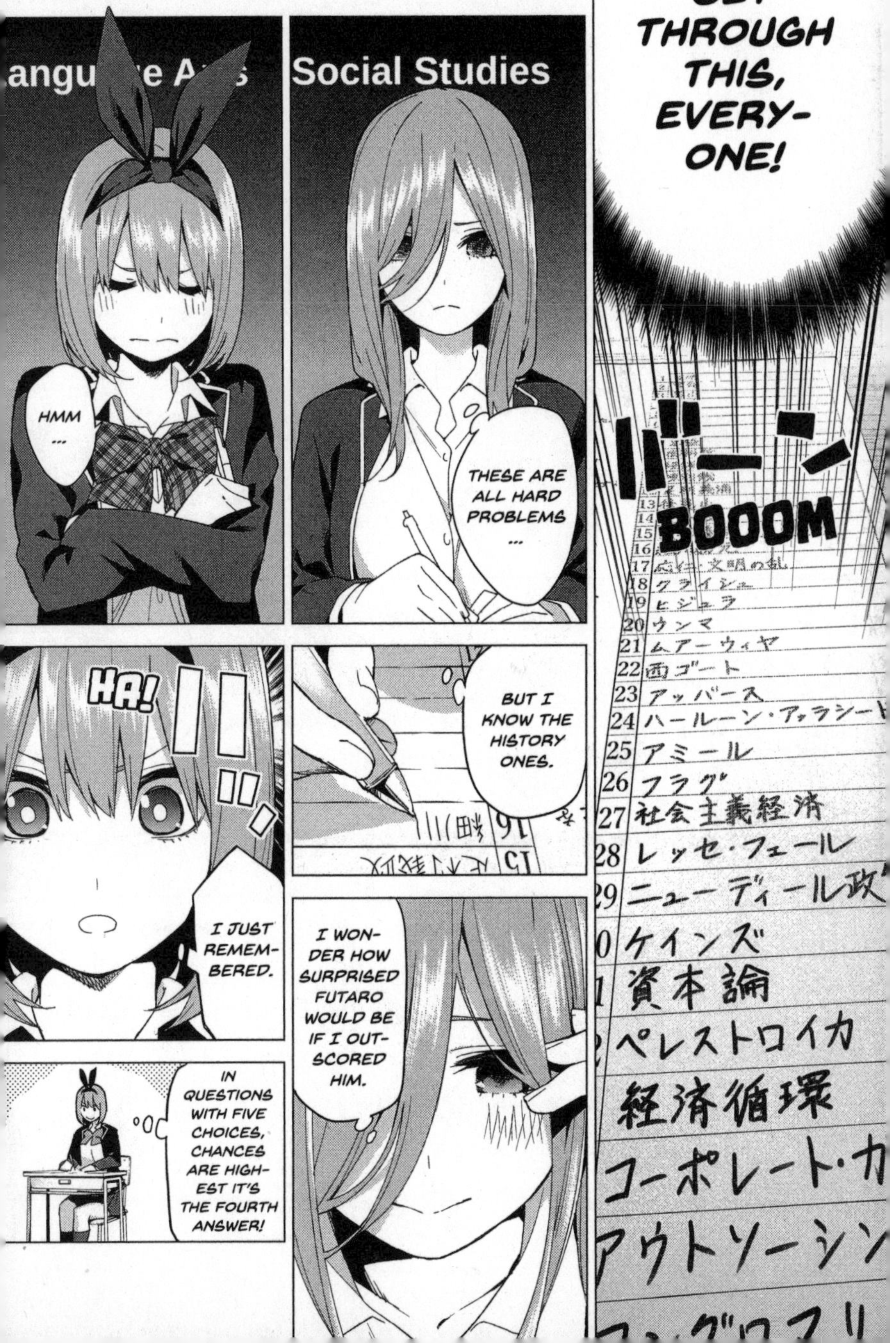
GET THROUGH THIS, EVERY-ONE!
BOOOM
Social Studies
THESE ARE ALL HARD PROBLEMS ...
HMM ...
BUT I KNOW THE HISTORY ONES.
HA!
I JUST REMEM-BERED.
I WON-DER HOW SURPRISED FUTARO WOULD BE IF I OUT-SCORED HIM.
IN QUESTIONS WITH FIVE CHOICES, CHANCES ARE HIGH-EST IT'S THE FOURTH ANSWER!

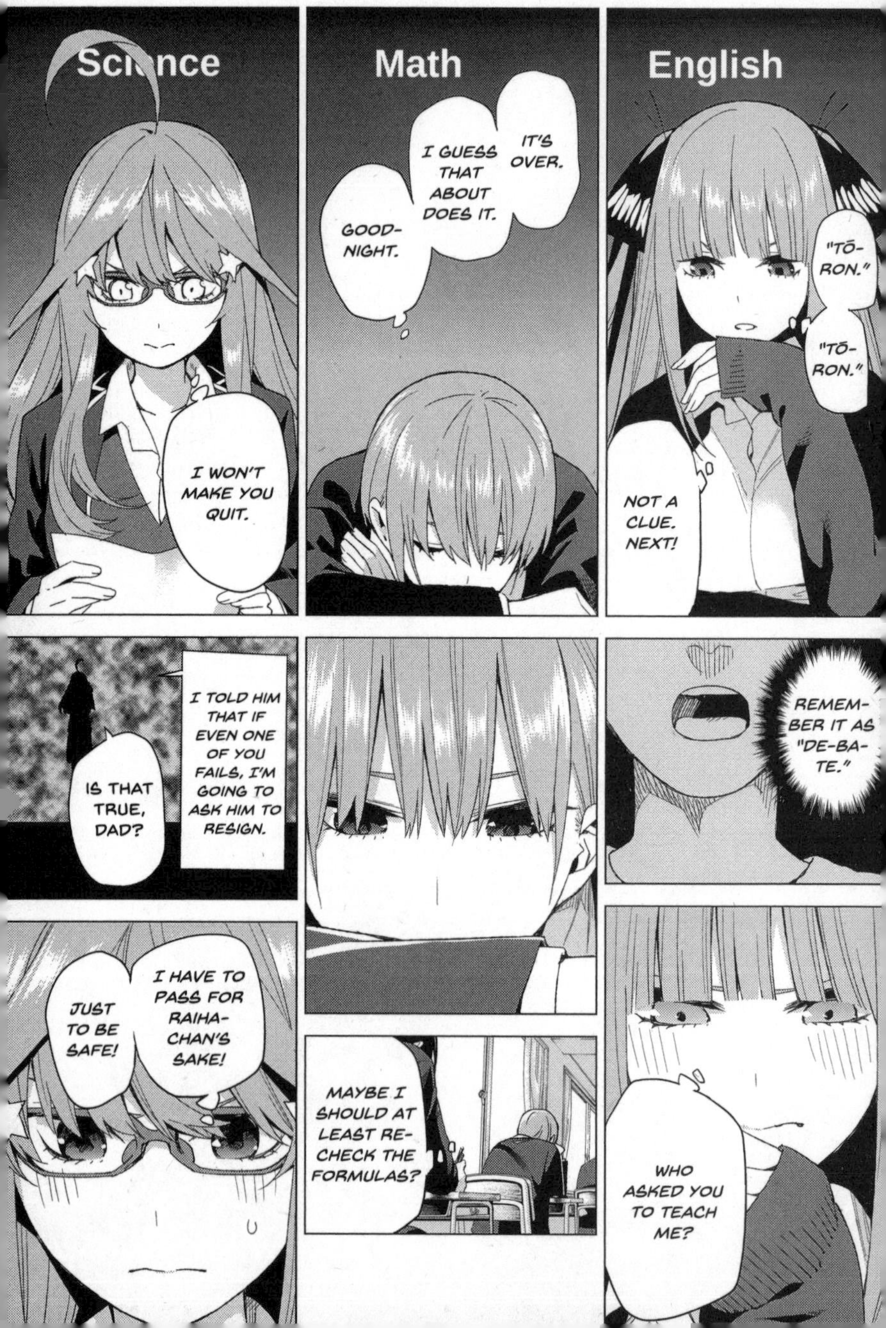
English
"TŌ-RON."
"TŌ-RON."
NOT A CLUE. NEXT!
Math
IT'S OVER.
I GUESS THAT ABOUT DOES IT.
GOOD-NIGHT.
Science
I WON'T MAKE YOU QUIT.
REMEMBER IT AS "DE-BA-TE."
I TOLD HIM THAT IF EVEN ONE OF YOU FAILS, I'M GOING TO ASK HIM TO RESIGN.
IS THAT TRUE, DAD?
WHO ASKED YOU TO TEACH ME?
MAYBE I SHOULD AT LEAST RE-CHECK THE FORMULAS?
I HAVE TO PASS FOR RAIHA-CHAN'S SAKE!
JUST TO BE SAFE!

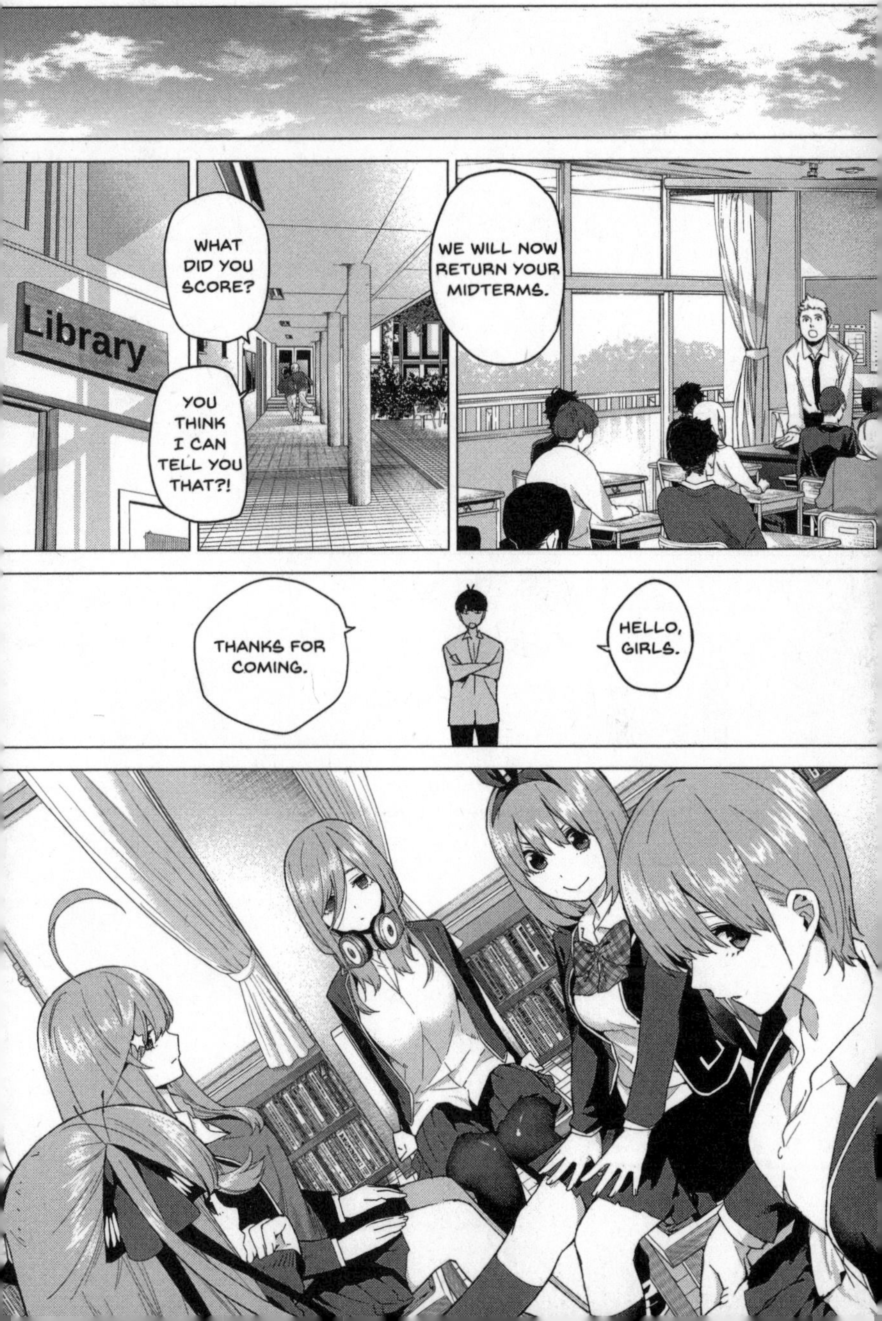
WE WILL NOW RETURN YOUR MIDTERMS.
WHAT DID YOU SCORE?
YOU THINK I CAN TELL YOU THAT?!
Library
HELLO, GIRLS.
THANKS FOR COMING.

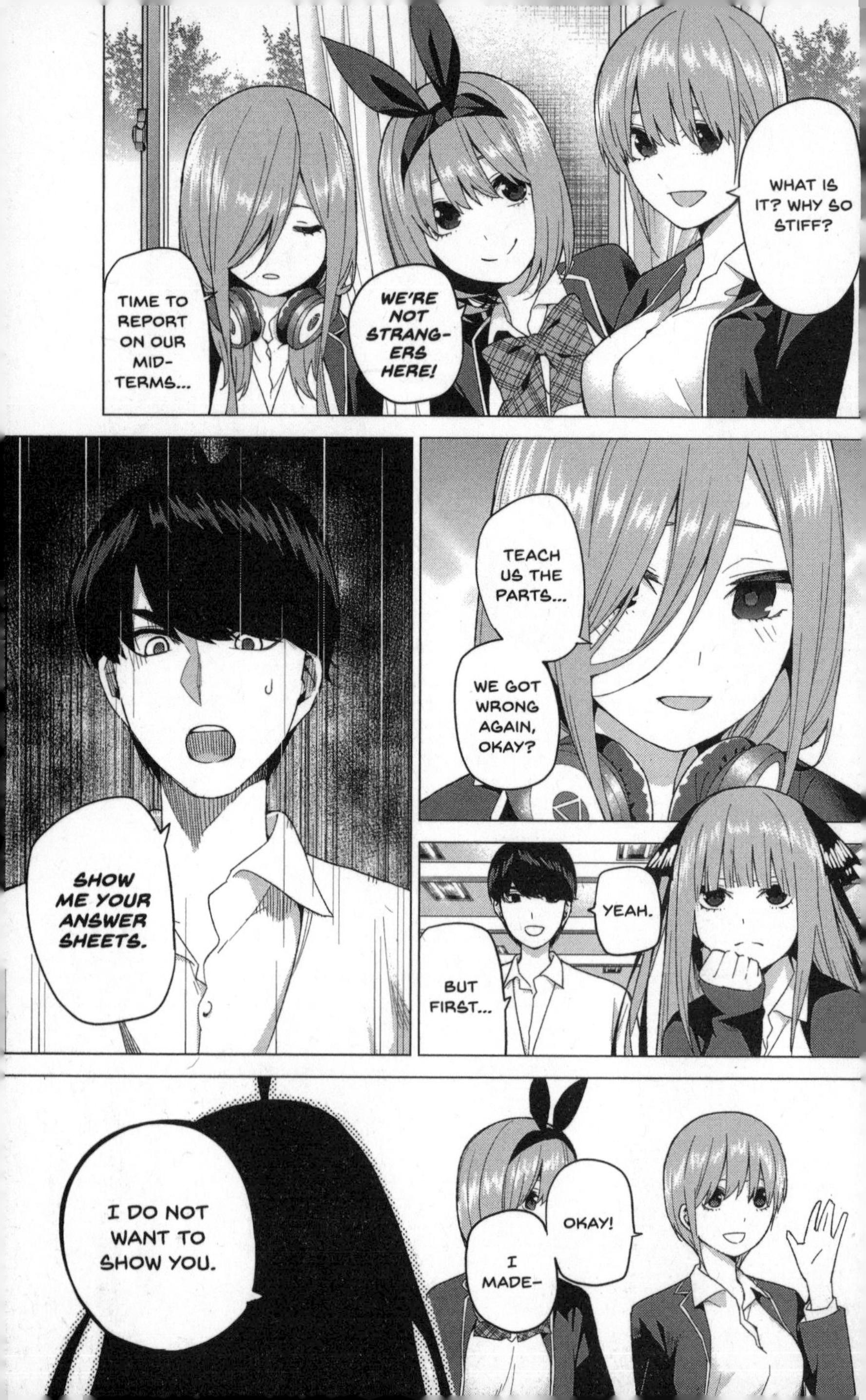
WHAT IS IT? WHY SO STIFF?
WE'RE NOT STRANGERS HERE!
TIME TO REPORT ON OUR MIDTERMS...
TEACH US THE PARTS...
WE GOT WRONG AGAIN, OKAY?
YEAH.
BUT FIRST...
SHOW ME YOUR ANSWER SHEETS.
OKAY!
I MADE-
I DO NOT WANT TO SHOW YOU.

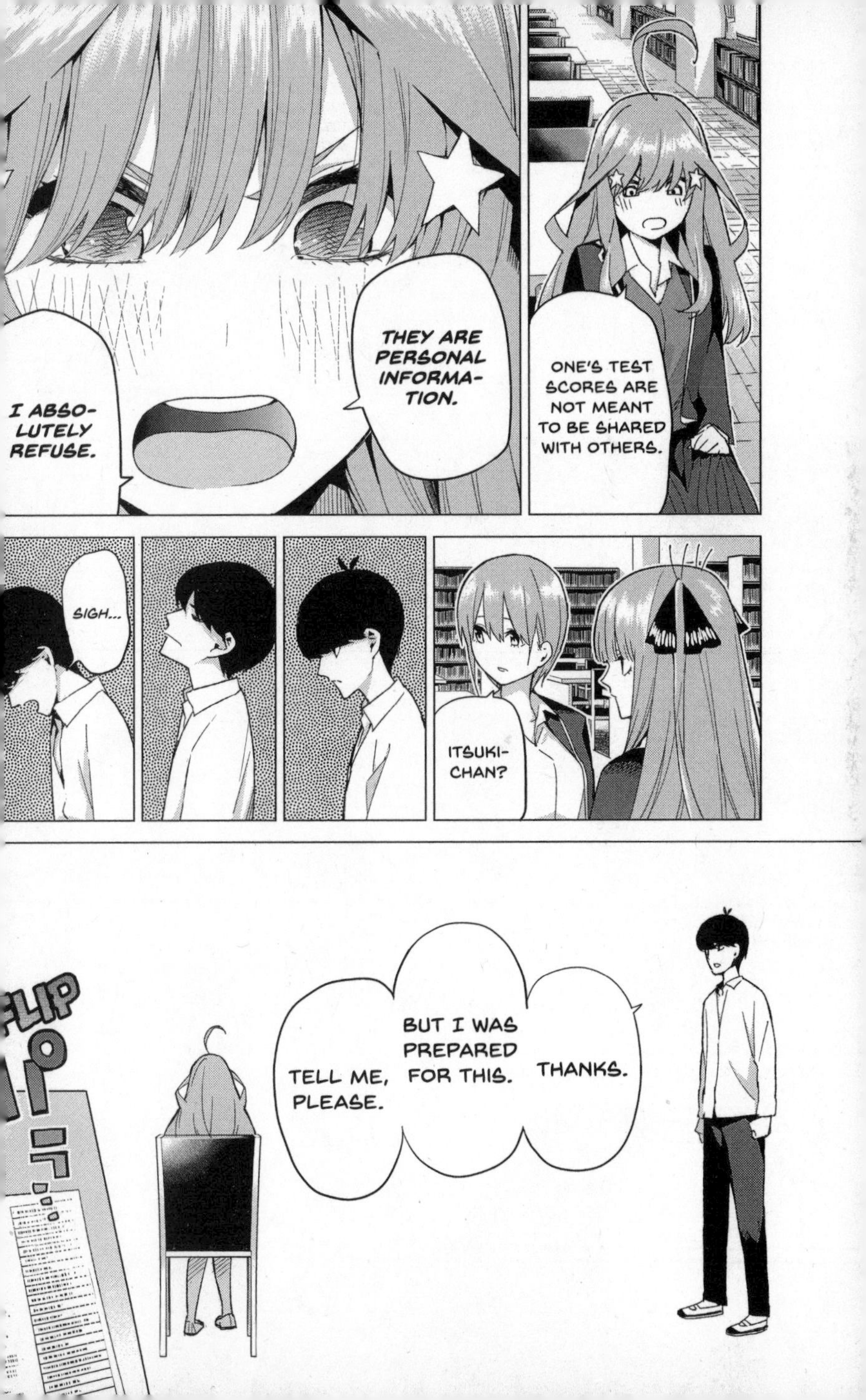
ONE'S TEST SCORES ARE NOT MEANT TO BE SHARED WITH OTHERS.
THEY ARE PERSONAL INFORMA-TION.
I ABSO-LUTELY REFUSE.
ITSUKI-CHAN?
SIGH...
THANKS.
BUT I WAS PREPARED FOR THIS.
TELL ME, PLEASE.
FLIP

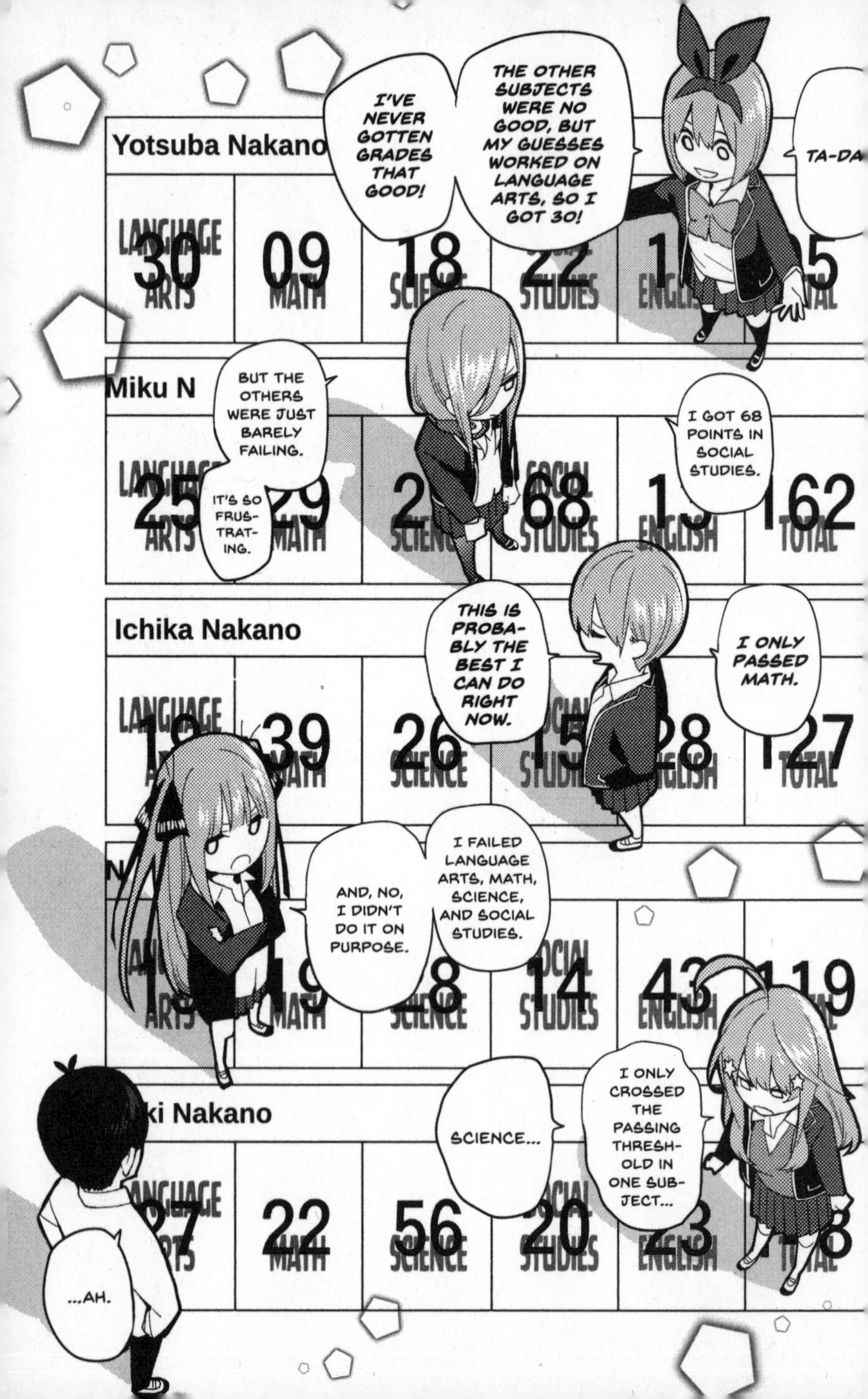
TA-DA
THE OTHER SUBJECTS WERE NO GOOD, BUT MY GUESSES WORKED ON LANGUAGE ARTS, SO I GOT 30!
I'VE NEVER GOTTEN GRADES THAT GOOD!
Yotsuba Nakano
LANGUAGE ARTS 30
MATH 09
18
Miku N
I GOT 68 POINTS IN SOCIAL STUDIES.
BUT THE OTHERS WERE JUST BARELY FAILING.
IT'S SO FRUS-TRAT-ING.
SOCIAL STUDIES 68
TOTAL 162
Ichika Nakano
I ONLY PASSED MATH.
THIS IS PROBABLY THE BEST I CAN DO RIGHT NOW.
MATH 39
SCIENCE 26
I FAILED LANGUAGE ARTS, MATH, SCIENCE, AND SOCIAL STUDIES.
AND, NO, I DIDN'T DO IT ON PURPOSE.
SOCIAL STUDIES 14
ENGLISH 43
ki Nakano
I ONLY CROSSED THE PASSING THRESH-OLD IN ONE SUB-JECT...
SCIENCE...
MATH 22
SCIENCE 56
...AH.

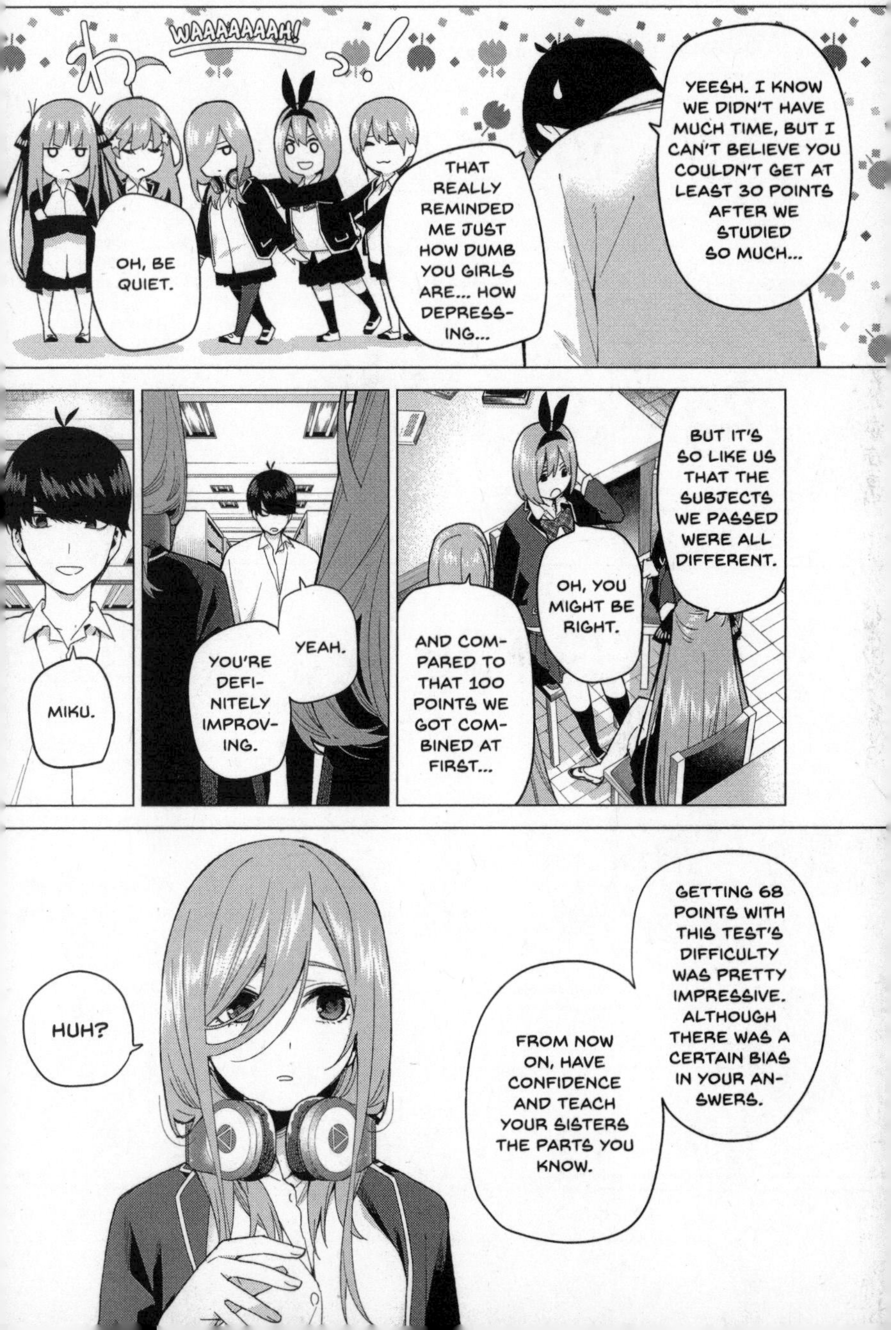

YEESH. I KNOW WE DIDN'T HAVE MUCH TIME, BUT I CAN'T BELIEVE YOU COULDN'T GET AT LEAST 30 POINTS AFTER WE STUDIED SO MUCH...
THAT REALLY REMINDED ME JUST HOW DUMB YOU GIRLS ARE... HOW DEPRESS-ING...
WAAAAAAAH!
OH, BE QUIET.
BUT IT'S SO LIKE US THAT THE SUBJECTS WE PASSED WERE ALL DIFFERENT.
OH, YOU MIGHT BE RIGHT.
AND COM-PARED TO THAT 100 POINTS WE GOT COM-BINED AT FIRST...
YEAH.
YOU'RE DEFI-NITELY IMPROV-ING.
MIKU.
GETTING 68 POINTS WITH THIS TEST'S DIFFICULTY WAS PRETTY IMPRESSIVE. ALTHOUGH THERE WAS A CERTAIN BIAS IN YOUR AN-SWERS.
FROM NOW ON, HAVE CONFIDENCE AND TEACH YOUR SISTERS THE PARTS YOU KNOW.
HUH?

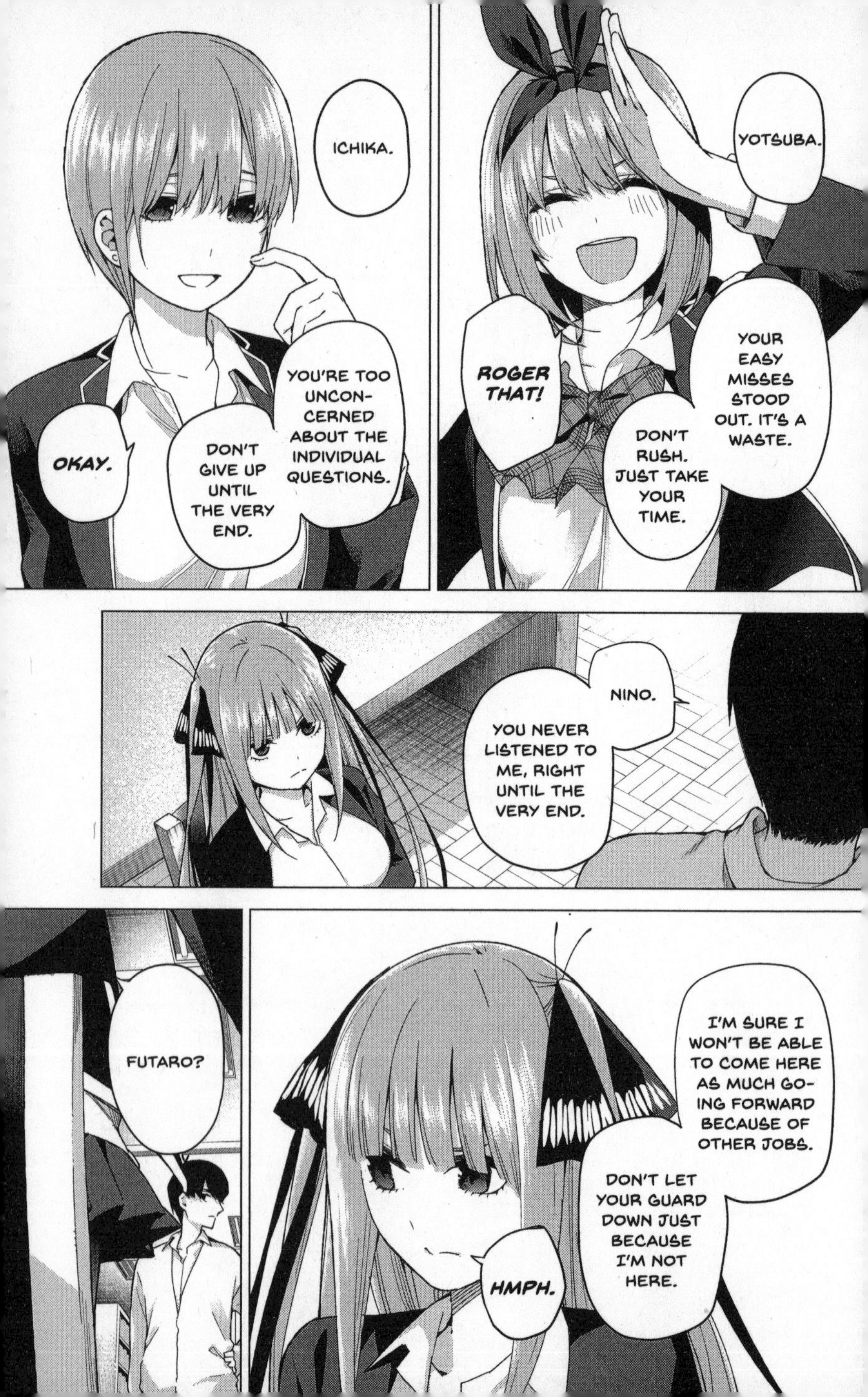
YOTSUBA.
YOUR EASY MISSES STOOD OUT. IT'S A WASTE.
DON'T RUSH. JUST TAKE YOUR TIME.
ROGER THAT!
ICHIKA.
YOU'RE TOO UNCON-CERNED ABOUT THE INDIVIDUAL QUESTIONS.
DON'T GIVE UP UNTIL THE VERY END.
OKAY.
NINO.
YOU NEVER LISTENED TO ME, RIGHT UNTIL THE VERY END.
I'M SURE I WON'T BE ABLE TO COME HERE AS MUCH GO-ING FORWARD BECAUSE OF OTHER JOBS.
DON'T LET YOUR GUARD DOWN JUST BECAUSE I'M NOT HERE.
HMPH.
FUTARO?

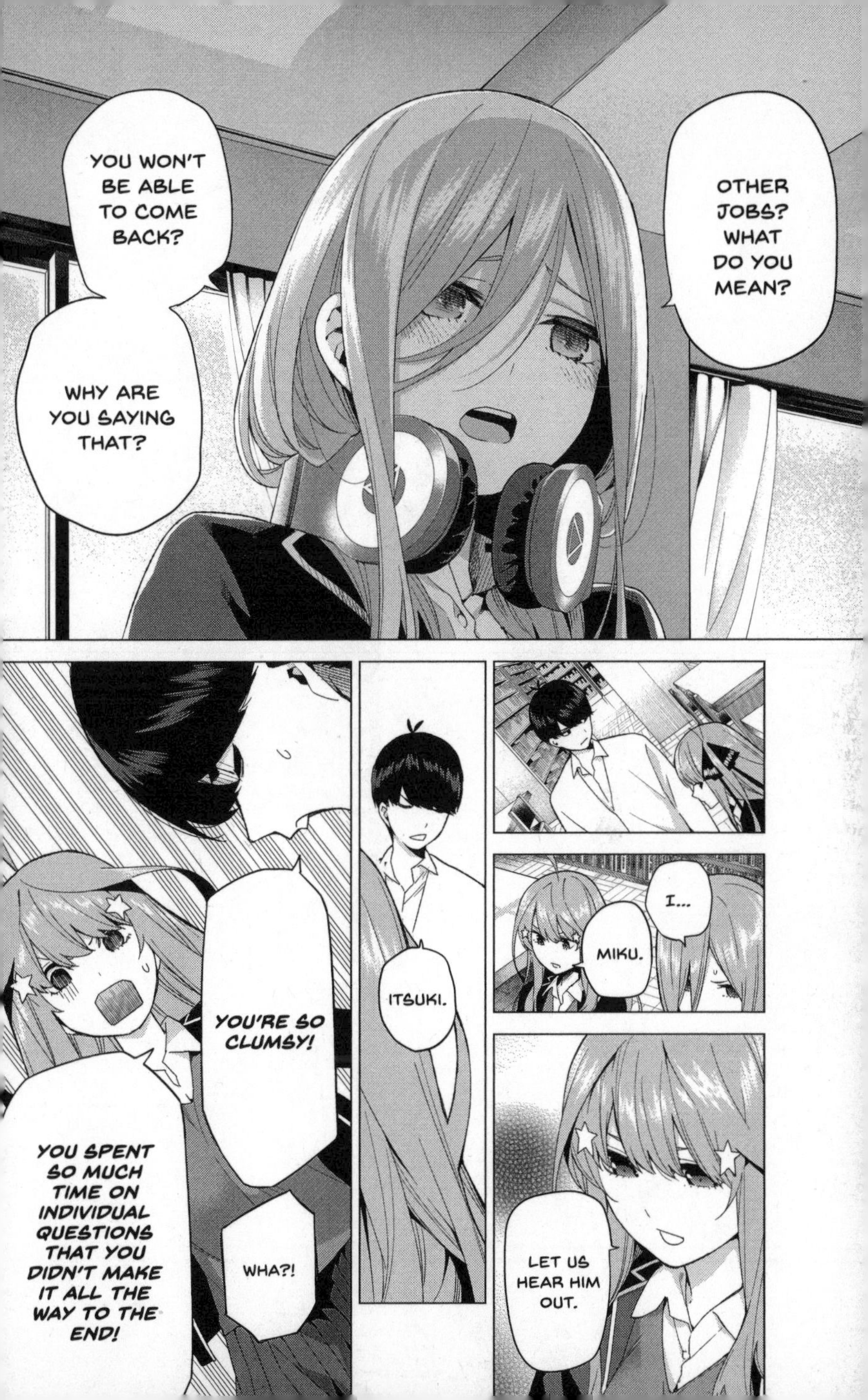
OTHER JOBS? WHAT DO YOU MEAN?
YOU WON'T BE ABLE TO COME BACK?
WHY ARE YOU SAYING THAT?
I...
MIKU.
LET US HEAR HIM OUT.
ITSUKI.
YOU'RE SO CLUMSY!
WHA?!
YOU SPENT SO MUCH TIME ON INDIVIDUAL QUESTIONS THAT YOU DIDN'T MAKE IT ALL THE WAY TO THE END!

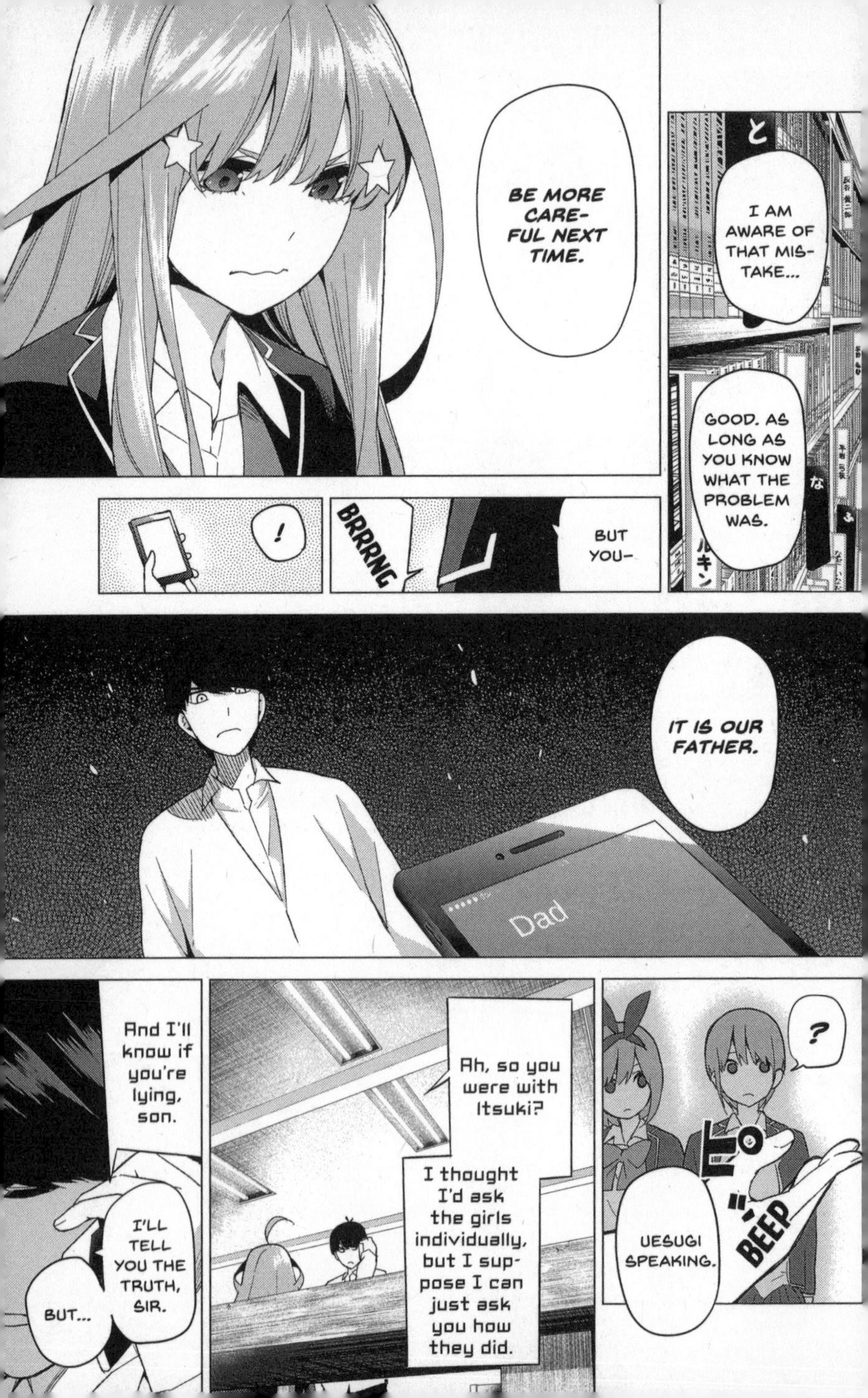
I AM AWARE OF THAT MIS-TAKE...
GOOD. AS LONG AS YOU KNOW WHAT THE PROBLEM WAS.
BE MORE CARE-FUL NEXT TIME.
BUT YOU-
BRRRNG
!
IT IS OUR FATHER.
Dad
?
BEEP
UESUGI SPEAKING.
Ah, so you were with Itsuki?
I thought I'd ask the girls individually, but I sup-pose I can just ask you how they did.
And I'll know if you're lying, son.
I'LL TELL YOU THE TRUTH, SIR.
BUT...

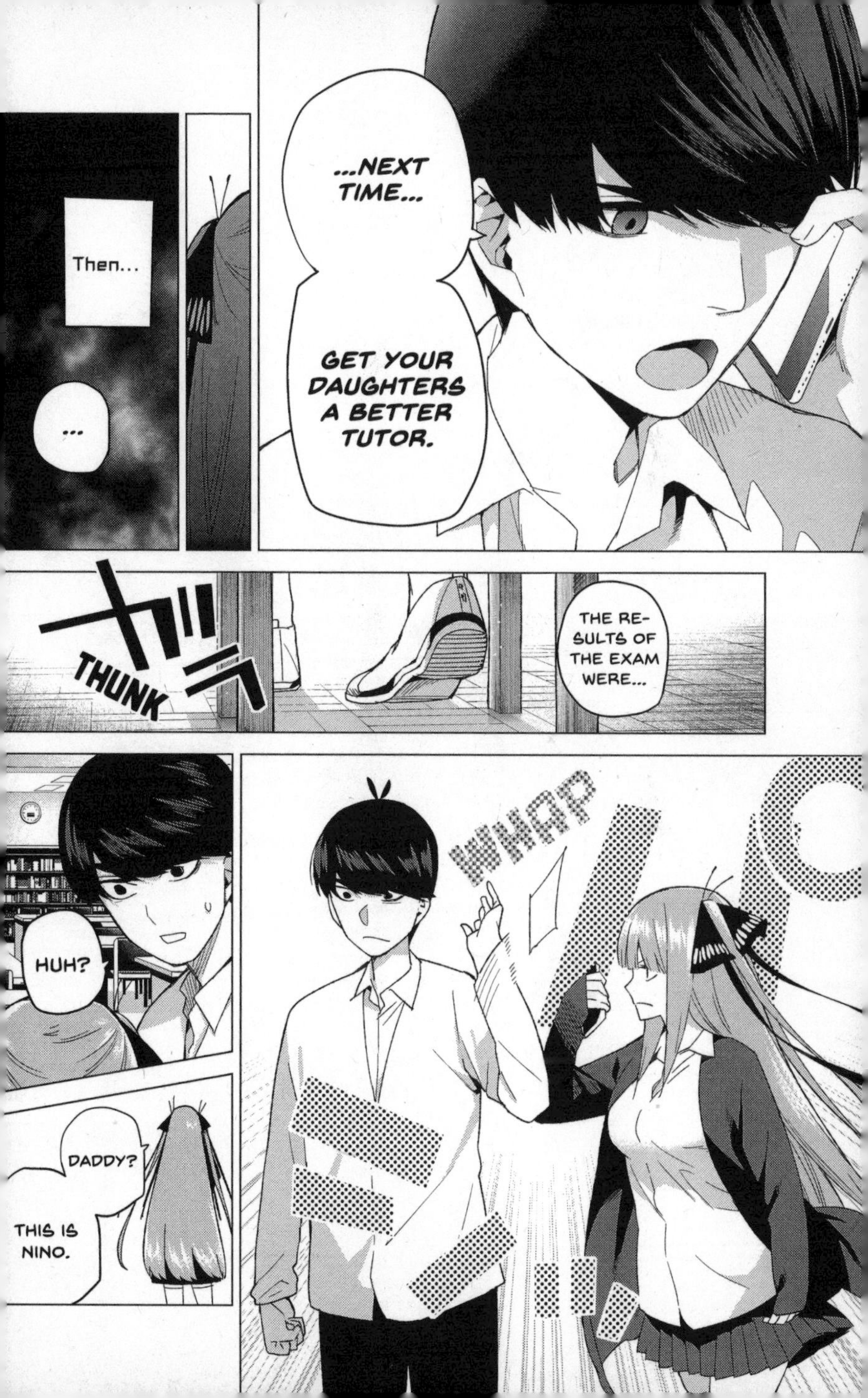
...NEXT TIME...
GET YOUR DAUGHTERS A BETTER TUTOR.
Then...
...
THE RE-SULTS OF THE EXAM WERE...
THUNK
WHAP
HUH?
DADDY?
THIS IS NINO.

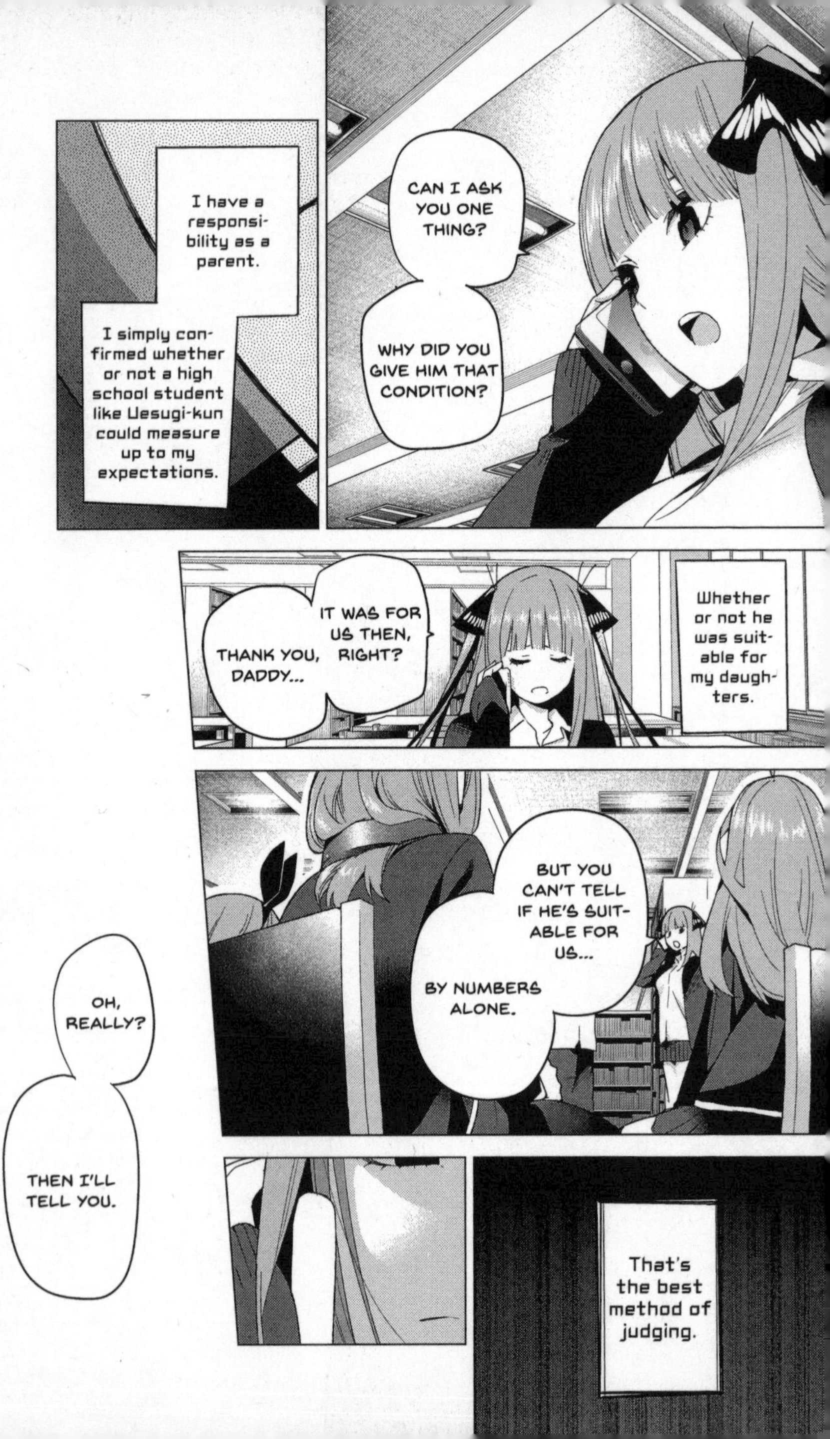
CAN I ASK YOU ONE THING?
WHY DID YOU GIVE HIM THAT CONDITION?
I have a responsibility as a parent.
I simply confirmed whether or not a high school student like Uesugi-kun could measure up to my expectations.
Whether or not he was suitable for my daughters.
IT WAS FOR US THEN, RIGHT?
THANK YOU, DADDY...
BUT YOU CAN'T TELL IF HE'S SUITABLE FOR US...
BY NUMBERS ALONE.
OH, REALLY?
THEN I'LL TELL YOU.
That's the best method of judging.

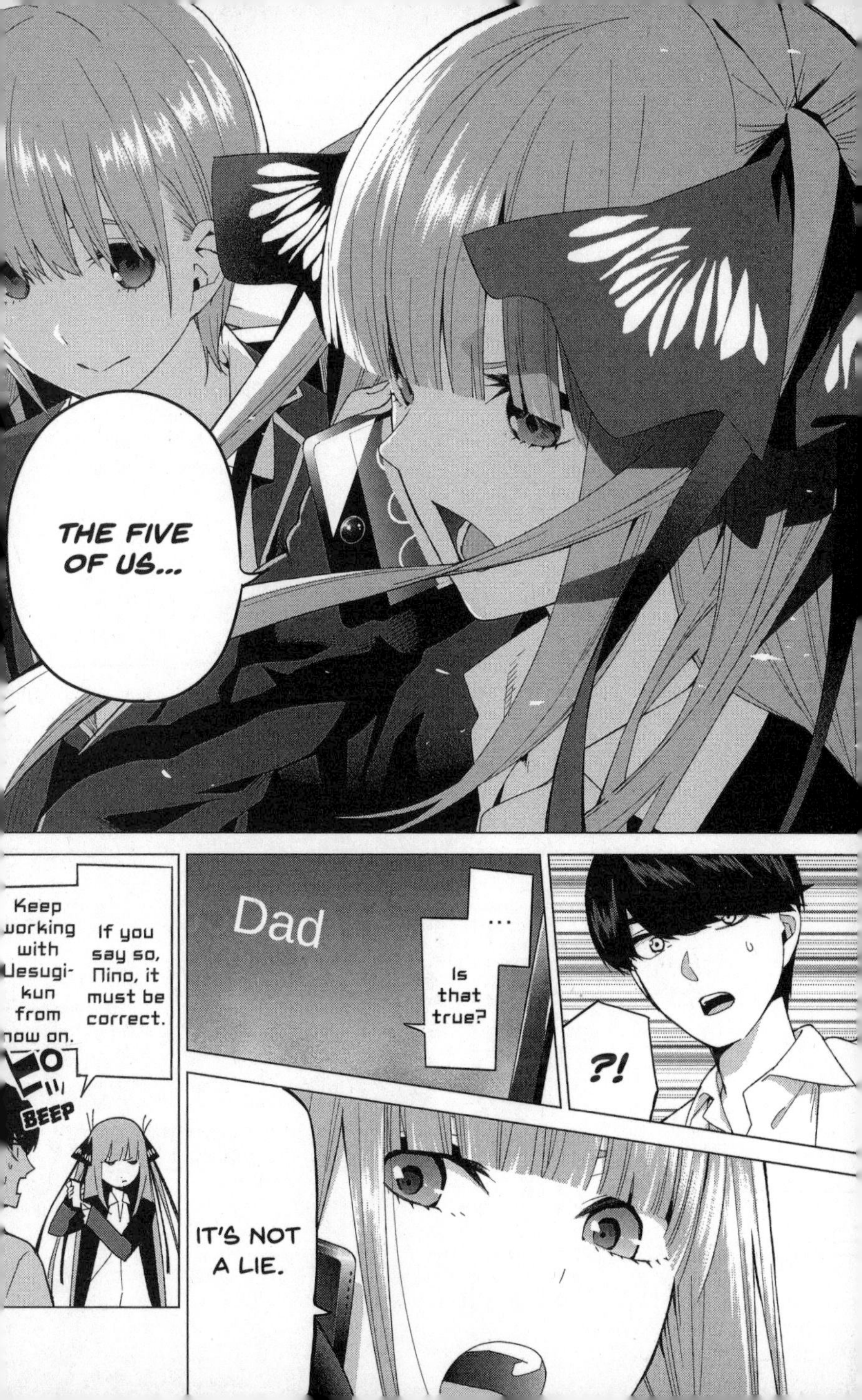
THE FIVE OF US...
?!
Dad
...
Is that true?
IT'S NOT A LIE.
If you say so, Nino, it must be correct.
Keep working with Uesugi-kun from now on.
BEEP

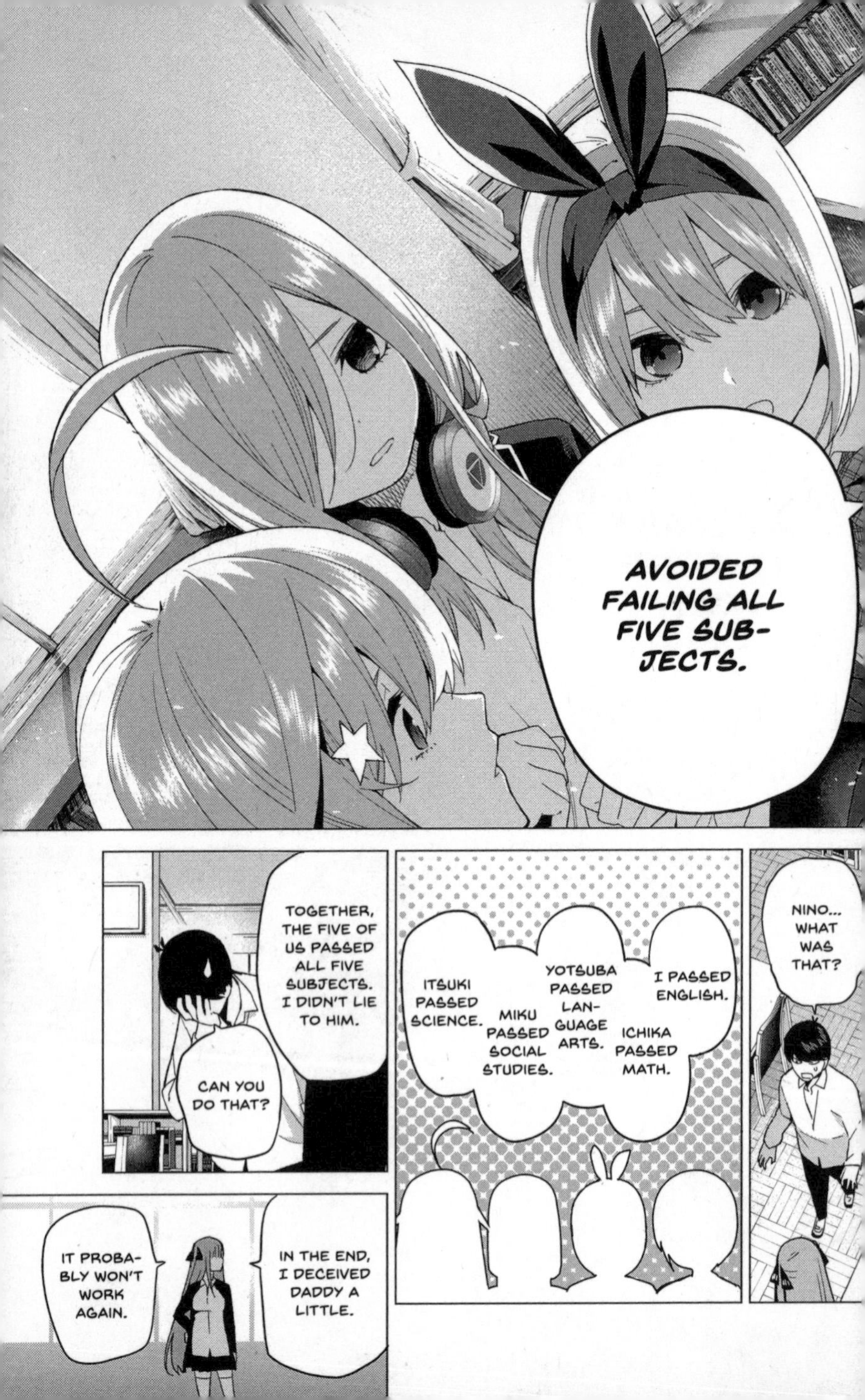

AVOIDED FAILING ALL FIVE SUBJECTS.
NINO... WHAT WAS THAT?
I PASSED ENGLISH.
ICHIKA PASSED MATH.
YOTSUBA PASSED LANGUAGE ARTS.
MIKU PASSED SOCIAL STUDIES.
ITSUKI PASSED SCIENCE.
TOGETHER, THE FIVE OF US PASSED ALL FIVE SUBJECTS. I DIDN'T LIE TO HIM.
CAN YOU DO THAT?
IN THE END, I DECEIVED DADDY A LITTLE.
IT PROBABLY WON'T WORK AGAIN.

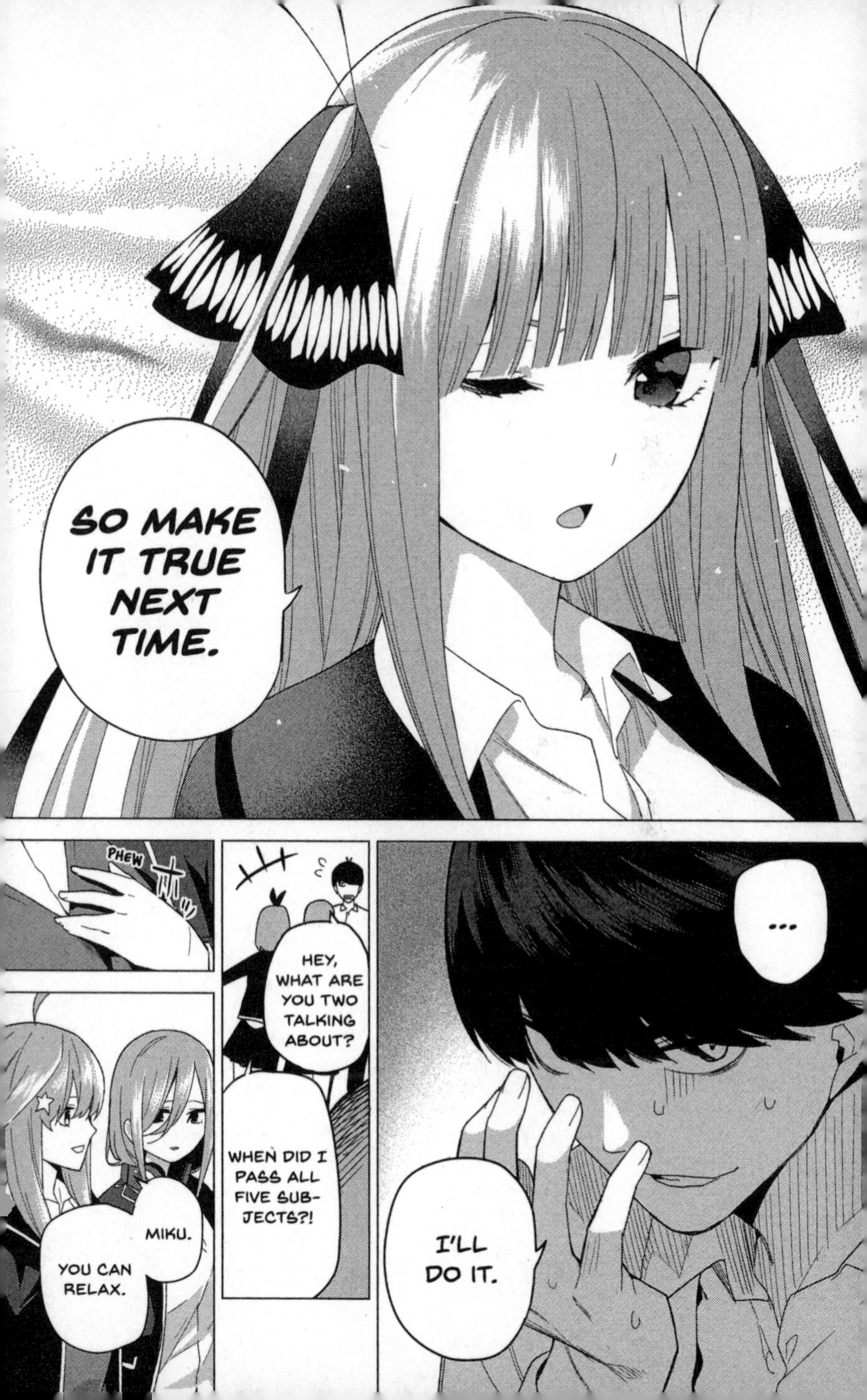
SO MAKE IT TRUE NEXT TIME.
...
I'LL DO IT.
HEY, WHAT ARE YOU TWO TALKING ABOUT?
WHEN DID I PASS ALL FIVE SUB-JECTS?!
PHEW
MIKU.
YOU CAN RELAX.

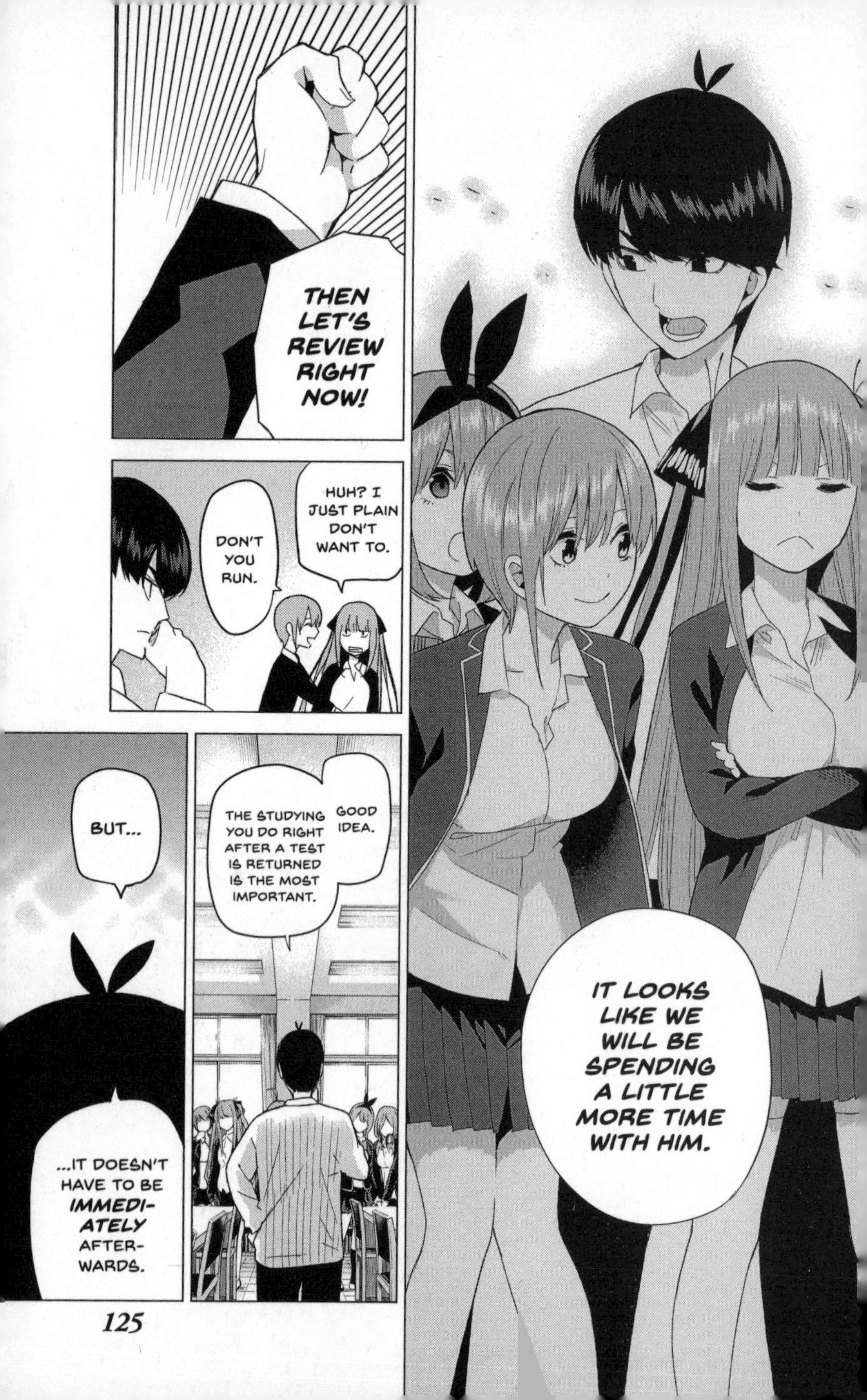
IT LOOKS LIKE WE WILL BE SPENDING A LITTLE MORE TIME WITH HIM.
THEN LET'S REVIEW RIGHT NOW!
HUH? I JUST PLAIN DON'T WANT TO.
DON'T YOU RUN.
GOOD IDEA.
THE STUDYING YOU DO RIGHT AFTER A TEST IS RETURNED IS THE MOST IMPORTANT.
BUT...
...IT DOESN'T HAVE TO BE *IMMEDIATELY* AFTERWARDS.

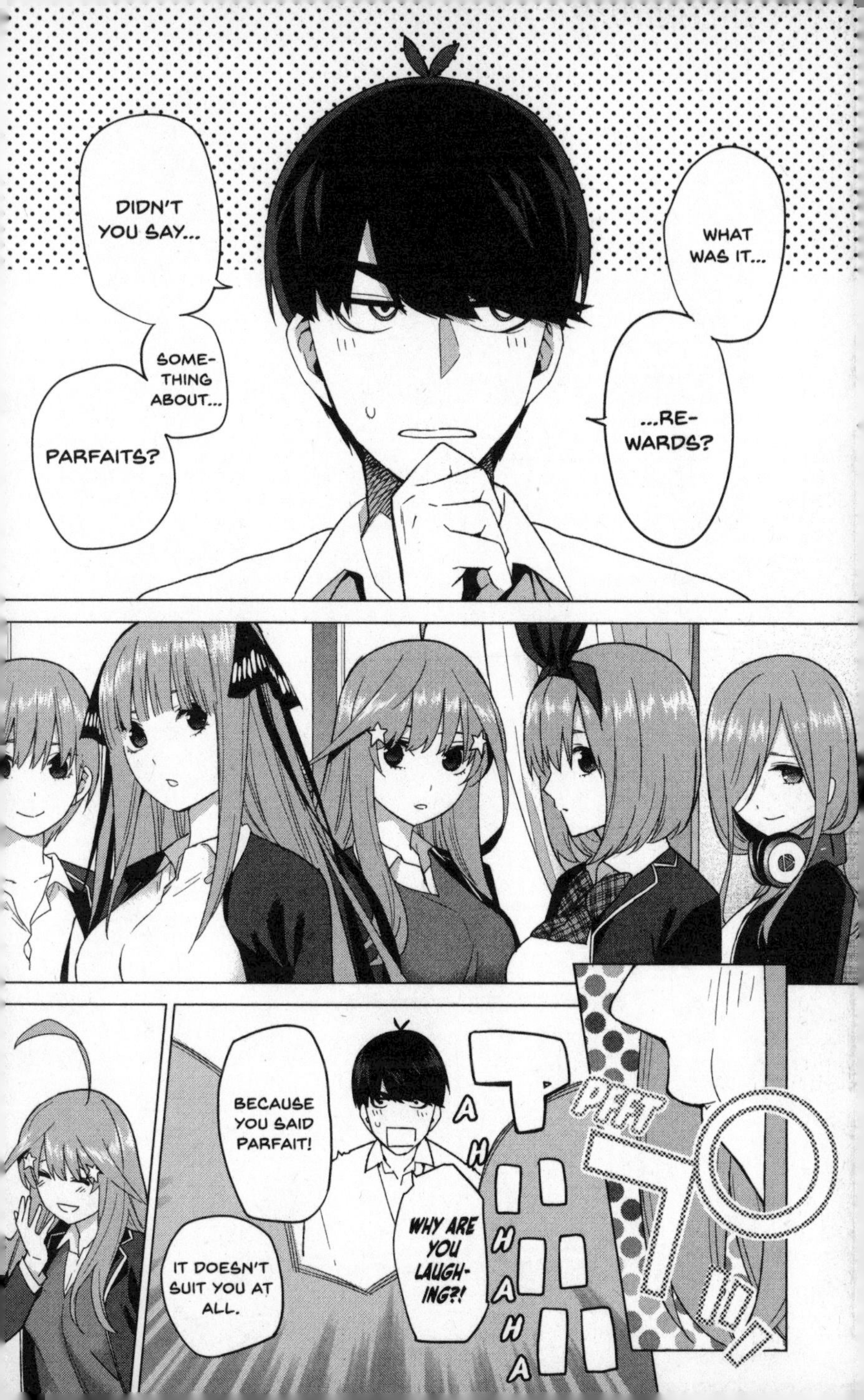
WHAT WAS IT...
...RE-WARDS?
DIDN'T YOU SAY...
SOME-THING ABOUT...
PARFAITS?
PFFT
AHAHAHA
WHY ARE YOU LAUGH-ING?!
BECAUSE YOU SAID PARFAIT!
IT DOESN'T SUIT YOU AT ALL.

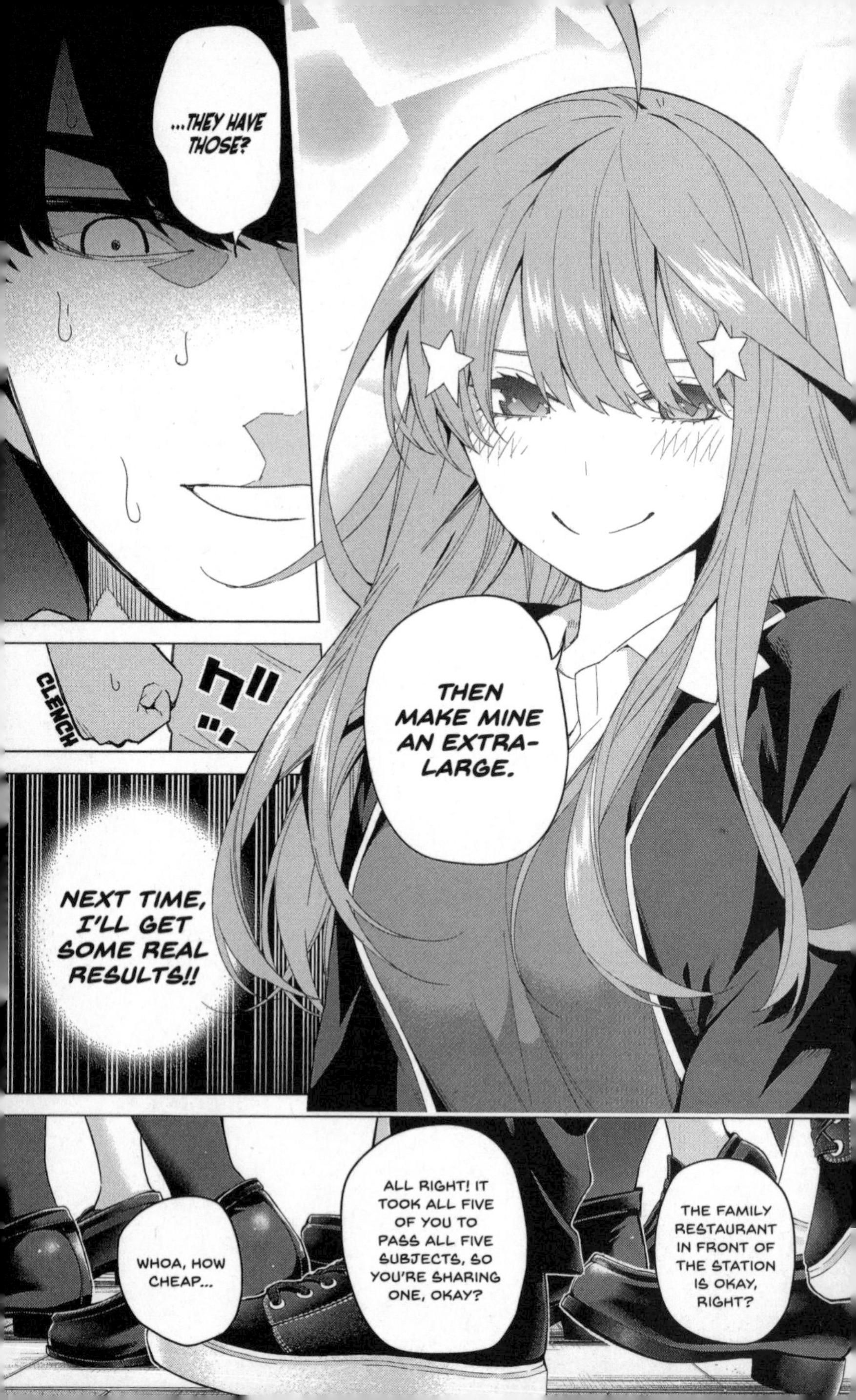
THEN MAKE MINE AN EXTRA-LARGE.
...THEY HAVE THOSE?
CLENCH
NEXT TIME, I'LL GET SOME REAL RESULTS!!
THE FAMILY RESTAURANT IN FRONT OF THE STATION IS OKAY, RIGHT?
ALL RIGHT! IT TOOK ALL FIVE OF YOU TO PASS ALL FIVE SUBJECTS, SO YOU'RE SHARING ONE, OKAY?
WHOA, HOW CHEAP...

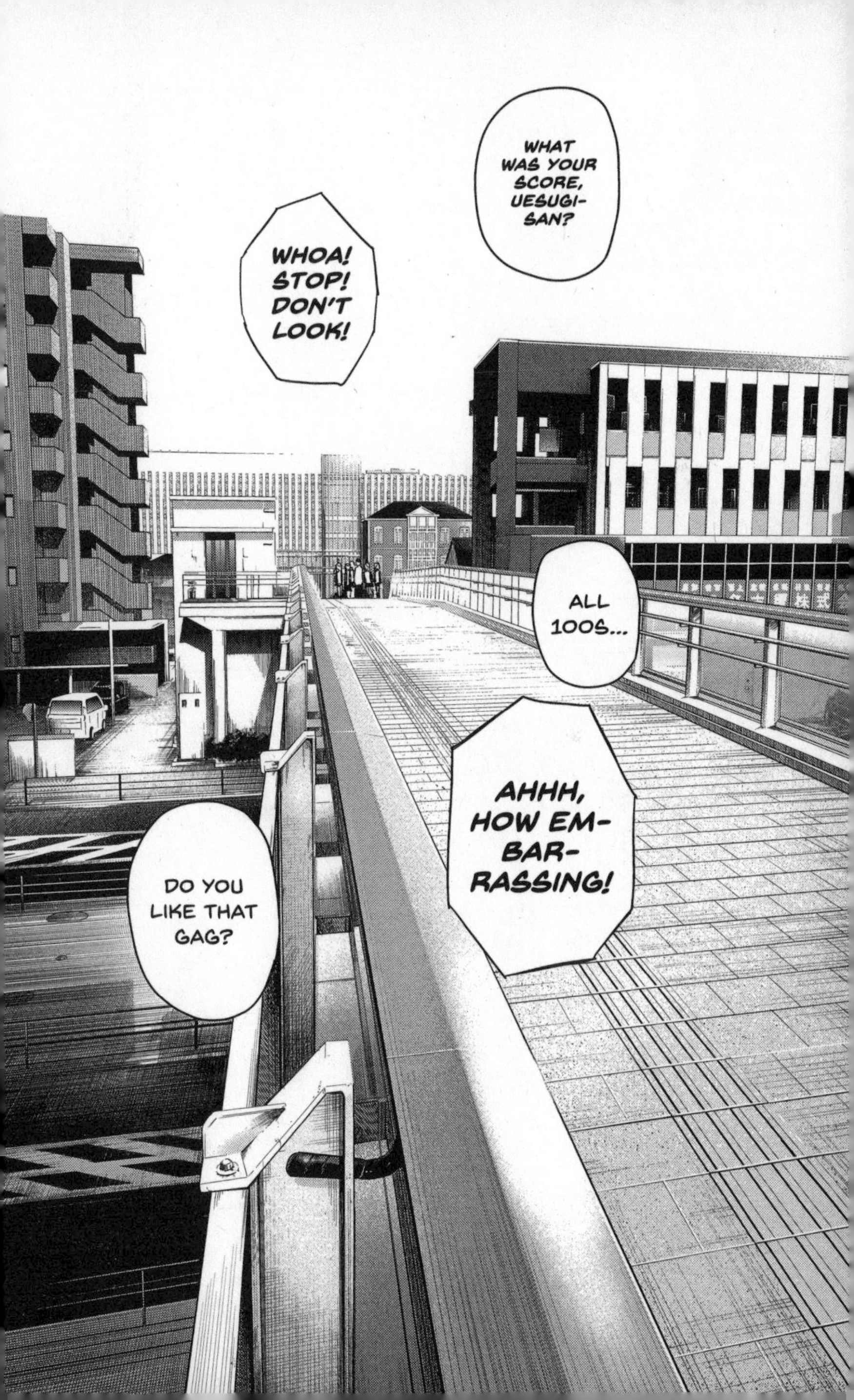
WHAT WAS YOUR SCORE, UESUGI-SAN?
WHOA! STOP! DON'T LOOK!
ALL 100S...
AHHH, HOW EM-BAR-RASSING!
DO YOU LIKE THAT GAG?

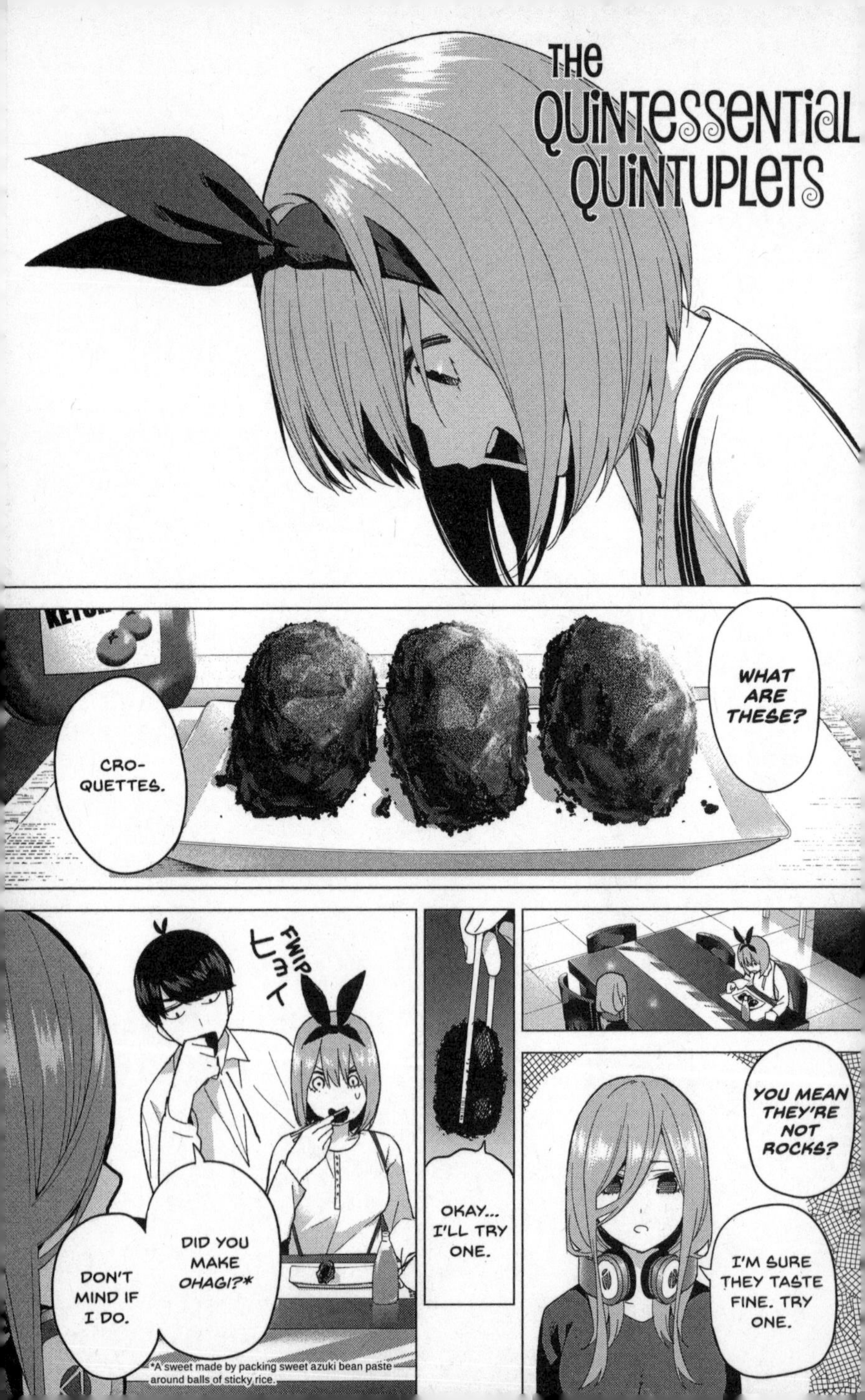
THE QUINTESSENTIAL QUINTUPLETS
WHAT ARE THESE?
CRO-QUETTES.
YOU MEAN THEY'RE NOT ROCKS?
I'M SURE THEY TASTE FINE. TRY ONE.
OKAY... I'LL TRY ONE.
FWIP ヒョイ
DID YOU MAKE OHAGI?*
DON'T MIND IF I DO.
*A sweet made by packing sweet azuki bean paste around balls of sticky rice.

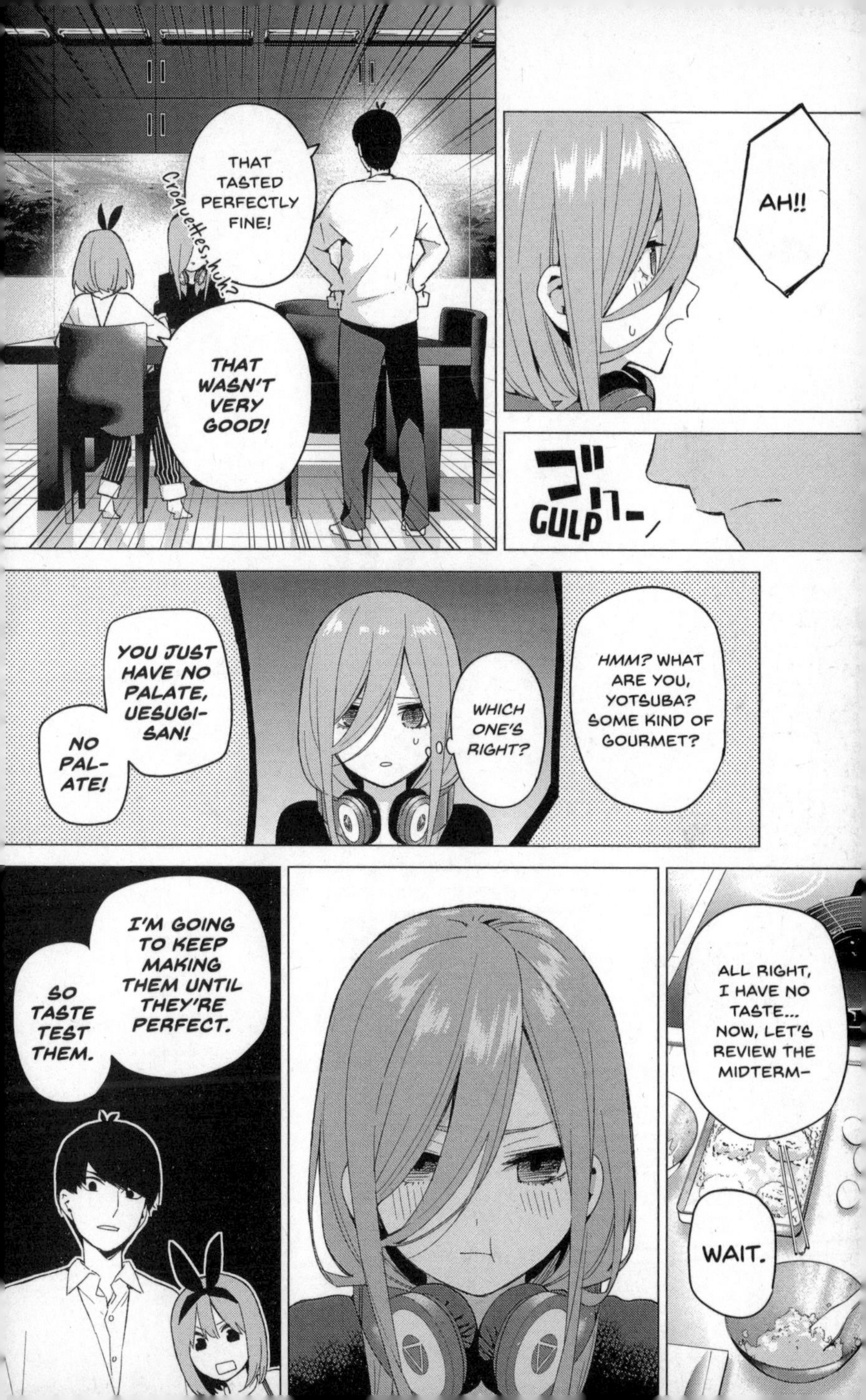

AH!!
GULP
THAT TASTED PERFECTLY FINE!
Croquettes, huh?
THAT WASN'T VERY GOOD!
HMM? WHAT ARE YOU, YOTSUBA? SOME KIND OF GOURMET?
WHICH ONE'S RIGHT?
YOU JUST HAVE NO PALATE, UESUGI-SAN!
NO PAL-ATE!
ALL RIGHT, I HAVE NO TASTE... NOW, LET'S REVIEW THE MIDTERM-
WAIT.
I'M GOING TO KEEP MAKING THEM UNTIL THEY'RE PERFECT.
SO TASTE TEST THEM.

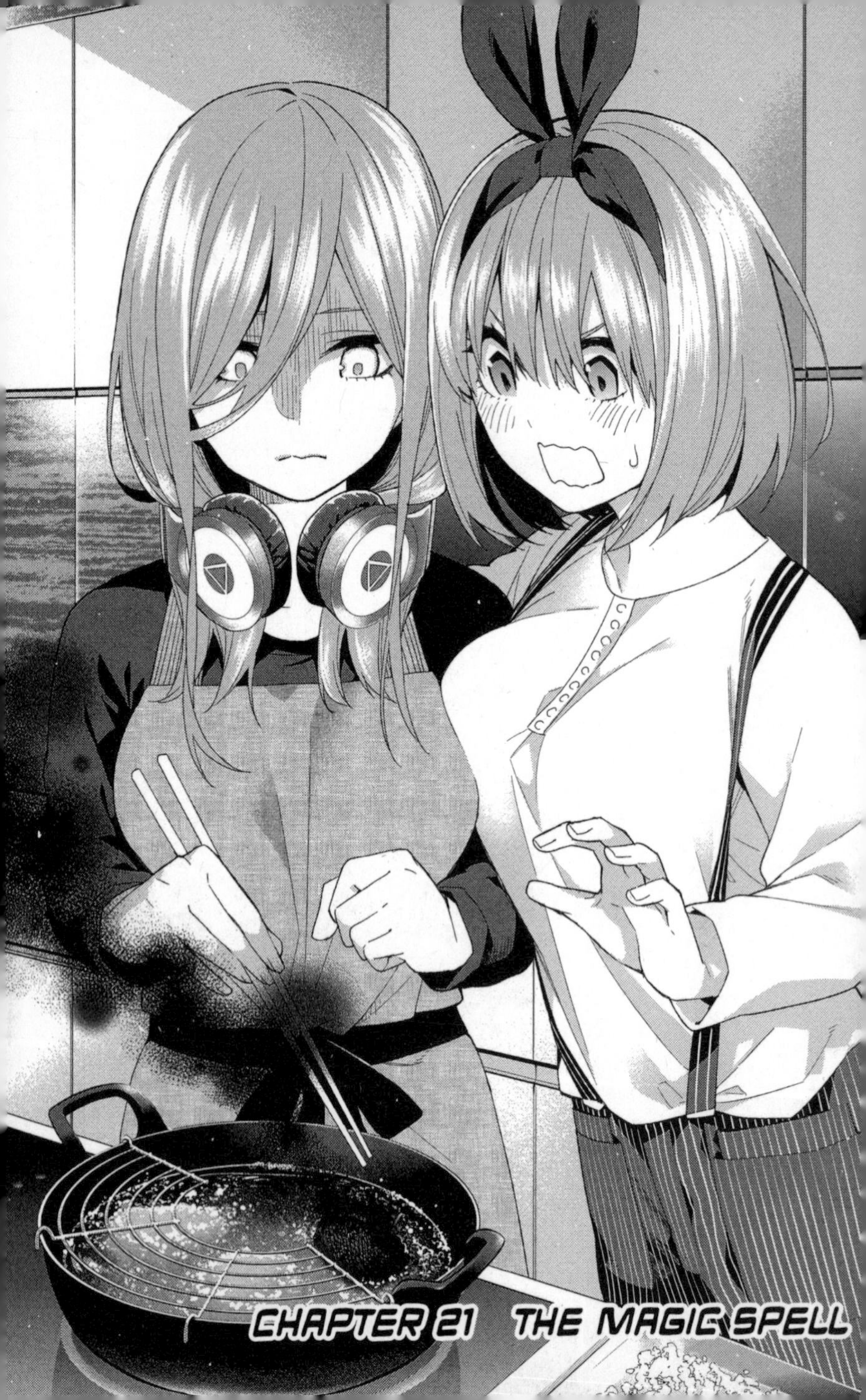
CHAPTER 21 THE MAGIC SPELL

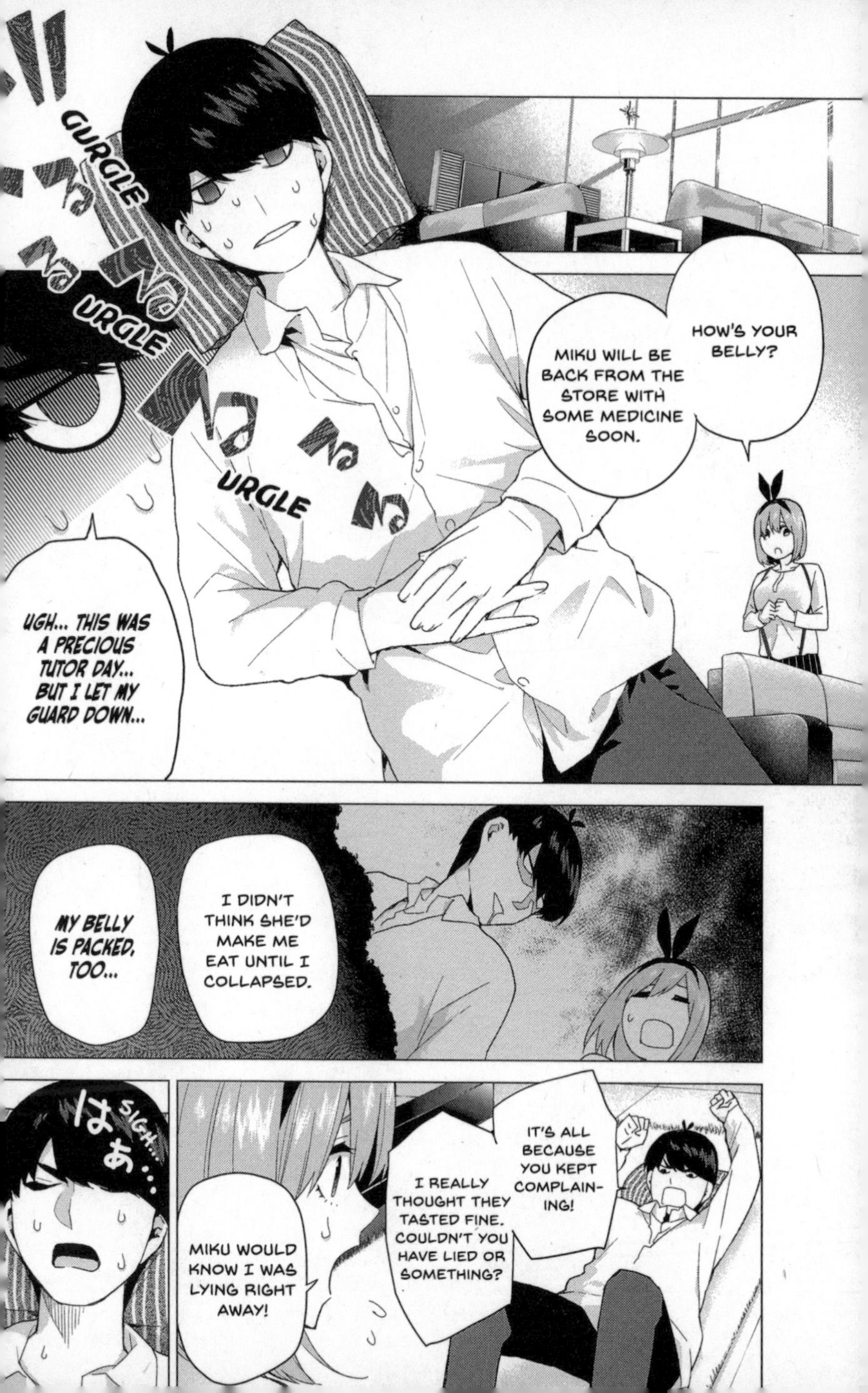
HOW'S YOUR BELLY?
MIKU WILL BE BACK FROM THE STORE WITH SOME MEDICINE SOON.
GURGLE
URGLE
URGLE
UGH... THIS WAS A PRECIOUS TUTOR DAY... BUT I LET MY GUARD DOWN...
I DIDN'T THINK SHE'D MAKE ME EAT UNTIL I COLLAPSED.
MY BELLY IS PACKED, TOO...
IT'S ALL BECAUSE YOU KEPT COMPLAINING!
I REALLY THOUGHT THEY TASTED FINE. COULDN'T YOU HAVE LIED OR SOMETHING?
MIKU WOULD KNOW I WAS LYING RIGHT AWAY!
はぁ…
SIGH...

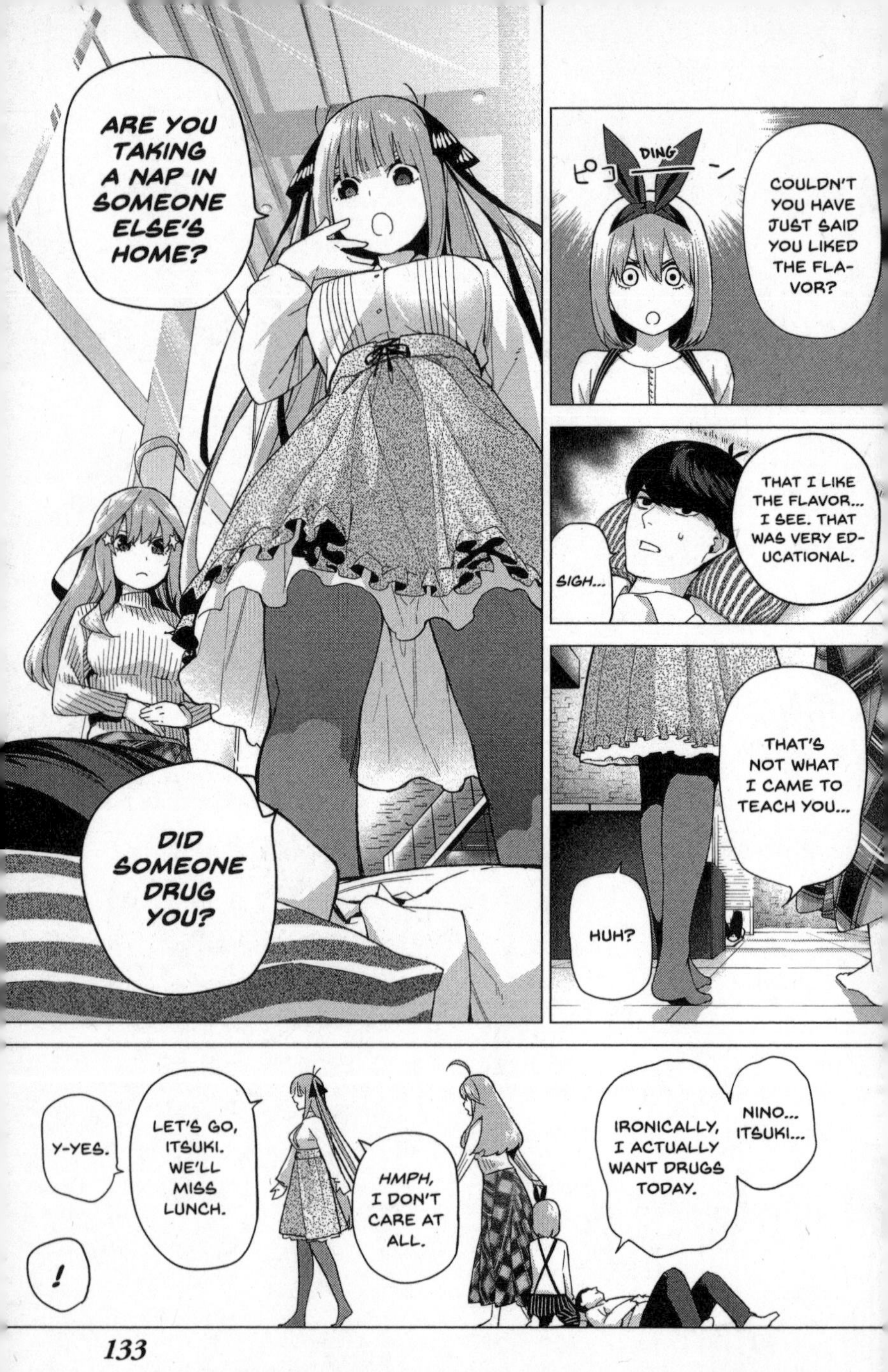
ピコ
DING
COULDN'T YOU HAVE JUST SAID YOU LIKED THE FLA-VOR?
THAT I LIKE THE FLAVOR... I SEE. THAT WAS VERY ED-UCATIONAL.
SIGH...
THAT'S NOT WHAT I CAME TO TEACH YOU...
HUH?
ARE YOU TAKING A NAP IN SOMEONE ELSE'S HOME?
DID SOMEONE DRUG YOU?
NINO... ITSUKI...
IRONICALLY, I ACTUALLY WANT DRUGS TODAY.
HMPH, I DON'T CARE AT ALL.
LET'S GO, ITSUKI. WE'LL MISS LUNCH.
Y-YES.
!

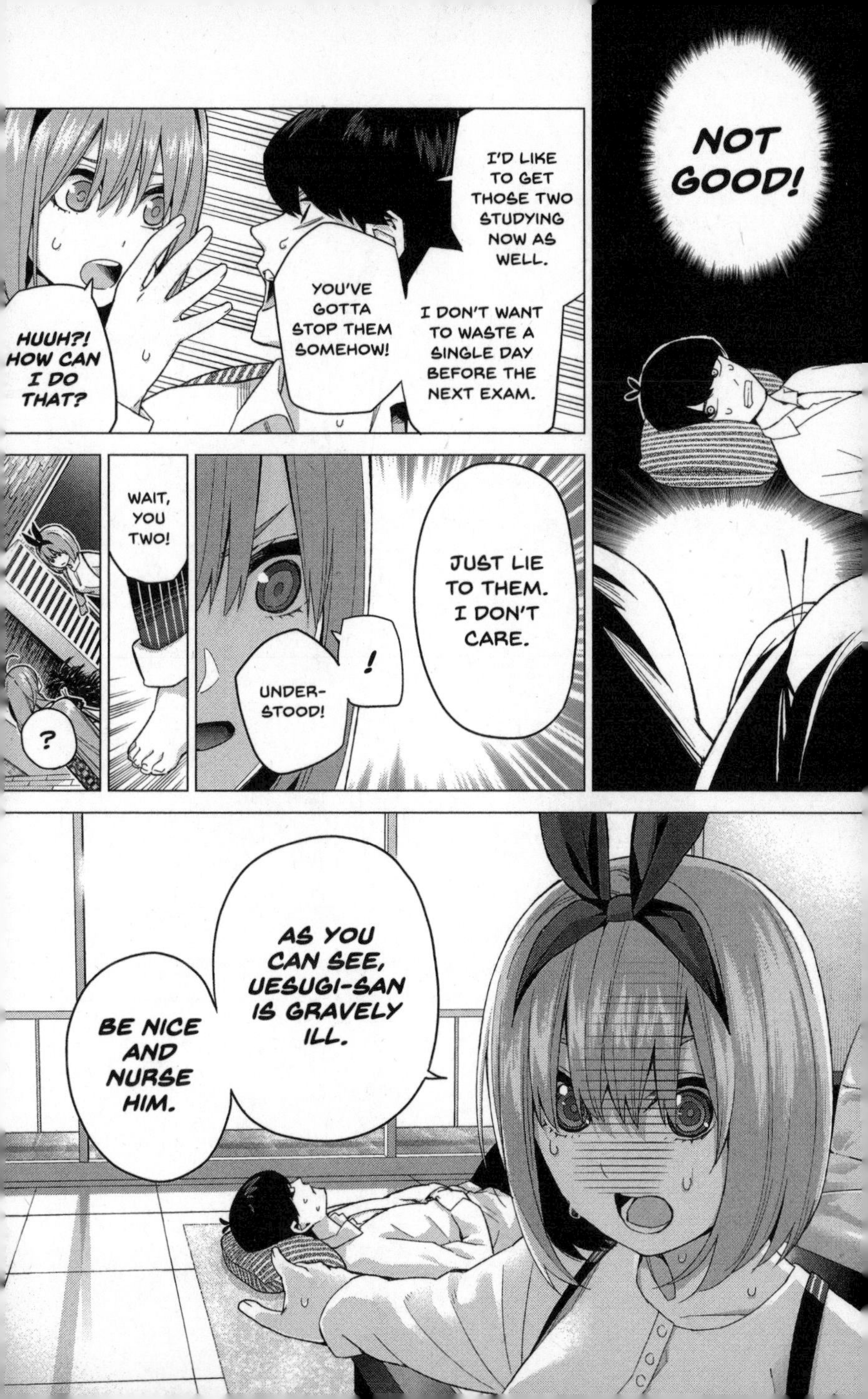
NOT GOOD!
I'D LIKE TO GET THOSE TWO STUDYING NOW AS WELL.
I DON'T WANT TO WASTE A SINGLE DAY BEFORE THE NEXT EXAM.
YOU'VE GOTTA STOP THEM SOMEHOW!
HUUH?! HOW CAN I DO THAT?
JUST LIE TO THEM. I DON'T CARE.
!
UNDER-STOOD!
WAIT, YOU TWO!
?
AS YOU CAN SEE, UESUGI-SAN IS GRAVELY ILL.
BE NICE AND NURSE HIM.

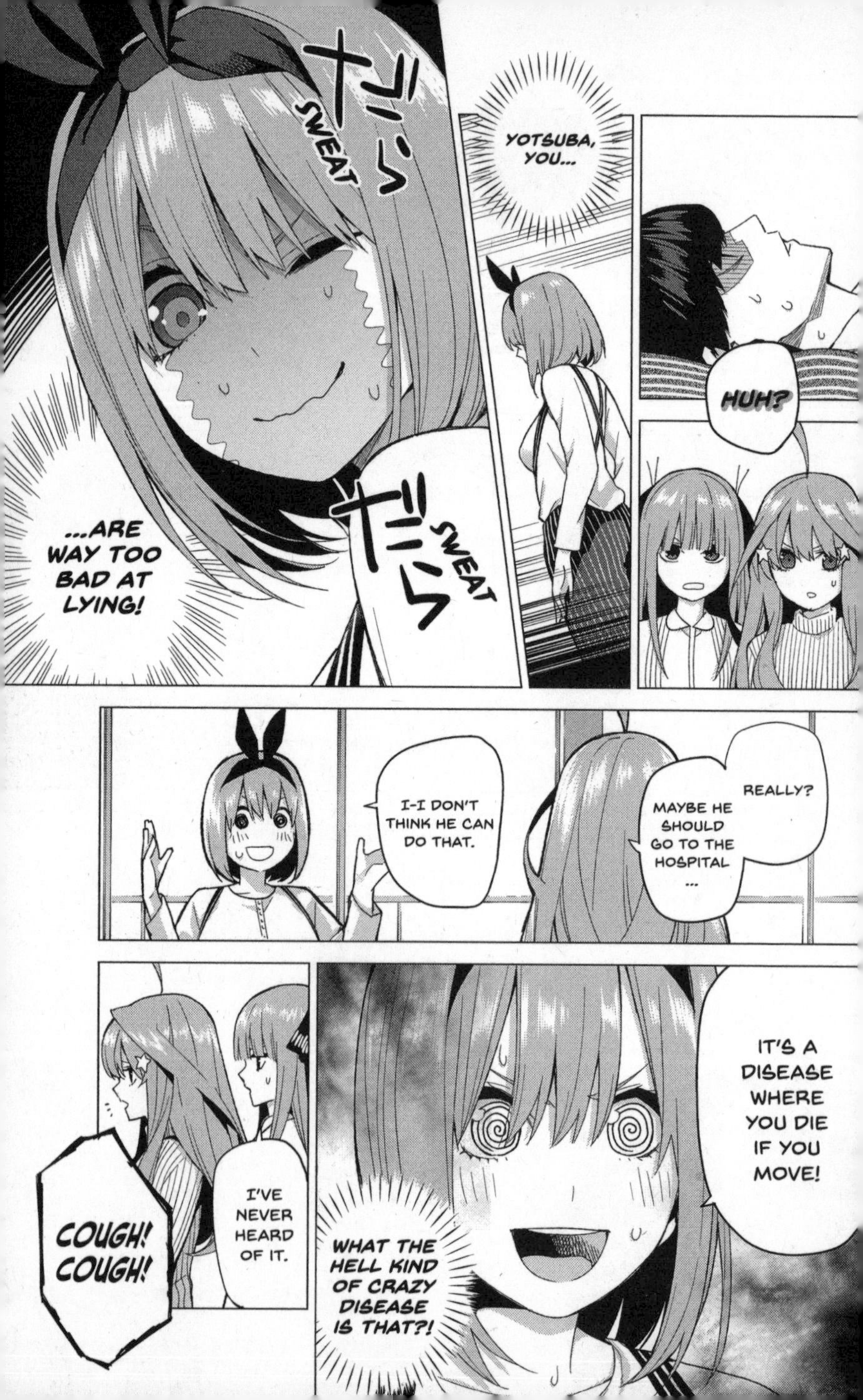
HUH?
YOTSUBA, YOU...
...ARE WAY TOO BAD AT LYING!
SWEAT
SWEAT
REALLY?
MAYBE HE SHOULD GO TO THE HOSPITAL...
I-I DON'T THINK HE CAN DO THAT.
IT'S A DISEASE WHERE YOU DIE IF YOU MOVE!
WHAT THE HELL KIND OF CRAZY DISEASE IS THAT?!
I'VE NEVER HEARD OF IT.
COUGH! COUGH!

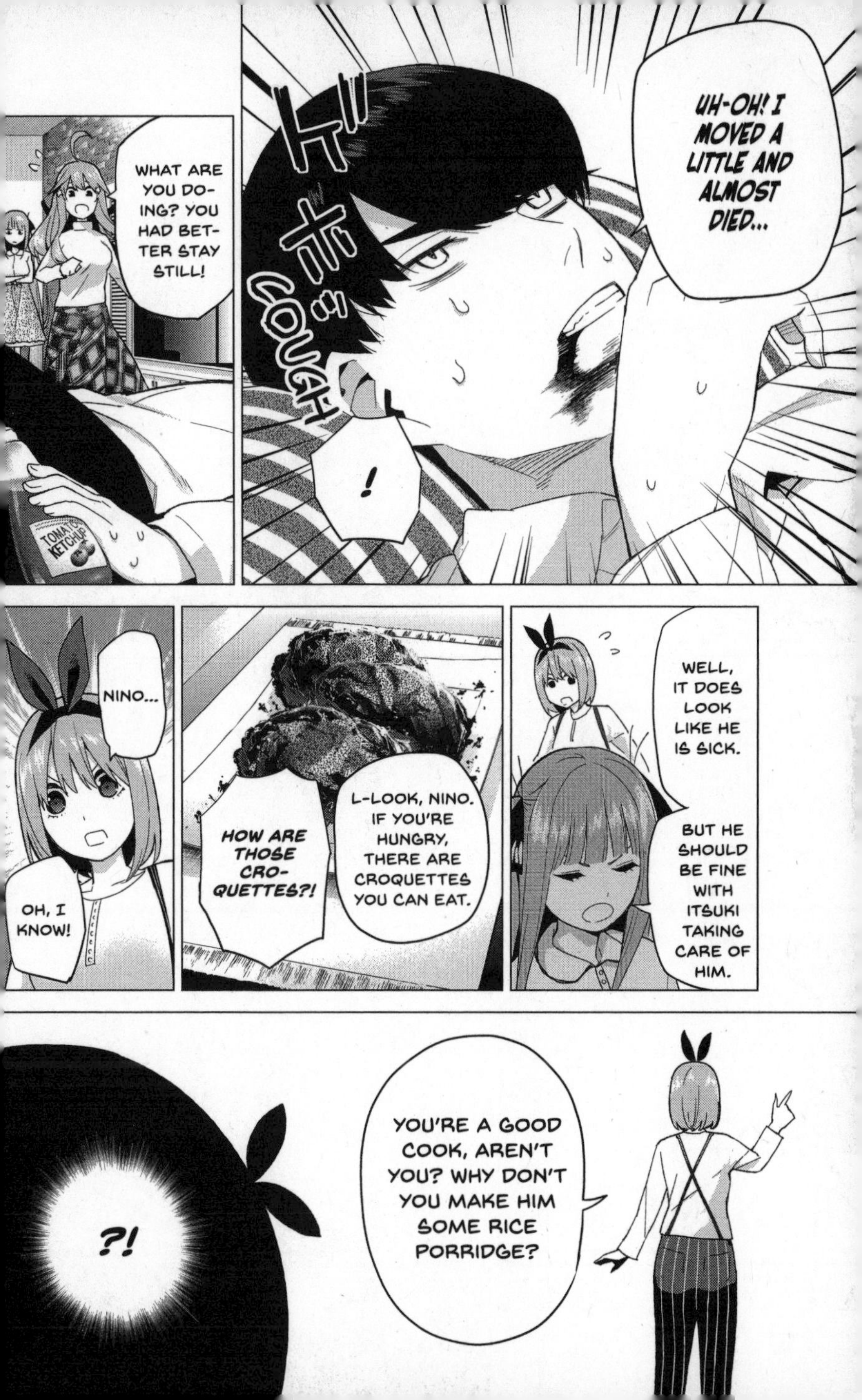
UH-OH! I MOVED A LITTLE AND ALMOST DIED...
COUGH
!
WHAT ARE YOU DOING? YOU HAD BETTER STAY STILL!
WELL, IT DOES LOOK LIKE HE IS SICK.
BUT HE SHOULD BE FINE WITH ITSUKI TAKING CARE OF HIM.
L-LOOK, NINO. IF YOU'RE HUNGRY, THERE ARE CROQUETTES YOU CAN EAT.
HOW ARE THOSE CROQUETTES?!
NINO...
OH, I KNOW!
YOU'RE A GOOD COOK, AREN'T YOU? WHY DON'T YOU MAKE HIM SOME RICE PORRIDGE?
?!

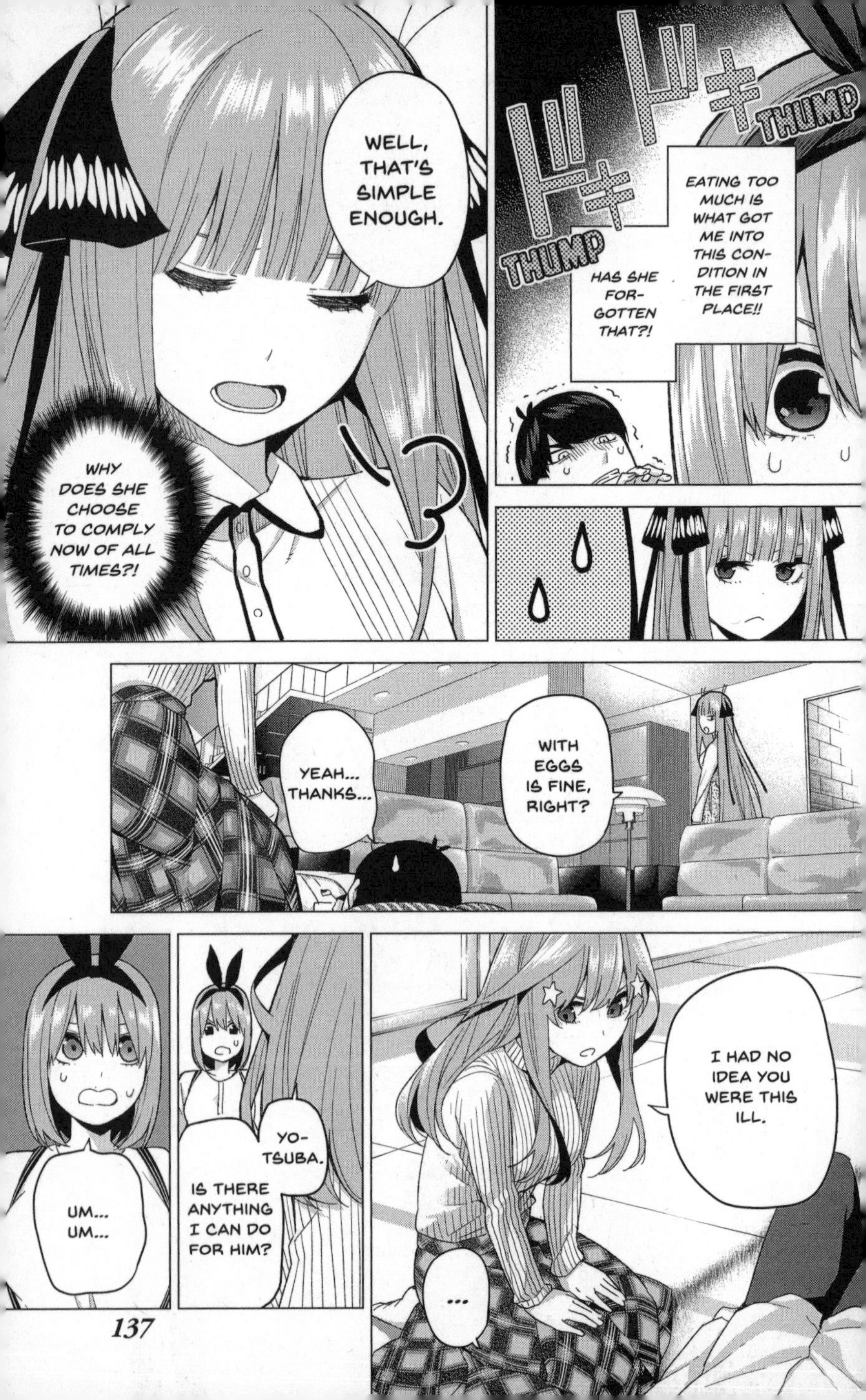
ドキ
THUMP
ドキ
THUMP
EATING TOO MUCH IS WHAT GOT ME INTO THIS CONDITION IN THE FIRST PLACE!!
HAS SHE FORGOTTEN THAT?!
WELL, THAT'S SIMPLE ENOUGH.
WHY DOES SHE CHOOSE TO COMPLY NOW OF ALL TIMES?!
WITH EGGS IS FINE, RIGHT?
YEAH... THANKS...
I HAD NO IDEA YOU WERE THIS ILL.
...
YOTSUBA.
IS THERE ANYTHING I CAN DO FOR HIM?
UM... UM...

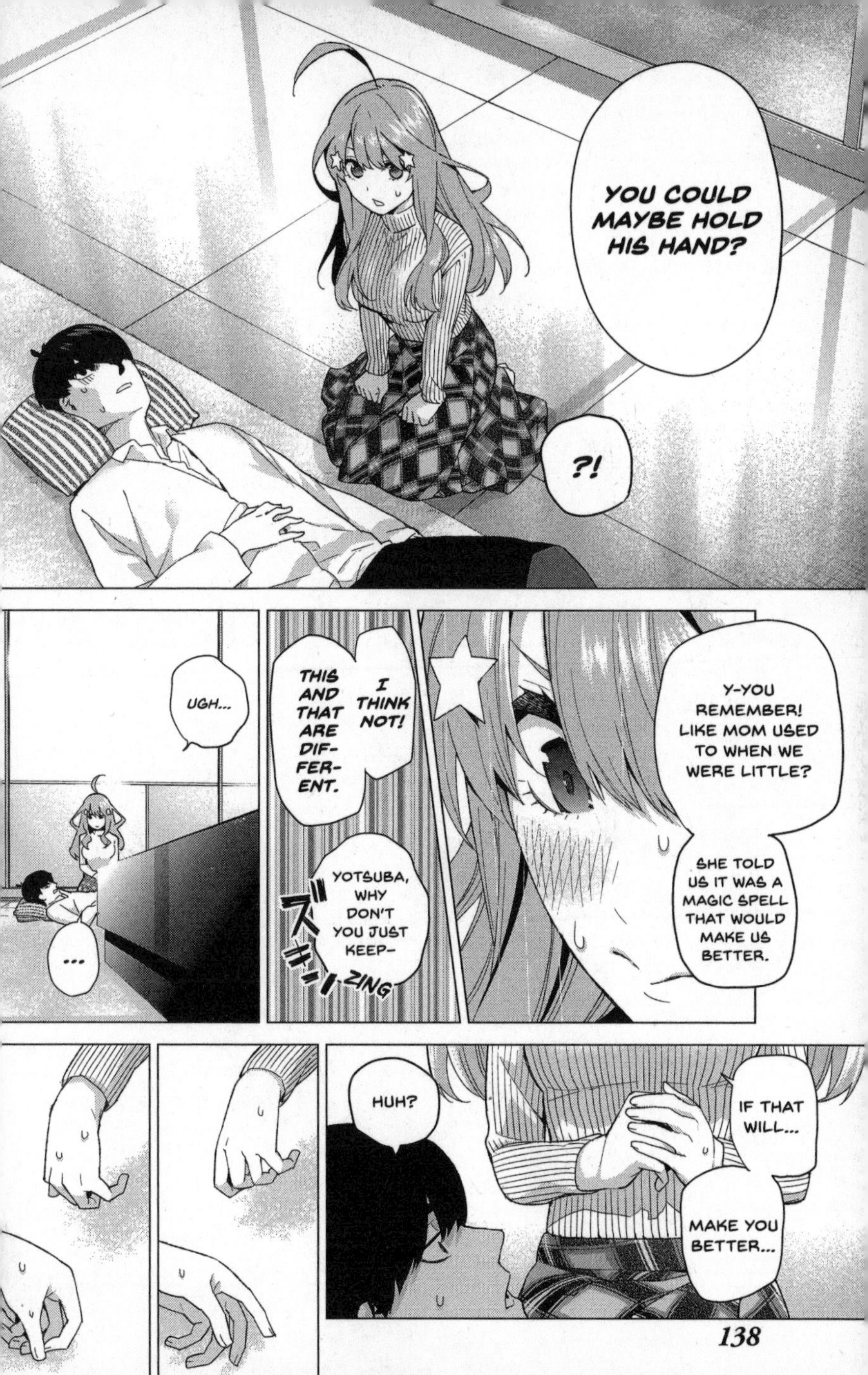
YOU COULD MAYBE HOLD HIS HAND?
?!
Y-YOU REMEMBER! LIKE MOM USED TO WHEN WE WERE LITTLE?
SHE TOLD US IT WAS A MAGIC SPELL THAT WOULD MAKE US BETTER.
I THINK NOT!
THIS AND THAT ARE DIF-FER-ENT.
YOTSUBA, WHY DON'T YOU JUST KEEP-
ZING
UGH...
...
IF THAT WILL...
HUH?
MAKE YOU BETTER...

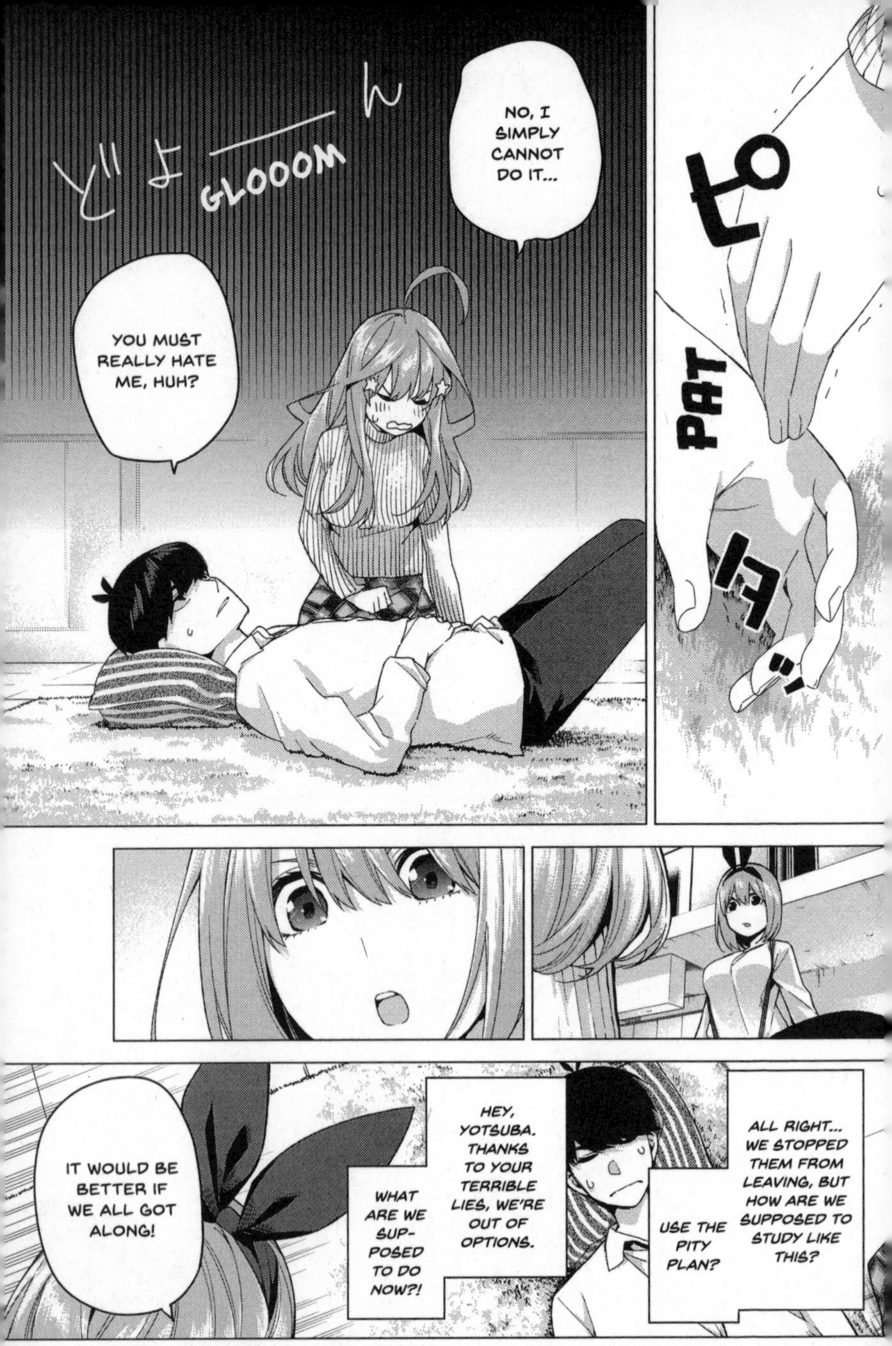
PAT
NO, I SIMPLY CANNOT DO IT...
GLOOOM
YOU MUST REALLY HATE ME, HUH?
ALL RIGHT... WE STOPPED THEM FROM LEAVING, BUT HOW ARE WE SUPPOSED TO STUDY LIKE THIS?
USE THE PITY PLAN?
HEY, YOTSUBA. THANKS TO YOUR TERRIBLE LIES, WE'RE OUT OF OPTIONS.
WHAT ARE WE SUP-POSED TO DO NOW?!
IT WOULD BE BETTER IF WE ALL GOT ALONG!

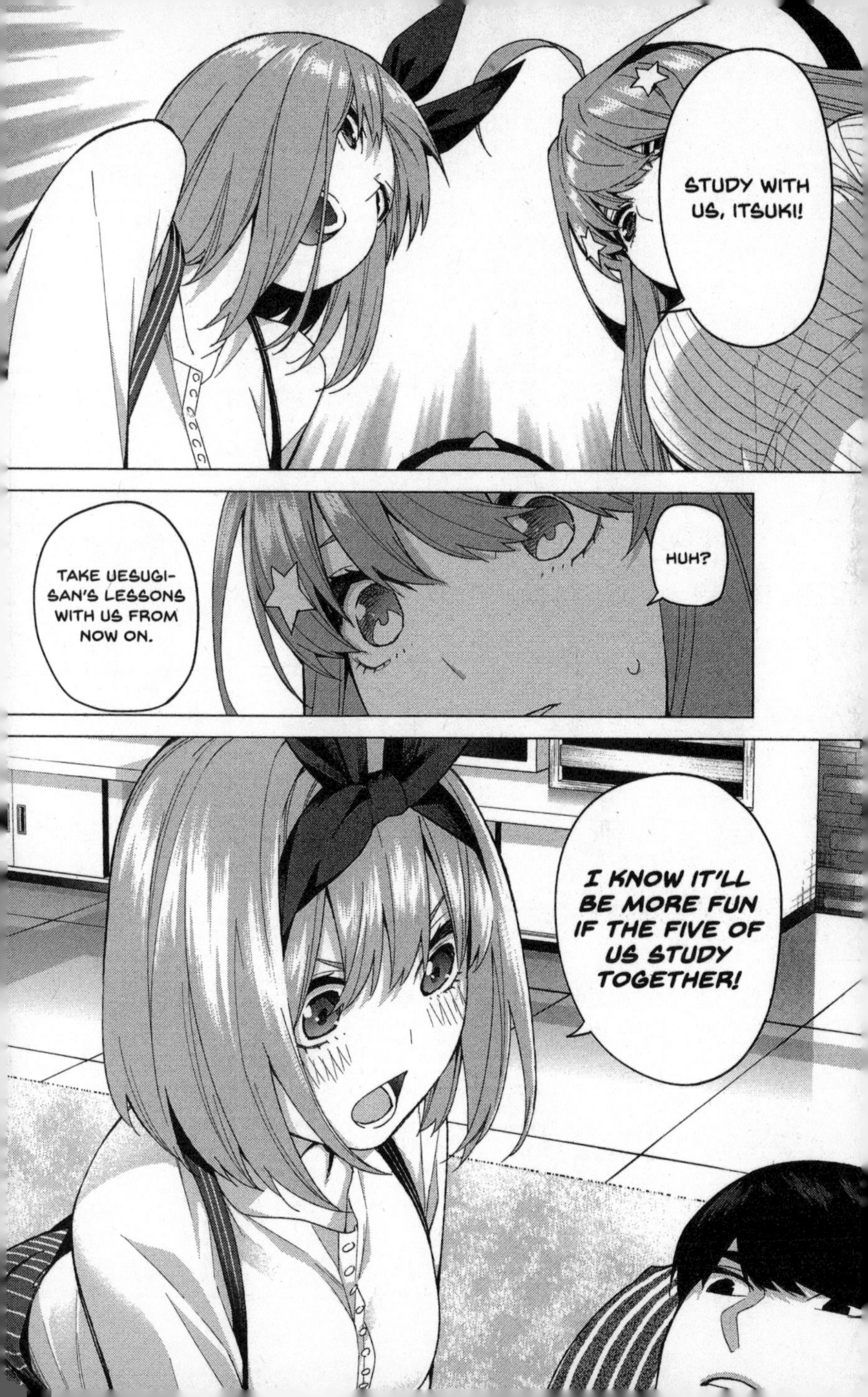
STUDY WITH US, ITSUKI!
HUH?
TAKE UESUGI-SAN'S LESSONS WITH US FROM NOW ON.
I KNOW IT'LL BE MORE FUN IF THE FIVE OF US STUDY TOGETHER!

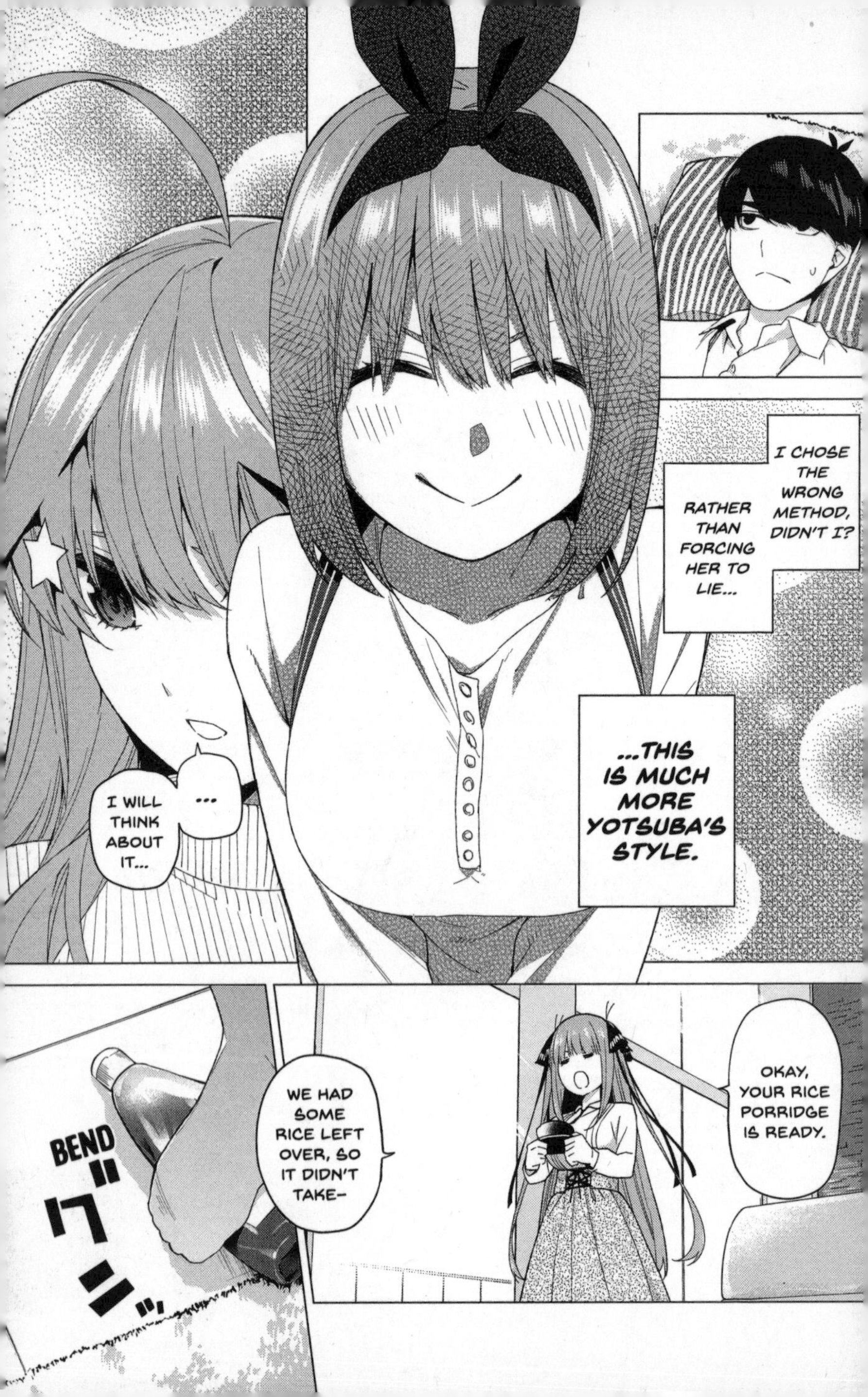
I CHOSE THE WRONG METHOD, DIDN'T I?
RATHER THAN FORCING HER TO LIE...
...THIS IS MUCH MORE YOTSUBA'S STYLE.
...
I WILL THINK ABOUT IT...
OKAY, YOUR RICE PORRIDGE IS READY.
WE HAD SOME RICE LEFT OVER, SO IT DIDN'T TAKE-
BEND
グッ

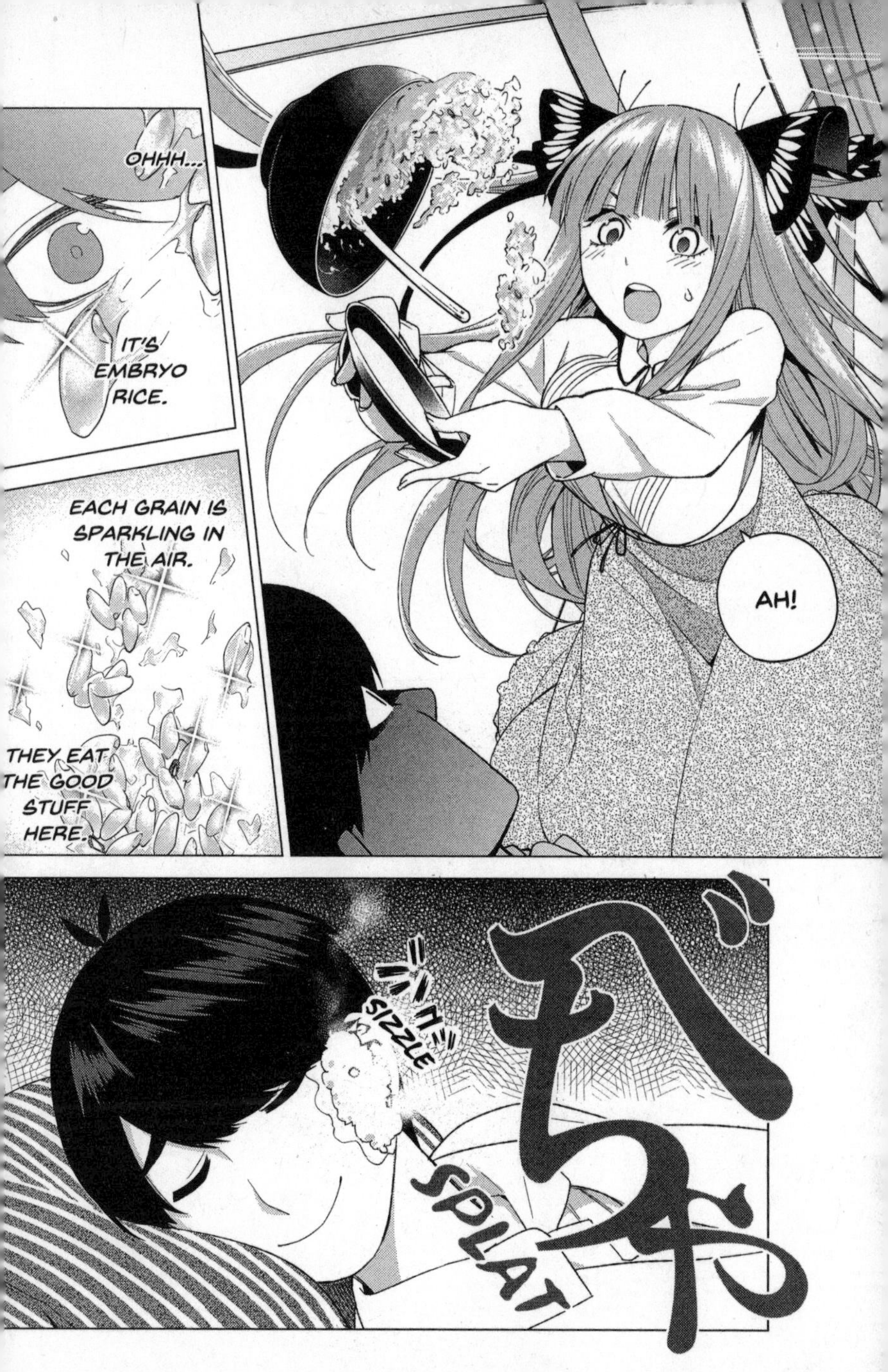
AH!
OHHH...
IT'S EMBRYO RICE.
EACH GRAIN IS SPARKLING IN THE AIR.
THEY EAT THE GOOD STUFF HERE.
SIZZLE
SPLAT

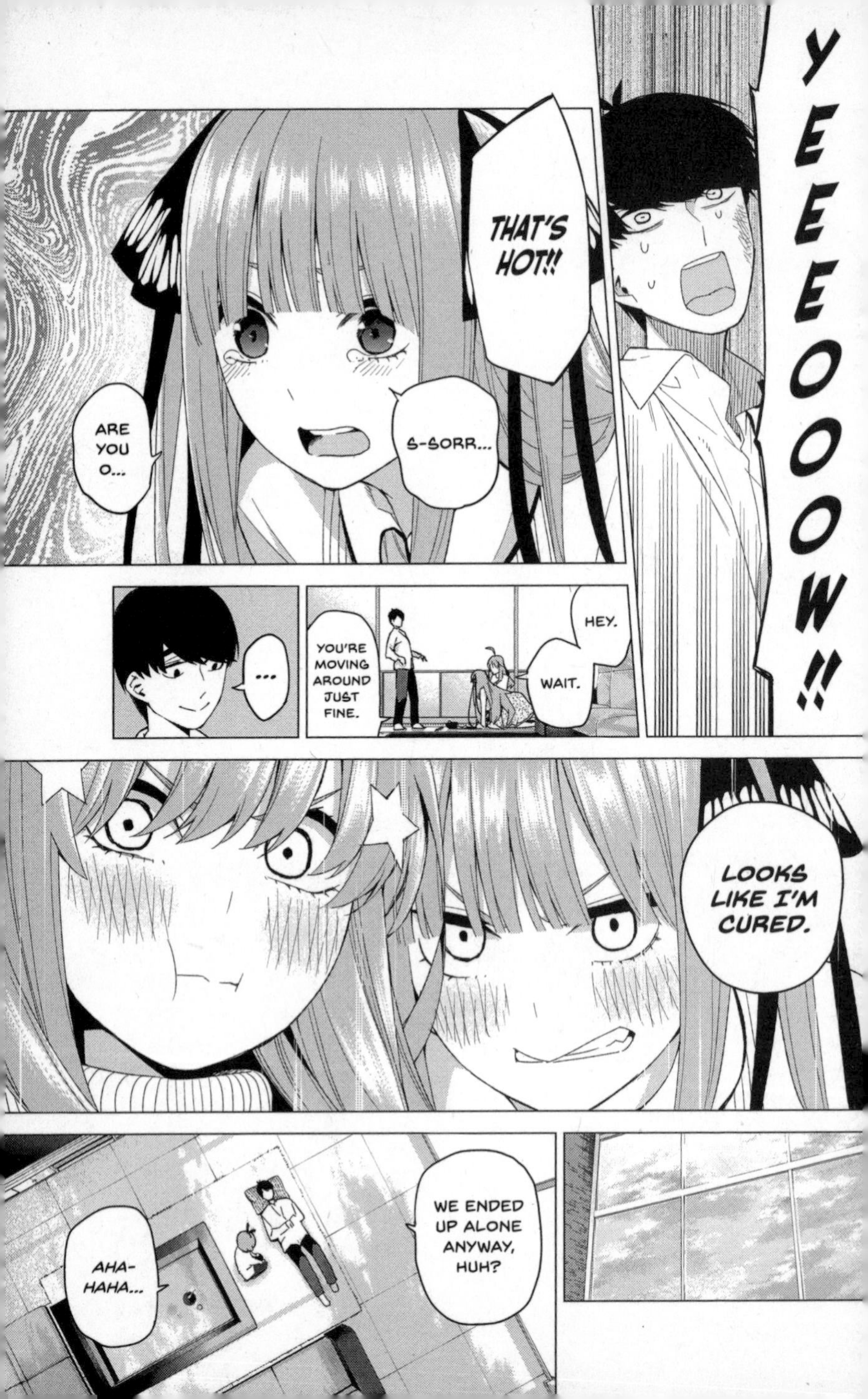
YEEEOOOOW!!
THAT'S HOT!!
S-SORR...
ARE YOU O...
HEY. WAIT.
YOU'RE MOVING AROUND JUST FINE.
...
LOOKS LIKE I'M CURED.
WE ENDED UP ALONE ANYWAY, HUH?
AHA-HAHA...

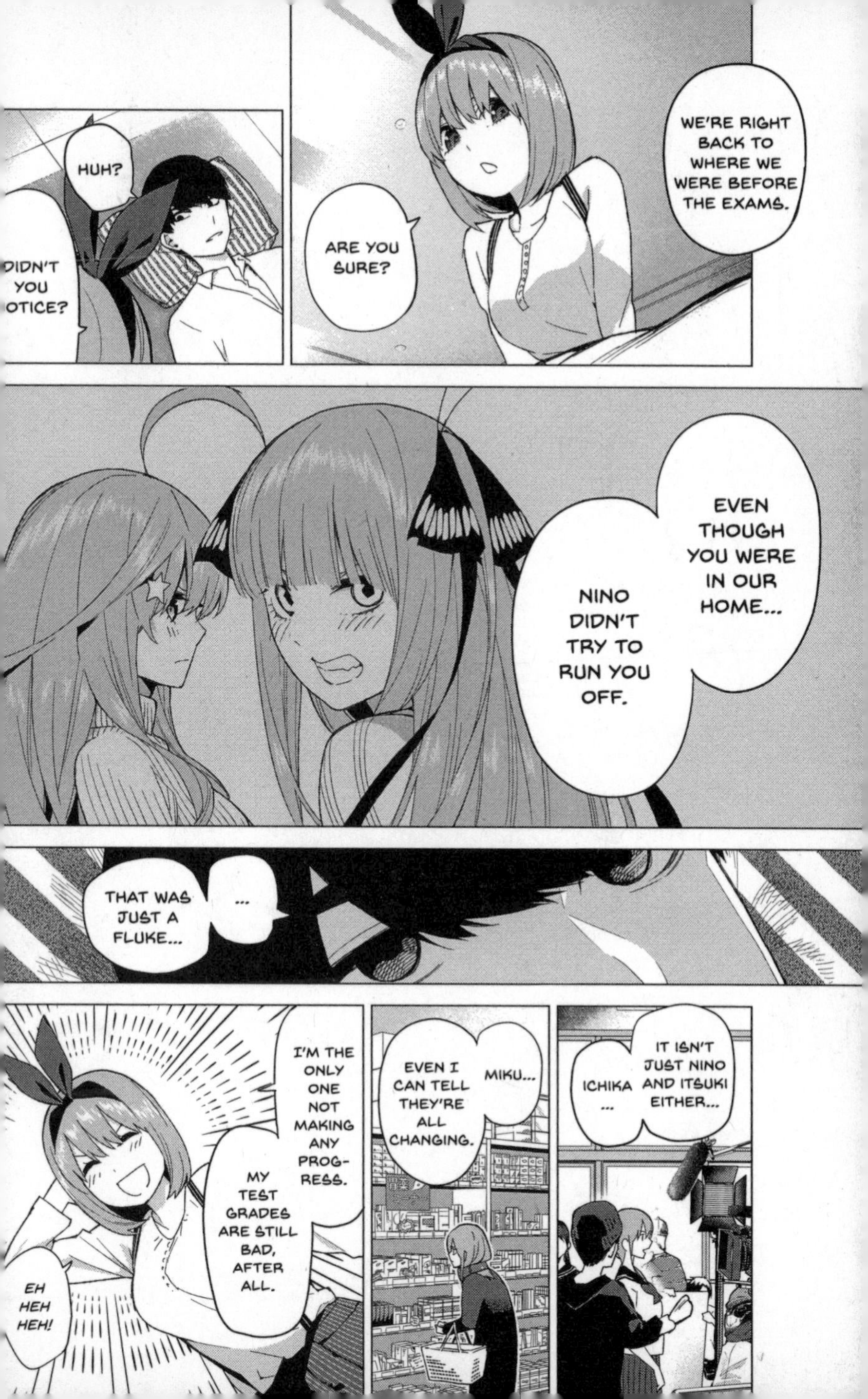
WE'RE RIGHT BACK TO WHERE WE WERE BEFORE THE EXAMS.
ARE YOU SURE?
HUH?
DIDN'T YOU OTICE?
EVEN THOUGH YOU WERE IN OUR HOME...
NINO DIDN'T TRY TO RUN YOU OFF.
...
THAT WAS JUST A FLUKE...
IT ISN'T JUST NINO AND ITSUKI EITHER...
ICHIKA ...
MIKU...
EVEN I CAN TELL THEY'RE ALL CHANGING.
I'M THE ONLY ONE NOT MAKING ANY PROG-RESS.
MY TEST GRADES ARE STILL BAD, AFTER ALL.
EH HEH HEH!

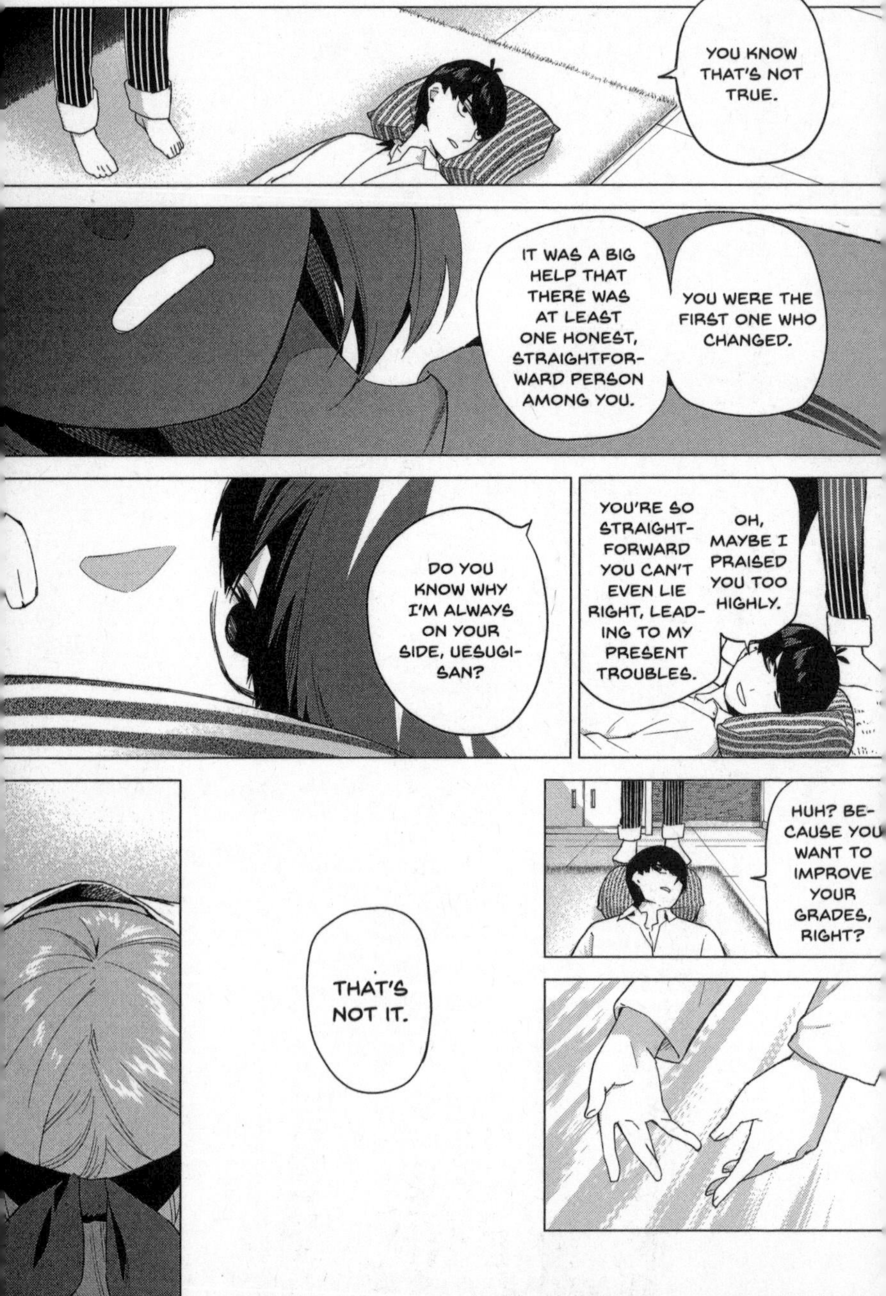
YOU KNOW THAT'S NOT TRUE.
YOU WERE THE FIRST ONE WHO CHANGED.
IT WAS A BIG HELP THAT THERE WAS AT LEAST ONE HONEST, STRAIGHTFOR-WARD PERSON AMONG YOU.
OH, MAYBE I PRAISED YOU TOO HIGHLY.
YOU'RE SO STRAIGHT-FORWARD YOU CAN'T EVEN LIE RIGHT, LEAD-ING TO MY PRESENT TROUBLES.
DO YOU KNOW WHY I'M ALWAYS ON YOUR SIDE, UESUGI-SAN?
HUH? BE-CAUSE YOU WANT TO IMPROVE YOUR GRADES, RIGHT?
THAT'S NOT IT.

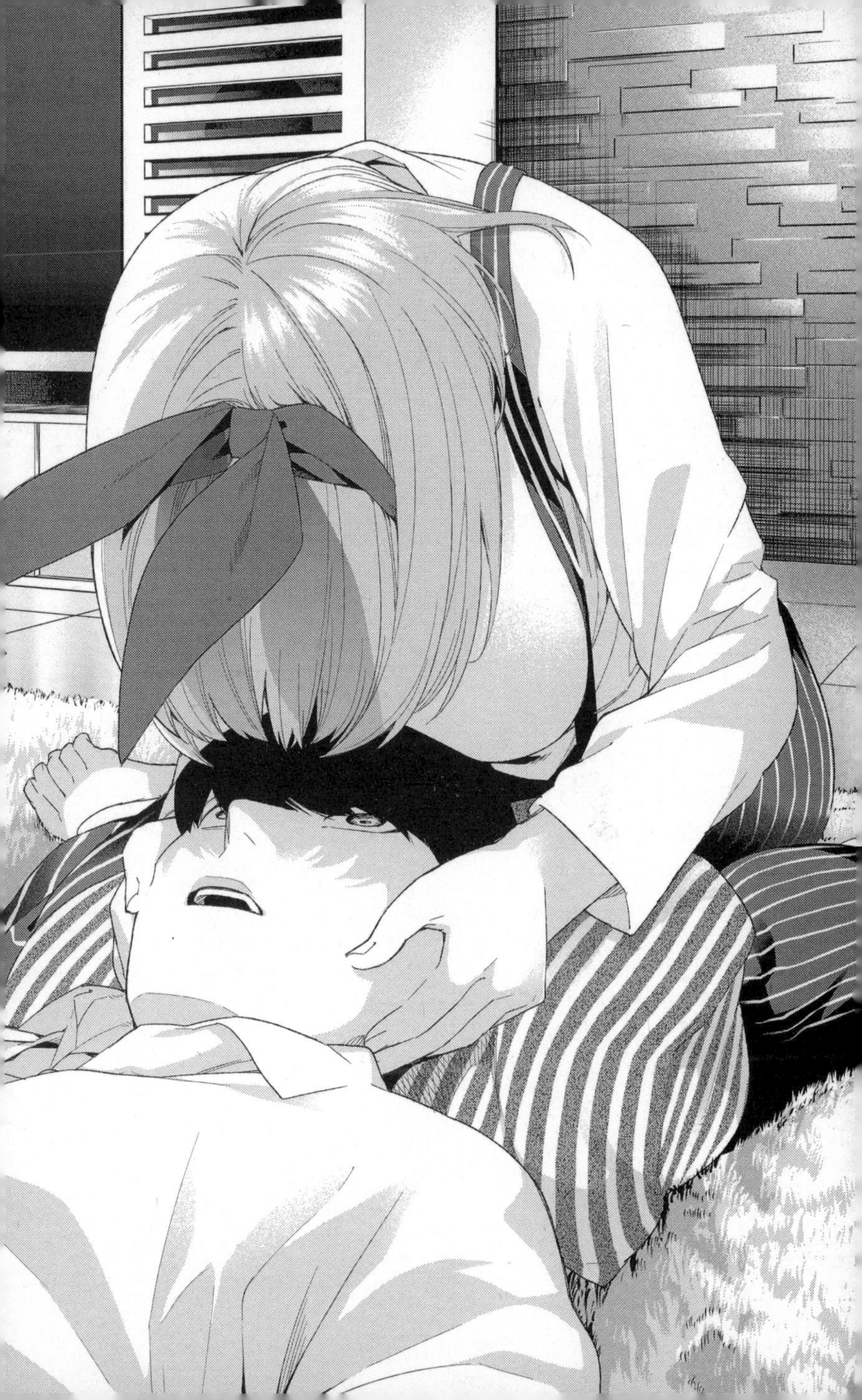

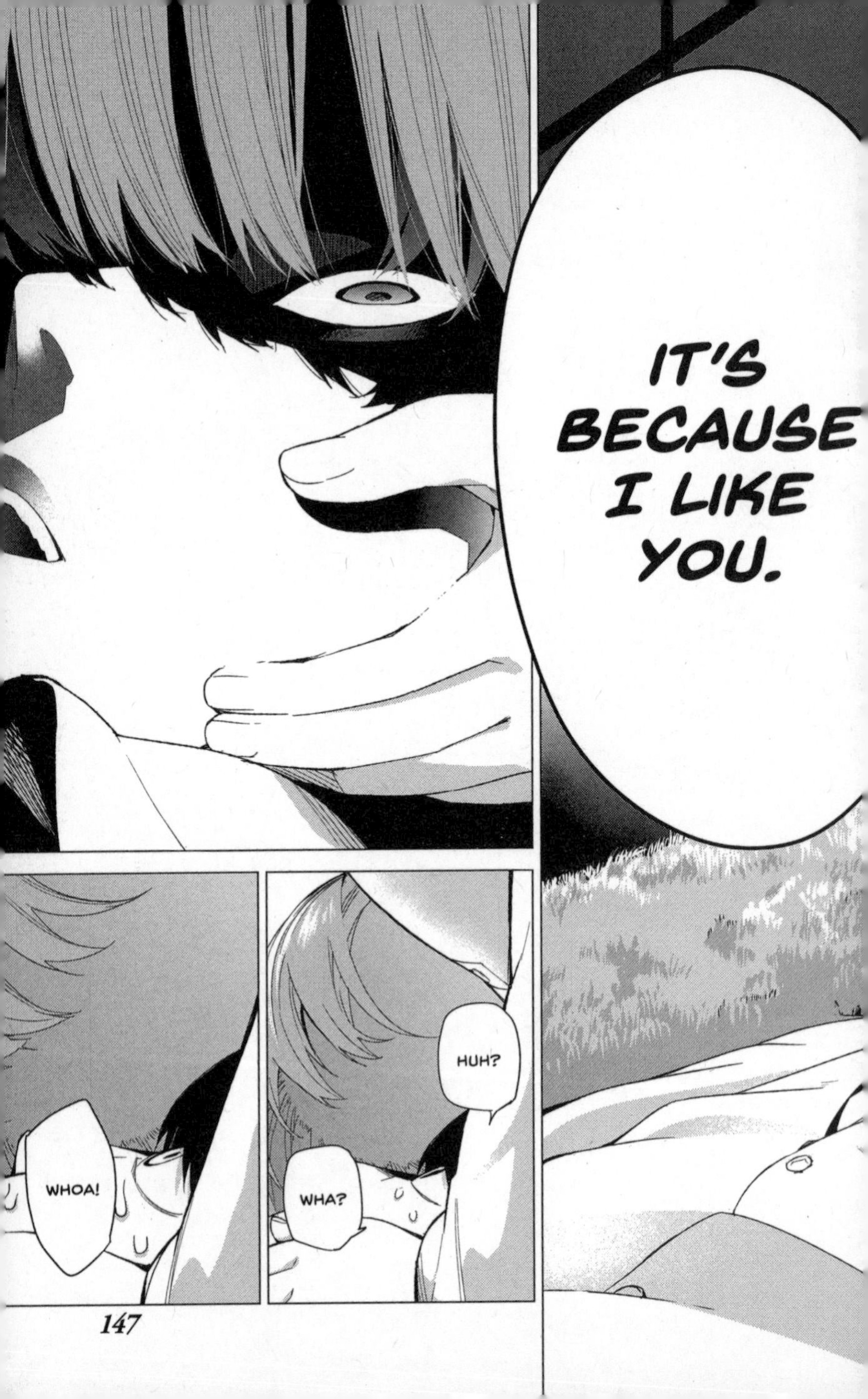

IT'S BECAUSE I LIKE YOU.
HUH?
WHA?
WHOA!

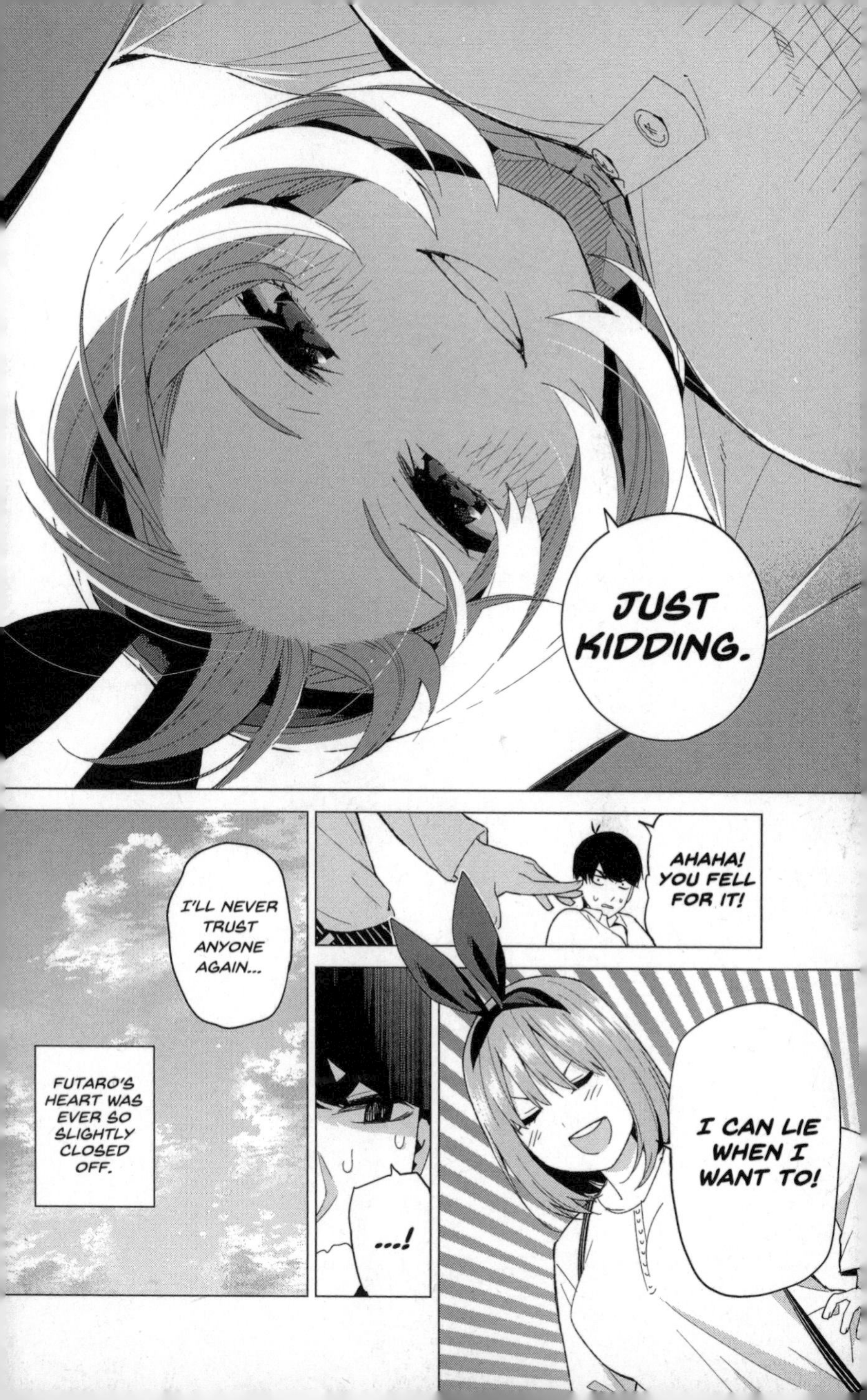
JUST KIDDING.
AHAHA! YOU FELL FOR IT!
I CAN LIE WHEN I WANT TO!
...!
I'LL NEVER TRUST ANYONE AGAIN...
FUTARO'S HEART WAS EVER SO SLIGHTLY CLOSED OFF.

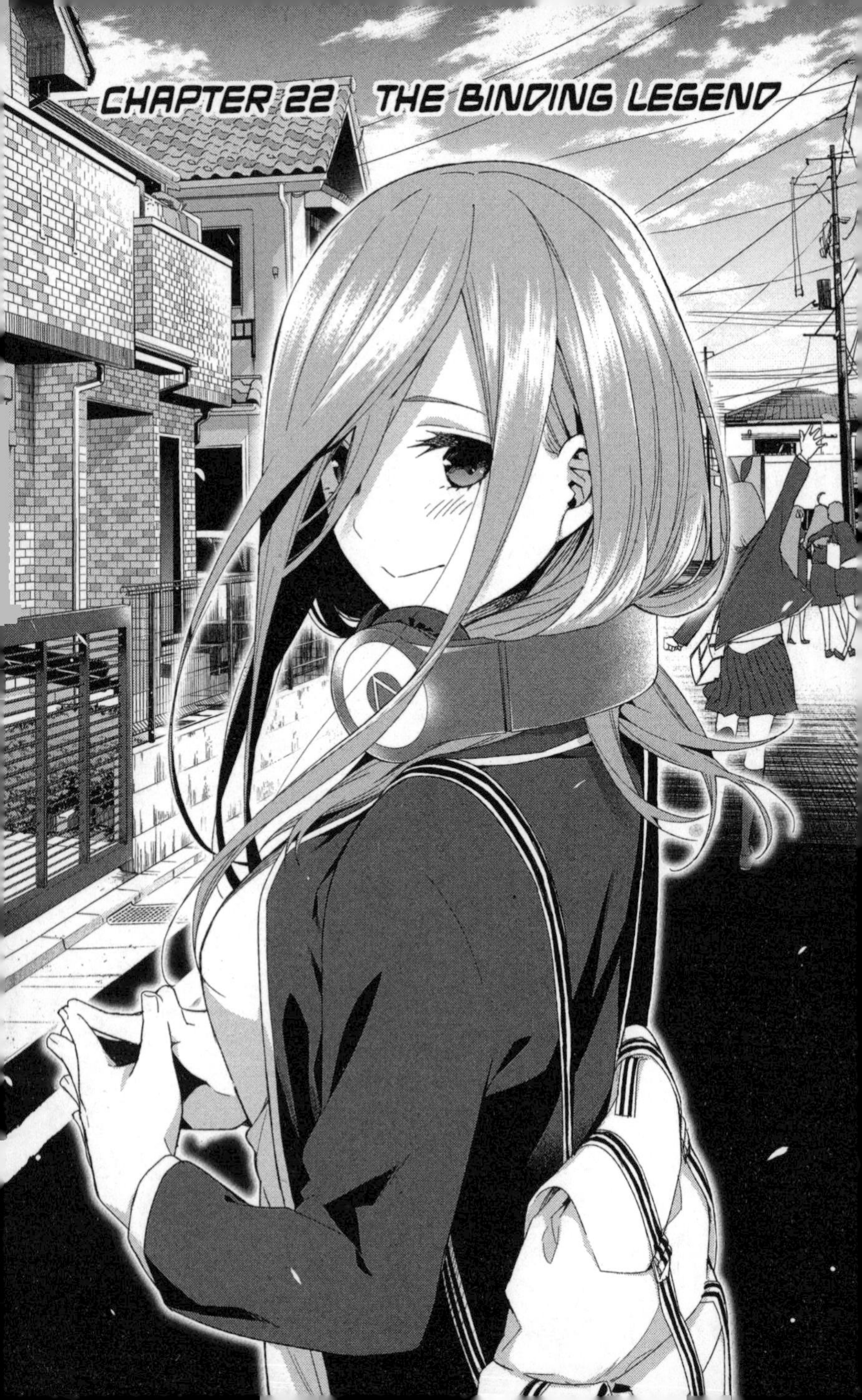
CHAPTER 22 THE BINDING LEGEND

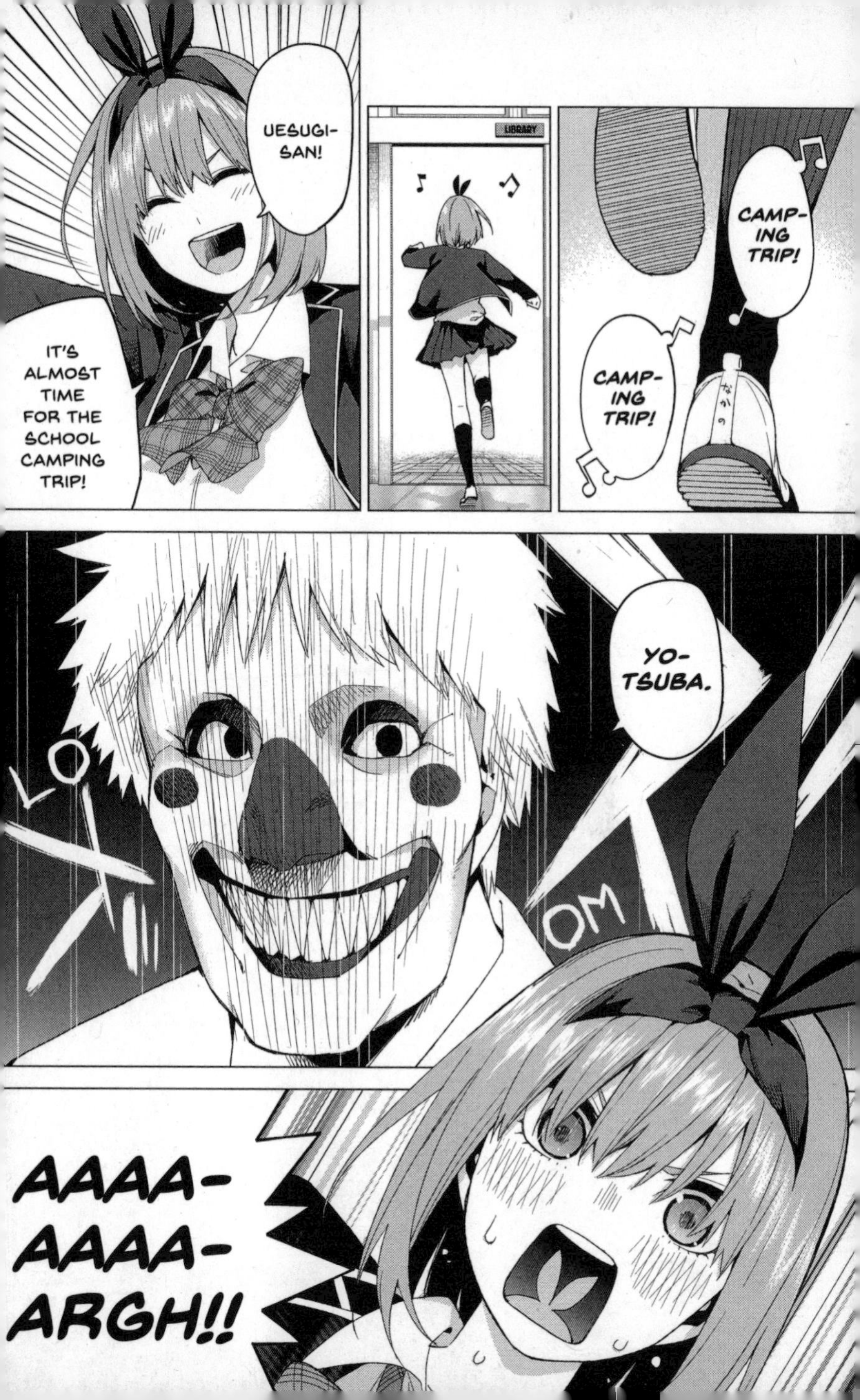
CAMP-ING TRIP!
CAMP-ING TRIP!
なかの
LIBRARY
UESUGI-SAN!
IT'S ALMOST TIME FOR THE SCHOOL CAMPING TRIP!
YO-TSUBA.
LOOM
AAAA-AAAA-ARGH!!

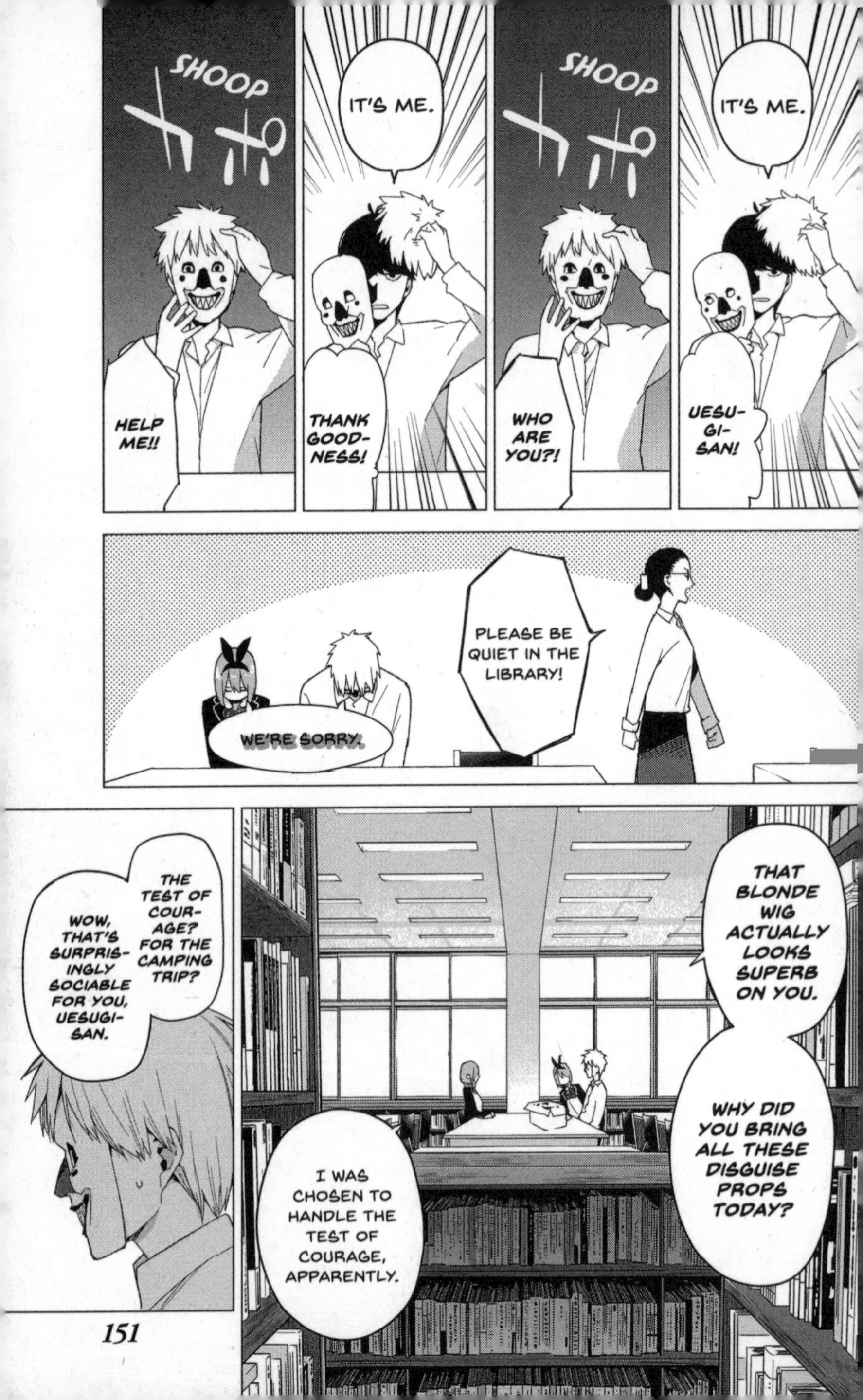
IT'S ME.
UESUGI-SAN!
SHOOP
WHO ARE YOU?!
IT'S ME.
THANK GOODNESS!
SHOOP
HELP ME!!
PLEASE BE QUIET IN THE LIBRARY!
WE'RE SORRY.
THAT BLONDE WIG ACTUALLY LOOKS SUPERB ON YOU.
WHY DID YOU BRING ALL THESE DISGUISE PROPS TODAY?
I WAS CHOSEN TO HANDLE THE TEST OF COURAGE, APPARENTLY.
THE TEST OF COURAGE? FOR THE CAMPING TRIP?
WOW, THAT'S SURPRISINGLY SOCIABLE FOR YOU, UESUGI-SAN.

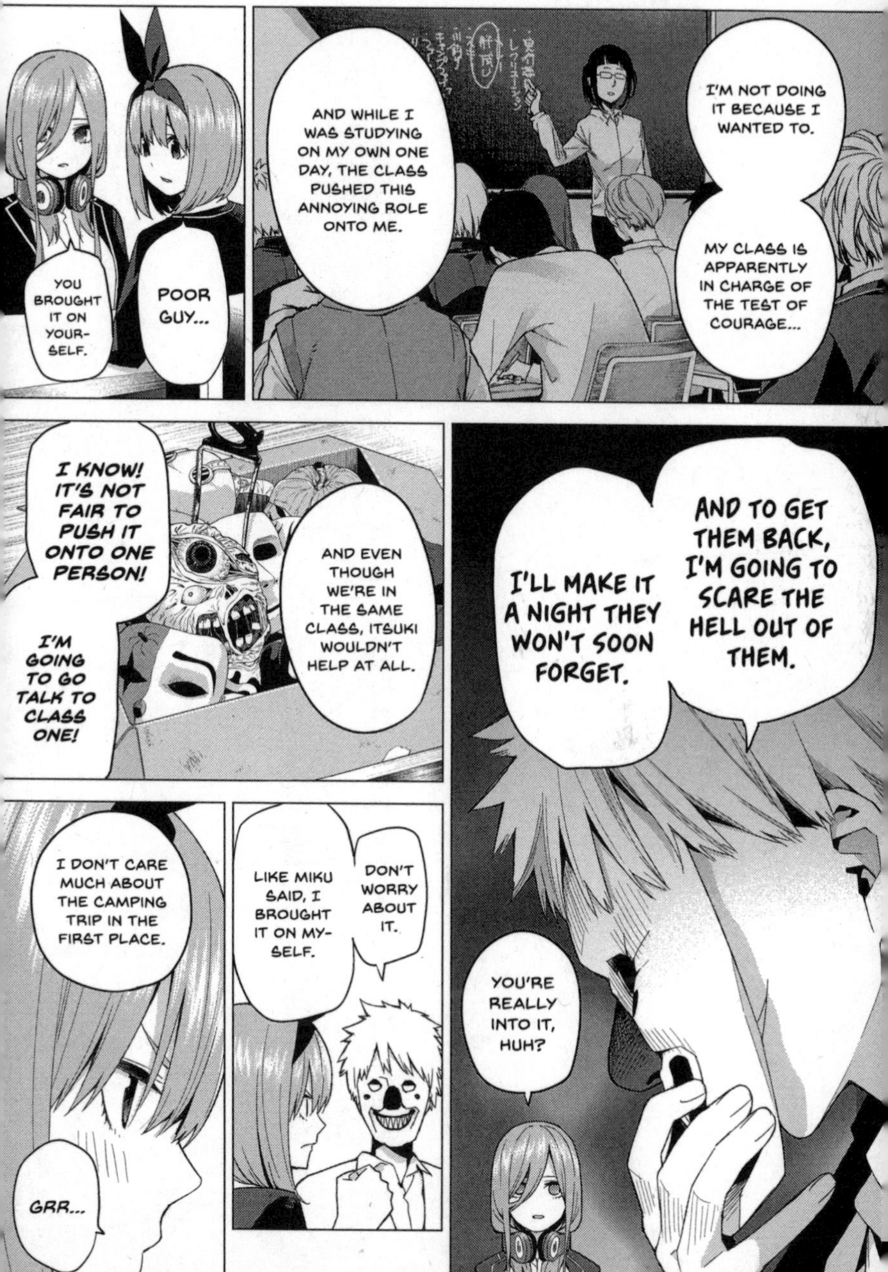
I'M NOT DOING IT BECAUSE I WANTED TO.
MY CLASS IS APPARENTLY IN CHARGE OF THE TEST OF COURAGE...
AND WHILE I WAS STUDYING ON MY OWN ONE DAY, THE CLASS PUSHED THIS ANNOYING ROLE ONTO ME.
POOR GUY...
YOU BROUGHT IT ON YOUR-SELF.
AND TO GET THEM BACK, I'M GOING TO SCARE THE HELL OUT OF THEM.
I'LL MAKE IT A NIGHT THEY WON'T SOON FORGET.
YOU'RE REALLY INTO IT, HUH?
AND EVEN THOUGH WE'RE IN THE SAME CLASS, ITSUKI WOULDN'T HELP AT ALL.
I KNOW! IT'S NOT FAIR TO PUSH IT ONTO ONE PERSON!
I'M GOING TO GO TALK TO CLASS ONE!
DON'T WORRY ABOUT IT.
LIKE MIKU SAID, I BROUGHT IT ON MY-SELF.
I DON'T CARE MUCH ABOUT THE CAMPING TRIP IN THE FIRST PLACE.
GRR...

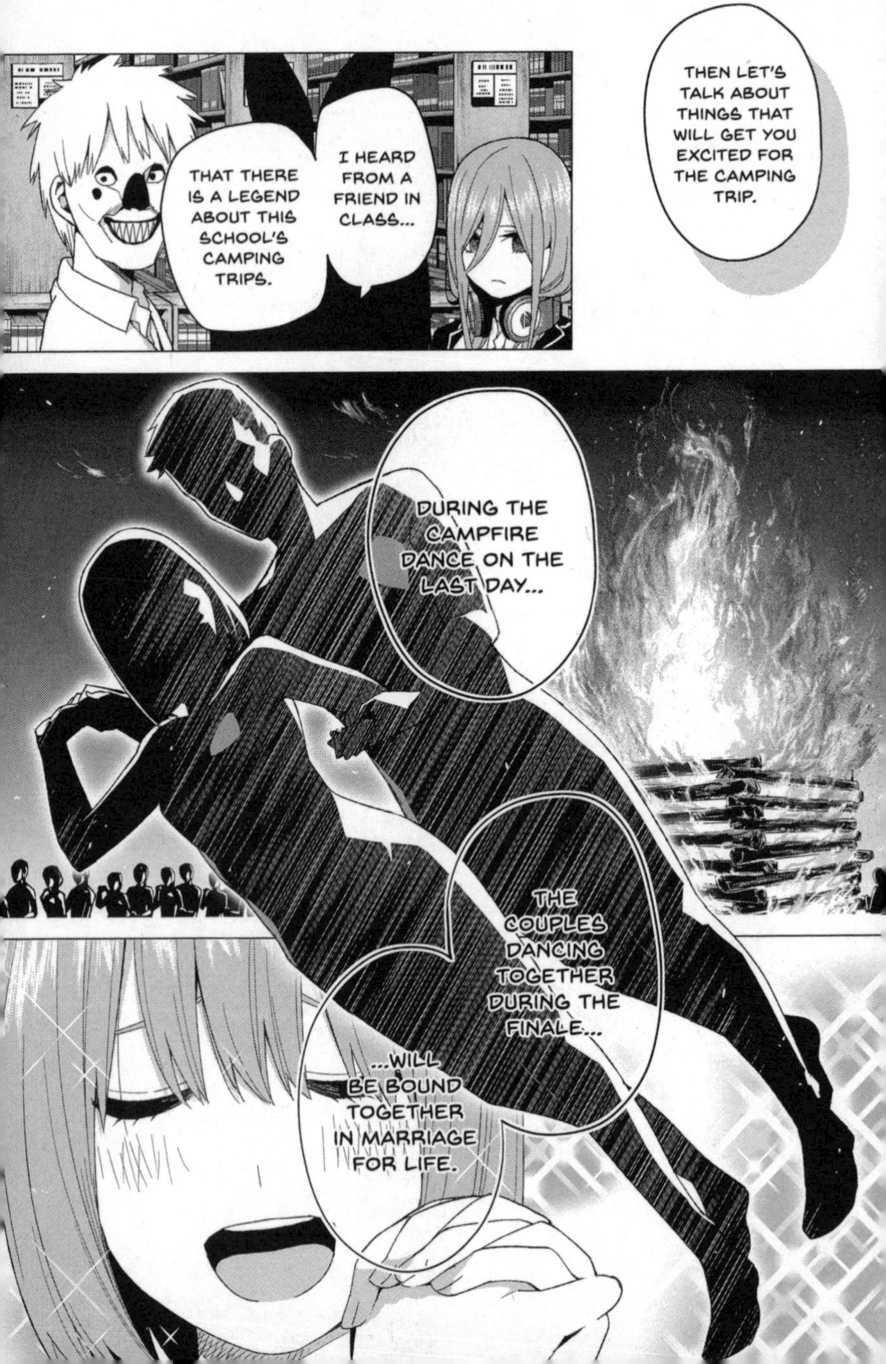
THEN LET'S TALK ABOUT THINGS THAT WILL GET YOU EXCITED FOR THE CAMPING TRIP.
I HEARD FROM A FRIEND IN CLASS...
THAT THERE IS A LEGEND ABOUT THIS SCHOOL'S CAMPING TRIPS.
DURING THE CAMPFIRE DANCE ON THE LAST DAY...
THE COUPLES DANCING TOGETHER DURING THE FINALE...
...WILL BE BOUND TOGETHER IN MARRIAGE FOR LIFE.

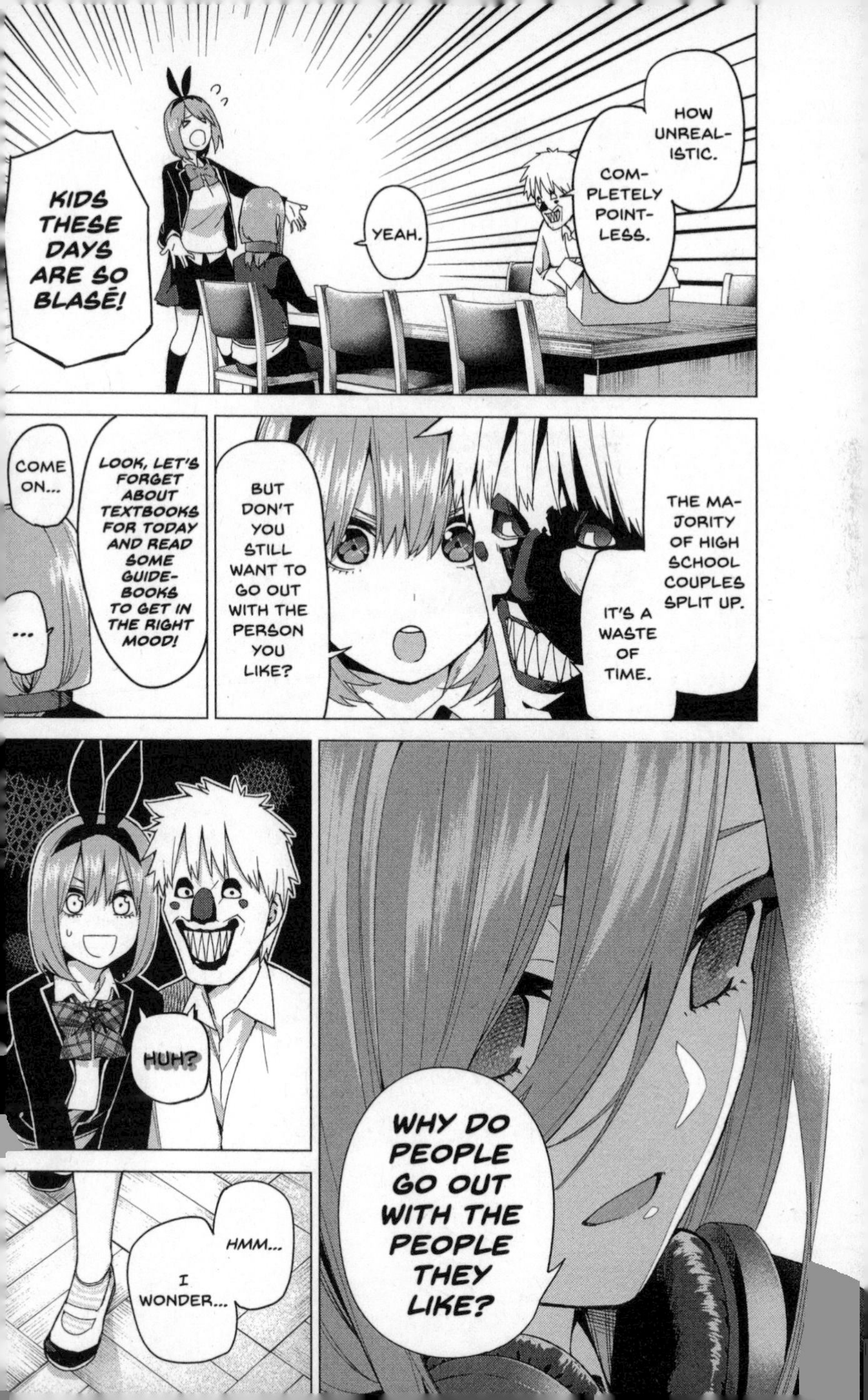
HOW UNREALISTIC.
COMPLETELY POINTLESS.
YEAH.
KIDS THESE DAYS ARE SO BLASÉ!
THE MAJORITY OF HIGH SCHOOL COUPLES SPLIT UP.
IT'S A WASTE OF TIME.
BUT DON'T YOU STILL WANT TO GO OUT WITH THE PERSON YOU LIKE?
LOOK, LET'S FORGET ABOUT TEXTBOOKS FOR TODAY AND READ SOME GUIDEBOOKS TO GET IN THE RIGHT MOOD!
COME ON...
...
WHY DO PEOPLE GO OUT WITH THE PEOPLE THEY LIKE?
HUH?
HMM... I WONDER...

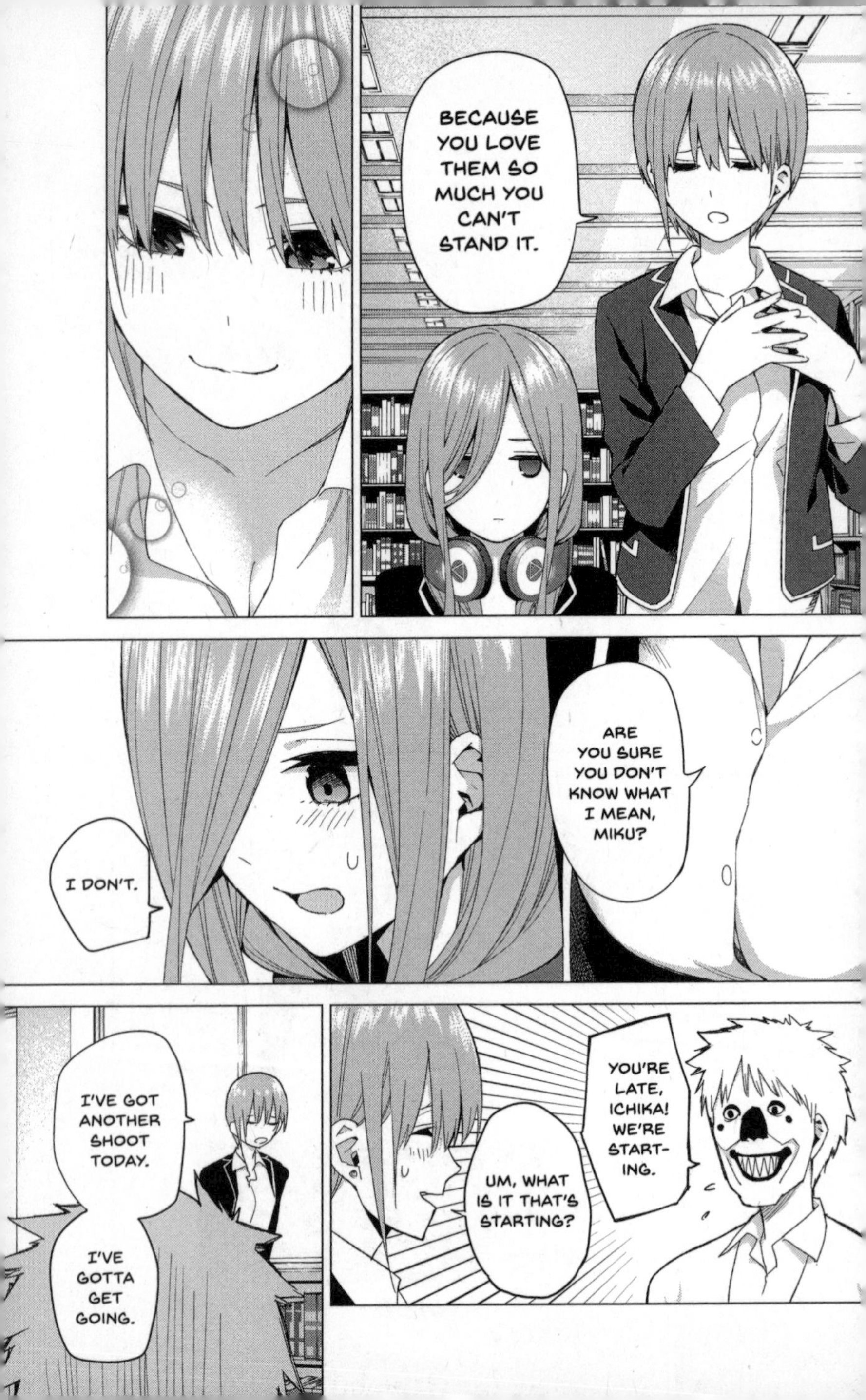
BECAUSE YOU LOVE THEM SO MUCH YOU CAN'T STAND IT.
ARE YOU SURE YOU DON'T KNOW WHAT I MEAN, MIKU?
I DON'T.
YOU'RE LATE, ICHIKA! WE'RE START-ING.
UM, WHAT IS IT THAT'S STARTING?
I'VE GOT ANOTHER SHOOT TODAY.
I'VE GOTTA GET GOING.

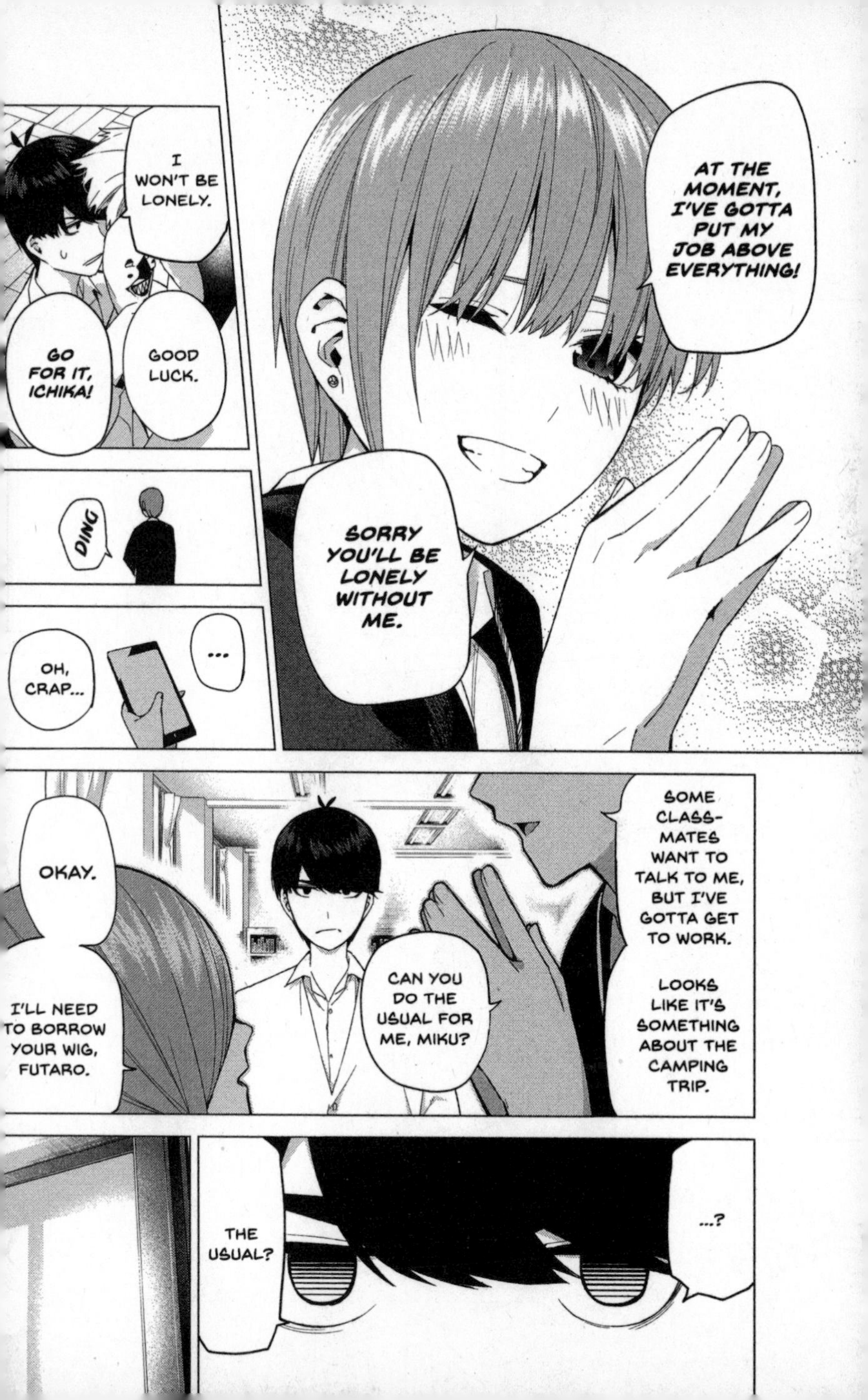
AT THE MOMENT, I'VE GOTTA PUT MY JOB ABOVE EVERYTHING!
SORRY YOU'LL BE LONELY WITHOUT ME.
I WON'T BE LONELY.
GOOD LUCK.
GO FOR IT, ICHIKA!
DING
...
OH, CRAP...
SOME CLASS-MATES WANT TO TALK TO ME, BUT I'VE GOTTA GET TO WORK.
LOOKS LIKE IT'S SOMETHING ABOUT THE CAMPING TRIP.
CAN YOU DO THE USUAL FOR ME, MIKU?
OKAY.
I'LL NEED TO BORROW YOUR WIG, FUTARO.
...?
THE USUAL?

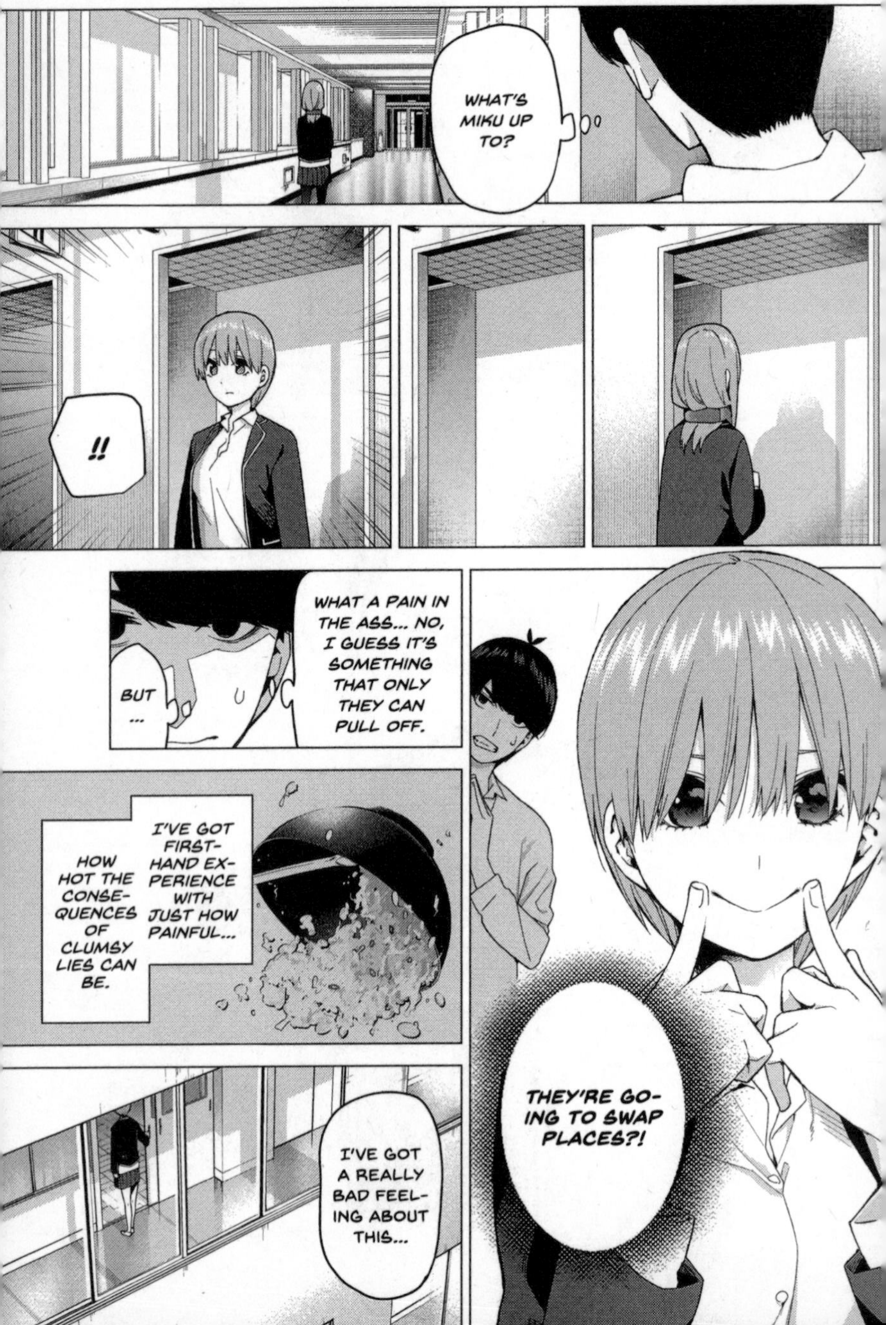
WHAT'S MIKU UP TO?
!!
THEY'RE GO-ING TO SWAP PLACES?!
WHAT A PAIN IN THE ASS... NO, I GUESS IT'S SOMETHING THAT ONLY THEY CAN PULL OFF.
BUT ...
I'VE GOT FIRST-HAND EX-PERIENCE WITH JUST HOW PAINFUL...
HOW HOT THE CONSE-QUENCES OF CLUMSY LIES CAN BE.
I'VE GOT A REALLY BAD FEEL-ING ABOUT THIS...

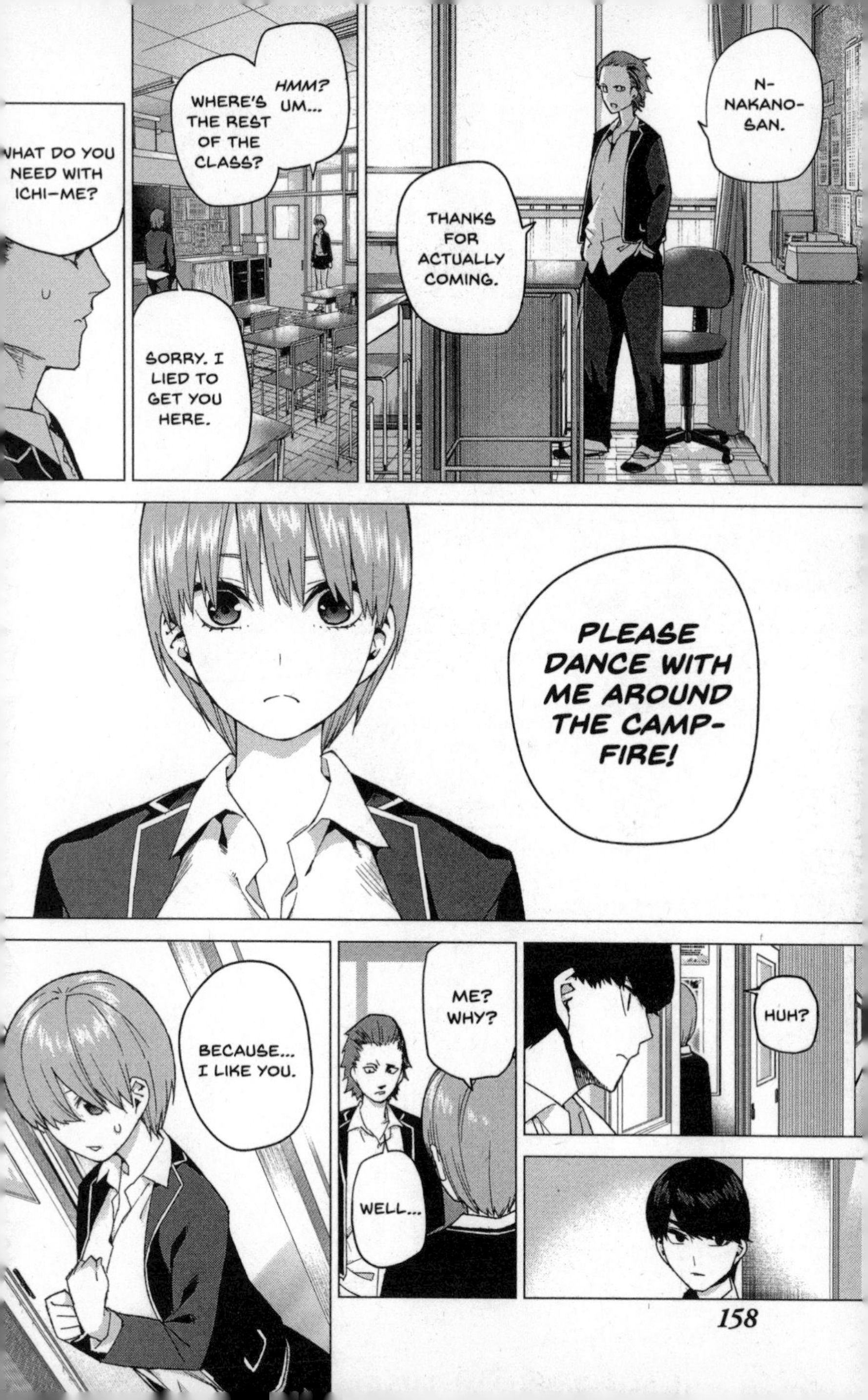
N-NAKANO-SAN.
THANKS FOR ACTUALLY COMING.
HMM? UM...
WHERE'S THE REST OF THE CLASS?
SORRY. I LIED TO GET YOU HERE.
WHAT DO YOU NEED WITH ICHI-ME?
PLEASE DANCE WITH ME AROUND THE CAMP-FIRE!
HUH?
ME? WHY?
WELL...
BECAUSE... I LIKE YOU.

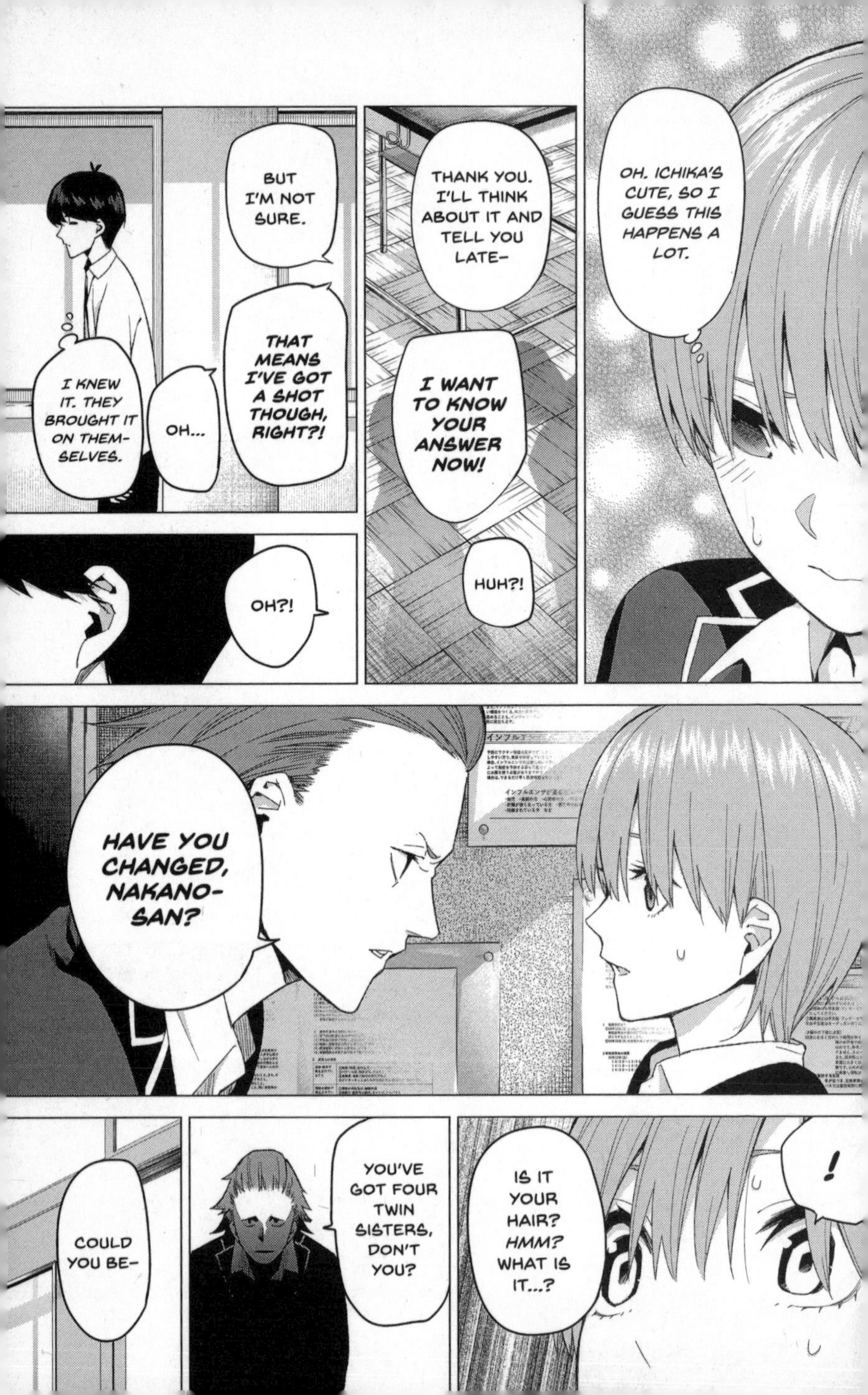
OH. ICHIKA'S CUTE, SO I GUESS THIS HAPPENS A LOT.
THANK YOU. I'LL THINK ABOUT IT AND TELL YOU LATE-
I WANT TO KNOW YOUR ANSWER NOW!
HUH?!
BUT I'M NOT SURE.
THAT MEANS I'VE GOT A SHOT THOUGH, RIGHT?!
OH...
I KNEW IT. THEY BROUGHT IT ON THEM-SELVES.
OH?!
HAVE YOU CHANGED, NAKANO-SAN?
!
IS IT YOUR HAIR? HMM? WHAT IS IT...?
YOU'VE GOT FOUR TWIN SISTERS, DON'T YOU?
COULD YOU BE-

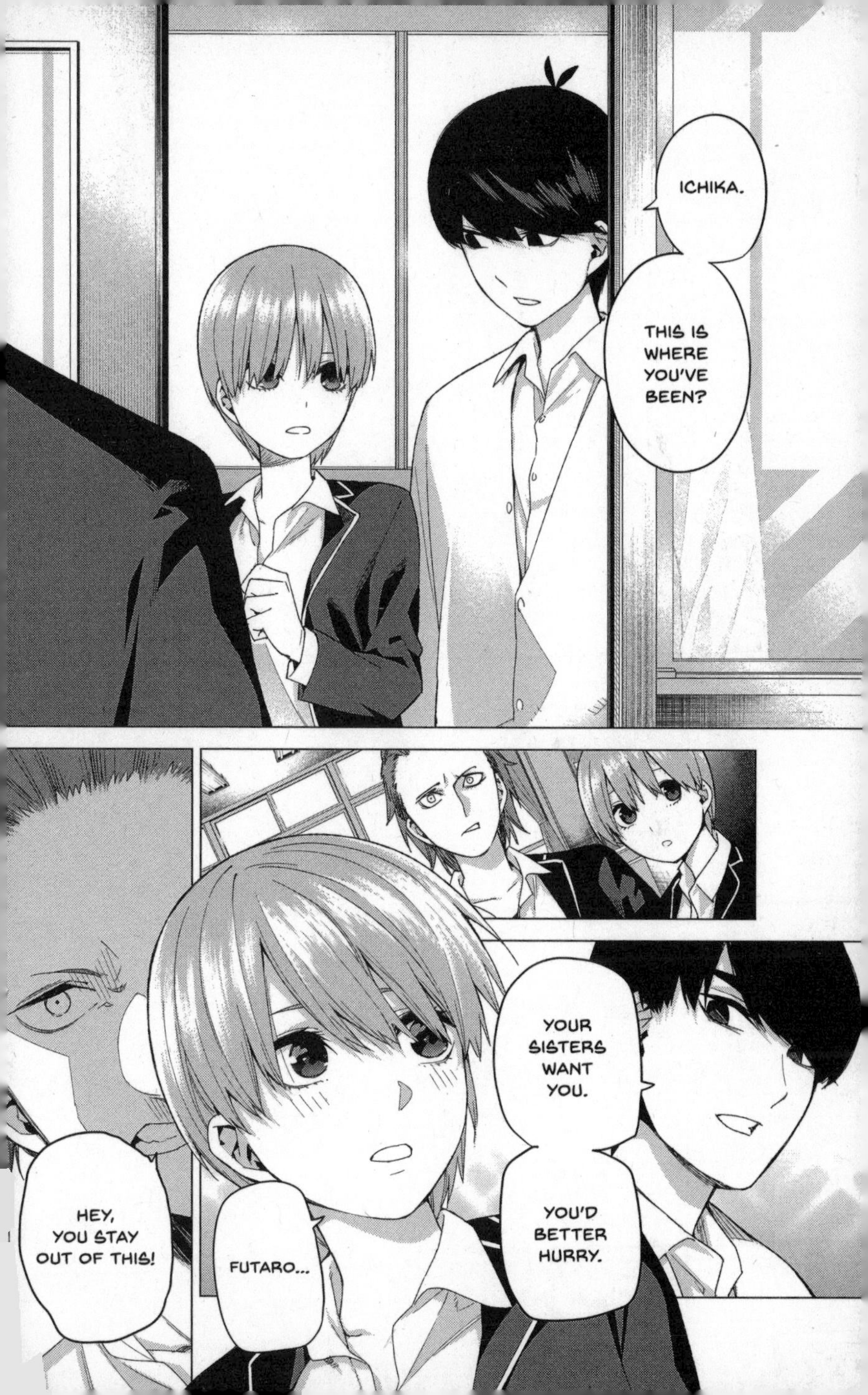
ICHIKA.
THIS IS WHERE YOU'VE BEEN?
YOUR SISTERS WANT YOU.
YOU'D BETTER HURRY.
FUTARO...
HEY, YOU STAY OUT OF THIS!

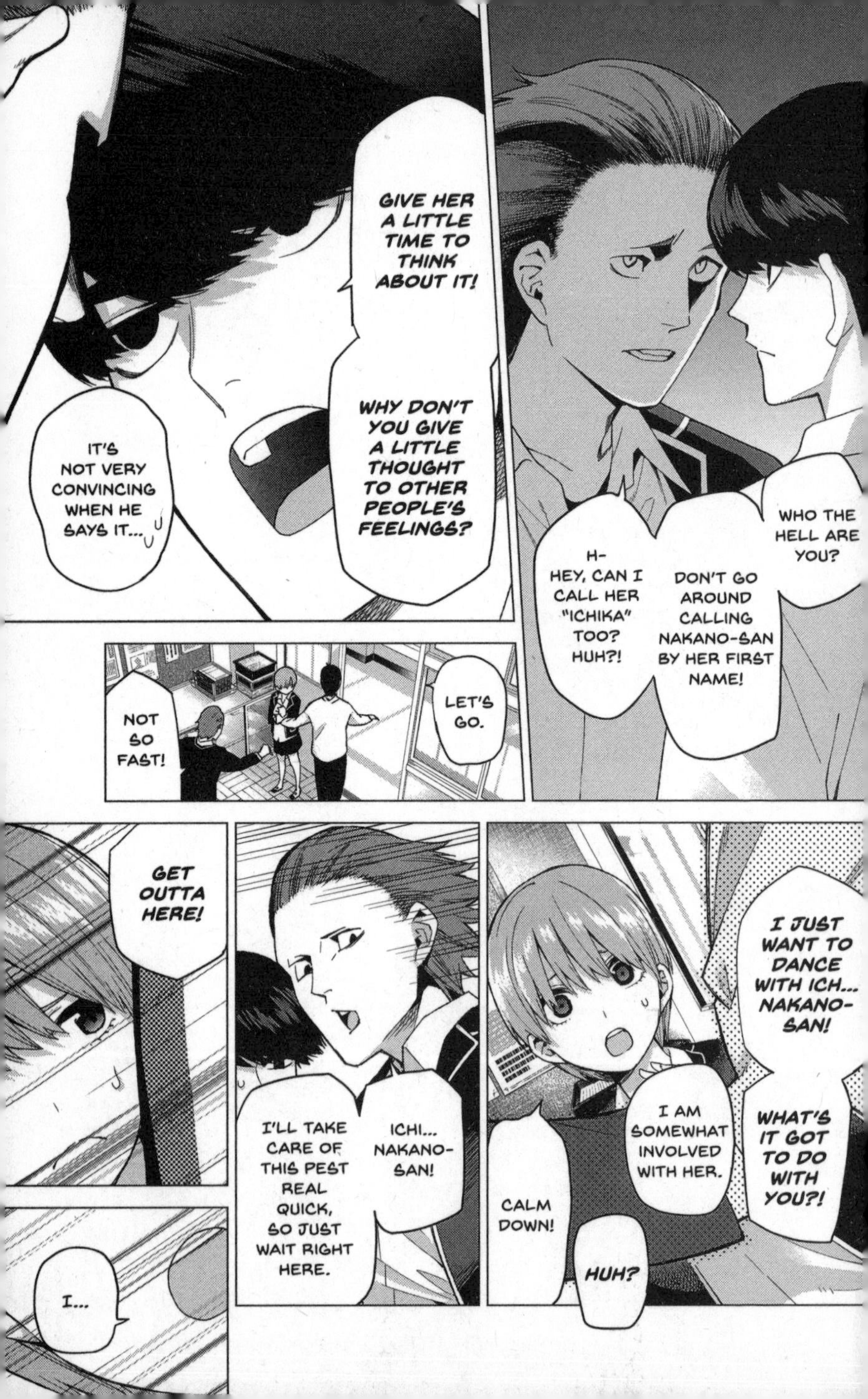
WHO THE HELL ARE YOU?
DON'T GO AROUND CALLING NAKANO-SAN BY HER FIRST NAME!
H- HEY, CAN I CALL HER "ICHIKA" TOO? HUH?!
GIVE HER A LITTLE TIME TO THINK ABOUT IT!
WHY DON'T YOU GIVE A LITTLE THOUGHT TO OTHER PEOPLE'S FEELINGS?
IT'S NOT VERY CONVINCING WHEN HE SAYS IT...
LET'S GO.
NOT SO FAST!
I JUST WANT TO DANCE WITH ICH... NAKANO-SAN!
WHAT'S IT GOT TO DO WITH YOU?!
I AM SOMEWHAT INVOLVED WITH HER.
CALM DOWN!
HUH?
ICHI... NAKANO-SAN!
I'LL TAKE CARE OF THIS PEST REAL QUICK, SO JUST WAIT RIGHT HERE.
GET OUTTA HERE!
I...

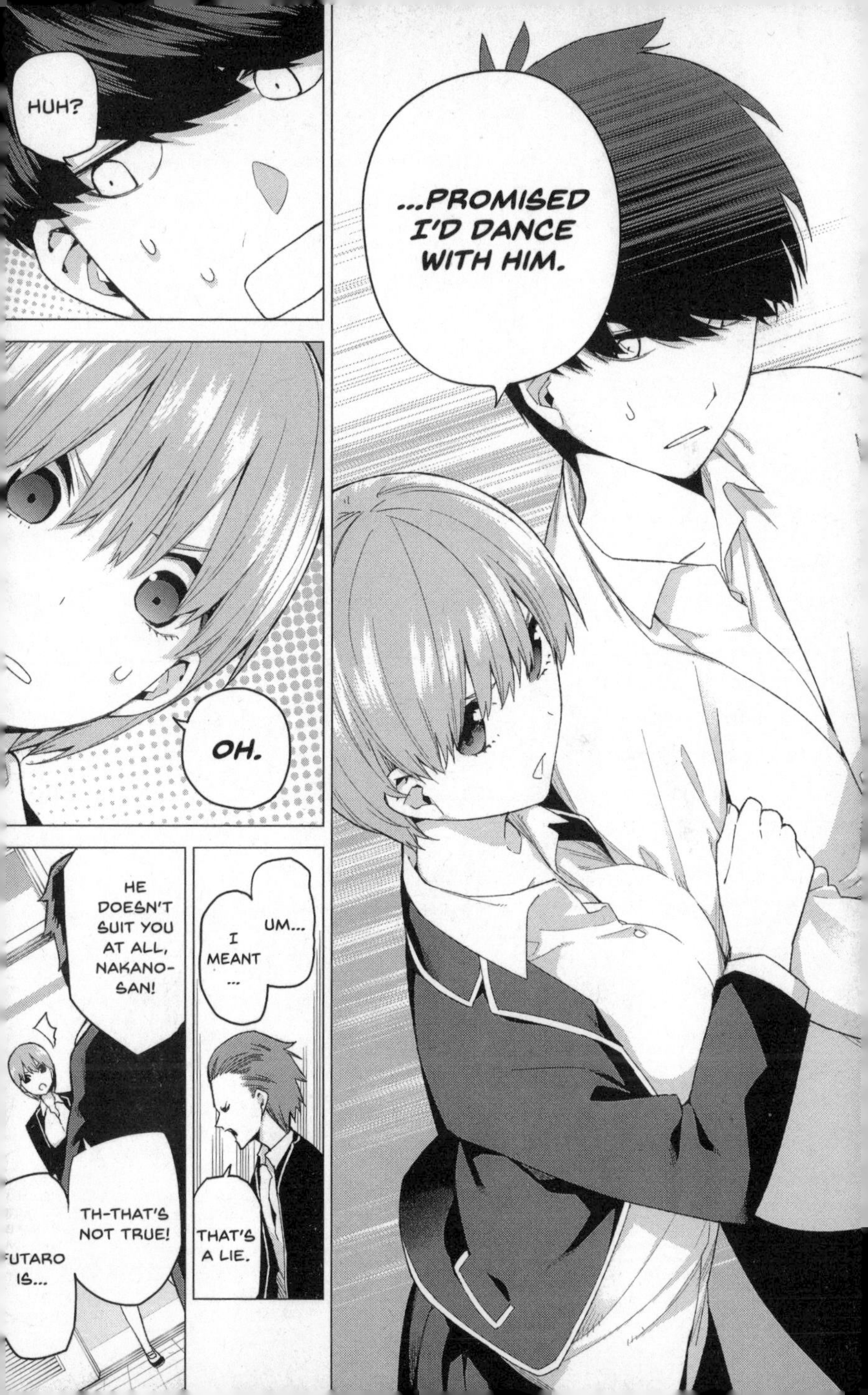
...PROMISED I'D DANCE WITH HIM.
HUH?
OH.
UM... I MEANT ...
THAT'S A LIE.
HE DOESN'T SUIT YOU AT ALL, NAKANO-SAN!
TH-THAT'S NOT TRUE!
FUTARO IS...

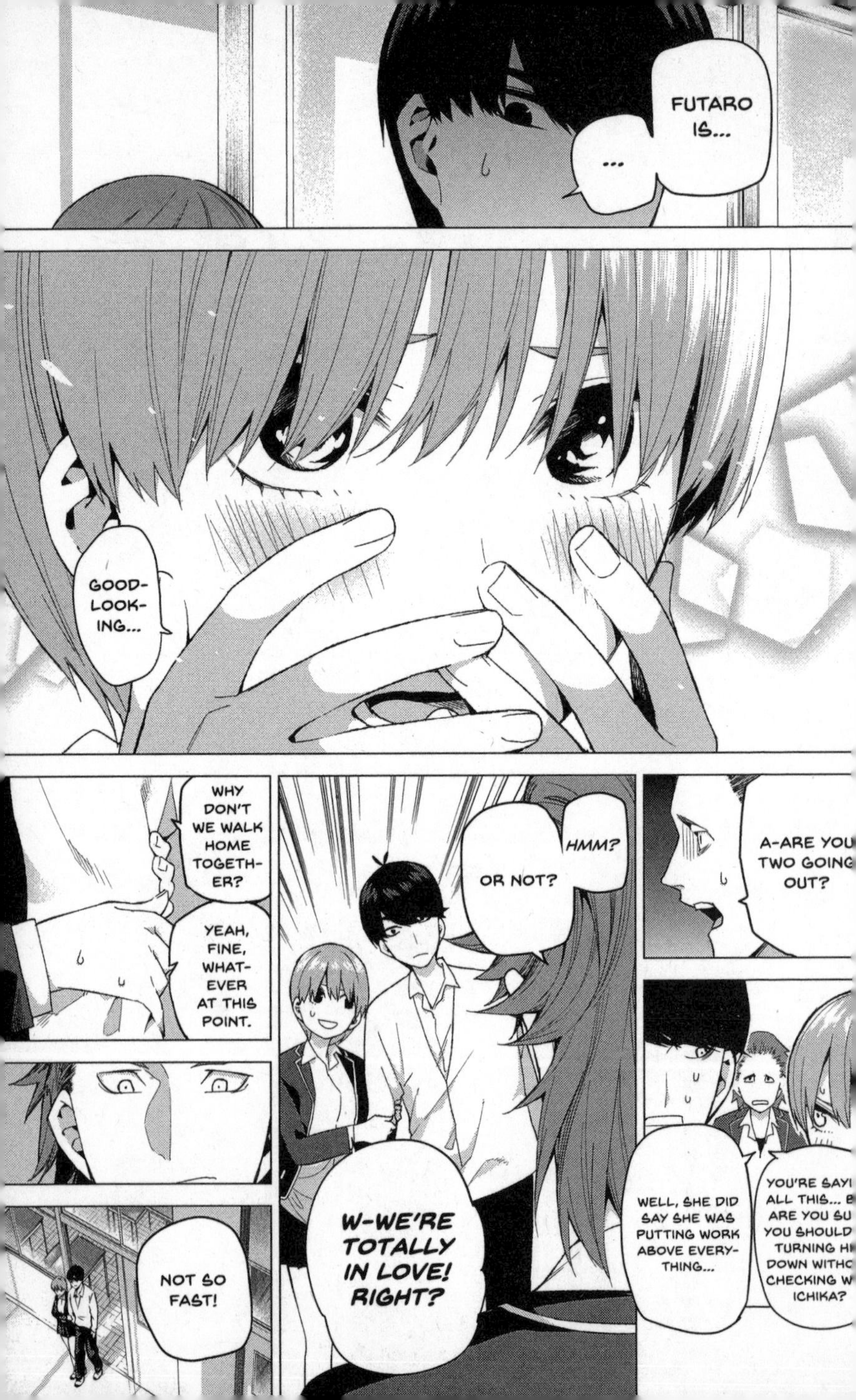
FUTARO IS...
...
GOOD-LOOKING...
A-ARE YOU TWO GOING OUT?
YOU'RE SAYI ALL THIS... B ARE YOU SU YOU SHOULD TURNING HI DOWN WITHO CHECKING W ICHIKA?
WELL, SHE DID SAY SHE WAS PUTTING WORK ABOVE EVERYTHING...
HMM?
OR NOT?
W-WE'RE TOTALLY IN LOVE! RIGHT?
WHY DON'T WE WALK HOME TOGETHER?
YEAH, FINE, WHATEVER AT THIS POINT.
NOT SO FAST!

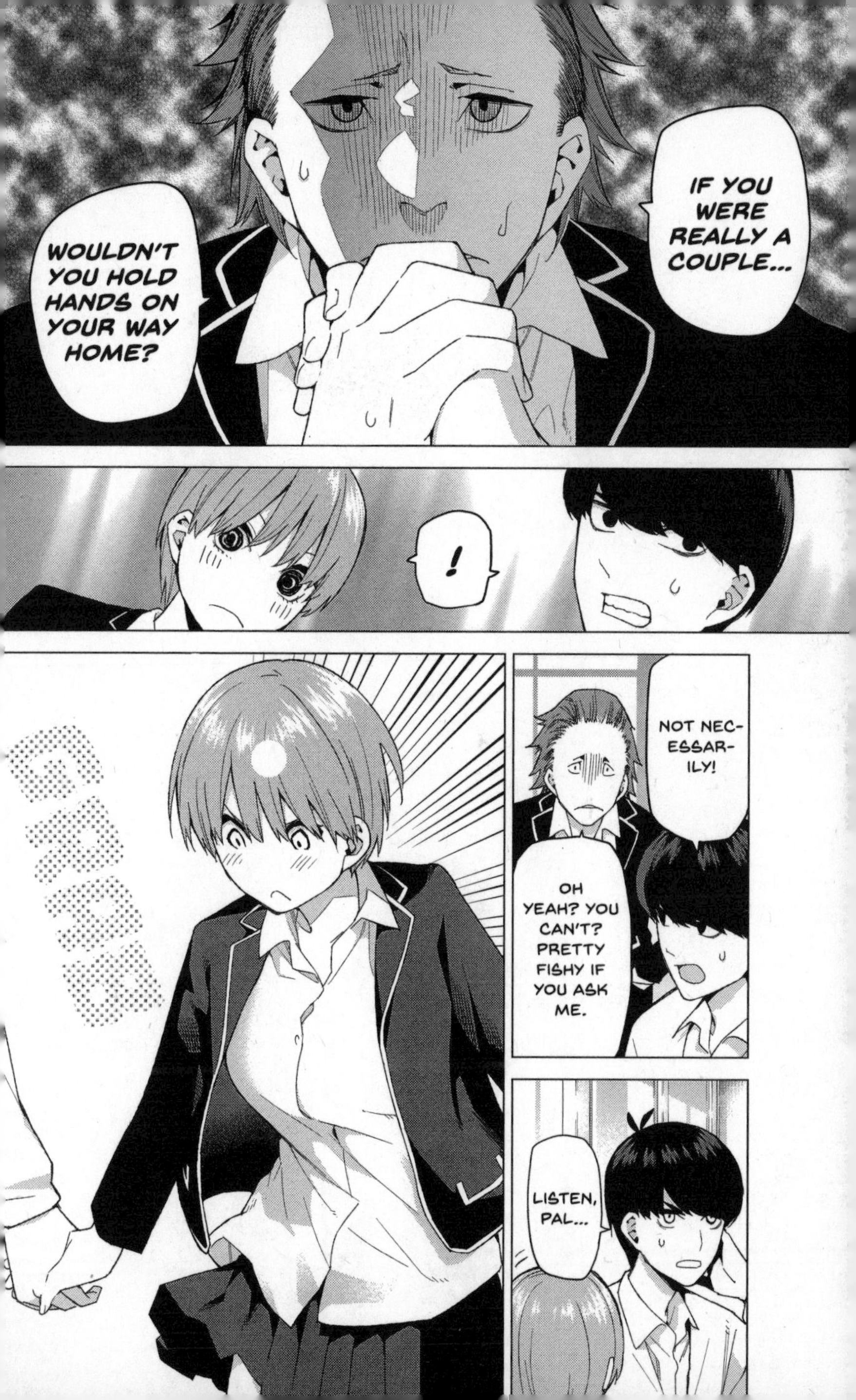
IF YOU WERE REALLY A COUPLE...
WOULDN'T YOU HOLD HANDS ON YOUR WAY HOME?
!
NOT NEC-ESSAR-ILY!
OH YEAH? YOU CAN'T? PRETTY FISHY IF YOU ASK ME.
LISTEN, PAL...

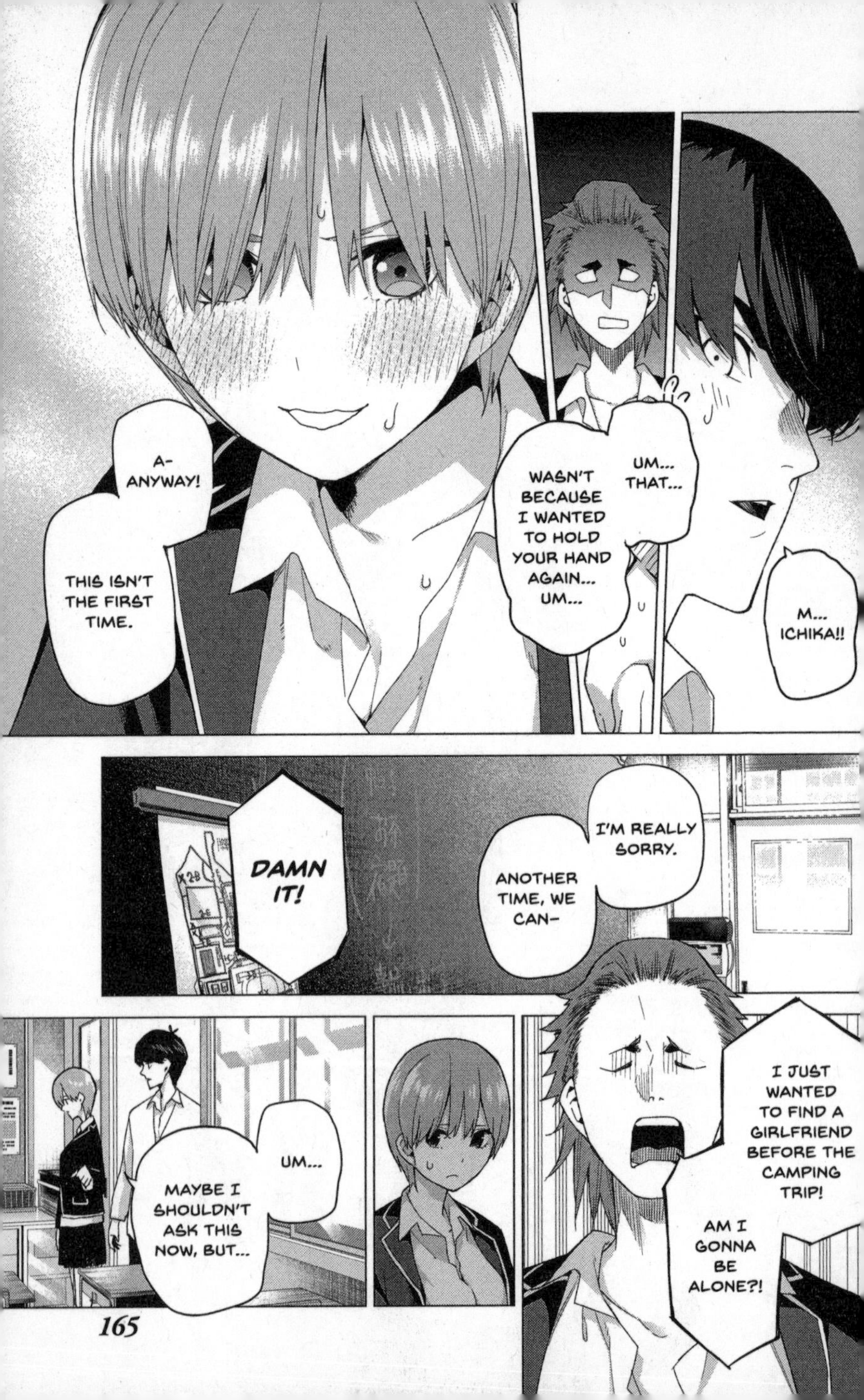
M... ICHIKA!!
UM... THAT...
WASN'T BECAUSE I WANTED TO HOLD YOUR HAND AGAIN... UM...
A- ANYWAY!
THIS ISN'T THE FIRST TIME.
I'M REALLY SORRY.
ANOTHER TIME, WE CAN-
DAMN IT!
I JUST WANTED TO FIND A GIRLFRIEND BEFORE THE CAMPING TRIP!
AM I GONNA BE ALONE?!
UM...
MAYBE I SHOULDN'T ASK THIS NOW, BUT...

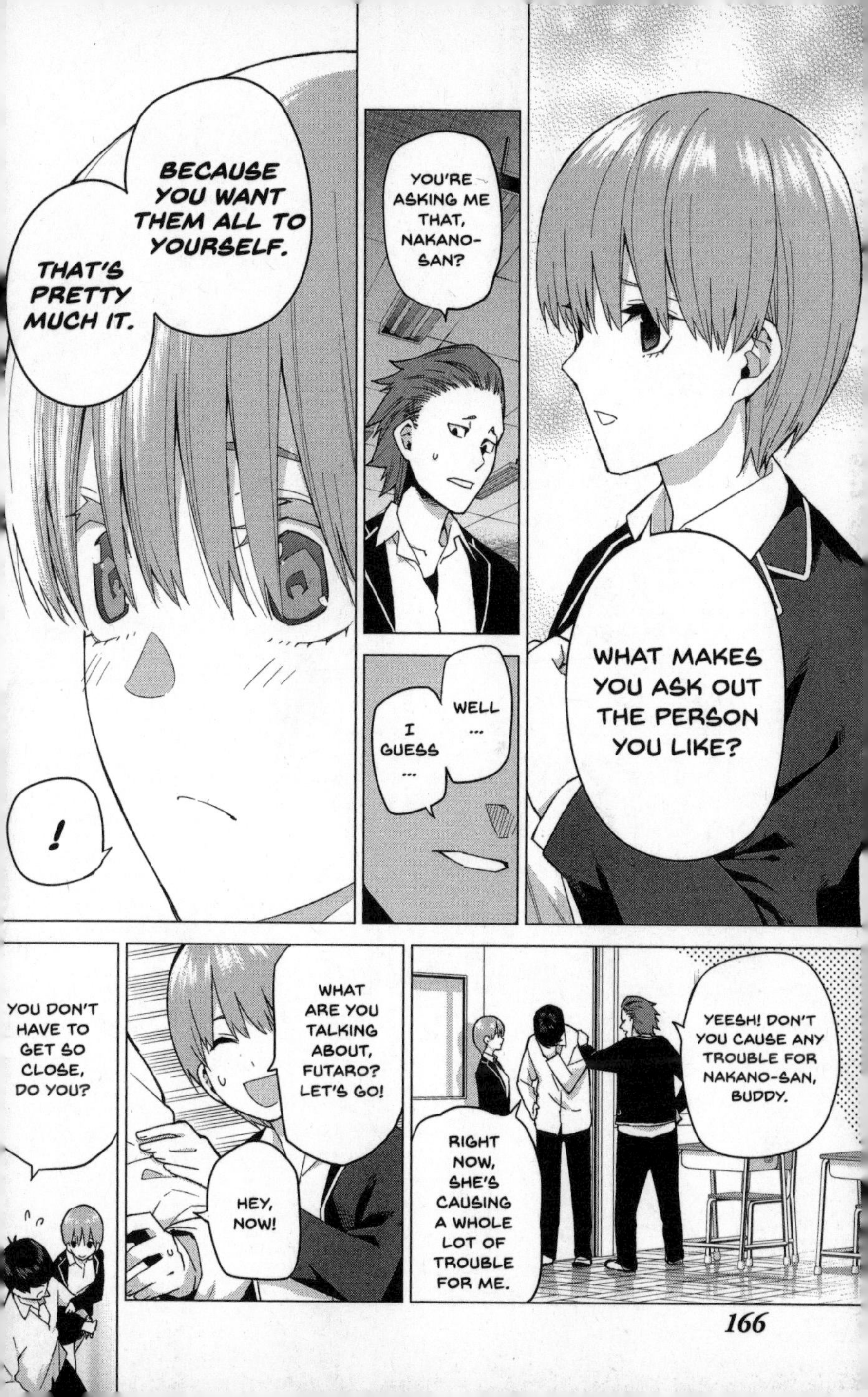
WHAT MAKES YOU ASK OUT THE PERSON YOU LIKE?
YOU'RE ASKING ME THAT, NAKANO-SAN?
WELL... I GUESS...
BECAUSE YOU WANT THEM ALL TO YOURSELF.
THAT'S PRETTY MUCH IT.
!
YEESH! DON'T YOU CAUSE ANY TROUBLE FOR NAKANO-SAN, BUDDY.
RIGHT NOW, SHE'S CAUSING A WHOLE LOT OF TROUBLE FOR ME.
WHAT ARE YOU TALKING ABOUT, FUTARO? LET'S GO!
HEY, NOW!
YOU DON'T HAVE TO GET SO CLOSE, DO YOU?

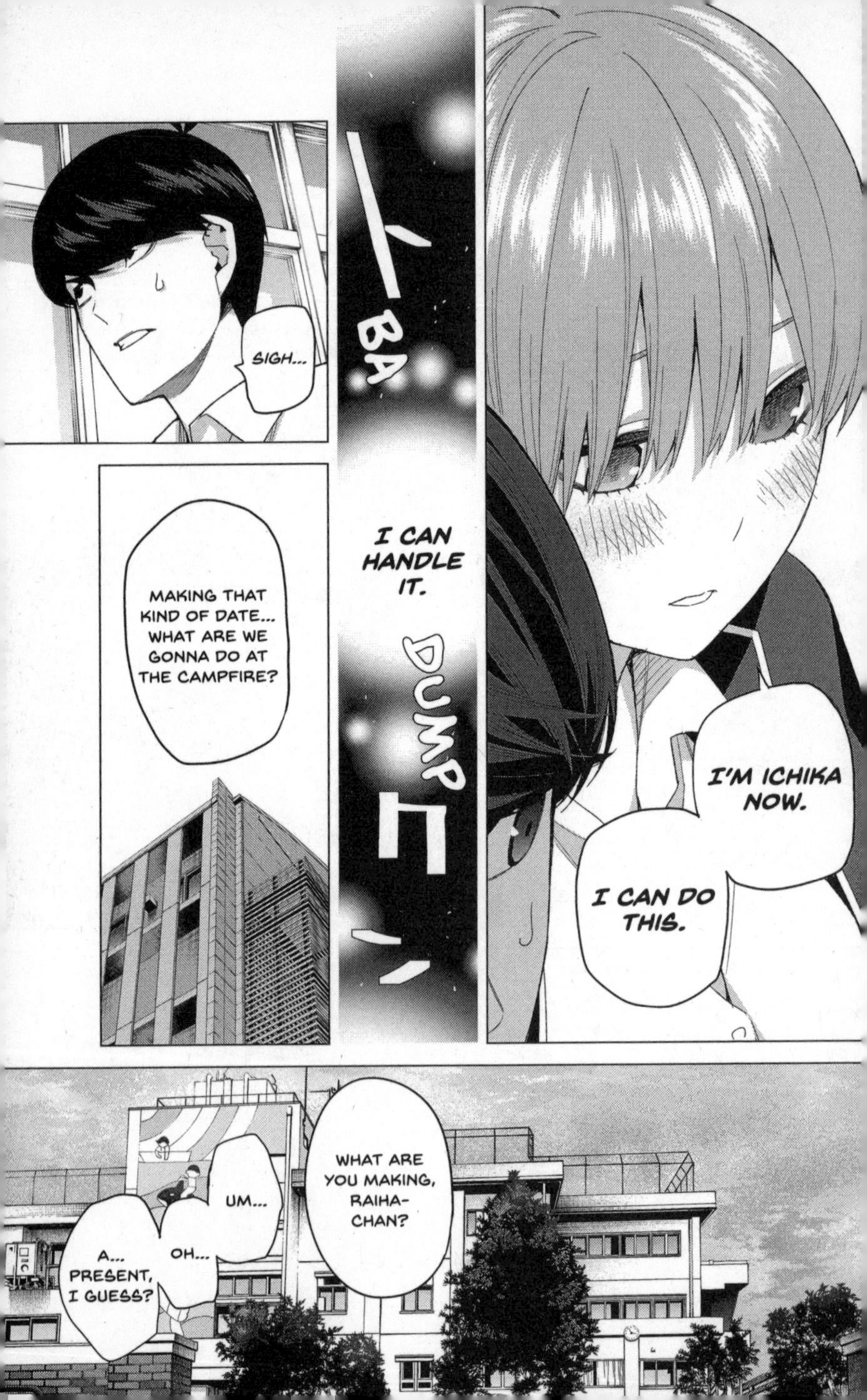
I'M ICHIKA NOW.
I CAN DO THIS.
BA
I CAN HANDLE IT.
DUMP
SIGH...
MAKING THAT KIND OF DATE... WHAT ARE WE GONNA DO AT THE CAMPFIRE?
WHAT ARE YOU MAKING, RAIHA-CHAN?
UM...
OH...
A... PRESENT, I GUESS?

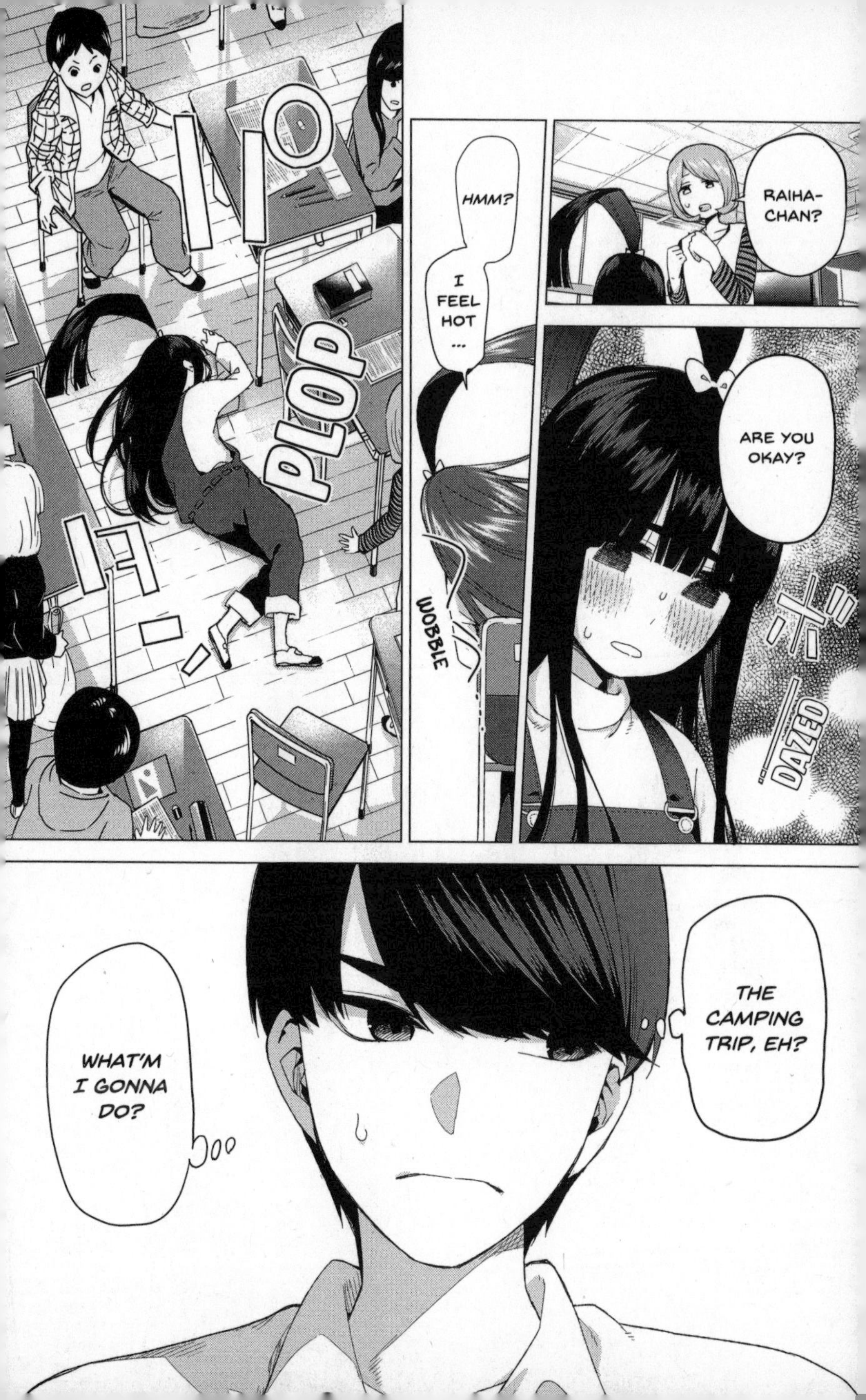
RAIHA-CHAN?
ARE YOU OKAY?
DAZED
HMM?
I FEEL HOT ...
WOBBLE
PLOP
THE CAMPING TRIP, EH?
WHAT'M I GONNA DO?

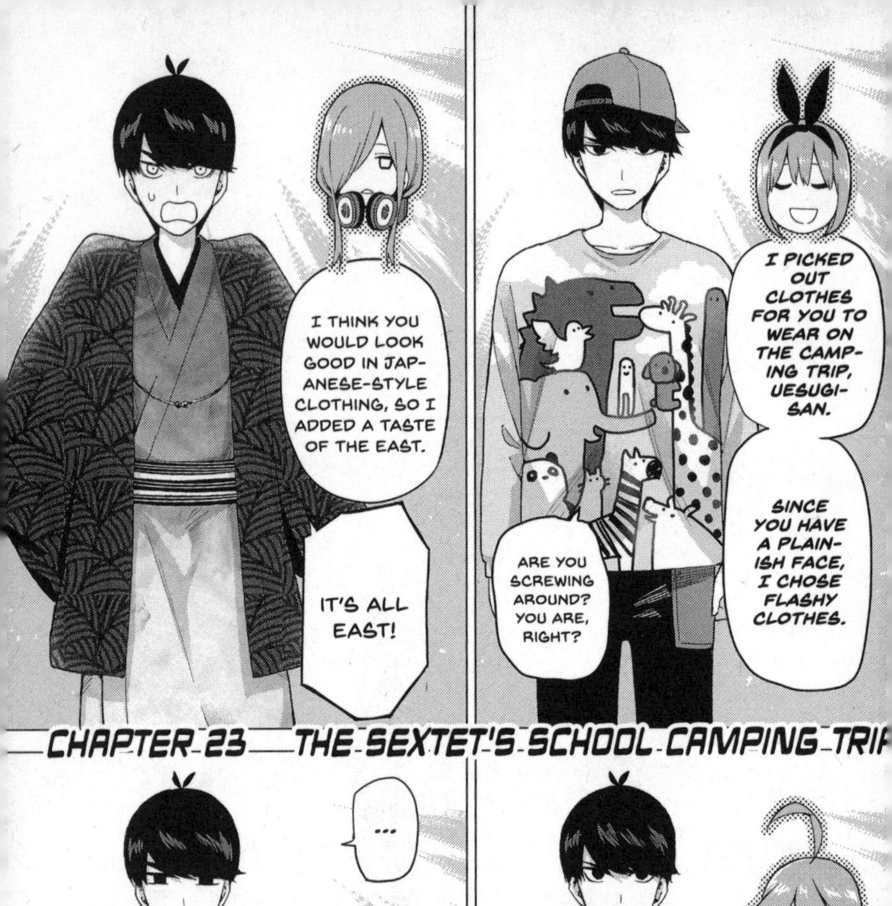
I PICKED OUT CLOTHES FOR YOU TO WEAR ON THE CAMPING TRIP, UESUGI-SAN.
SINCE YOU HAVE A PLAINISH FACE, I CHOSE FLASHY CLOTHES.
ARE YOU SCREWING AROUND? YOU ARE, RIGHT?
I THINK YOU WOULD LOOK GOOD IN JAPANESE-STYLE CLOTHING, SO I ADDED A TASTE OF THE EAST.
IT'S ALL EAST!

CHAPTER 23 THE SEXTET'S SCHOOL CAMPING TRIP

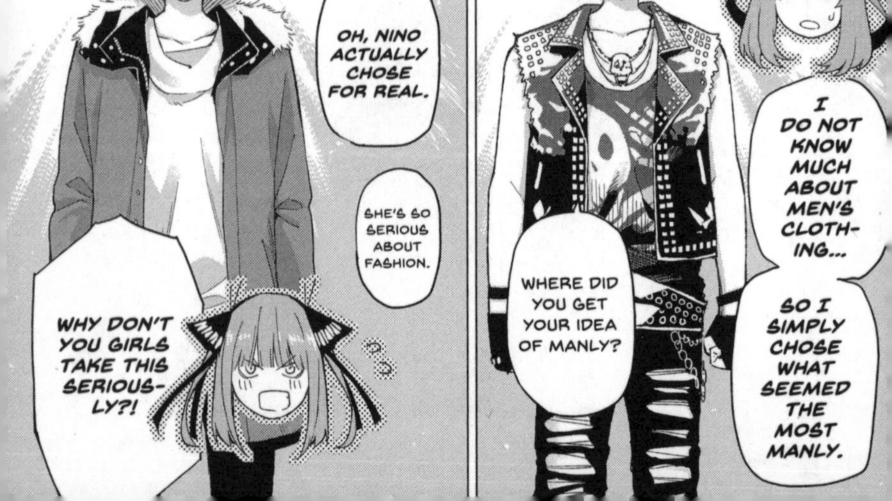
I DO NOT KNOW MUCH ABOUT MEN'S CLOTHING...
SO I SIMPLY CHOSE WHAT SEEMED THE MOST MANLY.
WHERE DID YOU GET YOUR IDEA OF MANLY?
...
OH, NINO ACTUALLY CHOSE FOR REAL.
SHE'S SO SERIOUS ABOUT FASHION.
WHY DON'T YOU GIRLS TAKE THIS SERIOUSLY?!

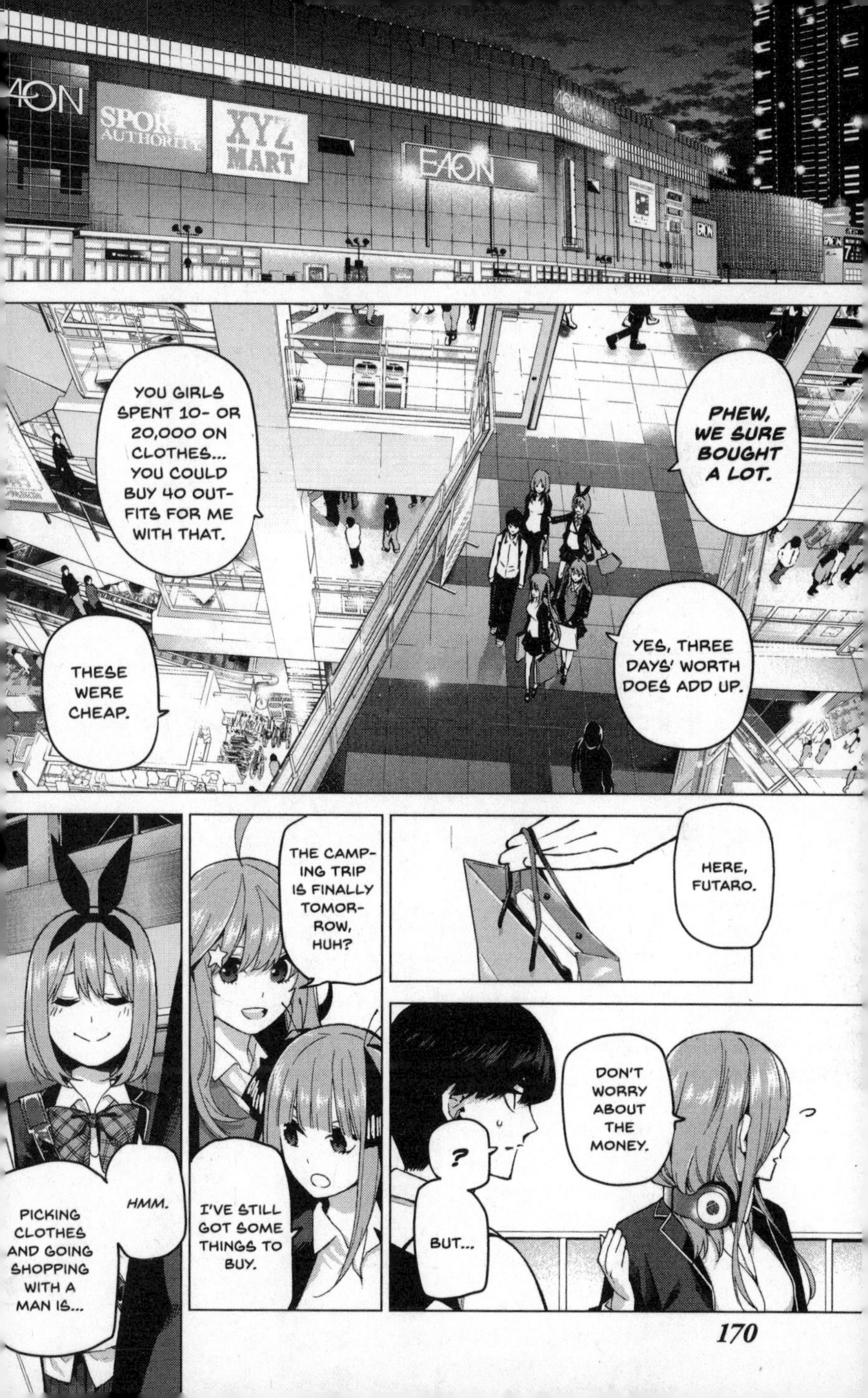
EAON
XYZ MART
PHEW, WE SURE BOUGHT A LOT.
YOU GIRLS SPENT 10- OR 20,000 ON CLOTHES... YOU COULD BUY 40 OUT-FITS FOR ME WITH THAT.
YES, THREE DAYS' WORTH DOES ADD UP.
THESE WERE CHEAP.
HERE, FUTARO.
DON'T WORRY ABOUT THE MONEY.
?
BUT...
THE CAMP-ING TRIP IS FINALLY TOMOR-ROW, HUH?
I'VE STILL GOT SOME THINGS TO BUY.
HMM.
PICKING CLOTHES AND GOING SHOPPING WITH A MAN IS...

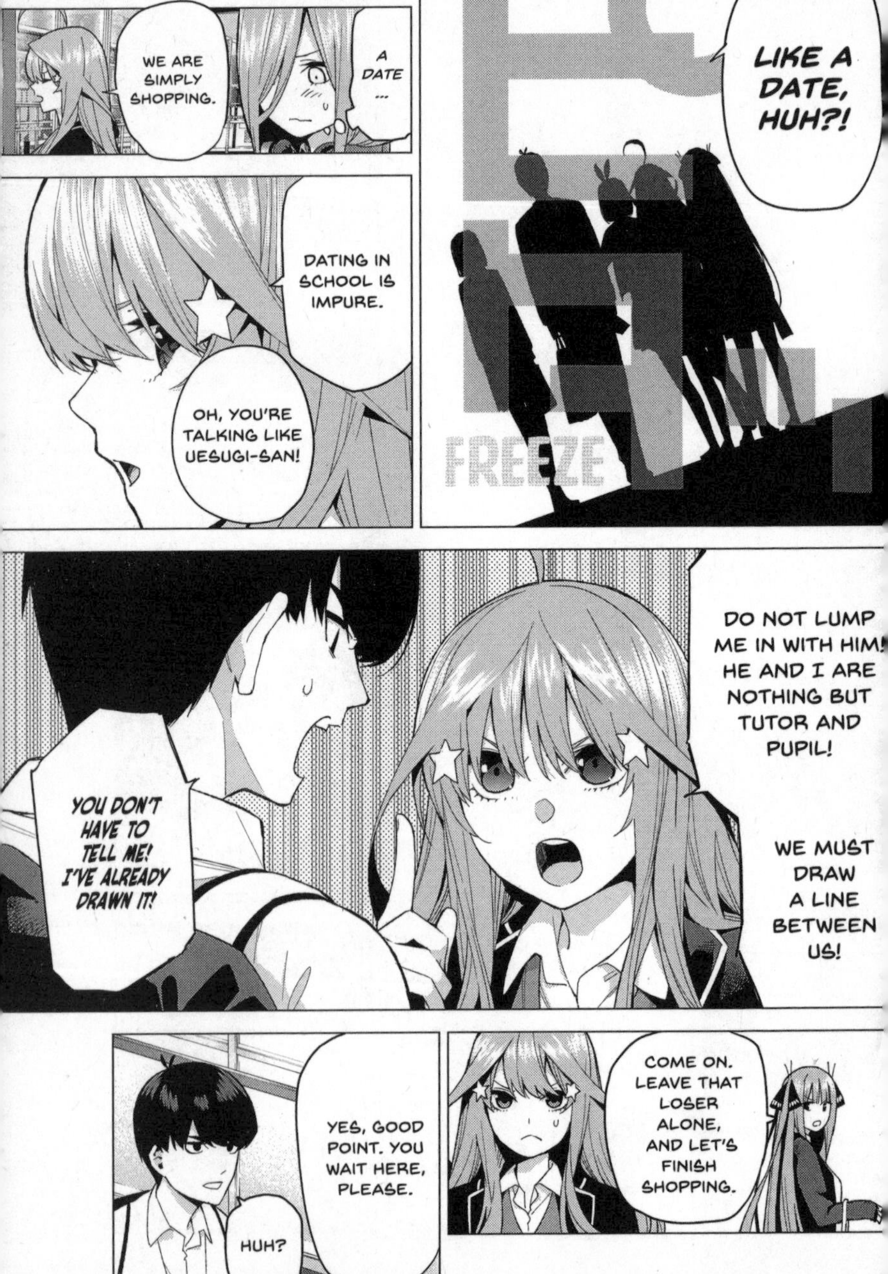
LIKE A DATE, HUH?!
FREEZE
A DATE ...
WE ARE SIMPLY SHOPPING.
DATING IN SCHOOL IS IMPURE.
OH, YOU'RE TALKING LIKE UESUGI-SAN!
DO NOT LUMP ME IN WITH HIM! HE AND I ARE NOTHING BUT TUTOR AND PUPIL!
WE MUST DRAW A LINE BETWEEN US!
YOU DON'T HAVE TO TELL ME! I'VE ALREADY DRAWN IT!
COME ON. LEAVE THAT LOSER ALONE, AND LET'S FINISH SHOPPING.
YES, GOOD POINT. YOU WAIT HERE, PLEASE.
HUH?

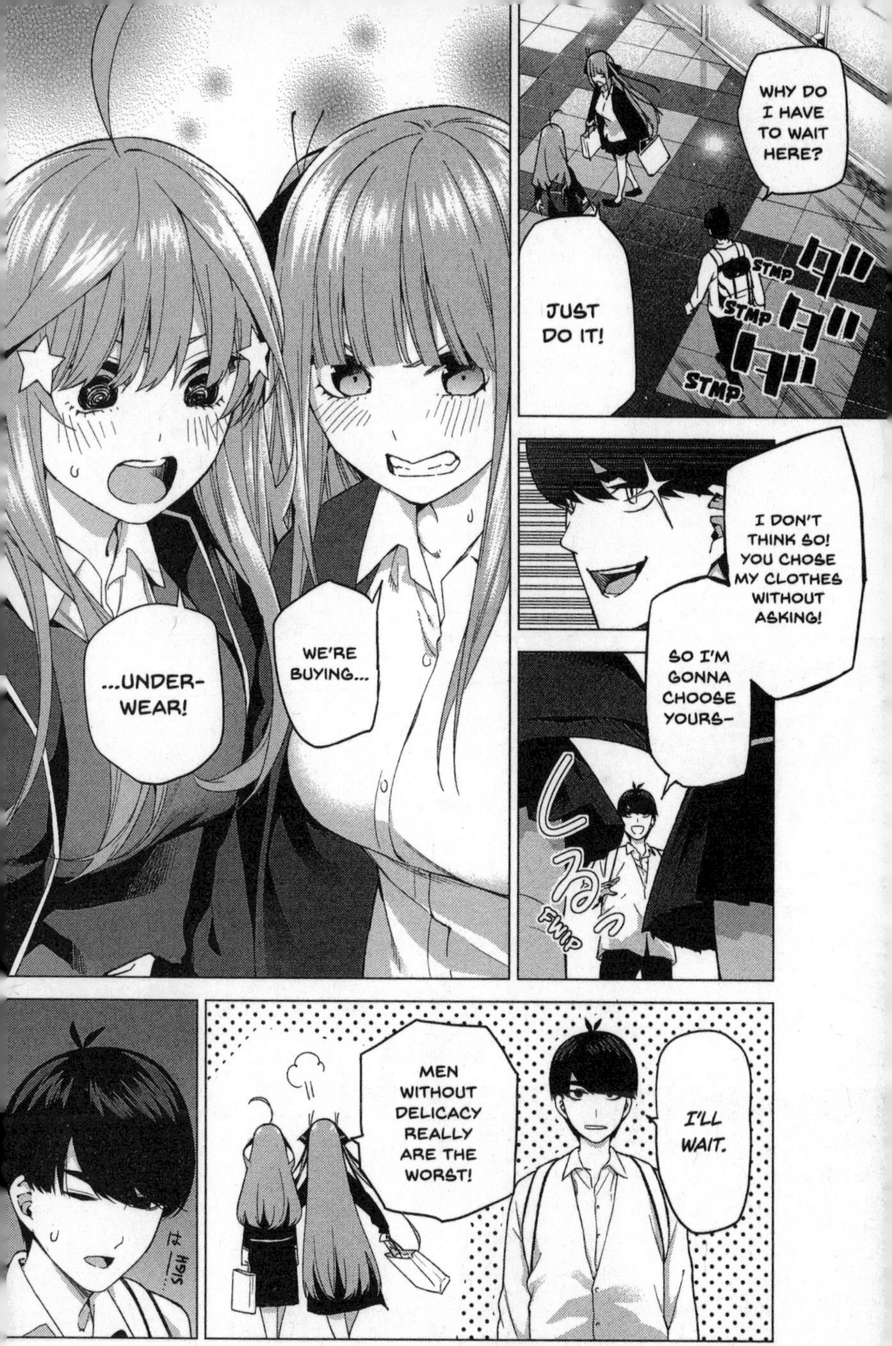

WHY DO I HAVE TO WAIT HERE?
JUST DO IT!
STMP
STMP
STMP
I DON'T THINK SO! YOU CHOSE MY CLOTHES WITHOUT ASKING!
SO I'M GONNA CHOOSE YOURS-
FWIP
WE'RE BUYING...
...UNDER-WEAR!
I'LL WAIT.
MEN WITHOUT DELICACY REALLY ARE THE WORST!
SIGH

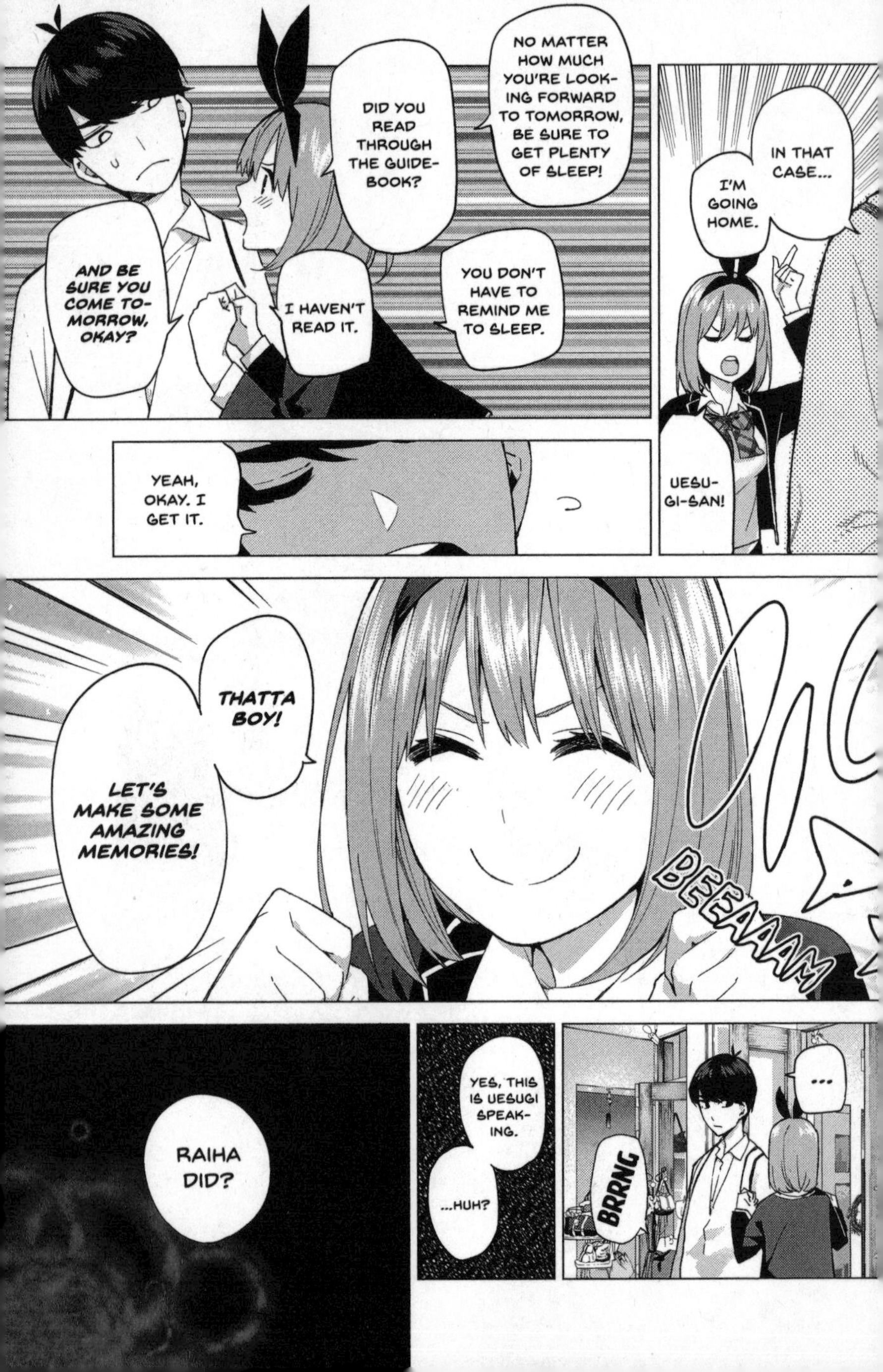
IN THAT CASE...
I'M GOING HOME.
UESUGI-SAN!
NO MATTER HOW MUCH YOU'RE LOOKING FORWARD TO TOMORROW, BE SURE TO GET PLENTY OF SLEEP!
DID YOU READ THROUGH THE GUIDEBOOK?
YOU DON'T HAVE TO REMIND ME TO SLEEP.
I HAVEN'T READ IT.
AND BE SURE YOU COME TOMORROW, OKAY?
YEAH, OKAY. I GET IT.
BEEAAAM
THATTA BOY!
LET'S MAKE SOME AMAZING MEMORIES!
...
YES, THIS IS UESUGI SPEAKING.
BRRNG
...HUH?
RAIHA DID?

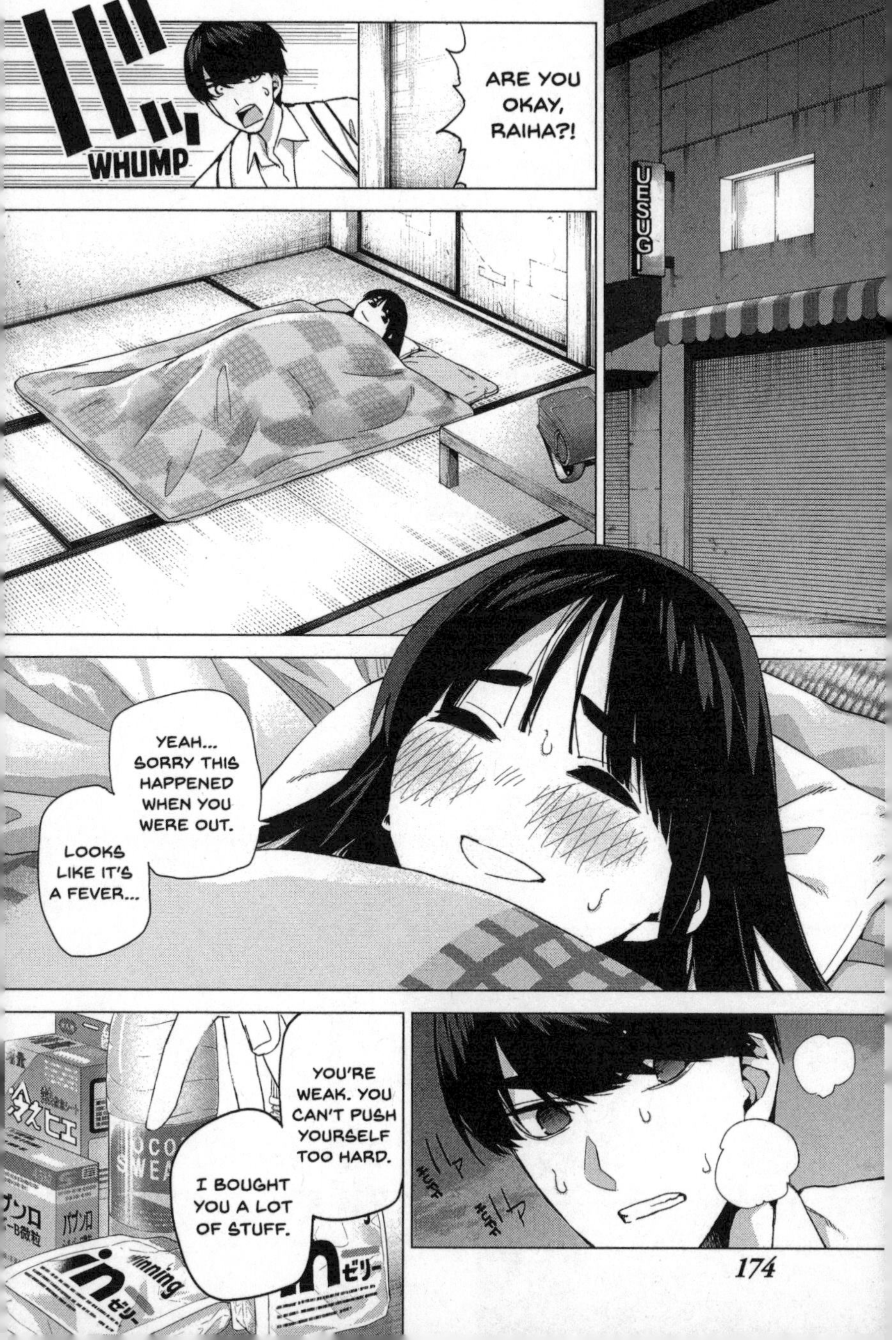
UESUGI
WHUMP
ARE YOU OKAY, RAIHA?!
YEAH... SORRY THIS HAPPENED WHEN YOU WERE OUT.
LOOKS LIKE IT'S A FEVER...
HUFF
HUFF
YOU'RE WEAK. YOU CAN'T PUSH YOURSELF TOO HARD.
I BOUGHT YOU A LOT OF STUFF.

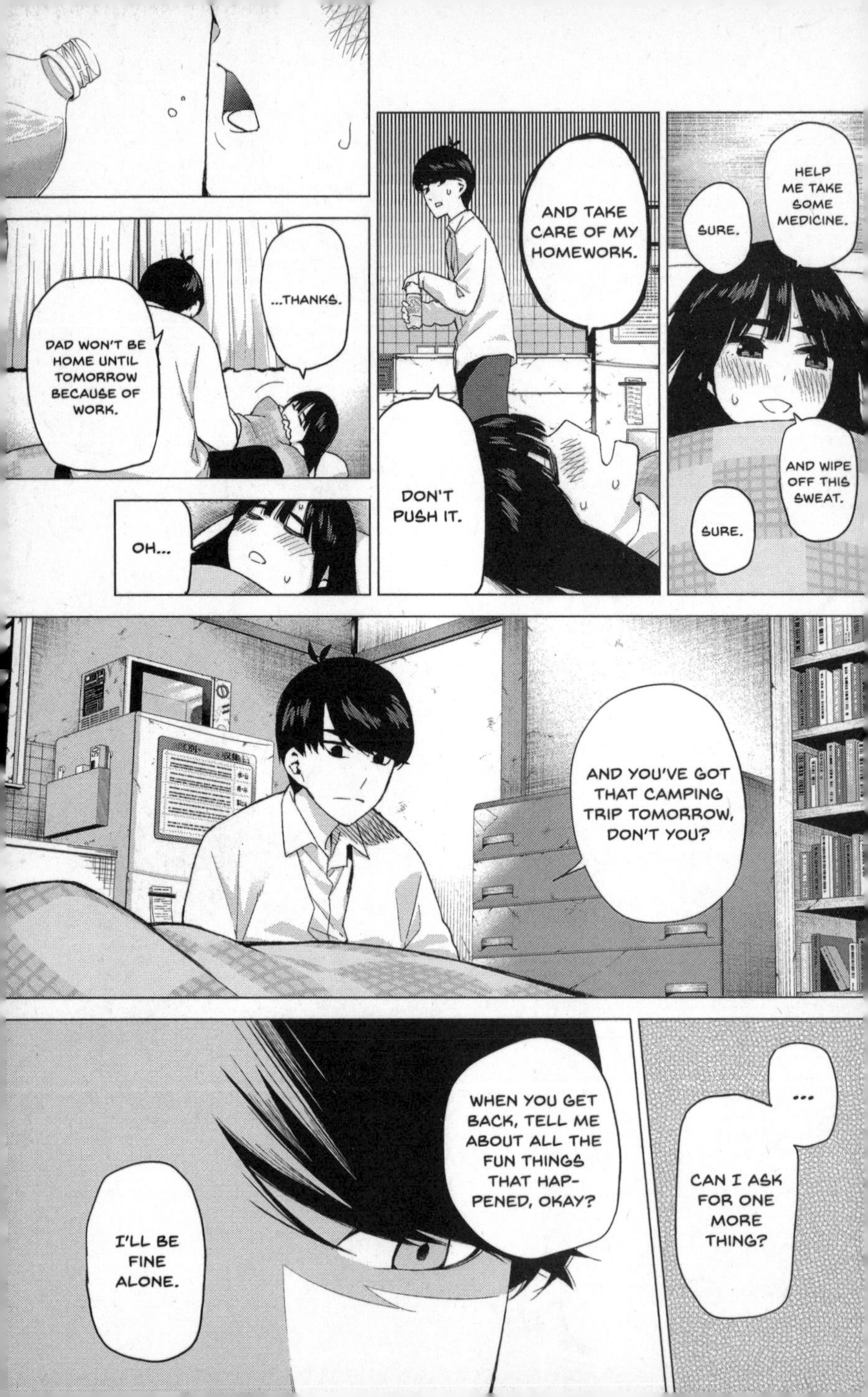
HELP ME TAKE SOME MEDICINE.
SURE.
AND WIPE OFF THIS SWEAT.
SURE.
AND TAKE CARE OF MY HOMEWORK.
DON'T PUSH IT.
...THANKS.
DAD WON'T BE HOME UNTIL TOMORROW BECAUSE OF WORK.
OH...
AND YOU'VE GOT THAT CAMPING TRIP TOMORROW, DON'T YOU?
...
CAN I ASK FOR ONE MORE THING?
WHEN YOU GET BACK, TELL ME ABOUT ALL THE FUN THINGS THAT HAP-PENED, OKAY?
I'LL BE FINE ALONE.

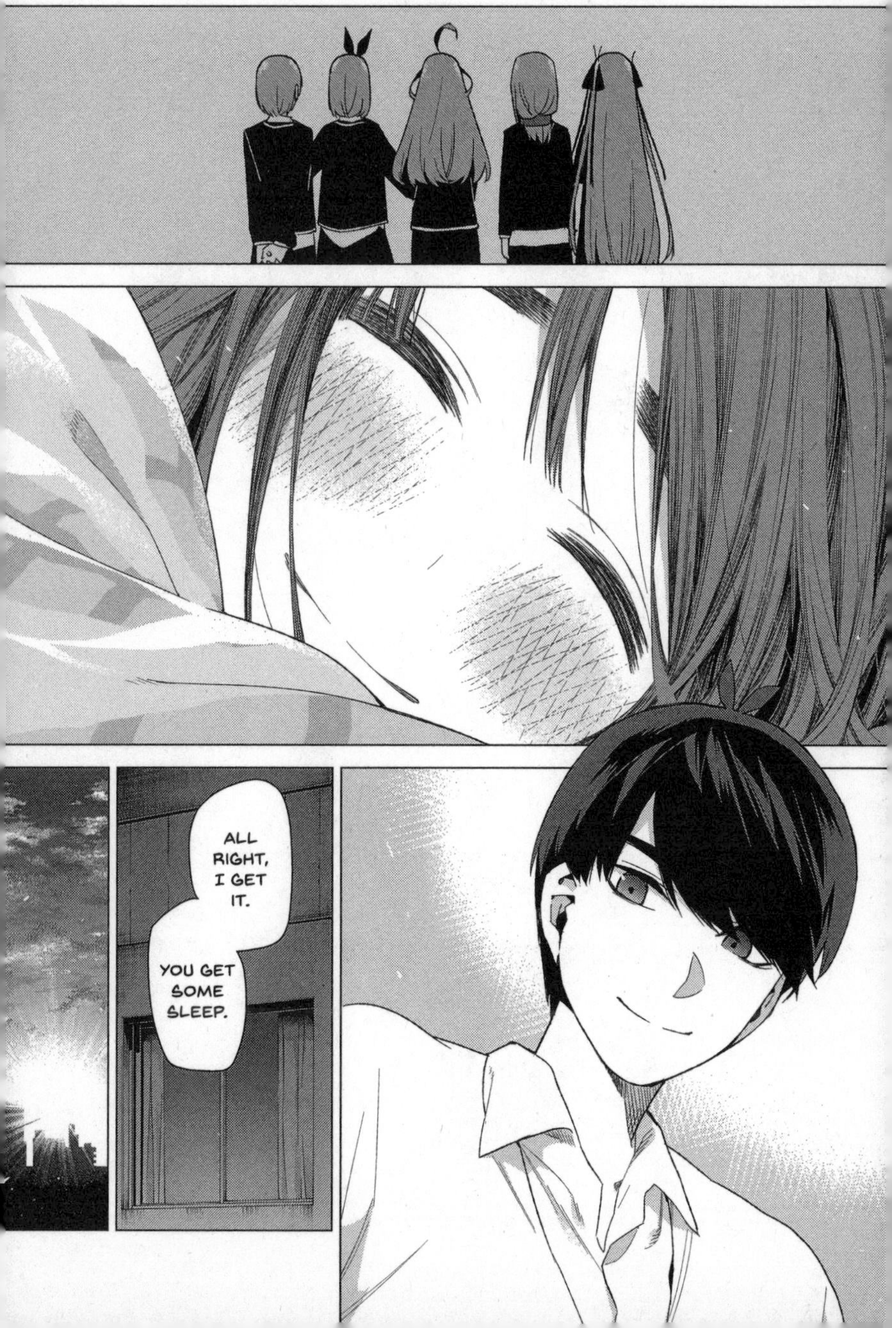
ALL RIGHT, I GET IT.
YOU GET SOME SLEEP.

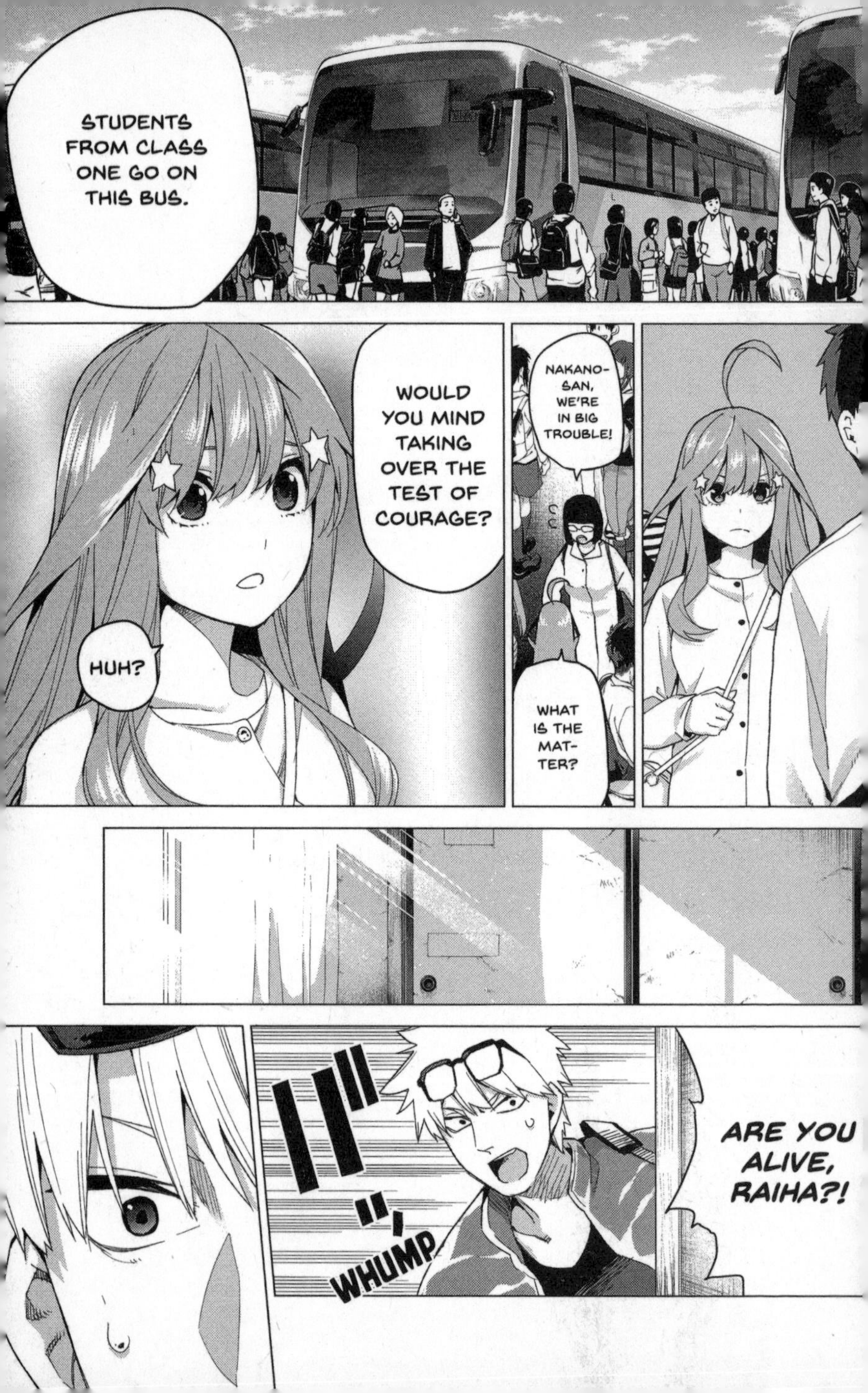
STUDENTS FROM CLASS ONE GO ON THIS BUS.
NAKANO-SAN, WE'RE IN BIG TROUBLE!
WHAT IS THE MATTER?
WOULD YOU MIND TAKING OVER THE TEST OF COURAGE?
HUH?
ARE YOU ALIVE, RAIHA?!
WHUMP

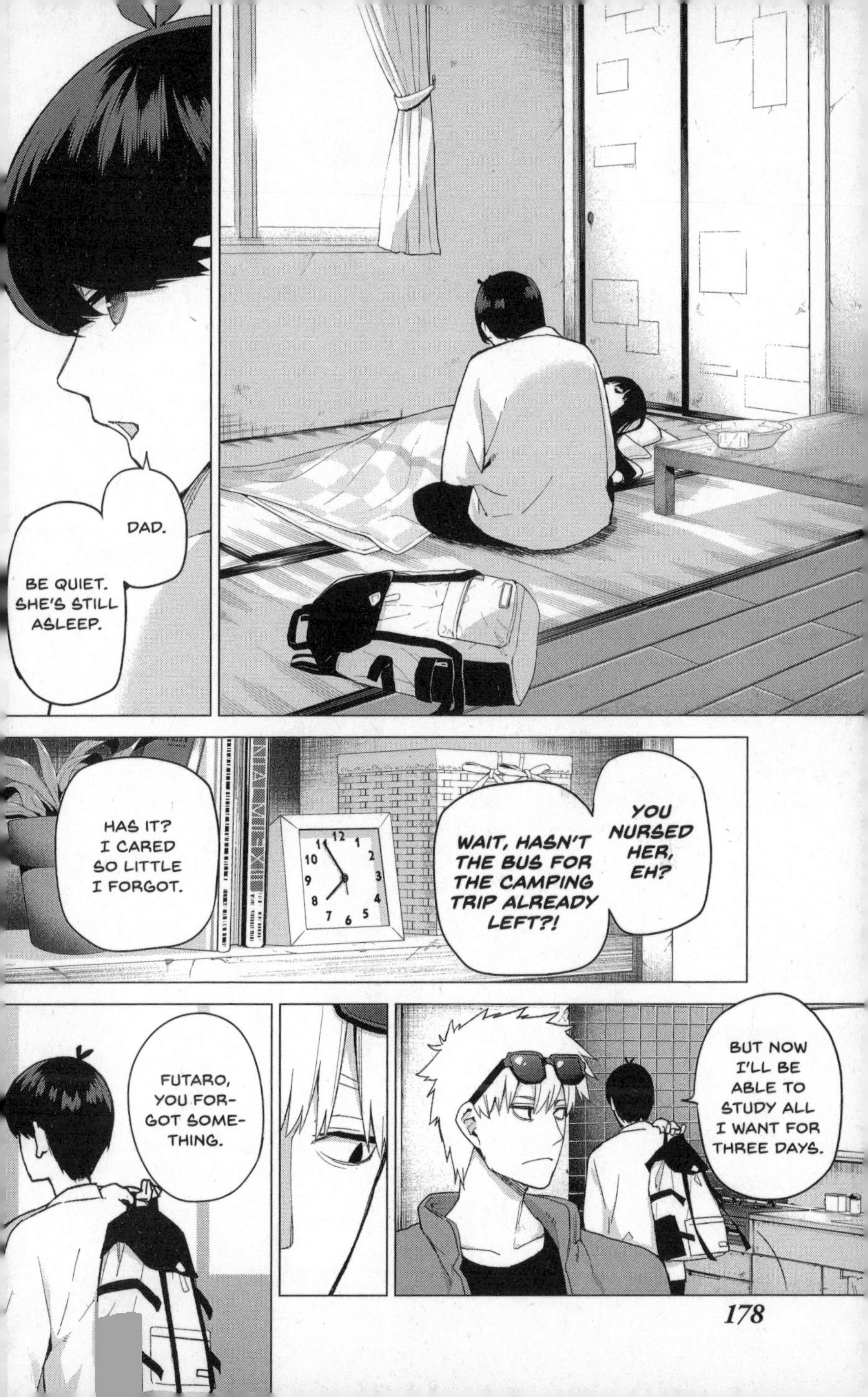
DAD.
BE QUIET. SHE'S STILL ASLEEP.
YOU NURSED HER, EH?
WAIT, HASN'T THE BUS FOR THE CAMPING TRIP ALREADY LEFT?!
HAS IT? I CARED SO LITTLE I FORGOT.
BUT NOW I'LL BE ABLE TO STUDY ALL I WANT FOR THREE DAYS.
FUTARO, YOU FOR-GOT SOME-THING.

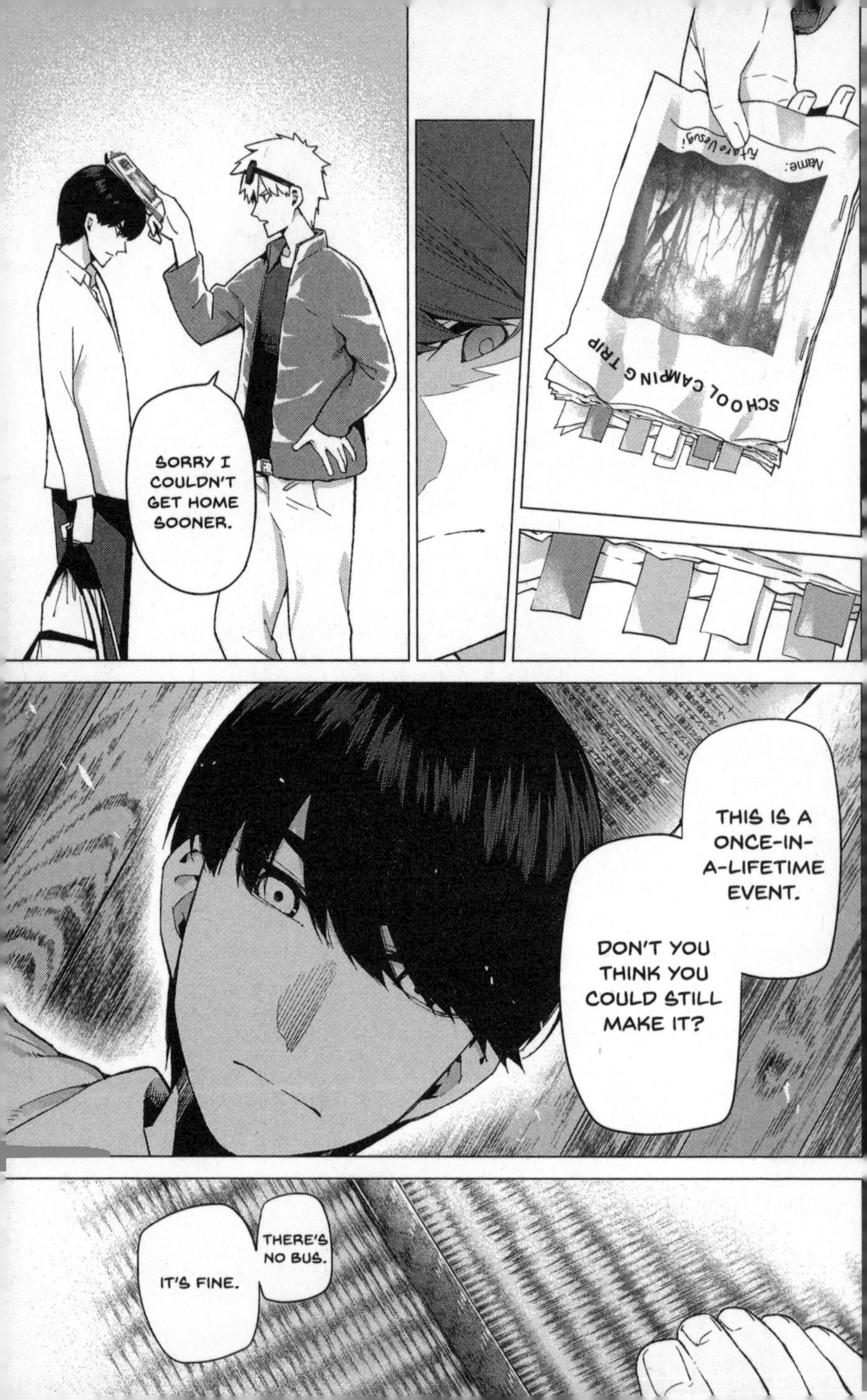
Name: Futaro Uesugi
SCHOOL CAMPING TRIP
SORRY I COULDN'T GET HOME SOONER.
THIS IS A ONCE-IN-A-LIFETIME EVENT.
DON'T YOU THINK YOU COULD STILL MAKE IT?
THERE'S NO BUS.
IT'S FINE.

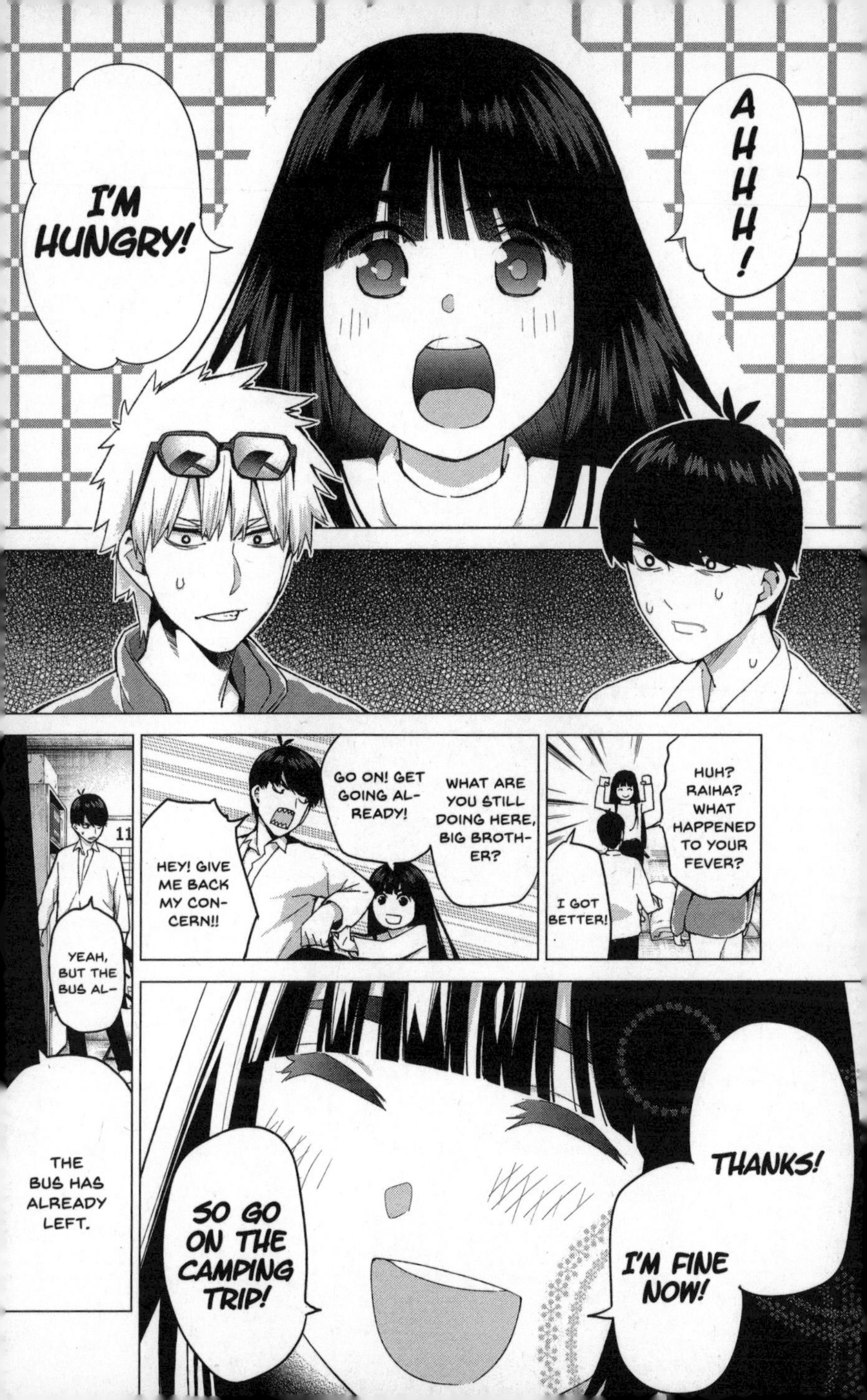

AHHHH!
I'M HUNGRY!
HUH? RAIHA? WHAT HAPPENED TO YOUR FEVER?
I GOT BETTER!
WHAT ARE YOU STILL DOING HERE, BIG BROTHER?
GO ON! GET GOING AL-READY!
HEY! GIVE ME BACK MY CON-CERN!!
THANKS!
I'M FINE NOW!
SO GO ON THE CAMPING TRIP!
YEAH, BUT THE BUS AL—
THE BUS HAS ALREADY LEFT.

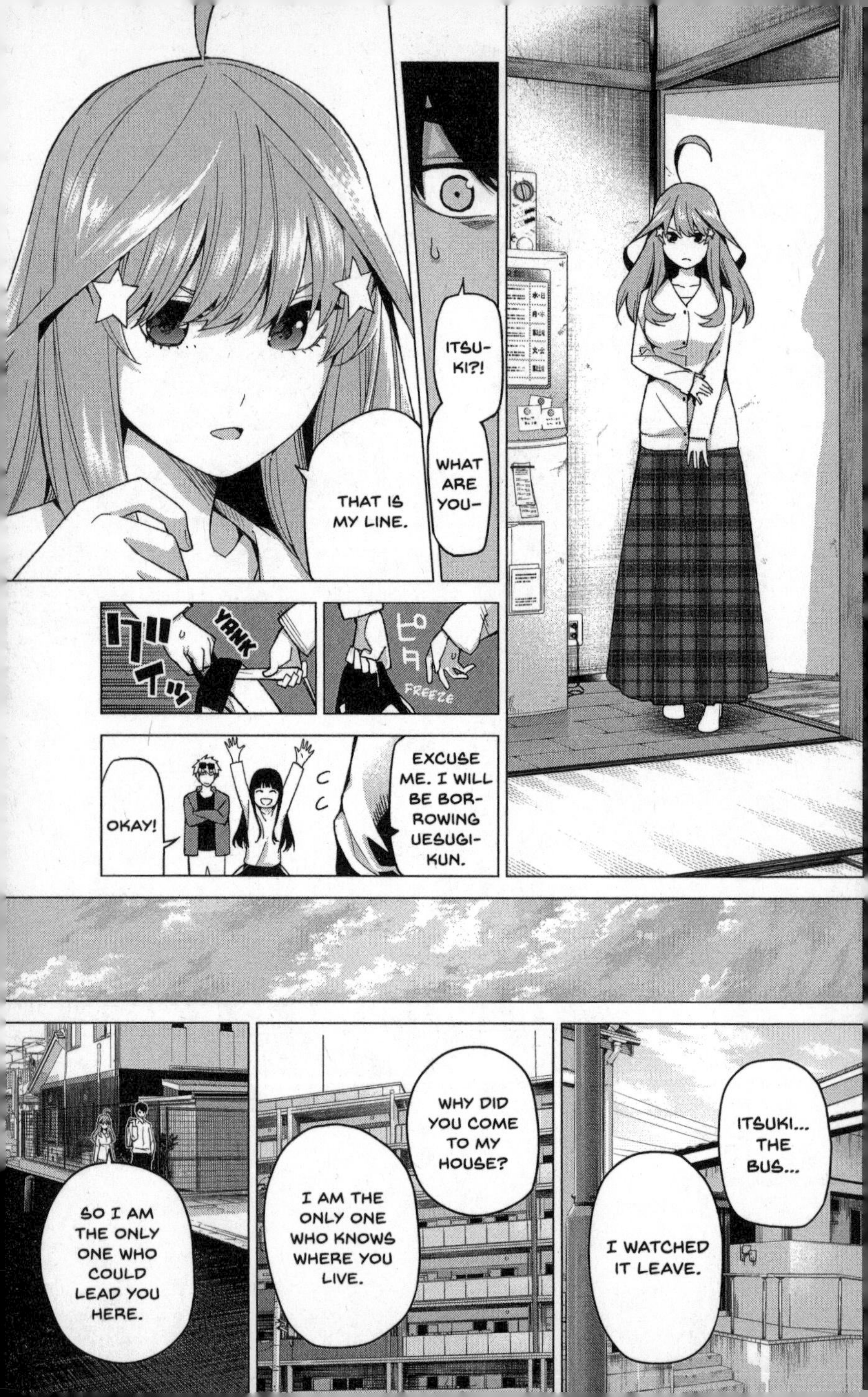
ITSUKI?!
WHAT ARE YOU—
THAT IS MY LINE.
ピタ
FREEZE
グイッ
YANK
EXCUSE ME. I WILL BE BORROWING UESUGI-KUN.
OKAY!
ITSUKI... THE BUS...
I WATCHED IT LEAVE.
WHY DID YOU COME TO MY HOUSE?
I AM THE ONLY ONE WHO KNOWS WHERE YOU LIVE.
SO I AM THE ONLY ONE WHO COULD LEAD YOU HERE.

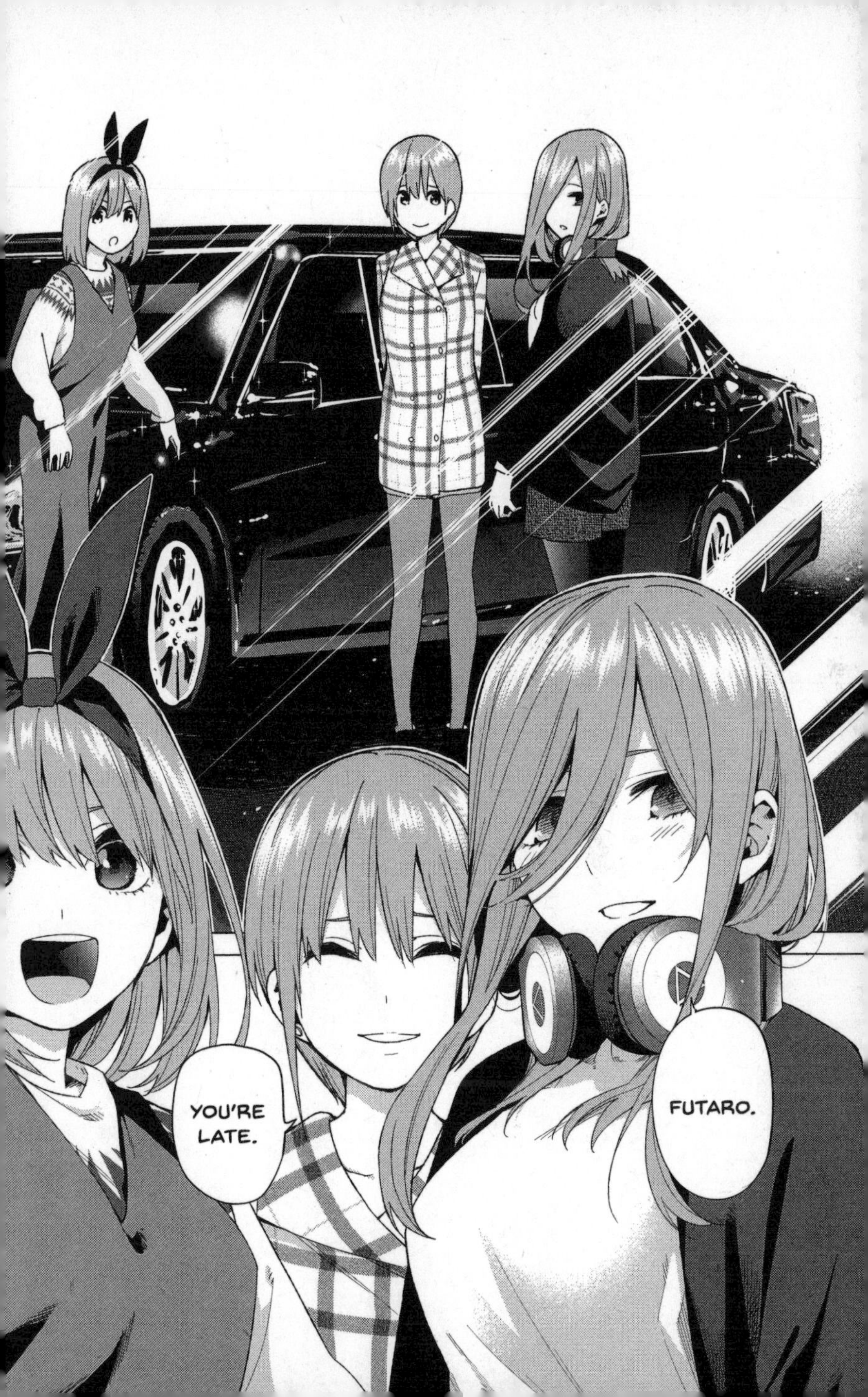
FUTARO.
YOU'RE LATE.

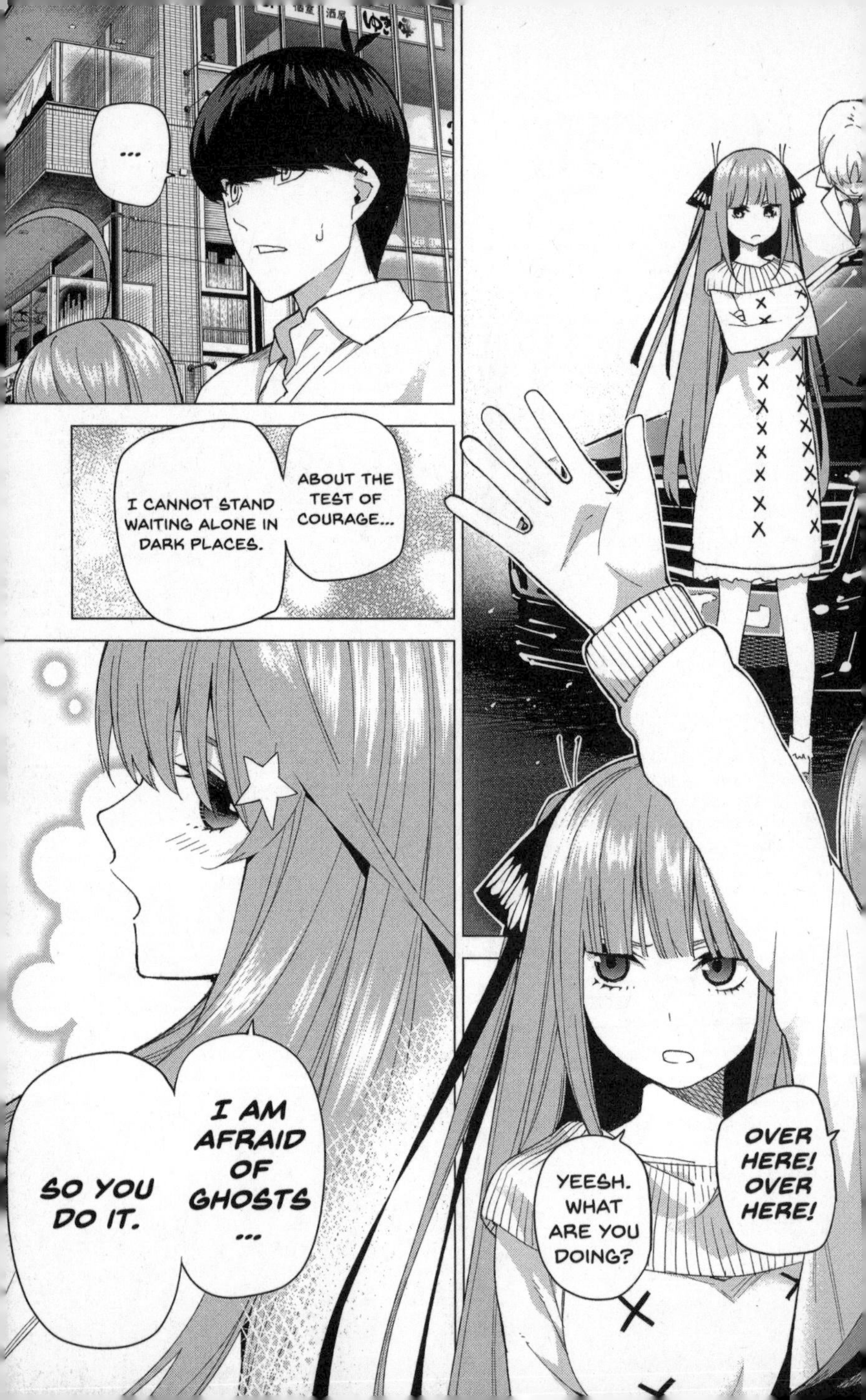
OVER HERE! OVER HERE!
YEESH. WHAT ARE YOU DOING?
...
ABOUT THE TEST OF COURAGE...
I CANNOT STAND WAITING ALONE IN DARK PLACES.
I AM AFRAID OF GHOSTS ...
SO YOU DO IT.

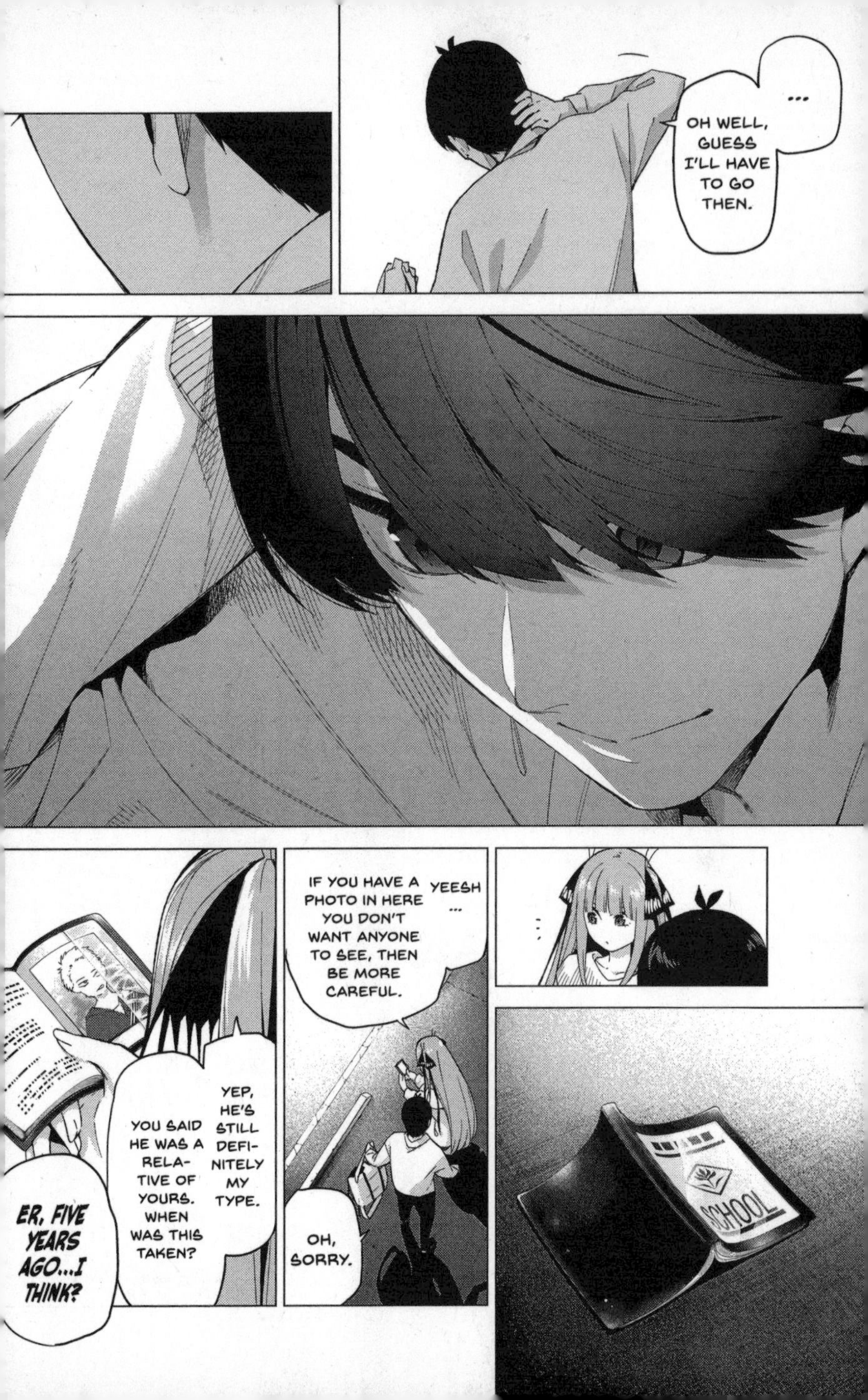
...
OH WELL, GUESS I'LL HAVE TO GO THEN.
...
SCHOOL
YEESH ...
IF YOU HAVE A PHOTO IN HERE YOU DON'T WANT ANYONE TO SEE, THEN BE MORE CAREFUL.
OH, SORRY.
YEP, HE'S STILL DEFI-NITELY MY TYPE.
YOU SAID HE WAS A RELA-TIVE OF YOURS. WHEN WAS THIS TAKEN?
ER, FIVE YEARS AGO...I THINK?

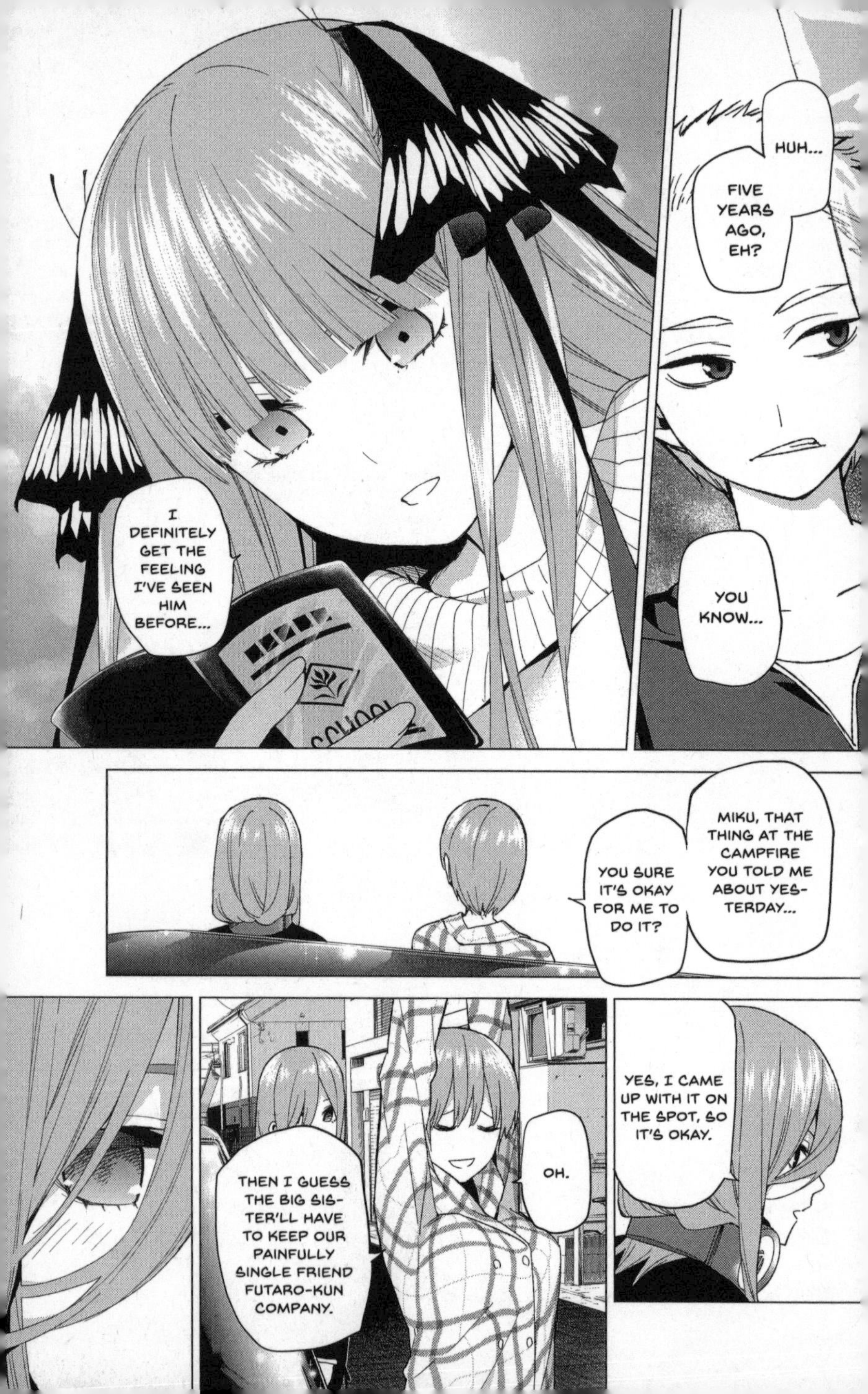
HUH...
FIVE YEARS AGO, EH?
YOU KNOW...
I DEFINITELY GET THE FEELING I'VE SEEN HIM BEFORE...
MIKU, THAT THING AT THE CAMPFIRE YOU TOLD ME ABOUT YES-TERDAY...
YOU SURE IT'S OKAY FOR ME TO DO IT?
YES, I CAME UP WITH IT ON THE SPOT, SO IT'S OKAY.
OH.
THEN I GUESS THE BIG SIS-TER'LL HAVE TO KEEP OUR PAINFULLY SINGLE FRIEND FUTARO-KUN COMPANY.

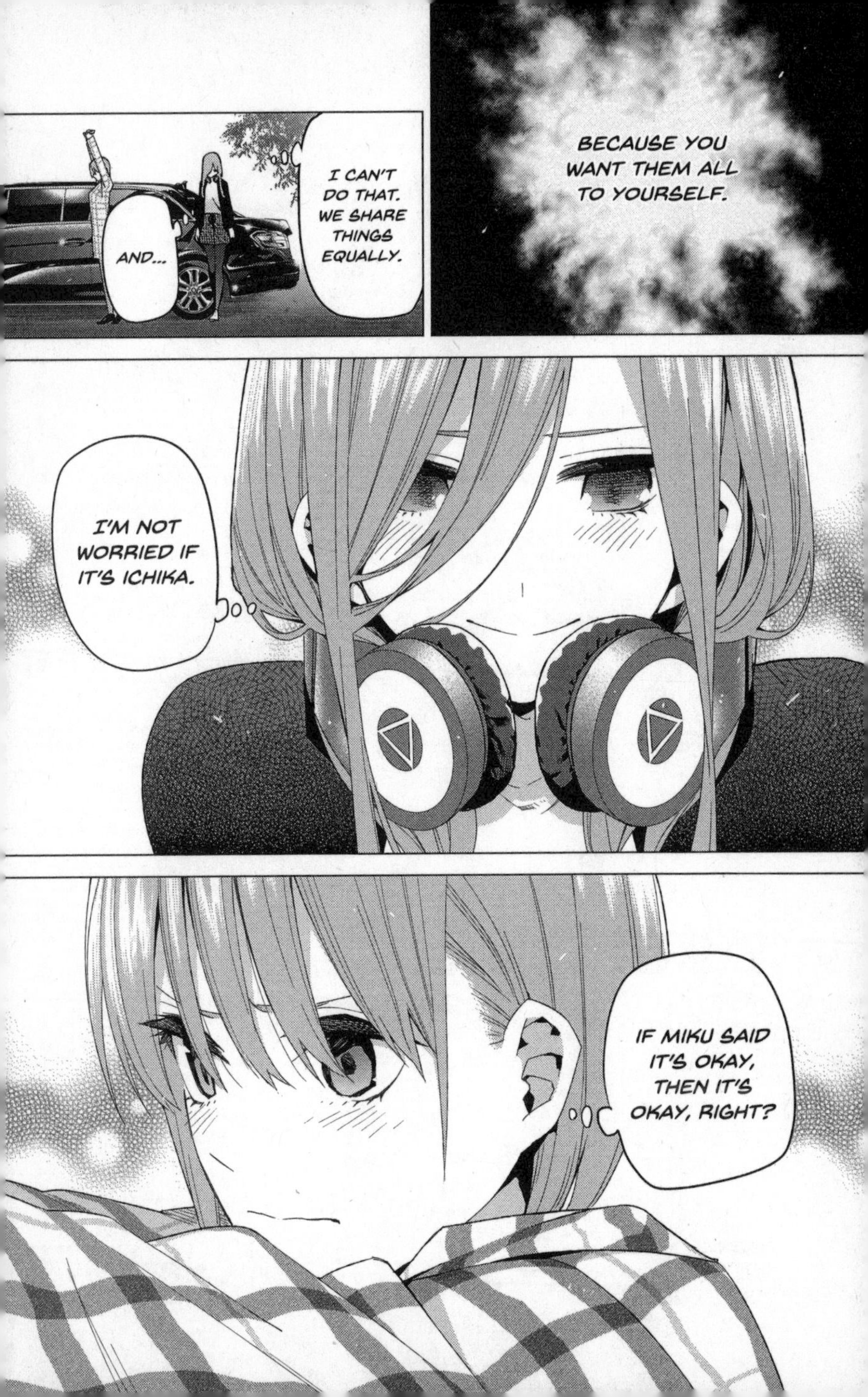
BECAUSE YOU WANT THEM ALL TO YOURSELF.
I CAN'T DO THAT. WE SHARE THINGS EQUALLY.
AND...
I'M NOT WORRIED IF IT'S ICHIKA.
IF MIKU SAID IT'S OKAY, THEN IT'S OKAY, RIGHT?

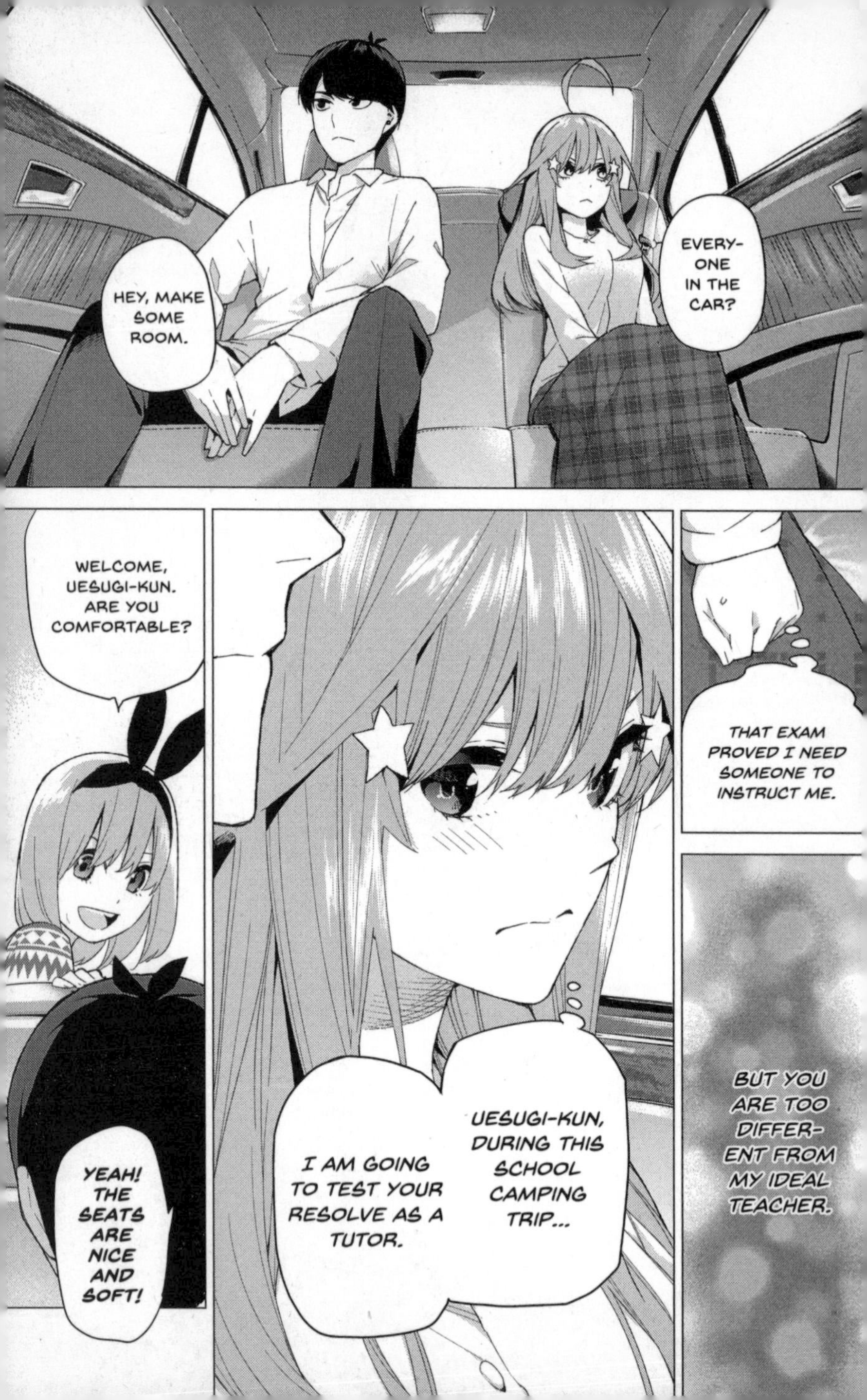
EVERY-ONE IN THE CAR?
HEY, MAKE SOME ROOM.
THAT EXAM PROVED I NEED SOMEONE TO INSTRUCT ME.
BUT YOU ARE TOO DIFFER-ENT FROM MY IDEAL TEACHER.
UESUGI-KUN, DURING THIS SCHOOL CAMPING TRIP...
I AM GOING TO TEST YOUR RESOLVE AS A TUTOR.
WELCOME, UESUGI-KUN. ARE YOU COMFORTABLE?
YEAH! THE SEATS ARE NICE AND SOFT!

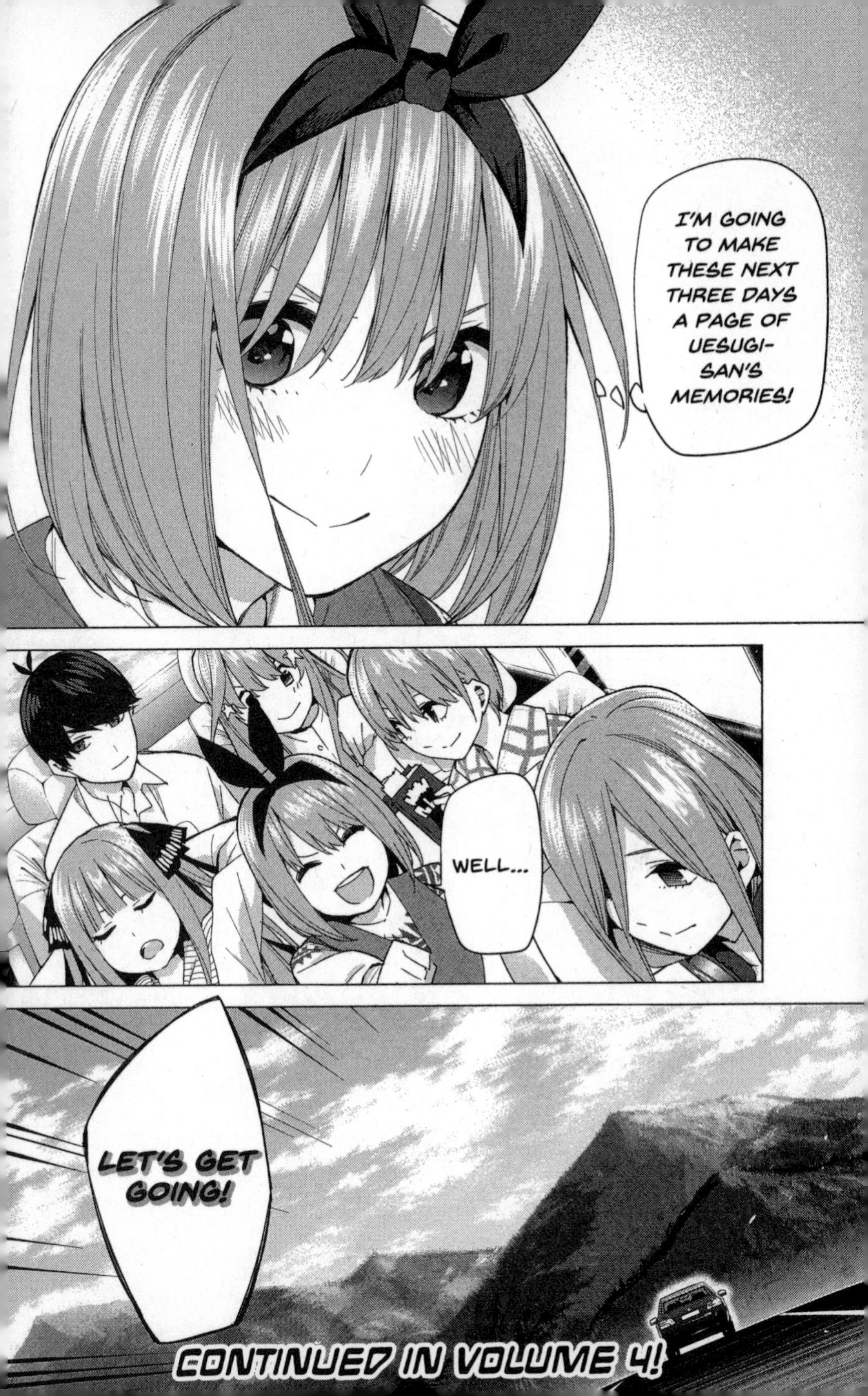
I'M GOING TO MAKE THESE NEXT THREE DAYS A PAGE OF UESUGI-SAN'S MEMORIES!
WELL...
LET'S GET GOING!
CONTINUED IN VOLUME 4!

EXTRA BONUS COMIC

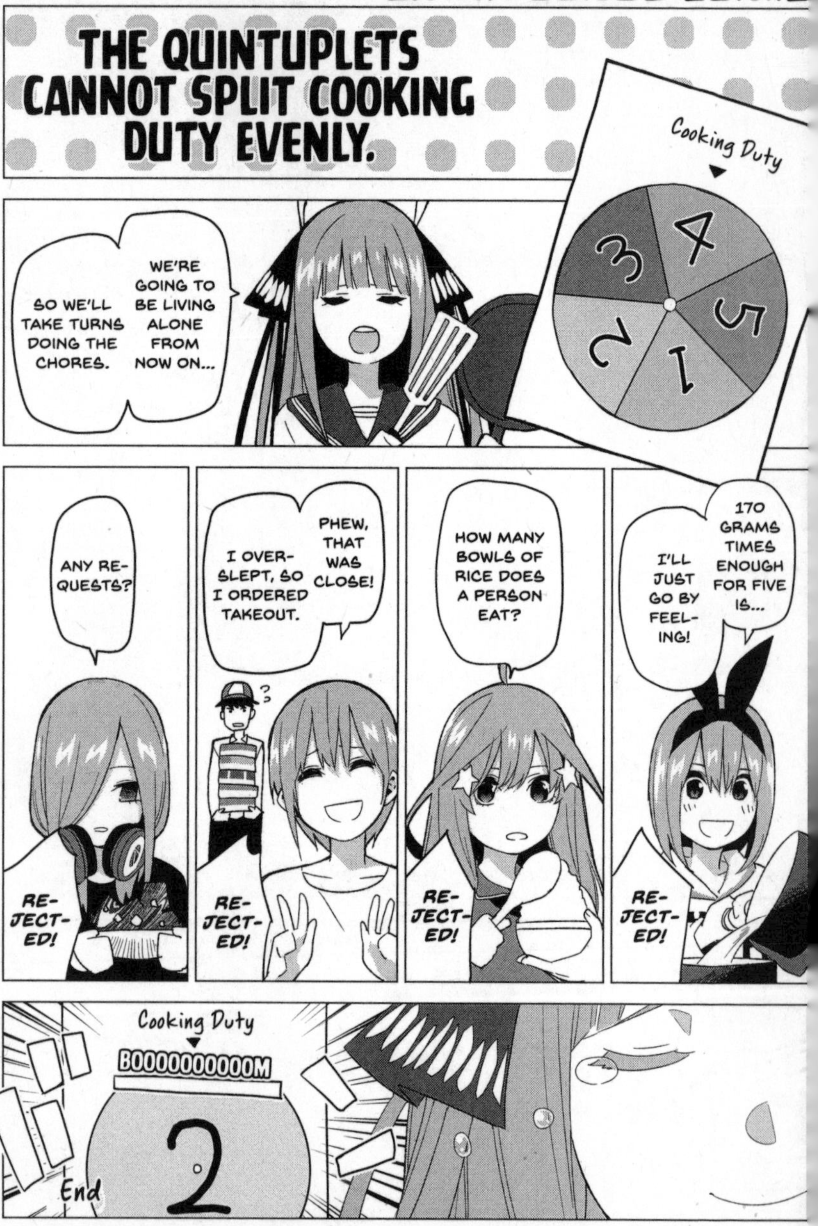
THE QUINTUPLETS CANNOT SPLIT COOKING DUTY EVENLY.
Cooking Duty
3 4 5 1 2
WE'RE GOING TO BE LIVING ALONE FROM NOW ON...
SO WE'LL TAKE TURNS DOING THE CHORES.
170 GRAMS TIMES ENOUGH FOR FIVE IS...
I'LL JUST GO BY FEEL-ING!
RE-JECT-ED!
HOW MANY BOWLS OF RICE DOES A PERSON EAT?
RE-JECT-ED!
PHEW, THAT WAS CLOSE!
I OVER-SLEPT, SO I ORDERED TAKEOUT.
RE-JECT-ED!
ANY RE-QUESTS?
RE-JECT-ED!
Cooking Duty
BOOOOOOOOOOM
2
End

Staff Ueno Hino Ogata Cho

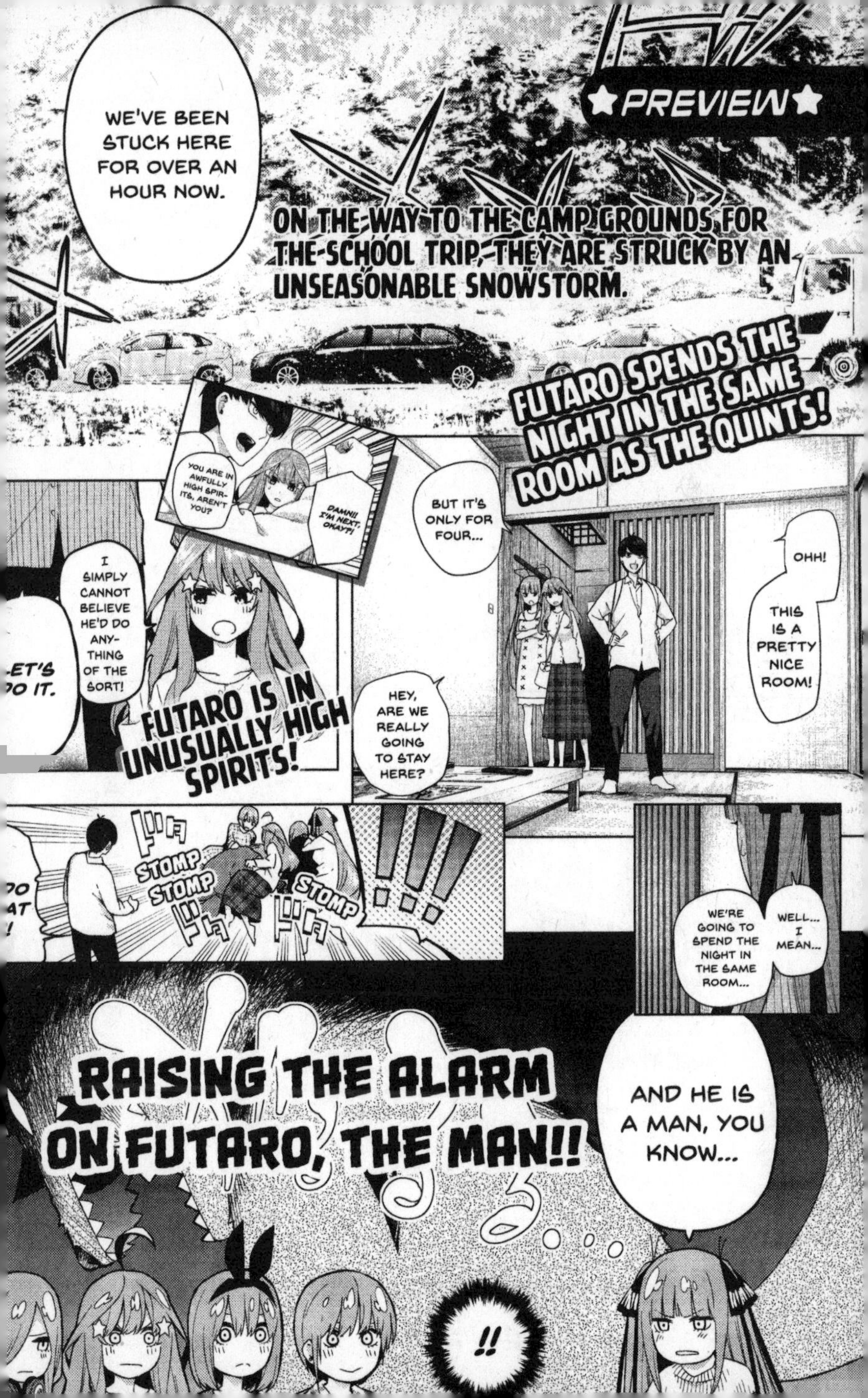
★PREVIEW★
ON THE WAY TO THE CAMP GROUNDS FOR THE SCHOOL TRIP, THEY ARE STRUCK BY AN UNSEASONABLE SNOWSTORM.
WE'VE BEEN STUCK HERE FOR OVER AN HOUR NOW.
FUTARO SPENDS THE NIGHT IN THE SAME ROOM AS THE QUINTS!
OHH! THIS IS A PRETTY NICE ROOM!
BUT IT'S ONLY FOR FOUR...
HEY, ARE WE REALLY GOING TO STAY HERE?
DAMN!! I'M NEXT, OKAY?!
YOU ARE IN AWFULLY HIGH SPIRITS, AREN'T YOU?
I SIMPLY CANNOT BELIEVE HE'D DO ANYTHING OF THE SORT!
FUTARO IS IN UNUSUALLY HIGH SPIRITS!
WELL... I MEAN...
WE'RE GOING TO SPEND THE NIGHT IN THE SAME ROOM...
!!!
STOMP
STOMP STOMP
AND HE IS A MAN, YOU KNOW...
RAISING THE ALARM ON FUTARO, THE MAN!!
!!

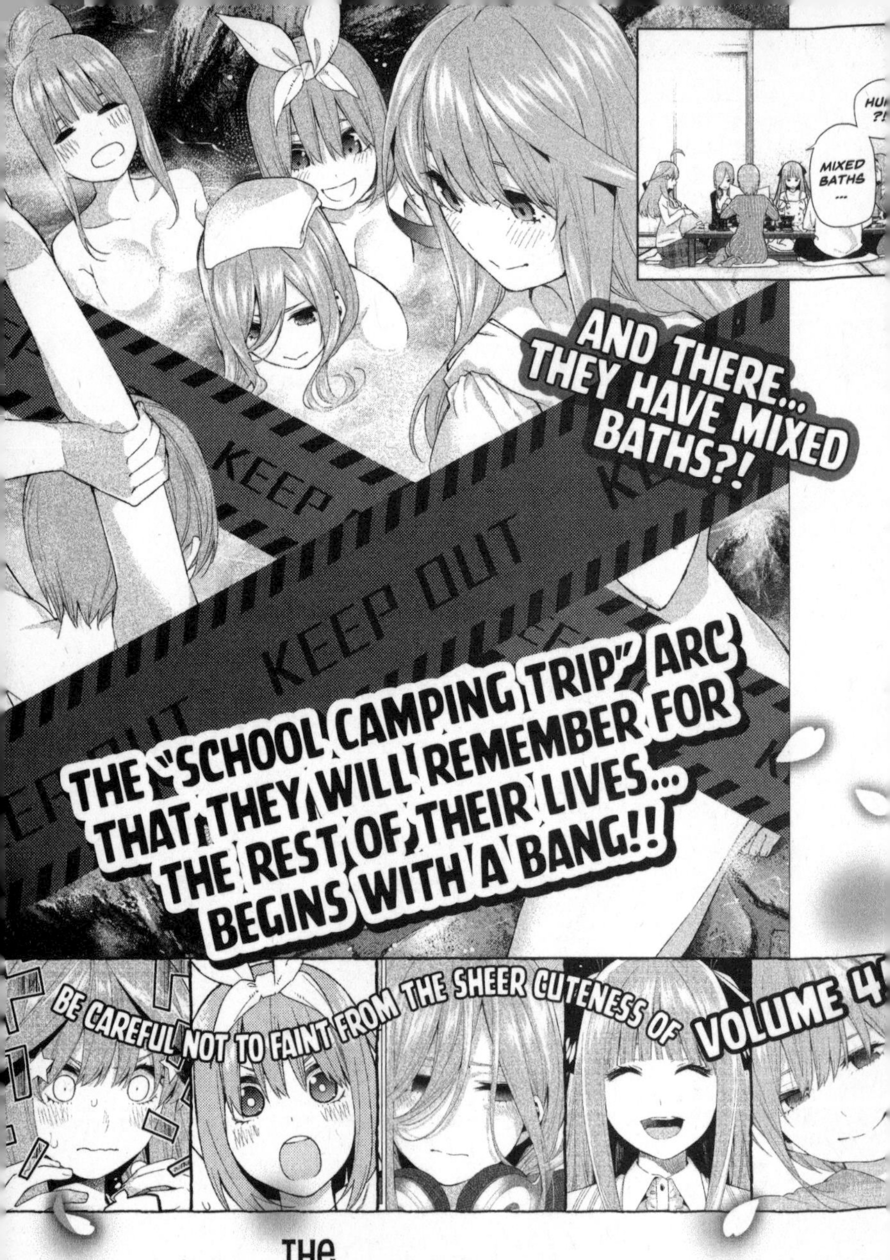
MIXED BATHS ...
AND THERE... THEY HAVE MIXED BATHS?!
KEEP OUT
THE "SCHOOL CAMPING TRIP" ARC THAT THEY WILL REMEMBER FOR THE REST OF THEIR LIVES... BEGINS WITH A BANG!!
BE CAREFUL NOT TO FAINT FROM THE SHEER CUTENESS OF VOLUME 4

THE QUINTESSENTIAL QUINTUPLETS 4

A Kodansha Comics Trade Paperback Original.

Published in the United States by Kodansha Comics,
an imprint of Kodansha USA Publishing, LLC, New York.

Publication rights for this English edition arranged through Kodansha Ltd., Tokyo.

First published in Japan in 2018 by Kodansha Ltd., Tokyo,
as Gotoubun no Hanayome volume 3.

Cover Design: Saya Takai (RedRooster)

ISBN 978-1-63236-776-1

Printed in the United States of America.

www.kodanshacomics.com

9 8 7 6 5 4 3 2 1

Translation: Steven LeCroy
Lettering: Jan Lan Ivan Concepcion
Additional Layout: Belynda Ungurath
Editing: David Yoo, Thalia Sutton
Editorial Assistance: YKS Services LLC/SKY Japan, INC.
Kodansha Comics Edition Cover Design: Phil Balsman